Seeking Equality

Seeking Equality
The Political Economy of the Common Good in the United States and Canada

John Harles

UNIVERSITY OF TORONTO PRESS

Copyright © University of Toronto Press 2017
Higher Education Division

www.utppublishing.com

All rights reserved. The use of any part of this publication reproduced, transmitted in any form or by any means, electronic, mechanical, photocopying, recording, or otherwise, or stored in a retrieval system, without prior written consent of the publisher—or in the case of photocopying, a licence from Access Copyright (the Canadian Copyright Licensing Agency), 320–56 Wellesley Street West, Toronto, Ontario, M5S 2S3—is an infringement of the copyright law.

LIBRARY AND ARCHIVES CANADA CATALOGUING IN PUBLICATION

Harles, John C., author
    Seeking equality : the political economy of the common good in the United States and Canada / by John Harles.

Includes bibliographical references and index.
Issued in print and electronic formats.
ISBN 978-1-4426-3430-5 (hardcover).—ISBN 978-1-4426-3429-9 (softcover).—
ISBN 978-1-4426-3431-2 (EPUB).—ISBN 978-1-4426-3432-9 (PDF)

1. Equality—Canada. 2. Equality—United States. 3. Canada—Economic conditions. 4. United States—Economic conditions. 5. Canada—Social conditions. 6. United States—Social conditions. I. Title.

HM821.H37 2017   305.0971   C2017-903601-7
                                        C2017-903602-5

We welcome comments and suggestions regarding any aspect of our publications—please feel free to contact us at news@utphighereducation.com or visit our Internet site at www.utppublishing.com.

North America
5201 Dufferin Street
North York, Ontario, Canada, M3H 5T8

2250 Military Road
Tonawanda, New York, USA, 14150

ORDERS PHONE: 1-800-565-9523
ORDERS FAX: 1-800-221-9985
ORDERS E-MAIL: utpbooks@utpress.utoronto.ca

UK, Ireland, and continental Europe
NBN International
Estover Road, Plymouth, PL6 7PY, UK
ORDERS PHONE: 44 (0) 1752 202301
ORDERS FAX: 44 (0) 1752 202333
ORDERS E-MAIL: enquiries@nbninternational.com

Every effort has been made to contact copyright holders; in the event of an error or omission, please notify the publisher.

The University of Toronto Press acknowledges the financial support for its publishing activities of the Government of Canada through the Canada Book Fund.

Tables 2.1, 2.13 OECD (2016), *In It Together: Why Less Inequality Benefits All.* www.oecd.org/social/income-distribution-database.htm; 2.3. 2.8, 2.9, 2.10, 2.15, 2.16 OECD (2016), "Income Distribution and Poverty". www.stats.oecd.org; 2.5 OECD (2014), ""Focus on Top Incomes and Taxation in OECD Countries: Was the crisis a game changer?". http://www.oecd.org/social/OECD2014-FocusOnTopIncomes.pdf; 3.5, 3.6, 3.10, 3.11 Courtesy of The Pew Charitable Trusts.3.9 OECD (2015), *Education at a Glance 2015: OECD Indicators*; 4.1, 4.2, 4.3 World Values Survey. http://www.worldvaluessurvey.org; 6.1, 6.2, 6.3 © Richard Wilkinson and Kate Pickett, 2009, *The Spirit Level: Why Greater Equality Makes Societies Stronger*, Bloomsbury Press, an imprint of Bloomsbury Publishing Plc. Reproduced by permission of Penguin Books Ltd.

Contents

Figures and Tables   vii
Acknowledgments   ix

Introduction   1

1   Distribution   13

2   Mobility   55

3   Values   102

4   Policy   145

5   Why It Matters   174

Conclusion   214

Bibliography   229
Index   273

Figures and Tables

Figures

1.1 Rising Income Inequality—Gini Coefficients in OECD Countries, 1985 and 2013   14
1.2 Gini Coefficients of Inequality for Disposable Income (Post-Transfer and Tax), 2013   15
1.3 Ratio of Top versus Bottom Decile Share for Disposable Income (Post-Transfer and Tax), 2013   16
1.4 Canada and US Income Shares of Top 1 Percent of Earners, 1913–2015   16
1.5 Increase in Income Share of Top 1 Percent of Earners, 1981–2012   17
1.6 Gini Coefficients of Inequality for Market and Disposable Incomes, 2013   22
1.7 US and Canadian Gini Coefficients, Post-Tax and Transfer, 1980–2011   22
1.8 Reduction in Inequality (Gini Coefficients) after Transfers and Taxes   23
1.9 Real Median Household Market Income, United States and Canada, 1984–2013   24
1.10 Gini Coefficients of Inequality for Income (Disposable) and Wealth, 2012   30
1.11 Wealth Share for Top Net Worth Households, 2010   30
1.12 Wealth Inequality in the United States, 1913–2014   31
1.13 Poverty Rate before and after Taxes and Transfers, Poverty Line 50 Percent of Median Household Income   36
1.14 Mean Poverty Gap after Taxes and Transfers, Poverty Line 50 Percent of Median Household Income, 1983–2012   36
2.1 Generational Change in Median Family Income (Matched Parent–Child Pairs)   68
2.2 US Adult Children Income Quintile Rank by Parents' Income Quintile Rank   69
2.3 Earnings Deciles of US and Canadian Sons Compared to Fathers' Earning Deciles   70

2.4   Income Elasticities for OECD Countries   71
2.5   The Great Gatsby Curve—the Correlation between High Inequality and Low Mobility   73
2.6   Relative Earnings of Tertiary-Educated Workers by Level of Education   79
2.7   Absolute Family Income and Wealth Mobility by Education and Parents' Quintile   80
2.8   Relative Family Income and Wealth Mobility by Education and Parents' Quintile   81
2.9   Percent Achieving a Bachelor's Degree by Age 24, per Family Income Quartile   82
3.1   AmericasBarometer: Agreement That the State Should Reduce Inequality   128
3.2   General Social Survey: Percent of Americans Saying That the Government Should Reduce Income Differences between the Rich and the Poor, 1978–2014   129
3.3   Environics: Percent of Canadians Saying That the Government Should Reduce the Gap between the Rich and the Poor, 1986–2011   130
5.1   Health and Social Problems and Inequality   178
5.2   Life Expectancy and Income Inequality   180
5.3   Infant Mortality and Income Inequality   180

Tables

1.1   Growth in Real Household Income Share by Quintile, United States and Canada   19
1.2   Growth in Real Mean Household Income by Quintile, United States and Canada   21
2.1   Average Disposable Household Income and Income Growth by Quintile, Selected Years, 1986–2011   59
2.2   Relative Income Mobility by Quintile Movement   62
2.3   Percentage of Children with Gross Family Income Exceeding that of Their Parents   66
3.1   World Values Survey Questions on Income Equality   124
3.2   World Values Survey Questions on Preference for Markets: Private versus Government Ownership of Business   126
3.3   World Values Survey Questions on Preference for Markets: Economic Competition   127
4.1   Key Differences in US/Canadian Welfare Reform Legislation   157

Acknowledgments

WRITING A BOOK CAN BE A LONG AND LONELY BUSINESS, with ample time for introspection. Even a moment's reflection, however, is enough to recognize my debt of gratitude to the many people who walk behind the words and ideas on these pages. As I note elsewhere in this volume, "We are not entirely our own creation. Instead, we are the evolving sum of the forces at work upon us—of parents and children, spouses and partners, neighbors and friends, teachers and coaches, co-workers and co-religionists, and a host of others who intersect with our lives at various points." If *Seeking Equality* makes a positive contribution to civic dialogue and understanding, it is because I have had accomplices.

This book's origins are in a chapter on inequality that David Thomas and David Biette asked me to contribute to the fourth edition of their text *Canada and the United States: Differences that Count* (University of Toronto Press, 2014). If they had realized how much foundational research was necessary to produce that essay they might have had second thoughts, but I am deeply grateful for their confidence. The two Davids also introduced me to my principal editor, Michael Harrison of the University of Toronto Press (UTP). Throughout the project, Michael has been reassuring, patient, and prompt in responding to my every question—one could not ask for a better guide across the publishing terrain. Others at UTP have been equally generous: Mat Buntin, Sarah Adams, and Julia Cadney. The same is true of Anna Del Col and Beate Schwirtlich, who are responsible for the book's striking cover. As many Torontonians will know, it incorporates an excerpt from the art deco frieze work on the old Toronto Stock Exchange building. Charles Comfort, the artist who designed the frieze in the mid-1930s, intended it to express the unity of capital and labor, as members of representative occupations strode from right to left toward a common Canadian prosperity. The stonemason who executed Comfort's plan may have had other ideas: a closer look shows that the top-hatted figure—a banker or broker—appears to have his hand in the pocket of the workingman in front of him. My copy editor, Leanne Rancourt, was a pleasure to work with; she made my prose much more fluent than if left to me alone.

Components of *Seeking Equality* have appeared in different form at various symposia and seminars. The "Inequality and Redistribution" panel of the 2014 Midwest Political Science Association conference deserves special mention, given the good feedback offered by its discussant, Michael Albertus of the University of Chicago, and convener, Stephen Nelson of Northwestern University. Leo Panitch of York University, Toronto, was kind enough to comment on a chapter-length distillation of the manuscript, as was Harvey Simmons, professor emeritus from York; the book is far better for their input. Observations by UTP's anonymous reviewers were also helpful and heartening—I have incorporated almost all of their suggestions, though on occasion my stubbornness prevailed. Invaluable direction in locating and deciphering official measures of economic inequality was provided by Aaron Cobet and Vera Crain of the United States Bureau of Labor Statistics, as well as by Marc Frenette, Louise Marmen, Brian Murphy, and especially Yuri Ostrovsky of Statistics Canada, who mined unpublished evidence on intergenerational income mobility for my benefit. They testify to the excellence of our public statistical services and the talented people who staff them. Diana Elliot of the Pew Charitable Trusts was just as gracious, offering important comparative perspective and nuance.

At Messiah College I have been privileged to mentor exceptional research assistants who have faithfully obliged my requests to find and interpret discrete data and documents—now they can see how it all fits together: Victoria Falkner, Alejandro Garcia, Johnathan Hershey, Morgan Lee, Christina McIntyre, Xu Ren, and Hanna Nussbaum Ruth. They and their classmates will have anticipated several of the arguments in this book, given the abbreviated versions that sometimes appear in the courses I teach; our discussions keep me honest. But if a more systematic treatment persuades a few students, here and elsewhere, that wrestling with economic equality is worth the effort—indeed, that it is essential to democracy and justice—I will count my work a success. Teaching in a department alongside congenial colleagues is its own reward. Dean Curry and Paul Rego must have tired hearing about the draft manuscript and wondered about the length of time necessary to complete it, though they are far too decent to have complained.

Inevitably, close friends and family also shape the writing process. I remember my mentors, Dick Rung of Wheaton College and the late Jim Sharpe of Nuffield College, Oxford, whose exacting academic standards were always leavened by good humor and encouragement, and whose nurturing continued long after my graduation—they are a model for all of us who teach. Charles Kupfer, Henry Rhoads, and Harvey Simmons have helped me think more clearly about the subjects addressed here—and not only when we discuss politics, since amity is its own tonic. Walter and Jan Harles have had the good sense to occasionally disagree with their son's opinions, yet they are steadfast in their support of him; to use an idiom of this book, they were chosen wisely. Ellen Harles shouldered the inconveniences of *Seeking*

Equality more than anyone, including having the majority of it written at our kitchen table; I hope she will find most of the disruption justified. In August 1995, shortly before we were to leave Canada, having spent an extraordinary year on transfer from our jobs and lives in the United States, she gave birth to our son at the Wellesley Hospital in Toronto. Since then, whenever I think about Canada, the United States, and the connections between them, the political is profoundly personal—which is to say that this book is for Tristan, Canadian and American.

Introduction

> So when the question is raised whether some
> attempt to establish greater equality may not be
> desirable … (t)hey rear, and snort, and paw the air,
> and affirm with one accord that the suggestion
> is at once wicked and impracticable.
> R.H. Tawney, *Equality*[1]

Of all the concepts considered by students of politics, equality must be one of the most contested. Its protean nature is sufficiently frustrating that even staunch advocates count equality among the endangered species of ideals.[2] Nevertheless, equality—more precisely economic inequality—is very much a concern of the moment. A recent global survey finds that the publics of rich democratic countries increasingly consider inequality the greatest threat to the world—more troublesome than disease, environmental degradation, religious and ethnic strife, or the prospect of nuclear war.[3] This should come as no surprise. The issue resonates because the gap between the haves and have-nots is not simply a problem of abstract intellectual interest but touches concretely on the ability of ordinary people to live fulfilling lives. And while income disparities have narrowed in developing economies, not so in advanced industrial states like Canada and the United States where they are reaching levels not seen since the 1920s.[4]

Pope Francis may have done as much as anyone to increase global awareness of the injustice that derives from a skewed distribution of economic resources. His mission manifesto, *Evangelii gaudium*, attacks "the idolatry of money" and calls the unfettered market "a new tyranny." In the same way, whatever else can be said about the Occupy Movement, its rallying cry that "we are the 99 percent" helped focus attention on the political and economic significance of wide discrepancies in income and wealth. Undoubtedly one of the more startling headlines of the last few years must be "Davos: Income Inequality on World Economic Forum Agenda," referring to the annual meeting of the great and the good in the Swiss Alps, 80 billionaires strong.[5] Yet a growing number of global financial elites now warn about the disruptive consequences of large economic imbalances—among them the head of the International Monetary Fund, the governor of the Bank of England, and the CEO of Goldman Sachs, the investment banking house not particularly known for its magnanimity.[6]

Public opinion leaders in North America have followed suit. Former president Barack Obama called the chasm between economic elites and the rest the "defining challenge of our time," maintaining in his second inaugural address that the United States "cannot succeed when a shrinking few do very well and a growing many barely make it."[7] And equality was front and center in the 2016 presidential primary season, though most enthusiastically championed by Bernie Sanders, the senator from Vermont who made it the cornerstone of his challenge to the eventual Democratic nominee, Hillary Clinton.[8] Her Republican nemesis, Donald Trump, the real-estate magnate who went on to win the general election, said little explicitly about economic equality during his campaign, perhaps as befits a multi-billionaire born to extraordinary privilege.[9] Still, election analysts credit Trump's victory partly to his support among a disaffected white working class, which voted for him in significantly greater numbers than his Republican predecessor, Mitt Romney, four years earlier.[10] Trump's antiestablishment message, including skepticism of immigration and international trade agreements that allegedly disadvantaged American workers, was a potent appeal to individuals feeling excluded from the benefits of national economic growth and vulnerable to a global market whose fundamentals are rapidly changing. Whether that constituency will be adequately represented by a president and cabinet whose combined net worth—estimated at over $13 billion—is the greatest by far of any administration in recent history and whose economic leadership includes high-ranking executives from the very Wall Street institutions excoriated by candidate Trump as elitist and corrupt remains to be seen.[11]

Canadian politicians are more circumspect. To be fair, they may have less to talk about since distributional differences are not quite as conspicuous north of the border. During his nine-year tenure, Prime Minister Stephen Harper said little about economic inequality, which had leveled out by the time his Conservative government took power in 2006.[12] If leaders of Canada's major opposition parties were more concerned, in the 2015 federal election they seemed relatively subdued when it came to speaking and strategizing on equality's behalf.[13] Still, compared to other rich democratic countries, Canada remains in the lower half of the income and wealth equality tables, and by some measures its middle-class incomes are stagnating. That fact has not been lost on the Liberal Party government of Justin Trudeau nor its New Democratic Party rivals, the traditional parties of the center-left/left, who put inequality back on the legislative agenda once the post-election Parliament was convened.[14] Among the Trudeau government's initial measures were means-testing what had been Canada's universal child benefit—in effect, siphoning cash from the top 10 percent of earners and progressively redistributing it to others—and increasing income taxes on the top 1 percent of earners to pay for a middle-class tax cut. Canada's newspaper of record, the *Globe and Mail*, took note, its editorial page advising the Liberals to "Stop Whacking the One Percent."[15]

Attention by book publishers has intensified as well. According to Google Books's Ngram Viewer, a rough and ready scan of words and phrases appearing in over 5 million English language volumes through 2008, the frequency of the phrase "economic inequality" has more than doubled since 1970 and that of "income inequality" has more than quadrupled.[16] Interest has only accelerated since the 2013 publication of Thomas Piketty's bestseller, *Capital in the Twenty-First Century*, a study that reviewers have called "enthralling," "revolutionary," and "groundbreaking" while hailing its French economist author as "a modern Marx."[17] At 577 pages in its English language translation, it is not for the faint-hearted. Exemplary in its empirical rigor and statistically informed historical analysis, the text details the long-term processes whereby in advanced industrial countries income, wealth, and power have become progressively concentrated in the hands of the super-rich. Yet as Piketty cautions, even the most sophisticated quantitative exploration of the economic forces behind inequality can tell only part of the story. There is always a subjective and psychological dimension to inequality, he notes, as democratic publics make decisions about the appropriate distribution of economic resources.[18] Thus Piketty insists on the importance of the cultural and governmental context of economic decision making along with the "political, normative, and moral purpose" of the discipline of economics, avenues of inquiry he invites other scholars to consider as well.[19] And he encourages social scientists in other fields not to "leave the study of economic facts to economists" or to "flee in horror the minute a number rears its head."[20]

The present volume takes up the challenge. Its author is a political scientist who wishes to assess the hard evidence of economic inequality by offering political context and meaning for what the data reveal. Hence, the analysis begins by posing empirical questions about the distribution of economic resources in the United States and Canada, including the political factors that account for the differences between them, and goes on to indicate why, for practical reasons as well as those more philosophical, high levels of inequality are a bad thing. Insofar as book titles can be instructive, *Seeking Equality: The Political Economy of the Common Good in the United States and Canada* suggests that (1) as the practice of politics and economics is integrated, so must be their study, especially in light of the power relationships influencing the division of a country's material resources; (2) acting in the common good—trying to enhance the well-being of each member of the political community and doing so equally—is a proper object of democratic government; and (3) equality is an aspiration worth pursuing, a concept at the heart of social and economic justice even if it is difficult to fully realize. Consequently, economic arrangements that permit the few to be consistently advantaged at the expense of the many demand moral scrutiny.

Within certain academic circles this additional normative emphasis may not be entirely welcome.[21] Social scientists can be reluctant to consider the evaluative implications of their research, not wishing to conflate the "is" with the "ought." But the social purpose of social science cannot be forgotten. Compelling work in politics and economics must be able to pass the "so what?" test: How are what we study, the things we discover, and the conclusions we draw relevant to the average citizen? How do they bear on the substance of the life we share? Or again, with respect to more immediate concerns, why is a yawning gap between the very rich and the rest cause for civic anxiety … and what can be done about it? At the end of this book, one hopes readers will know.

The Approach

Comparison is at the heart of social science—the only way in which students of politics can aspire to make even tentative generalizations about political life. That alone may recommend the method adopted here: to relate the shape and significance of economic inequality across two states, the United States and Canada.[22] Yet this is a pairing of a certain kind, in which the many similarities between the countries being studied serve to highlight the variations between them. A key difference, detailed in the pages that follow, is that on every standard measure of economic equality—the distribution of income and wealth, middle-class well-being, the poverty rate, upward economic mobility—Canada does better than the United States. Isolating the factors responsible is more daunting. Interdependent historical, institutional, and macroeconomic forces are clearly at work, as is the momentum of past policy choices. But the hypothesis ventured here is that cultural factors are also part of the mix. Specifically, there are marked distinctions of value between Canadians and Americans regarding how best to look after the most economically vulnerable members of society. In effect, Canada has a more equal distribution of economic resources than the United States because Canadians care more about the disadvantages of people at the bottom of the income scale, are less disposed to protect the prerogatives of those at the top, and have a greater willingness to use the instruments of government to redress each.

A "most similar systems" research design has a further practical advantage.[23] There is a natural political curiosity between Canada and the United States because each country presents a viable image of what the other might be. American politicians and policy wonks may find, say, progressive Scandinavian models of political economy to be of limited relevance, but Canada is a closer run thing.[24] When two states have so much in common, their policy regimes are unlikely to appear so exotic as to be nontransferable. Thus, for an American audience who thinks a little more economic equality might be a good idea, the Canadian experience can be especially instructive. It's harder to dismiss the lessons to be learned when two countries have intersecting histories; share a long, peaceful, and (until late) permeable border; confront common geographical barriers to economic and political development; experience similar waves of large-scale immigration and thus high levels of ethnoracial diversity; draw on a shared and largely British political heritage, modified by the territorial decentralization of power that is federalism; adopt parallel forms of political economy that tend to favor market-based solutions to social problems; possess interdependent economies, including the largest and most comprehensive bilateral trading relationship in the world; and have almost always been on the same side in the defining foreign policy engagements of the last century.

Canada and the United States are not carbon copies—demographically, culturally, and politically the French fact in the former and increasingly the Hispanic one in the latter have made certain of that. So, too, in the way in which the legacy of slavery and Jim Crow continues to plague the American struggle for racial equality, including economic equality. But given that the two countries are alike in so many other respects, an astute observer may wonder why Canadians are able to enjoy more equal economic outcomes than Americans. One response, not entirely satisfactory, is that this is largely a problem of scale. Presumably, the administrative apparatus necessary to reconfigure the allocation of desirable public goods grows more convoluted the larger a citizenry gets. On this logic, since Canada's population is around one-tenth the size of the United States, its governments can more easily intervene to correct for the inequities of the market. The problem is that the reverse argument is just as potent. Certainly the magnitude of the American population is not simply a liability but also a potential asset, inasmuch as 325 million people can bring more resources to bear on the problems of inequality than 35 million. Moreover, if population size is decisive, it's unclear which countries offer the United States a better match. For students of advanced industrial democracy it's hardly acceptable that Indonesia, Brazil, and Pakistan—the next runners-up in sheer number of residents—are the most likely candidates for comparison.

An Overview of the Argument

Explanations for cross-border differences in economic distribution are to be found elsewhere, not principally in failures of bureaucracy but of national will.

Subsequent chapters marshal support for that claim. Drawing on evidence from domestic and international statistical agencies, Chapter 1 relates that over the past few decades inequalities of income and wealth have increased in virtually all the advanced industrial economies. The United States and Canada are at the forefront of the trend, though the former is a considerably more unequal place than the latter. Globalization and the rapid development of information technology are among the principal culprits, but discrete national policies can deflect their most severe consequences—policies that have had a greater ameliorative effect in Canada. High levels of inequality might be less worrisome if one could be confident of moving up the ladder of economic success. Yet Chapter 2 reveals that across multiple indicators mobility is lower in the United States than in Canada. That is particularly the case with respect to income elasticity, the degree to which parents' earnings advantages are passed on to their children. By that benchmark, Canada has one of the highest and the United States one of the lowest rates of upward mobility among all rich democratic states. North of the border, the economic status of the household in which a young person is raised does relatively little to determine his or her chances of a comfortable life in adulthood, including access to what is most often the prerequisite of prosperity: a university degree. South of the border, it's more important to choose your parents wisely.

Causal questions remain. Chapter 3 speculates that distinctions in economic distribution and mobility are influenced by contrasting political cultures. Dominant historical patterns of belief, constitutional practices, and contemporary public opinion polls suggest that Canadians are more inclined than Americans to value the well-being of the community over the individual, support equality in general and economic equality in particular, and see the state as having an important redistributive role. Canadians also operate within a Westminster model of parliamentary government, an institutional arrangement that can more quickly accommodate proposed changes in the allocation of economic goods, provided a critical mass of public officials and citizens are supportive. By contrast, the hyper-fragmentation of power in the American constitutional system serves as a braking mechanism on redistributive initiatives, typically preserving a status quo favorable to economic elites. To see what these structural and ideational tendencies look like in action, Chapter 4 addresses the Canadian and American experience with welfare reform, a policy field that was overhauled in the mid-1990s and whose evolution suggests how each country treats its neediest members. Reliance on the market to lift welfare recipients out of destitution has been central to the US reform agenda, where social assistance has been increasingly privatized. Canada has been a kinder and gentler place, keener to make certain that the burdens of reform are shouldered evenly by the people and governments subject to them and retaining a social safety net that is better funded and more comprehensive than its American counterpart.

Economic equality is a concept that requires defending—its value is not self-evident. Chapter 5 lays out the reasons for thinking that in the present North American circumstances more of it would be better. It argues that a productive, healthy, socially cohesive, democratic, and just society requires Canadian and American polities to move in an egalitarian direction. But the United States must move further. A way forward is outlined in the Conclusion, which specifies the kinds of economic policies conducive to a widely shared prosperity. Since Canada has implemented more of them, Americans would be wise to consider their neighbor's example. Institutional tweaks to the operation of democracy are required as well, particularly when it comes to reducing the ability of private money to buy political influence. Yet perhaps the hardest transformation to affect, and the most necessary, will be a change in the dominant civic outlook. For Americans used to prioritizing individual autonomy over community obligation, and more likely to see an active state as an agent of coercion than an aid to economic emancipation, it is a tall order. Nevertheless, value preferences change over time. And if cultural variables do have a significant influence on policy outcomes, as this analysis maintains, then a given economic distribution is not foreordained. Instead, it matters what people think about the kind of life they wish to share. Believers in democracy and in justice should be cheered.

An Ideal of Equality

What follows is not chiefly a work of political theory. It does not in any comprehensive way outline the features of a perfectly just social and economic arrangement or the character of the state that must nurture it.[25] Yet an ideal of equality does percolate below the surface of these pages. While grasping it is not essential to the majority of the argument—not until the book's final two chapters at any rate—it may be helpful for readers to know briefly what that view is.

What equality requires in any distributive decision is rarely obvious. Consider the account of King Solomon in the Hebrew Scriptures, a morality tale expressed in various ways and across multiple cultures.[26] Confronted with a dilemma in which two women claim to be the mother of the same infant boy, Solomon proposes to divide the child in half, giving each plaintiff an equal share. Immediately the birth mother relents, not wishing her son to be harmed.[27] Recognizing true sacrificial love, the kind only a mother can express, the king awards the baby to the woman willing to let him go. In the standard interpretation, the story celebrates a ruler's wisdom. But there is another lesson, one less remarked upon: In the application of justice, strict equality is not always a good thing. Sameness of treatment can lead to deeply unsatisfactory results.

Answering the question of *who* is to be made equal is the first problem. A natural response is to make everyone equal, though this is not as straightforward as it seems. In light of the different aptitudes and capacities possessed by any two people, making them equal in some relevant respect may require unequal remedies. A tall person and a person of shorter stature will both need suitable clothes for the winter, for example, but not the same amount of fabric to keep warm. Moreover, as contemporary theorists of equality often point out, in the present era of identity politics equality's mandate is no longer simply to make the quality of people's lives fundamentally alike in terms of economic circumstances, political power, social status, and so on. Instead, it is to recognize, institutionalize, and promote their difference equally.[28] Thus, in the interest of equality, unequal treatment will be extended to members of a particular social group according to their gender, ethnicity, race, sexuality, or disability. And yet if all people should be regarded equally, meaning differently, one might reasonably ask whether equality amounts to much.

Despite the paradox, egalitarians believe in a profound similarity between human beings. According to some, the common denominator is the capacity to reason, for others the vulnerability to suffering, for still others a glimpse of the divine. Whatever the source, this irreducible quality, a matter of conviction as much as fact, is the basis for believing that the things that divide people are less important than the essential dignity that unites them.[29] The second challenge of equality, then, determining *what* is to be made equal, must be disciplined by recognition of the equal and intrinsic worth of all. As the British political economist R. H. Tawney writes, equality insists that whereas people "differ profoundly as individuals in capacity and character, they are equally entitled as human beings to consideration and respect, and that the well-being of a society is likely to be increased if it so plans its organization that, whether their powers are great or small, all its members may be equally enabled to make the best of such powers as they possess."[30]

The concept of equality advocated in this book follows Tawney's lead. Its answer to the "what" question of equality is that ideally the basic material needs people require to enjoy satisfying lives of their own choosing should be equally met. This is at the core of what is sometimes called a *capabilities perspective* on distributive justice, which tries to square an individual's freedom to pursue a meaningful plan of life with an equal claim to the resources making it possible.[31] In a democratic state, the full slate of what is necessary will be fashioned by civic dialogue and the vagaries of the policymaking process, though at a minimum food, clothing, shelter, medical care, education, work, and recreation seem indispensable. To be sure, it is an ideal, a standard to be kept in mind as political decisions are made about how best to allocate the goods most important to a fulfilling life, though no less persuasive for that.

How such necessities are to be obtained, that is, the appropriate mix of private and public provision, is a further issue for democratic debate. By their nature, markets have an uneasy relationship with equality, insofar as economic competition for labor, capital, and consumers is spurred by unequal financial inducements.[32] Indeed, as this book will argue, escalating market-driven inequalities in rich democratic countries merit serious public attention. Governments must be expected to play a major role in advancing their citizens' equal well-being in large part because markets are poorly equipped to do so. Equal opportunity will be part of the public arsenal, giving individuals similar tools for economic, social, and political advancement and trusting that the outcomes will be favorable. It will not be enough. That kind of equality inevitably leads to uneven results that prejudice future opportunities—especially when markets are the principal register of the financial rewards individuals are deemed to deserve for their economic efforts.[33] So the state, especially the democratic state, will need to be vigilant. Indeed, democratic governments should be uniquely attuned to issues of distributive justice since they too rest on a moral foundation of respect for the inherent equality of all.[34] This relationship between economic and political equality—and economic and political power—is close and reciprocal. If economic disparities grow too deep, the democratic ideal of a citizen's equal influence in the political decision-making process is threatened. And if democracy is corrupted, so is the chance for ordinary citizens to be treated justly, which is to say equally, with regard to the requirements of a good life.

Concluding Remarks

Readers will not venture far into these pages before recognizing that slightly more attention is given to the American than the Canadian engagement with inequality. Availability of national data is the smaller part of the reason. Repositories of American economic statistics tend to be more numerous and their holdings more extensive than for Canadian counterparts. The elimination of Canada's mandatory long-form census between 2006 and 2015—a major source of comprehensive and high-quality economic information—was especially unfortunate. But the principal reason is simply that compared to Canada the United States is in greater jeopardy from the malevolent effects of inequality. Canadians cannot be complacent. Among advanced industrial states Canada is still in the lower half of the economic equality rankings, and it continues to struggle with the realities of poverty and low-income status—to which Indigenous peoples and visible minorities are disproportionately exposed. Yet from the perspective of those Americans who desire a more even-handed division of economic goods, the Canadian record is enviable. If there are comparative lessons to be learned, then it is the United States who must learn them.

It will not be easy. Political conversations about redistribution never are—especially when the proposal is to take something from one group of people and give it to another. But in the United States, for cultural and historical reasons, resistance is unusually intense. Derisive public officials and their allies regularly raise the specter of "class war" to shame supporters of a more equitable distribution of economic resources.[35] Never mind that extending health insurance as a right of citizenship or taxing millionaires at a rate no less than middle-income families is hardly the storming of the Winter Palace.[36] Nor that class is invoked by protégés of privilege in the most imprecise and eccentric way. In the name of national solidarity, it is insisted, the perquisites of the well-to-do must be preserved.

The truth, as this book will convey, is quite the reverse. In many ways a kind of class war has already begun, conducted by the rich against the rest. And in the United States, the rich are winning.

Notes

1 Tawney, *Equality*, 44.
2 For instance, see Dworkin, *Sovereign Virtue*, 1.
3 Pew Research Center, "Middle Easterners See Religious and Ethnic Hatred as Top Global Threat."
4 Lakner and Milanovic, "Global Income Distribution." Global wealth distribution is a different story. According to a report by Oxfam, the richest 1 percent now possess more wealth than the rest of the world combined. Hardoon, Ayele, and Fuentes-Nieva, "An Economy for the 1%."
5 Fleury, "Davos: Income Inequality on World Economic Forum Agenda."
6 Monaghan, "IMF Chief Says Banks Haven't Changed since Financial Crisis"; Carney, "Inclusive Capitalism"; Song, "Goldman Sachs CEO."
7 "Obama's Second Inaugural Speech."
8 See, for instance, Nyhan, "Why Republicans Are Suddenly Talking about Income Inequality."
9 Kessler, "Trump's False Claim He Built His Empire with a 'Small Loan' from His Father."
10 According to exit polling, Trump performed better than Romney among white men with no college degree by 18 percentage points; among individuals with family income under $30,000 by 16 points; among high school graduates or less by 12 points; and among individuals with family income between $30,000 and $50,000 by 6 points. These were not the typical Trump voters, who tended

to be better off economically than non-Trump voters, even with comparable levels of education and after controlling for race (since white people on average are richer than non-whites). Hillary Clinton still won more votes than Trump from individuals making under $30,000 (by 12 points) and between $30,000 and $50,000 (by 9 points). But the large inroads Trump made among whites of modest income and education certainly contributed to his victory. Turnout also had a bearing. Not only did Trump mobilize Republican-inclined working-class voters in larger-than-expected numbers, but Clinton failed to do so among their Democratic counterparts, lagging the share of those who had gone to the polls for Barack Obama in the previous two elections. See Huang, Jacoby, Strickland, and Lai, "Election 2016: Exit Polls"; Tyson and Maniam, "Behind Trump's Victory"; Cohn, "Why Trump Won Working Class Whites"; Kilibarda and Roithmayr, "The Myth of the Rust Belt Revolt."

11   Rocheleau, "Trump's Cabinet Picks so Far Worth a Combined $13b."
12   It should be noted that a House of Commons Committee on Income Inequality was created in 2012 by virtue of a private member's bill shepherded by a Liberal MP. The committee reported in 2013, recommending changes to the tax code, including the working income tax benefit, preserving (though not increasing) social assistance benefits, and encouraging educational opportunity. No action was taken by the Conservative government.
13   Extending publicly funded child care, increasing the child tax benefit and the minimum wage, and closing tax loopholes for stock options were among the modest inequality-fighting proposals offered by the major opposition parties. See, for instance, Tsalikis, "What Canada's Election Campaign Has Missed"; Yakabuski, "There Is No Middle in the Middle Class Debate."
14   Raj, "Income Inequality Back in Focus for Liberals, NDP as Parliament Returns."
15   "Stop Whacking the One Percent."
16   Google Books, "Ngram Viewer," https://books.google.com/ngrams.
17   Wolf, "'Capital in the 21st Century'"; Cowen, "Capital Punishment"; Krugman, "Why We're in a New Gilded Age"; "Capitalism and Its Critics: A Modern Marx." It should be said that *The Economist* did not intend the association with Marx as a compliment.
18   Piketty, *Capital in the Twenty-First Century*, 2.
19   Ibid., 574.
20   Ibid., 575.
21   See, for instance, the discussion in Flyvberg, *Making Social Science Matter*.
22   On how rare the comparative approach to inequality has become among US-trained political scientists, see Stepan and Linz, "Comparative Perspectives on Inequality and the Quality of Democracy in the United States."
23   Przeworski and Teune, *The Logic of Comparative Social Inquiry*.
24   See, for example, the discussion in Edsall, "Why Can't America Be Sweden?" Or consider the following exchange from an October 2015 Democratic presidential primary debate:

BERNIE SANDERS: [W]hen you look around the world, you see every other major country providing health care to all people as a right, except the United States. You see every other major country saying to moms that, when you have a baby, we're not gonna separate you from your newborn baby, because we are

going to have—we are gonna have medical and family paid leave, like every other country on Earth. Those are some of the principles that I believe in, and I think we should look to countries like Denmark, like Sweden and Norway, and learn from what they have accomplished for their working people. ...
HILLARY CLINTON: I think what Senator Sanders is saying certainly makes sense in the terms of the inequality that we have. But we are not Denmark. I love Denmark. We are the United States of America. And it's our job to rein in the excesses of capitalism so that it doesn't run amok and doesn't cause the kind of inequities we're seeing in our economic system. But we would be making a grave mistake to turn our backs on what built the greatest middle class in the history. ("The CNN Democratic Debate Transcript, Annotated")

25 The Oxford economist Sir Anthony Atkinson takes a similar approach in his recent book of proposals to turn the tide of inequality: "I am not seeking a transcendental solution. I shall not discuss the ultimate question of the socially just allocation of power. Rather I start from the pragmatic concern that current levels of inequality are too high and that this outcome in part reflects the fact that the balance of power is weighted against consumers and workers." Atkinson, *Inequality: What Can Be Done?* 124.

26 I Kings 3:16–28. The story has numerous parallels in ancient Greek, Indian, and Chinese folktales. Perhaps its most famous contemporary interpretation is the German playwright Bertolt Brecht's *The Caucasian Chalk Circle*. Barton and Muddiman, *The Oxford Bible Commentary*, 236.

27 According to the Midrash, the traditional rabbinical commentaries on the Hebrew Scriptures, the two women are widows, mother and daughter-in-law. At issue is the ancient Jewish custom whereby, if at all possible, a widowed woman was obligated to marry her brother-in-law. In this instance the daughter-in-law would need to wait until the infant son of her mother-in-law had come of age. Wishing to be free of such constraints, the woman who had lost her child concocted the story of the stolen baby. Presumably it explains why she is unconcerned if he should die.

28 Squires, "Equality and Difference."
29 Guttman, "Equality."
30 Tawney, *Equality*, 46–47.
31 Sen, *The Idea of Justice*; Nussbaum, *Creating Capabilities*, 28.
32 Rae, *Equalities*, 26.
33 See, for instance, ibid., 64–76; Charvet, "The Idea of Equality as a Substantive Principle of Society."
34 Dahl, *Democracy and Its Critics*, 83–84.
35 For instance, Rushe, "Obama's Millionaire Tax Is Class War, Say Republicans"; "The War over Class War."
36 Taxing millionaires at a rate no lower than middle-income families is the gist of the famous "Buffett Rule," named for Warren Buffett, the billionaire investor who thought it shameful that he should be able to pay proportionately less income tax than his administrative assistant.

1
Distribution

CANADA AND THE UNITED STATES have a more unequal distribution of income and wealth than most rich democratic countries. Yet when it comes to the degree of that inequality, the United States has few rivals. On every major distributional indicator Canada fares better—if by that one means is more equal—than its American neighbor. At the summit of the inequality tables, the United States makes for an easy target.

The present chapter lays the empirical foundations for such observations, focusing on income, the middle class, wealth, and poverty. It concludes with a brief analysis of the factors driving rising levels of inequality across the advanced industrial economies since the late 1970s, particularly in North America: globalization, the deregulation of the financial industry, the rapid development of information technology, changing family dynamics, and public policy. That discussion is especially pertinent to the strategies a concerned citizen might endorse as a means to greater economic equity, the subject of the Conclusion in this book.

Two brief methodological observations are in order. First, when considering income inequality it is important to keep in mind what kind of income is at issue: *market* income, roughly all cash earnings before government taxes and transfers; *gross* income, total monetary income after transfers but before taxes; or *disposable* income, post-tax and transfer earnings, that is to say, where one stands after the full distributional impact of a government's fiscal policy. The discussion that follows tries to be conscientious in specifying which of these definitions is being used.[1]

Second, by multiplying the number of countries and cases to be considered, comparative social science presents its own challenges, all the more so when it comes to assessing the kind of economic data offered here. Statistical agencies in different countries collect similar information in different ways, and a variety of approaches can be used within a single agency. The present analysis is sensitive to these idiosyncrasies by choosing the closest available cross-national common denominators, for instance, when squaring data from Statistics Canada and the US Census Bureau, but it recognizes the limitations.[2] Various tables and footnotes specify the sources; whether too many liberties have been taken is up to others. Most often, data are used that have already been harmonized by comparatively inclined think tanks and international research centers, such as the Organisation for Economic

Co-operation and Development (OECD), the Luxembourg Income Study database, the World Wealth and Income Database, and Credit Suisse's Global Wealth Databook. Inasmuch as these rely on statistics collected by discrete national governments, here too the smoothing is imperfect. Best, one suspects, to live carefully with the ambiguities.

Income

Over the last three decades, income inequality has increased in virtually all advanced industrial states. Among the 34 member countries of the OECD, a group that includes the world's most prosperous democracies, the average disposable income of the richest tenth of the population is now almost 10 times that of the poorest tenth. The Gini coefficient, the statistic most often used to express the distribution of household income, has risen across the great majority of those states. On a scale of zero to one, where zero indicates perfect equality in that each citizen has the same amount of income and one indicates perfect inequality in that all income would go to a single person, the aggregate OECD Gini for household earnings after government transfers and taxes has increased from 0.29 in the mid-1980s to 0.32 by 2014, a jump of more than 10 percent. As Figure 1.1 indicates, the rate of increase varies between countries, but there is no doubt that inequality is ascendant.[3]

Figure 1.1 Rising Income Inequality—Gini Coefficients in OECD Countries, 1985 and 2013

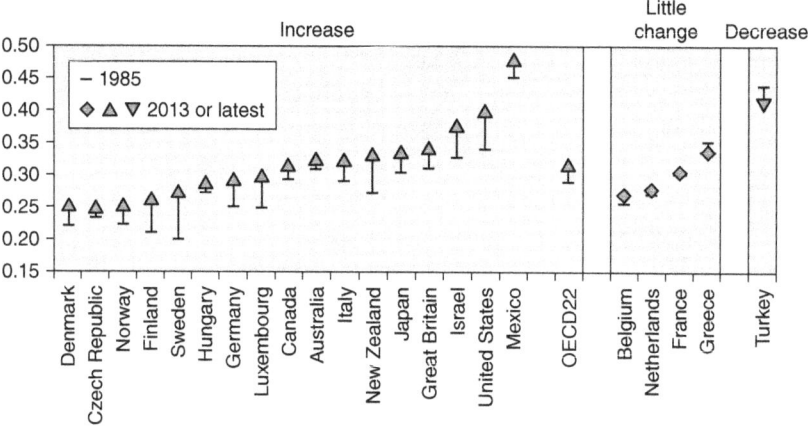

Note: Income refers to household disposable income, adjusted for household size.

Source: OECD, *In It Together*, p. 24, Figure 1.3.

North American economies have trended in the same direction, though with respect to the distribution of income and wealth the United States is a significantly more unequal place than Canada. To be sure, among advanced industrial states the United States has the highest level of income inequality of all. (The OECD considers Mexico, Turkey, and Chile—member states with even greater inequality than the United States—to be "emerging" as opposed to "advanced" economies). That is true as measured by its Gini coefficient as well as the relative income stake of the top 90 percent versus the bottom 10 percent of American earners, the former now commanding a share more than 18 times larger than that of the latter. By contrast, for the last two decades Canada has tended to track the average Gini for OECD members. And whereas Canada's top 10 percent receive 9.3 times more income share than the poorest 10 percent, that is still roughly half of the equivalent ratio in the United States (Figures 1.2 and 1.3).

Things have not always been this way. Across the last century, income distribution for affluent individuals in North America has followed a U-shaped pattern. As Figure 1.4 shows, that trajectory has been especially pronounced for those at the very top of the income scale—the richest 1 percent of all earners. In the 1920s, Canadian and American earnings disparities were

Figure 1.2 Gini Coefficients of Inequality for Disposable Income (Post-Transfer and Tax), 2013

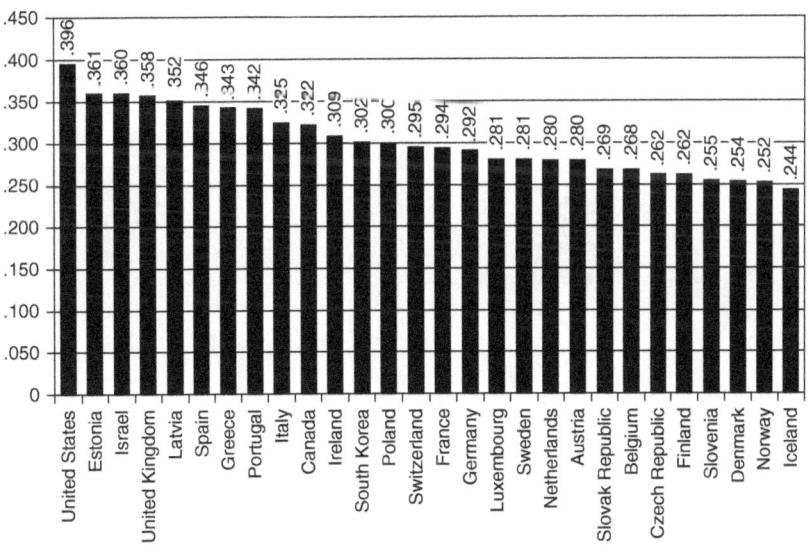

OECD average (2013) = 0.315

Source: OECD, "Income Distribution and Poverty."

Figure 1.3 Ratio of Top versus Bottom Decile Share for Disposable Income (Post-Transfer and Tax), 2013

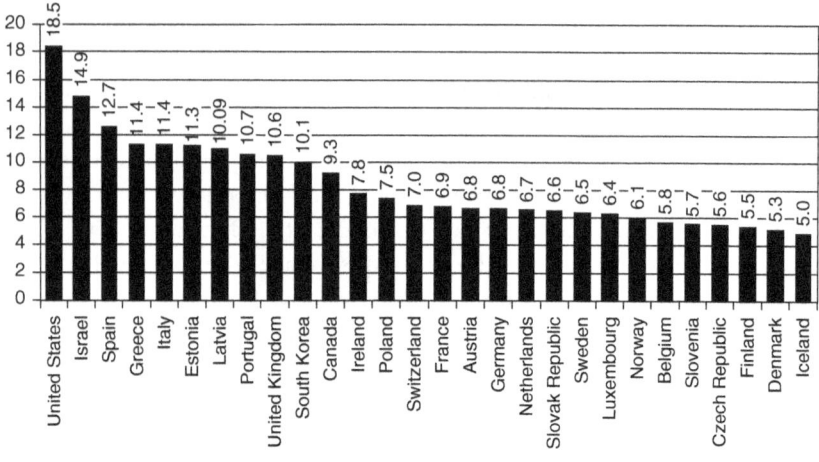

OECD average (2013) = 8.9

Source: OECD, "Income Distribution and Poverty."

Figure 1.4 Canada and US Income Shares of Top 1 Percent of Earners, 1913–2015

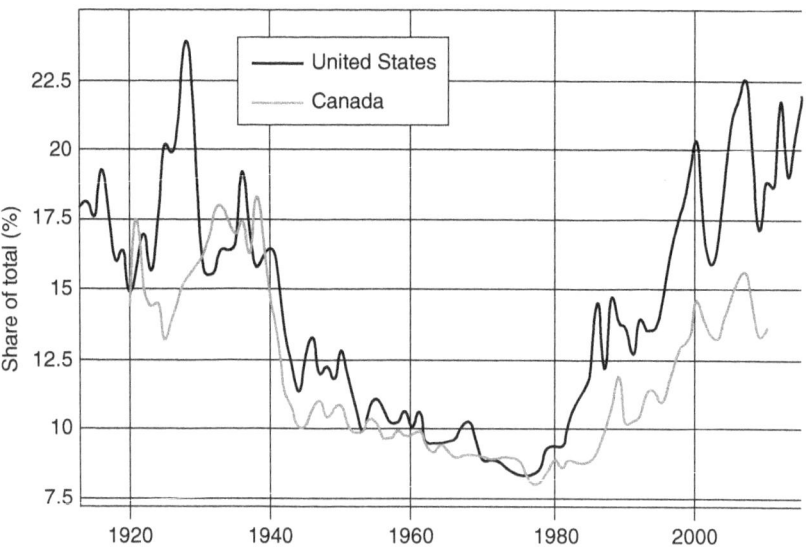

Note: This graph displays gross income (post-transfers but pre-tax) exclusive of capital gains.

Source: World Wealth and Income Database.

almost as skewed as they are at present. But from the late 1930s until the early 1950s, each country's income gaps began to compress, after which they held fairly constant through the mid-1970s. Since then, income inequality has increased on either side of the border to the degree that in the United States it once again rivals that of the late Gilded Age, a phenomenon the American economist Paul Krugman calls the "Great Divergence."[4]

It is not quite back to the future. To begin, the source of contemporary inequality is different. In the 1920s, the richest individuals received much of their income from wealth—returns on capital investments in property, stocks and bonds, savings, and so on. That is still an important and increasingly lucrative part of the revenue of the well-to-do. But now individuals at the highest rungs of the income ladder are being paid a considerably greater part of their earnings in wages, salaries, and benefits, leaving less generously compensated members of lower tiers far behind.[5] Further, between the early 1930s and the late 1970s, the most economically successful Canadians often accrued a larger portion of gross national income than did their American peers. Since then, the gap in income share has steadily grown to the advantage of the Americans.[6] Though the direction of change is the same, the United States seems to be racing ahead of Canada—indeed, ahead of all other advanced economies—in the income inequality sweepstakes (Figure 1.5).[7]

Figure 1.5 Increase in Income Share of Top 1 percent of Earners, 1981–2012

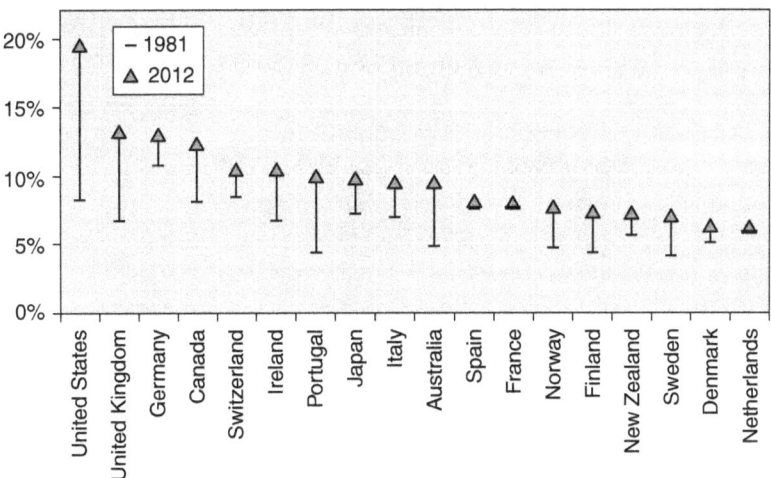

Note: Incomes refer to post-transfer but pre-tax incomes, excluding capital gains (except for Germany).

Source: OECD, "Focus on Top Incomes and Taxation in OECD Countries," 1.

Dig into the North American data a little further and one gets a better sense of just how disproportionate things are. Since the beginning of the Great Divergence, inequalities in the fraction of national income accumulated by leading Canadian and American earners have accelerated. According to the World Wealth and Income Database (WID), from 1975 to 2010 gross income share (income before taxes but after government transfers) jumped for the highest tenth of Canadian earners by 10 percent, the top 1 percent by 54 percent, and the top 0.1 percent by 127 percent. Their American counterparts have done better still—47 percent for the highest tenth, 127 percent for the top 1 percent, and a staggering 273 percent for the richest 0.1 percent. The result is a virtual law of increasing disproportion in that the higher up the income ladder one goes, the greater the extent of inequality. So in 2010, the last year for which the WID has parallel income data for Canada and the United States, of all national earnings received, the top tenth of American earners secured 45 percent and the top centile got 19 percent; although it was not quite as steep, Canadians followed the same distributional path—the top tenth garnered 41 percent and the top centile received 13 percent of total income. Concentration of income at the heights of the American distributional ladder continues unabated: In 2015 the leading tenth of households commanded half of all US income, the top centile had a 22-percent stake, and the richest 0.1 percent of Americans collected an 11-percent share.[8]

Not only do the rich continue to get extraordinarily richer, but people of modest means are losing ground as well. Consider the allocation of gross earnings according to household income quintile. When one divides a country's income distribution scale into five 20-percent bands from poorest to richest, what is the share of income accounted for by each? Table 1.1 displays the results. Predictably, the portion going to individual quintiles increases as one climbs from the bottom of the income scale to the top. But from 1980 onward, it is only families in the highest fifth whose piece of the earnings pie has grown, and even then an increasingly bigger wedge is being claimed by the richest among them. The income share of all other tiers has contracted—increasingly so in the United States as one descends the distributional ladder. Indeed, from the early years of the Great Divergence to the present, the evolution of American income share has been perfectly skewed. Earners who found themselves in the lowest four quintiles in 1980 were in an even weaker distributional position by the early 2010s, with each quintile worse off—in other words, less equal—than the one above it.

Income share is one thing, real income growth another. A household might be part of an income tier that is losing overall earnings share yet still improve its material well-being. As long as the economic health of those on the lower rungs of the income ladder was improving significantly, a

Table 1.1 Growth in Real Household Income Share by Quintile, United States and Canada

	United States				
	Income Share			Percent Income Share Growth	
	1980	2000	2013	1980–2013	2000–2013
Lowest 20%	4.2%	3.6%	3.2%	−23.8%	−11.1%
Second 20%	10.2	8.9	8.4	−17.6	−5.6
Middle 20%	16.8	14.8	14.4	−14.2	−2.7
Fourth 20%	24.7	23.0	23.0	−6.8	0.0
Highest 20%	44.1	49.8	51.0	15.6	2.4
Top 5%	16.5	22.1	22.2	34.5	0.4
Top 1%	10.0	21.5	20.0	100.0	−6.9
	Canada				
	Income Share			Percent Income Share Growth	
	1980	2000	2011	1980–2011	2000–2011
Lowest 20%	4.3%	4.1%	4.1%	−4.6%	0.0%
Second 20%	10.9	9.5	9.6	−11.9	1.0
Middle 20%	17.9	15.6	15.3	−14.5	−1.9
Fourth 20%	25.2	23.9	23.8	−5.5	−0.4
Highest 20%	41.8	47.0	47.2	12.9	0.4
Top 5%	19.5*	25.7	25.1	28.7**	−2.3
Top 1%	7.4*	12.7	11.7	58.1**	−7.8

*Statistics Canada data for 1982.
**Statistics Canada data for 1982–2011.

Note: Comparable data are available only for pre-tax income.

Sources: US Census Bureau, "Selected Measures of Household Income Dispersion, 1967–2013" (constant 2013 US dollars); for the top 1 percent of US income earners, World Wealth and Income Database, http://wid.world; Statistics Canada, "Market, Total and After-Tax Income"; Statistics Canada, "High Income Trends of Tax Filers in Canada."

declining relative share might not matter so much. Questions of distribution aside, then, what can be said of mean household gross income in each quintile over time? Since 1980, as Table 1.2 reveals, the typical family among the highest 20 percent of earners has secured the greatest benefit by far of any growth in inflation-adjusted earnings—a jump of 48 percent in the United States and 33 percent in Canada. Among the richest vigintile and centile that growth has been spectacular, rising by 47.1 percent and 79.7 percent in

Canada, and 72.3 percent and 156 percent in the United States. Progress for the average household in each of the bottom three quintiles, however, has been halting, not only lagging far behind the highest two income quintiles in each country but in some instances experiencing hardly any real growth at all. Considering what is at stake, it is the fate of the bottom quintile where cross-border differences may be the most striking. While real income growth has been meager for the poorest Americans, it has increased by more than 13 percent for the poorest Canadians.[9]

Narrowing the time frame modifies the larger story. Since 2000, the average household in each Canadian quintile has gained in real terms, with the lowest two—by a slim margin—gaining the most. Conversely, the "noughties" was the first decade since the US Census began to collect data on income distribution in which mean household income declined for Americans in every income tier, the degree of regress being magnified the lower one is on the scale. At least in terms of income growth, the twenty-first century has been much harder on poorer than richer Americans, who in all events are far better equipped to handle any economic downturn. They are also likely to recover more quickly. Between 2009 and 2010, as the US economy began to emerge from a two-year recession, the top 1 percent of American households garnered 93 percent of all the increase in income produced.[10] Such resilience is to be expected; of all US income growth between 1979 and 2011, 84 percent went to the richest centile.[11]

With respect to income share, from an egalitarian perspective the twenty-first century has again been kinder in Canada than in the United States. Over the last decade or so the bottom three American quintiles have lost proportionately more than their Canadian counterparts. The reverse is true for the top Canadian earners, who have ceded more ground (see Table 1.1). It is also the case that the Canadian income scale is somewhat more compact than the American—the distance between the share of the lowest and highest fifth of earners is not quite as great. And in terms of purchasing power parity (PPP), a measure economists use to determine how much income is needed in each country to buy a common set of goods and services, the greater strength of the US dollar means that, on average, members of the highest Canadian income quintile, even more so the very top of Canadian earners, make considerably less than their American counterparts (Table 1.2).[12] Indeed, as Table 1.1 suggests, it is among the richest 1 percent of earners where distributional differences between the United States and Canada are the most egregious.

In neither place, however, is fiscal policy especially progressive. When measured by reductions in the Gini coefficient, as Figure 1.6 indicates, the economic impact of the state in Canada and the United States is below

Table 1.2 Growth in Real Mean Household Income by Quintile, United States and Canada

	United States		
	Mean income	Mean income growth	
	2013	1980–2013	2000–2013
Lowest 20%	$11,651	4.0%	−15.1%
Second 20%	$30,509	5.6	−11.0
Middle 20%	$52,322	9.8	−8.4
Fourth 20%	$83,519	18.9	−5.9
Highest 20%	$185,206	47.9	−3.7
Top 5%	$322,343	72.3	−5.5
Top 1%	$923,043	156.0	−2.5
	Canada		
	Mean income	Mean income growth	
	2011	1980–2011	2000–2011
Lowest 20%	$15,500	13.1%	12.3%
Second 20%	$35,900	3.4	11.4
Middle 20%	$57,700	0.7	9.0
Fourth 20%	$89,100	11.2	10.0
Highest 20%	$176,900	32.9	11.0
Top 5%	$216,400	47.1★	5.4
Top 1%	$504,600	79.7★	−0.7

★Statistics Canada data for 1982–2011.

Sources: US Census Bureau, "Selected Measures of Household Income Dispersion, 1967–2013" (constant 2013 US dollars); for the top 1 percent of US income earners, World Wealth and Income Database, http://wid.world; Statistics Canada, "Market, Total and After-Tax Income"; Statistics Canada, "High Income Trends of Tax Filers in Canada."

peer-country norms. The latest data indicate that among OECD members the average decrease in Gini due to transfers and taxes is 35 percent; in Canada it is 28 percent, and in the United States it is 23 percent. By that standard, the United States, along with Israel and South Korea, is one of the least redistributive of all advanced industrial democracies.[13] This helps explain why over the last three decades there has been a steady rise in income inequality in the United States but not in Canada, where the largest uptick in the Gini occurred between 1989 and 2000, having leveled off since then (Figure 1.7). Relative to Canada, the United States starts from a more unequal position in terms of market income and does less to compensate for it (Figure 1.8).[14] The result is that while inequalities in disposable income have

Figure 1.6 Gini Coefficients of Inequality for Market and Disposable Incomes, 2013

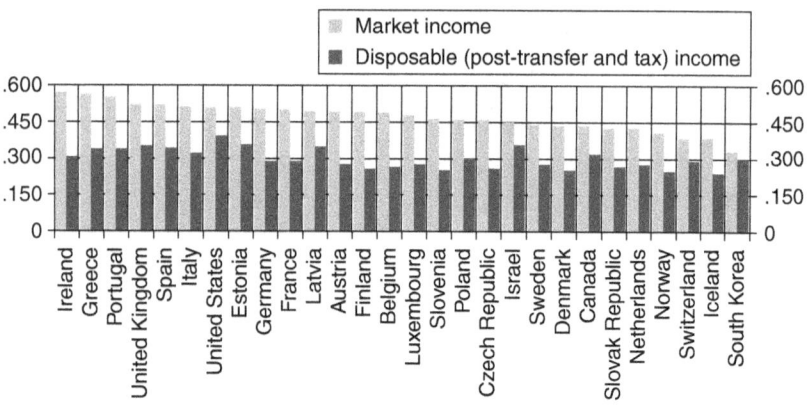

Source: OECD, "Income Distribution and Poverty."

Figure 1.7 US and Canadian Gini Coefficients, Post-Tax and Transfer, 1980–2011

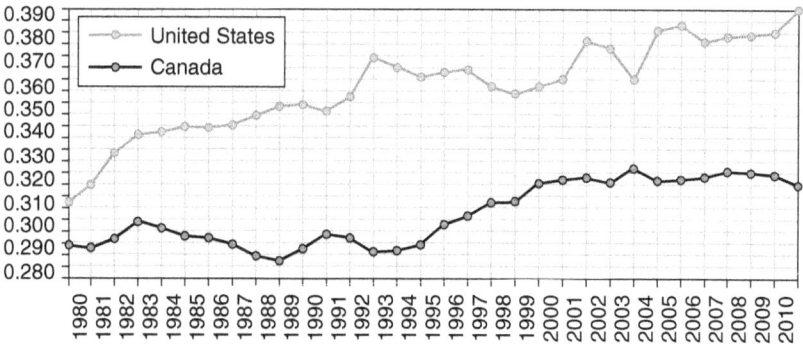

Source: OECD, "Income Distribution and Poverty."

grown in both countries, the distance between them has widened. Even if Canada and the United States are in the second division of income reallocation, in a straight two-country contest, Canada does better.

The Middle Class

Uncertain income growth—relative and absolute—feeds the anxieties of North American publics about the middle class. And we are all middle class now, or at least we think we are. So in a 2012 survey, the polling firm

Figure 1.8 Reduction in Inequality (Gini Coefficients) after Transfers and Taxes

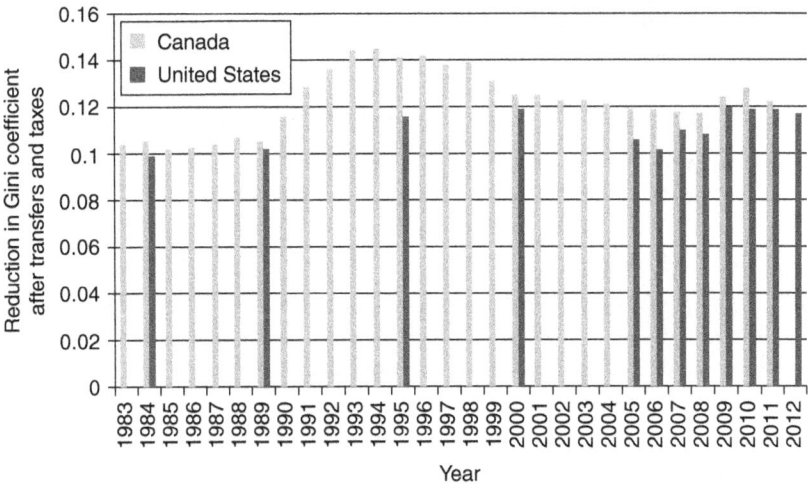

Note: US data available only for select years before 2005.
Source: OECD, "Income Distribution and Poverty."

Environics asked Canadians to self-identify in terms of class; only 1 percent of respondents claimed to be upper class and 5 percent lower class, but 93 percent said they were lower-middle, middle, or upper-middle class.[15] That same year the Pew Research Center posed a similar question to Americans, with much the same result: 89 percent of those surveyed answered that they were a subset of the middle class, with 2 percent saying they were upper class and 7 percent lower class.[16] When "middle" is used so expansively that anyone who is not among the most conspicuously affluent members of society seems to qualify, the economic predicament of households from the bottom of the income scale almost to the top becomes cause for middle-class concern. Reasonably well-off families and desperately poor ones alike can feel vulnerable to an economy in which the growth in earnings for the average household in the bottom four income quintiles is overwhelmed by that of the top—and dramatically so with respect to the richest 1 percent—or in which the income share of the leading fifth of families alone is expanding, with those at the heights of the income ladder again receiving the greatest part of the gain.

More precise markers of middle-class distress aren't hard to find. At the risk of irritating sociologists, political economists, and others who insist on more complex and exacting definitions, as a proxy let's examine median household market income, the earnings of a household at the midpoint of the income distribution scale. As Figure 1.9 demonstrates, in inflation-adjusted terms, that midpoint household in Canada and the United States earns only a little more now than it did in 1984—an additional $1,700 in Canada but just over $250 more in the United States. During the last decade for which national data are available, the Canadian record is better, but that of the United States is worse. From 2001 to 2011, the median Canadian household's income increased by $2,300, whereas between 2003 and 2013 the earnings of its US counterpart declined by almost $4,000. If families in both countries continue to struggle with the escalating costs of housing, health care, education, and child care, which are the foundations of a middle-class life, it is not for a lack of growth in the national accounts. Over the last two decades, the Canadian and US economies have expanded at reasonable rates—outpacing their Japanese and European competitors, for instance. But if a rising tide of economic growth is supposed to lift all boats, in America the boats at the very middle of the income distribution are not rising at all. Indeed, they are sinking.[17]

Figure 1.9 Real Median Household Market Income, United States and Canada, 1984–2013

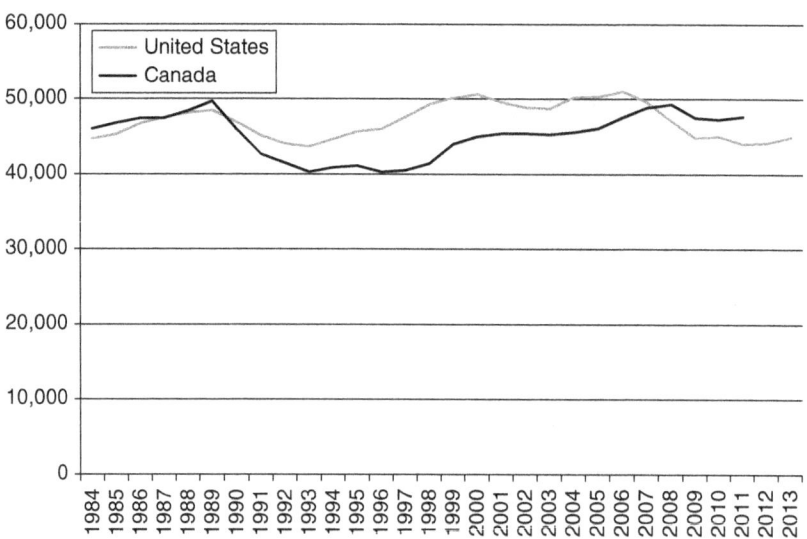

Note: Adjusted for inflation, US 2011 and Canadian 2011 dollars.

Sources: US Census Bureau, "Median Household Income, by Definition of Income: 1979 to 2003"; Statistics Canada, "Market Income, Government Transfers, Total Income, Income Tax and After-Tax Income."

Alternatively, consider the situation of the middle three income quintiles. Since 1980, gross (pre-tax) income share has decreased for that cohort by 5.9 percent in the United States and 5.3 percent in Canada (Table 1.1). The big winner in share gains over the same period—in fact the only winner—is the richest 20 percent, with the top 1 percent of its households leading the charge.[18] Refine the analysis to the middle fifth of the income distribution and the direction of change is the same. The share of before-tax income accounted for by American households contracted by 2.4 percent—and for Canadian families by slightly more. On the other hand, when one considers average earnings as opposed to income share, the news isn't all bad (Table 1.2). Over the last three decades or so, the typical family in the middle quintile of the American income distribution has seen its income rise by almost 10 percent in inflation-adjusted terms, while the earnings of a similarly situated Canadian household have been stagnant. Yet the twenty-first century has been harder on middle-income Americans, whose real earnings have dropped by more than 8 percent, and kinder to Canadians, for whom incomes have risen by almost 9 percent. Such fluctuations in fortune are reason alone for American angst. The evidence on real hourly wage rates ratchets up the worry. Since the Great Divergence, while the hourly compensation of American workers at the nineteeth percentile and above has skyrocketed, their compatriots in the lower half of the income distribution have been running in place, barely able to maintain the value of their earnings from year to year.[19]

Recent evidence indicates that in an absolute sense the Canadian middle class is now better off than the American. It is a development that has captured the attention of the press on both sides of the border. Drawing on data from the Luxembourg Income Study (LIS) database, one of the principal research centers harmonizing income and wealth inequality data on a cross-national basis, in April 2014 the *New York Times* was the first to announce that, based on real median per capita disposable income, the "American Middle Class Is No Longer the World's Richest," having been supplanted by its Canadian equivalent.[20] At virtually the same time, the American journal of political commentary *The Atlantic* confirmed that "Canada is officially home to the richest middle class on the planet," and this despite the fact that per capita gross domestic product (GDP) is almost 20 percent greater in the United States—an anomaly explained, according to the magazine, by higher American income inequality.[21] Unusual enough for the American media to pursue Canadian-themed stories, but a few days later the British newspaper *The Guardian* weighed in with an article titled "How America's Middle Class Fell Behind Its Canadian Neighbours."[22] The likely suspects, in the *Guardian's* view, are the higher cost of a university education, a lack of academic preparedness among young people, the higher price and lower coverage of health care, a lower minimum wage, astronomical CEO pay, and the limited distributional effect of American fiscal policy. Canada's newsweekly *Maclean's* offered a quick rejoinder in "Eight Charts [That] Explain Why Canada's Middle Class Is Richer than America's," giving macroeconomic factors the principal credit rather than relatively more generous Canadian social spending.[23] Yet referencing a *New York Times* article on "The Shrinking American Middle Class" in early 2015, Toronto's *Globe and Mail* reassured readers that it was "So Far Just a US Story," again citing Canada's system of public education and single-payer health care as among the major reasons for middle-class buoyancy north of the border.[24]

It is important to note that the Canadian advantage is based on PPPs for disposable income, that is to say, cash earnings after public transfers (for pensions, welfare, unemployment compensation, etc.) and taxes. The value of benefits like health insurance are not included, which, given Canada's publicly administered single-payer system of universal health care, means that out-of-pocket medical costs are far lower for the average Canadian than American family—a further comparative bonus. Of course, variations in the way in which North American governments directly redress economic inequality aren't the only reason for the Canadian edge. A better-educated and thus more competitive workforce, the entry of more women into full-time employment, higher median wages, the greater relative strength of labor unions, and even higher housing values and lower mortgage rates north of the border are among the additional factors that play a role. But transfer and tax policy influences the overall disbursement of national prosperity, which certainly can affect the middle class's sense of well-being.

Granted, the specific redistributive impact is more modest for families in middle-income quintiles than for those occupying the highest and lowest rungs of the earnings ladder. Statistics Canada finds that when 2011 market income is converted to disposable income, the household earnings share for the middle fifth of Canadians increases by only 1.7 percent.[25] For the same year, the US Congressional Budget Office estimates that the boost for the American middle-income quintile is even less—just 1.2 percent.[26] Still, middle-income Canadians appear better situated than their American counterparts. Whereas the ratio between the 90th percentile of earners and the median household for disposable income in Canada has held constant over the last two decades, during the same period the top end of the US distribution has gradually moved away from the center. At the same time, the ratio between the median household and the 10th percentile of earners has been steady in Canada but has grown in the United States.[27] In other words, if one fixes median income as the reference point, the American distribution is stretching apart at the top and bottom deciles, whereas the Canadian distribution is stable.[28]

Relative to the median, the richest Americans are getting richer and the poorest Americans are getting poorer. But for the average Canadian household, the ranks of the truly well-to-do aren't quite so remote, and neither is the prospect of joining them—arguably an encouragement to the kind of open, fluid, and democratic society in which aspirations to affluence can be realized. On the other hand, the comparative narrowness of the interval between middle-income families and the poorest Canadian households could have the opposite effect. Whether the threat of falling into the ranks of the worst off should be more troubling for middle-class Canadians than Americans requires a more thorough consideration of economic mobility, the subject of the next chapter. At the moment, it is enough to point out that as a percentage of the total population, the number of impoverished Canadians is not as great, and in the aggregate their circumstances not as desperate, as their US neighbors. For middle-income Canadians who fear the worst, there may be some reassurance in that—likewise the benefit to social stability when an underclass isn't so far under.

Wealth

Income is only part of the inequality picture; the distribution of wealth is just as revealing. In the broadest sense, *wealth* is all of the assets that people own, including financial resources like savings and bank accounts, equities, bonds, mutual funds, pensions, or insurance policies, as well as physical assets such as places of residence, land, commercial buildings, machines, and inventory. *Net worth* is simply the value of that wealth minus debt. Income is part of what comprises wealth, in that earnings from labor in the form of wages, salaries, and bonuses add to an individual's net worth and can be invested for further financial gain, and because wealth produces income in the form of rents, interest, dividends, profits, capital gains, and royalties.[29] But as economists maintain, wealth is a stock, income a flow.

Among rich democratic countries like Canada and the United States, wealth is even less equally allocated than income. The reason, according to the French economist Thomas Piketty in his masterwork *Capital in the Twenty-First Century*, can be expressed in a basic equation: $r > g$, "where r stands for the average rate of return on capital, including profits, dividends, interest, rents and other income from capital expressed as a percentage of its total value, and g stands for the annual growth rate of the economy, that is the annual increase in income or output."[30] Piketty maintains that income from capital—which is virtually synonymous with wealth in the way he uses the term—always grows at a faster rate than does the economy as a whole. Consequently, such income tends to be more unequally distributed than are earnings from labor like wages and salaries. Drawing on the experience of advanced European economies, he argues that this ultimately leads to a "patrimonial" form of capitalism, in which progressively higher levels of inequality are driven more by the inheritance of vastly unequal economic resources than by big monetary rewards for excellence in entrepreneurship, technological innovation, or professional expertise:

> When the rate of return on capital significantly exceeds the growth rate of the economy ... then it logically follows that inherited wealth grows faster than output and income. People with inherited wealth need save only a portion of their income from capital to see that capital grow more quickly than the economy as a whole. Under such conditions it is almost inevitable that inherited wealth will dominate wealth amassed from a lifetime's labor by a wide margin, and the concentration of capital will attain extremely high levels—levels potentially incompatible with the meritocratic values and principles of social justice fundamental to modern democratic societies.[31]

Differences in savings rates—wealthier households tend to save more—as well as population growth—lower growth concentrates wealth by reducing the number of heirs with whom one's bequest can be shared—enhance the basic dynamic.[32] In such conditions, annual rates of returns on capital of only a few percent, when compounded over time, can result in extremely large increases on an initial investment. It is the basic mechanism whereby the rich, who are more able and more likely to make such investments, get richer still.

Piketty accepts that the role of inheritance can change depending on broader political, social, and economic conditions. For example, because of the physical destruction wrought by two world wars as well as ensuing budgetary and political reforms, the value of private wealth in Europe expressed as a percentage of national income plummeted from 1914 to 1950, and with it the associated economic inequalities. But the cataclysm of war—including its egalitarian consequences, intended and not—is unlikely to be repeated. As Piketty observes, the ratio of privately held capital to national income has since rebounded in Europe, assisted by relatively low levels of economic and demographic growth, so that family-held fortunes—"wealth accumulated in the past"—are once again inequality's motivating force.[33]

Across the twentieth century, a similar reduction of the wealth-to-income ratio occurred in North America, though without being as deep at its low point or as high at its apex. And over the last 40 years, American and Canadian rates of economic and population growth have been greater than in Europe. Consequently, since the late 1970s dramatic increases in income and wealth inequality in Canada and especially the United States have not been triggered as much by inheritance as by the extraordinarily high salaries commanded by a class of "super-managers," executives with superstar compensation packages who dominate the ranks of the ultra-rich.[34] In that respect it is labor income, not income from capital, that is behind contemporary North American inequality. Still, Piketty anticipates that as these leading earners pass on their economic advantages to their heirs, a process made easier by gentle estate taxes in the United States, an oligarchy based on inheritance may well be in Canada's and America's future. To put it more familiarly, for every Elon Musk there will also be a Paris Hilton and a Kim Kardashian.

As with income, the United States sits at or near the top of the wealth inequality tables, with Canada holding a more moderate position. Figure 1.10 shows the Gini coefficients of income and wealth for OECD countries. In all cases wealth inequality is greater than income inequality—which is unsurprising, given that it is a global phenomenon. Yet with the exception of Denmark, a true outlier since it has one of the most equal distributions of national income in the OECD, the United States is the most unequal of all rich democratic countries, with a wealth Gini index of 0.84; Canada, at 0.72, comes in at slightly above the OECD average.[35] With respect to the wealth shares of the 10 percent of households with the highest net worth, a preferred indicator of inequality among economic statisticians, the concentration of American capital is unparalleled (Figure 1.11).[36] Canada tracks OECD norms at a 50-percent share for the top 10 percent and a 16-percent share for the wealthiest 1 percent of its families. But the wealthiest decile of American families owns more than three-quarters of total US assets, with the richest centile owning 37 percent.[37]

Reliable long-term data on net worth are available only for the United States. Across the last century the distribution of American wealth at the top end has the same U-shaped appearance as it does for income, though at a higher magnitude. For the wealthiest 10 percent of individuals, from a peak share of 85 percent in the late 1920s, relative net worth declined to around 65 percent by the mid-1980s, after which it steadily rose, if not quite recapturing its original heights; the richest 1 percent have traversed the same general path (Figure 1.12). But since the Great Divergence, share growth at the very top of the distributional ladder has been startling. Between 1980 and 2014, the proportion of wealth held by the richest 1 percent of Americans increased by 64 percent, and that of the top 0.1 percent by 151 percent to over a fifth of all US assets.[38]

Less fortunate Americans, of course, have traced the reverse trajectory. In the middle of the twentieth century their share of national wealth grew in tandem with rising middle-class incomes, rates of home ownership, and

Figure 1.10 Gini Coefficients of Inequality for Income (Disposable) and Wealth, 2012

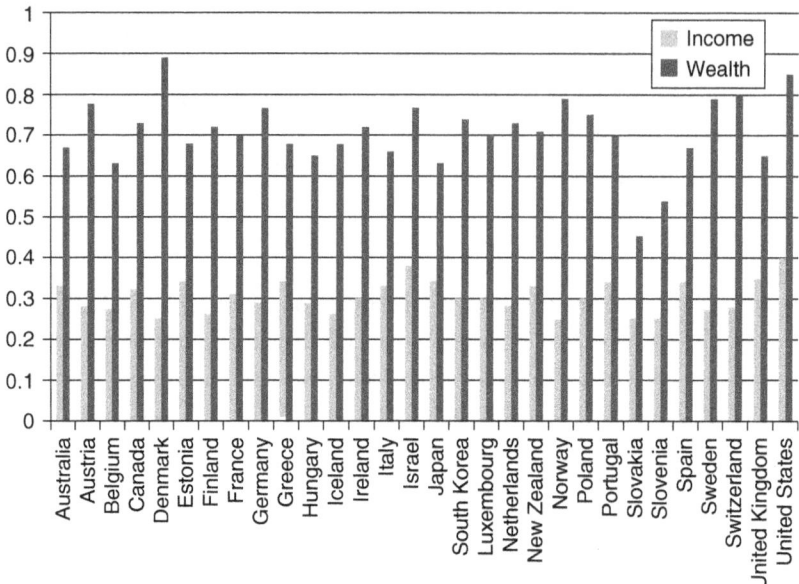

Note: The Credit Suisse estimates of wealth concentration may be slightly higher than those provided by national statistical agencies or international organizations like the OECD. Given that national surveys of wealth typically underreport high-wealth households, the authors of the *Global Wealth Databook* compensate by statistically adjusting the upper tail of the wealth distribution.

Sources: For income, OECD, "Income Distribution and Poverty"; for wealth, Shorrocks, Davies, and Lluberas, *Global Wealth Report, 2014*.

Figure 1.11 Wealth Share for Top Net Worth Households, 2010

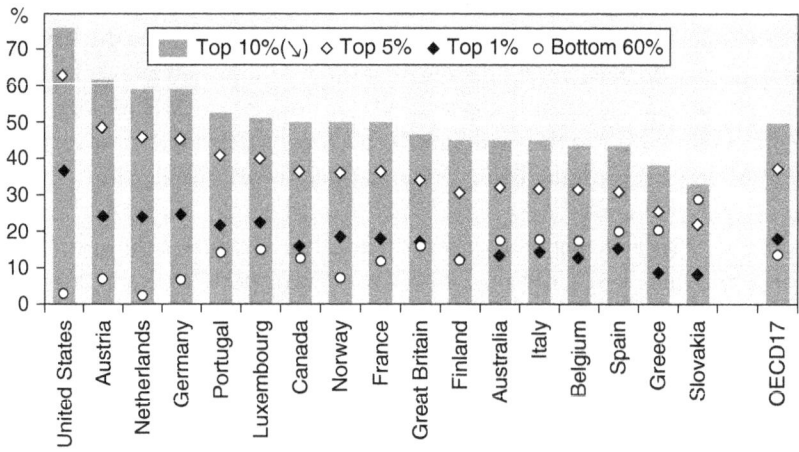

Note: Bottom 60 percent = the three lowest wealth quintiles when the wealth distribution is divided into fifths.

Source: OECD, *In It Together*, Table 6.7, OECD Wealth Distribution Database.

Figure 1.12 Wealth Inequality in the United States, 1913–2014

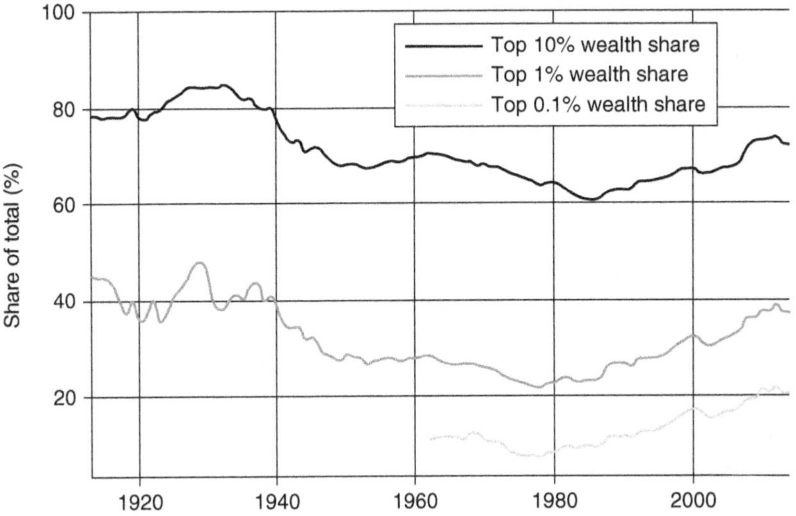

Source: World Wealth and Income Database.

participation in public and private pension funds. But since the Great Divergence these relative gains have been eroded. The US Federal Reserve confirms that between 1989 and 2013 the wealth share held by the top 10 percent of American households increased by 8.5 percent, while that of the bottom 90 percent of households decreased by the same amount. The latter now command around a quarter of total net worth in the United States—almost the same proportion as accounted for by the top 0.1 percent of American families alone.[39] It is no wonder that at roughly the same time the ratio between mean and median American household net worth expanded—an additional marker of inequality, since it indicates the greater relative concentration of wealth at the top end of the distribution, thus a higher average than median net worth. Once again the United States leads the OECD class, with a mean-to-median ratio in 2010 of 7.2; the closest Canadian comparable, for 2012, is below the OECD average at a far more modest 2.2.[40]

Households occupying particular tiers in the wealth distribution scale do not necessarily occupy exactly the same tiers in the income distribution scale, but the correlation is significant, especially at the margins. Since great wealth can generate great income (earnings that can be invested to produce even more wealth), the relationship is strongest at the top. According to the OECD, an average 45 percent of the households in rich democratic countries who are in the top fifth of the income ladder are also in the top fifth in terms of net worth, an association that is even stronger in Canada and the United States. Alternatively, 36 percent of households find themselves in both the lowest income and wealth quintiles.[41] More mobile households are unlikely to stray very far. A Canadian government study determined that more than three-quarters of families in a given income quintile are located in either the same net worth quintile or the one above or below it.[42] The growth dynamic for wealth according to income is little different than that pertaining to income alone. Between 1999 and 2012, for example, in the highest Canadian income quintile median wealth more than doubled; for the next highest tier it improved by 90 percent, but in the lowest one it grew by only 14.5 percent.[43]

To be fair, since the turn of the twenty-first century the share of wealth accruing to households at the heights of the North American wealth distribution has been relatively flat (in the United States) or diminished (in Canada). Given that securities have a major place in the portfolios of the richest Americans and Canadians, a temporary loss in the value of financial assets during the recent recession may be partly to blame.[44] Credit Suisse's Global Wealth Databook (GWD), a standard source on wealth inequality, suggests that between 2000 and 2014 the top 10 percent of US households in terms of net worth maintained its three-quarters stake, whereas the top 1 percent hovered around 38.5 percent. Over the same interval, the share of similarly positioned Canadian families contracted from 62 to 57 percent for the top 10 percent, and from 30 to 24 percent for the richest centile.[45] Statistics Canada data for the period confirm that the concentration of wealth in the top Canadian decile decreased, though in their calculations by around 2 percent.[46] Even in difficult economic times, inequalities in the allocation of wealth appear more resilient in the United States than in Canada.

One can easily lose perspective. Of late, the top household cohorts of the North American wealth distribution may not be decisively marching away from the rest, but when their superior wealth shares are translated into the monetary value of the assets they hold, the difference in sums is remarkable. Statistics Canada data for 2012 indicate that the wealthiest 10 percent of Canadian families had an average net worth of C$2.6 million, while the US Federal Reserve reports that in 2013 the average household in the same American decile was worth US$4 million.[47] Conversely, the least affluent 20 percent of Canadian households owe more than they own—on average $3,700 more—while the holdings of families in the next highest quintile are not much better off, with a modest mean net worth of $62,000. Worse still is the relative position of US households. American families in the bottom quartile of the prosperity schedule are on average $13,400 in the red; the mean for the next wealthiest 25 percent is less than $36,000.[48] Further, since the mid-2000s, the average real wealth for all but the top 10 percent of US households has declined, a condition, it should be noted, afflicting only the poorest fifth of Canadian families.[49] Data on wealth share are equally dismal. As calculated by the authors of the GWD, the bottom half of Canadian families command a 4.6 percent net worth share, their American counterparts just 1.3 percent, and in both countries the lowest quintile of households in effect have no wealth at all.[50]

Debt has wide implications in calculations of American and Canadian prosperity. US households are among the most indebted in the advanced industrial democracies, with Canadians in the middle of the pack. But both countries exceed rich democratic country norms when it comes to the proportion of households considered dangerously indebted. The OECD uses two indices to measure this: (1) the percent of households with debt-to-asset ratios above 75 percent, and (2) the percent of households with debt-to-income ratios above three. Roughly 16 percent of Canadian and 23 percent of American households fall into the first category, whereas 12 percent of Canadian and more than 16 percent of American families qualify for the second. In each case they are at the forefront of countries whose citizens are subject to the greatest financial risk.[51] That risk falls harder on occupants of some income strata than others. Average levels of indebtedness are progressively greater as one ascends the earnings ladder, as one would expect, given the easier access to credit and greater propensity to invest by those with more economic resources. But overindebted households are almost twice as likely to be found in the lower ranks of the income distribution as they are in the top 10 percent.[52]

The lion's share of that debt, around 80 percent of it in Canada and the United States, comes from mortgages on homes. With respect to wealth, housing is a double-edged sword. The value of one's principal residence is an important store of net worth, especially for householders of modest means. In North America as elsewhere, there is a strong relationship between growth in the median net worth of households and annual increases in the growth of house prices over time, a relationship more important across the income scale than growth in the savings rate or the return on financial assets. Investments like stocks and bonds are an important part of the portfolio of the top 10 percent of earners, the greater relative significance of which heightens wealth inequality between them and the rest.[53] Yet for the middle class, it is their homes that promise economic security.[54]

That is what makes them so vulnerable to bursts in housing price bubbles, as highly leveraged American home owners discovered during the last recession and its aftermath. For the bottom 90 percent of US households according to gross income, the average net value of their most important asset was slashed by a third, a quarter of all homes were pushed underwater (where the value of a property is less than the debt left on its mortgage) and 8 million into foreclosure, and the median net worth of American families declined by almost half to its lowest level in over 40 years.[55] From a pre-recession peak in 2004, US home-ownership rates fell five points to less than 64 percent by 2015, in the process driving up the price of rental housing to more than twice the rate of inflation and increasing the number of renters considered cost burdened (i.e., those who pay more than 30 percent of their income on rent, the standard measure of affordability) to half of the total.[56] By contrast, Canadian rates of home ownership have risen steadily over the last 40 years.[57] But there are ominous parallels with the United States. The relative prosperity of the Canadian middle class is built on extraordinary gains in net worth due to housing values. These increased by almost half in the last decade, a phenomenon attributed to cheap lines of credit, which is the means of buying into an overheated market. Canada's debt-to-disposable income ratio (1.63 in 2015) is now higher than even that of the United States. Largely a function of mortgage debt, it leaves all but the wealthiest Canadian families susceptible to a sudden collapse in housing prices or interest rate increases.[58]

As the example of mortgage debt suggests, stark differences between those at the upper reaches of the wealth distribution and the rest are of more than academic interest. They speak to the real-world economic vulnerability of large numbers of Canadians and Americans. Wealth offers a bulwark against the material insecurity that comes from the contingencies of life; a loss of income due to unemployment, sickness, and disability; or the financial pressures that come with changes in family status, like the birth of children, divorce, or the need to care for elderly parents. In these circumstances, wealth is an emollient, permitting families to smooth their spending patterns over time to meet unforeseen circumstances. It promises a decent standard of living in retirement. And it can be a legacy to one's children, enhancing their economic opportunity, often by helping them attend a college or university without fear of crushing loan repayments.

It is worrisome, then, that in a 2014 Environics poll 40 percent of Canadians report that their income is inadequate, that they are "stretched" and having a "hard time." So much so, according to respondents in Statistics Canada's Financial Capability Survey, that a third are not preparing financially for retirement, either on their own or through employer-based pension plans.[59] Americans are no different. In a recent US Federal Reserve survey, a third of non-retirees indicated they have no retirement savings or pension plan, and almost half of all respondents say they cannot cover an unexpected expense of even $400.⁶⁰ Opinion polls, of course, are of interest to social scientists mainly because of the frequency, not the veracity, of what is said. Yet in light of what the data on income and wealth distribution indicate, it is reasonable to consider that a significant percentage of North American households report having a hard time because so many of them *are* having a hard time. When a person owes more than he or she owns, and the real value of any assets one does have is diminishing—the predicament of the average family among the bottom fifth of Canadians and bottom fourth of Americans in terms of net worth—there is not much left for rainier days.

Poverty and Low-Income Status

That is particularly the case for the neediest of citizens, those deemed to be in poverty. Statistically, the determination of poverty is no easy thing. For comparative purposes, the most favored measure is relative: A family whose disposable income adjusted for household size is at least 50 percent below the national median is typically considered to be in poverty. By that criterion, the LIS finds that poverty rates in Canada are consistently lower than in the United States—12.5 percent versus 17 percent, respectively, in 2010, the last year for which joint data are available—and have held fairly constant over the previous 30 years.[61] Using the same rubric, the OECD confirms the relative standing of Canada and the United States (Figure 1.13). Both have poverty rates higher than the average OECD country, though only Israel has a greater share of its population in poverty than the United States, and in each case that rate has been fairly stable for a generation. Comparative social scientists are also interested in "poverty gaps," the average distance from the poverty line for the households beneath it expressed as a percentage of that line. By that account, too, the United States is more challenged than Canada, experiencing a depth of poverty that has intensified since the mid-1990s (Figure 1.14).

Confusingly, these internationally preferred definitions are not the ones that Canadian and American government agencies favor when they consider domestic poverty. Strictly speaking, Canada does not report an official level of poverty. Instead, Ottawa most often employs a different relative measure of economic difficulty called a "low-income cut-off" (LICO). LICO is the threshold beyond which a family would need to spend an additional 20 percent or more of its disposable income on food, clothing, or shelter than does the average household.[62] More recently, the Canadian government also calculates a "market basket measure" (MBM) of low-income status, an absolute indicator specifying the earnings a family would require after transfers and taxes to purchase a basket of goods that includes food, shelter, transportation, and other goods and services necessary to a basic standard of living. Poverty

Figure 1.13 Poverty Rate before and after Taxes and Transfers, Poverty Line 50 Percent of Median Household Income

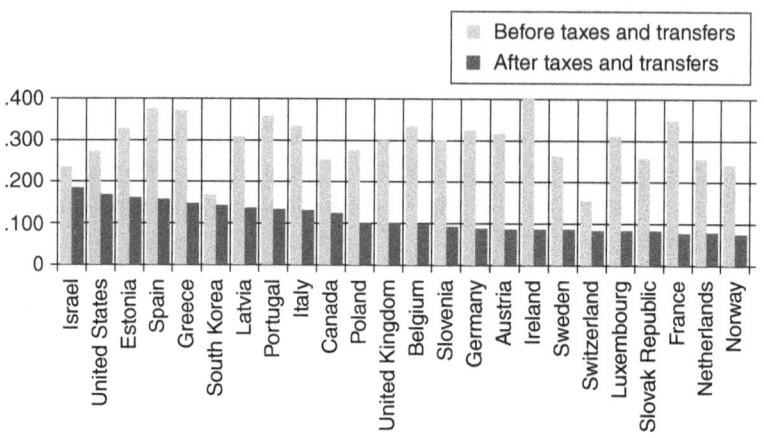

Source: OECD, "Income Distribution and Poverty."

Figure 1.14 Mean Poverty Gap after Taxes and Transfers, Poverty Line 50 Percent of Median Household Income, 1983–2012

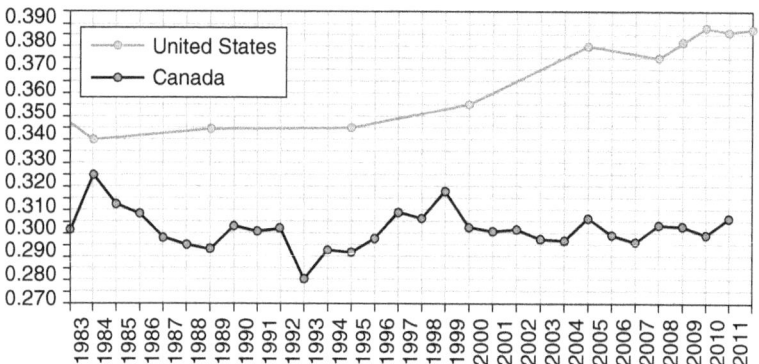

Source: OECD, "Income Distribution and Poverty."

rates vary according to these benchmarks, though the trend lines are broadly similar. In 2012, the LICO counted almost 10 percent of Canadians as having low-income status, whereas according to the MBM almost 13 percent qualified. Since the mid-1990s, the LICOs show that the percentage of low-income Canadians has diminished, with a slight uptick in 2012, while the MBM, in operation only since 2000, charts a more gently concave path.[63]

A specified monetary threshold, adjusted for family size and the age of family members, is used by the US Census Bureau to determine the

American poverty rate. This official measure represents three times the pre-tax income necessary to cover the cost of a minimum food diet—a standard first determined in 1963 and subsequently adjusted for inflation. The bureau counts only cash income before taxes in its calculations of family need, meaning that noncash public benefits like food stamps and rental vouchers, or tax advantages like the Child Tax Credit and the Earned Income Tax Credit that assist many working families, are not considered. By these standards, at 14.8 percent in 2014, the US poverty rate has not changed markedly over the last 50 years. Moreover, by government estimates, a significant percentage of Americans are deeply impoverished: 6.8 percent of all US residents live in families with an income less than one-half of the official poverty line.[64] Nevertheless, critics maintain that this official definition of poverty obscures the real progress that has been made in lifting low-income Americans out of economic distress, especially because noncash and tax benefits are a far more important part of the social safety net than they were when President Lyndon Johnson announced the war on poverty in 1964.[65] Consequently, in 2011 the US Census Bureau introduced a revised supplemental poverty measure (SPM) that takes into account such benefits and subtracts taxes, out-of-pocket medical expenses, commuting costs to work, and child care costs; expands the definition of family to include unmarried partners; and is sensitive to differences in the cost of housing based on geography. By these criteria, the poverty rate in the United States has declined by more than 10 points since the late 1960s and now stands at 15.3 percent, a half-point higher than the official measure.[66]

As these practices indicate, part of the debate concerning poverty/low-income rubrics concerns whether disposable or pre-tax cash income should be considered when constructing a poverty baseline. Internationally, in Canada, and with the advent of the SPM in America too, that question is being resolved in favor of the former. After all, it is a family's disposable income that indicates where they truly stand when it comes to securing the basic necessities of life. And the difference in the poverty rate between market and disposable income can be instructive. Tax and transfer policies are not the only explanation for the fall or rise of poverty over time, but they are important ones. So, as Figure 1.13 shows, in 2011 Canadian public efforts reduced market income poverty by more than half, whereas US tax and transfers reduced it by 40 percent—a further instance of the Canadian state's greater redistributive capacity.

The outstanding issue is whether absolute (the official US Census Bureau measure and the SPM; Canada's MBM) or relative measures (Canada's LICO) best capture the percentage of a population in economic distress. Absolute standards are intuitively appealing, in that they suggest the minimum economic requirements for a reasonable life and because they do not vary with the affluence of households farther up the income scale. But as noted, in advanced economies, especially for comparative purposes, it is relative measures that are most often used. Such indicators are more attuned to the fact that in rich democratic countries it is not so much survival that is at stake for the poor, but rather the requirements of a minimally respectable life as determined by the norms of the surrounding community. The Nobel Prize–winning economist Angus Deaton writes:

> The reality of poverty in America is about not having enough to participate fully in society, about families and their children not being able to live decent lives alongside neighbors and friends. Not being able to meet those social standards of decency is an *absolute* deprivation, but avoiding this absolute deprivation requires an amount of money that is relative in the sense that it must adjust to local standards. In wealthy countries like the United States, it is very hard to justify anything other than a *relative* poverty line.[67]

On this reading, social exclusion based on things like diet, housing, participation in the "right kind" of community activities, or the lack of consumer goods that confer acceptance are the hallmarks of poverty.

Inasmuch as inequality is also a relational concept, concerns about poverty and growing inequalities of income and wealth intersect. For most of the post-war period in Canada and the United States, problems of poverty and inequality have been conflated and the politics of redistribution assessed according to its impact on the poorest of citizens.[68] To be sure, in rich democratic countries the living standards of even the humblest members of society have improved. Technological innovation and globalized markets have made certain of it, bringing down the price of commodities, including communication and entertainment, which make life more enjoyable. Tempting, then, for defenders of the distributional status quo to argue that the poor have never had it so good. Yet it is an odd argument that celebrates the progress of the poor by historical metrics alone. Certainly low-income families in advanced industrial countries can thank their lucky stars that they no longer risk the workhouse or the debtor's prison, are less vulnerable to infectious diseases like cholera and typhoid, and use central heating to keep their places of residence warm instead of open fires and animal pelts. That's not really the point. For individuals sensitive to the moral imperatives of political economy, the immediate issue is the kind of life that poor households could have if economic resources were more fairly dispersed. In North America, the expanding prosperity of the well-to-do has not been widely shared, such that in a relative sense low-income families are falling behind. And as the price of food, shelter, health care, child care, and education escalates—the physical and mental foundations of upward economic mobility—they may be falling behind in an absolute sense, too. That is certainly the case in the United States, where many economists maintain that the principal cause of uneven progress against poverty has been the quickening of income and wealth inequality over the last few decades. So, in a study based on Census Bureau data from 1979 to 2007, among all the variables considered, income inequality was found to have the largest impact on the chances of an American falling into poverty—more than economic growth, education, family structure, or race.[69]

Canada's most economically disadvantaged citizens are not as compromised. Keith Banting and John Myles observe that in Canada "part of the paradox of the contemporary period has been the combination of rising inequality and stable or declining poverty."[70] It may be small comfort to Canadian anti-poverty organizations and their political allies who remain attentive in light of the spiraling cost of housing, prescription drugs, and other necessities. Canadians should think twice before indulging in self-congratulation. When it comes to the standard marks of inequality, among advanced industrial democracies Canada is middling or slightly worse (i.e., more unequal), and the redistributive effects of its tax and benefits system are significantly below average. Moreover, it has the highest rate of poverty for nonstandard workers—those in temporary or part-time work or who are self-employed—among all OECD countries.[71] In short, Canada has by no means escaped those forces making for greater income and wealth inequality, poverty included.

Yet compared to its American neighbor, the effects have not been as profound. To reiterate, the distance in income share between the top 10 percent and the bottom 10 percent of earners is far greater in the United States than in Canada (Figure 1.3). Since 1980, in both places income share growth has shrunk for all but the top 20 percent of earners, but in the United States declines for the lowest quintile have been five times as great (Table 1.1). During the same time, the real average income of the poorest Canadian quintile expanded by 13 percent, as opposed to just 4 percent for the poorest American (Table 1.2). In Canada and the United States, the least wealthy 20 percent of families in effect have zero net worth, owing more than they own, but American families in that predicament have on average three-and-a-half times more debt. Poverty rates are lower and the poverty gap is thinner in Canada, and while over the last 20 years that gap has leveled out in Canada, it has grown in the United States (Figures 1.13 and 1.14).

Doubtless any explanation for the Canadian advantage is multidimensional. But when it comes to those macroeconomic factors most often cited as driving down poverty—economic growth and the employment rate—Canada is not in a clearly stronger position. Since 1980, Canadian and American growth rates have tracked each other closely, as one would expect given the scale and interdependence of the economic relationship between the two countries. With respect to unemployment over the same period, if anything Canada's performance has been less favorable; American jobless rates have been higher than those in Canada only from 2009 to 2013.[72] Still, by internationally accepted standards, Canadian fiscal policy is consistently more successful at ameliorating low-income status (Figures 1.13 and 1.14).

The question is why this should be so. Perhaps poverty-fighting programs are more generous or better designed in Canada. Or maybe the social pathologies of the poor are more profound in the United States—that low-income Americans make worse choices, exhibit less personal responsibility, than their Canadian counterparts. It seems an unduly harsh analysis, given that more than 30 percent of all poor people in the United States are children and that a combination of dysfunctional schools, substandard housing, crime-addled neighborhoods, limited access to healthy food and regular medical attention, inadequate job training, and the scarcity of well-paying low- or semi-skilled jobs restricts the economic options of the rest. People in low-income status do not make choices in a vacuum; their circumstances limit what behaviors are desirable and feasible. So does the legacy of racial prejudice. It can be no coincidence that African-Americans and Hispanics are two-and-a-half times more likely to be in poverty than other Americans.[73]

Poverty is more than a character flaw, but lack of it could yet be a character virtue. Canada may do better than the United States when it comes to poverty reduction partly because Canadians care more about fellow citizens of modest means and try harder to redress their deprivation. That different sets of political values help explain the redistributive inclinations of Canada and the United States is a possibility explored in Chapters 3 and 4.

How Did This Happen?

Economists disagree as to the weighting of the factors responsible for burgeoning inequalities. The integration of the world economy through enhanced trade and investment and the mobility of capital and labor is part of the answer. As *New York Times* columnist Thomas Friedman famously observed, in a globalized world rich democratic countries are forced to put on a "golden straitjacket" of decision making, implementing those initiatives—free trade, balanced budgets, tax cuts, privatization, modest economic regulation, and so on—required to secure the confidence of international financial markets.[74] Certainly globalization has had many positive economic outcomes. Overall it has helped raise the standard of living for people in developing countries, even those who are very poor, though serious questions about exploitative wages and working conditions persist.[75] But in post-industrial states like Canada and the United States, while a global economy may deliver a greater variety of consumer goods at lower prices than ever before—a boon to citizens of modest means—for many it has meant job insecurity, diminished wages and benefits, and reduced hence less progressive levels of taxation as countries restructure their economies to maintain competitive advantage.

Beginning in the 1980s, such commitments took ideological form as neoliberalism, a philosophy encapsulating the new small government/business-first mood and influencing political parties across the traditional left-right spectrum, especially in the Anglo-Celtic democracies—the United Kingdom, Australia, New Zealand, Ireland, Canada, and the United States. A concomitant was the deregulation of financial institutions. When the Bretton Woods fixed currency exchange rate system ended in the 1970s, the opening of global capital markets, combined with the relaxation of domestic controls over credit and generous lending practices, sparked a renewed dynamism in the finance sector. "Credit became the world's greatest growth industry," writes Andrew Lansley, not a matter of expanding real productivity and innovation but of "paper chasing paper."[76] Compensation skyrocketed for individuals who knew how to ride the new financial wave. Between 1981 and 2006, among the top 1 percent of income earners in Canada, the share working in finance increased faster than for any other economic sector, doubling to almost 11 percent of the total. So did average pay—the highest for any industry group represented in the richest centile.[77] Americans working in finance were just as successful. From 1979 to 2005, their share among the top 1 percent of income earners almost doubled to 14 percent—again, the highest growth rate among all industry sectors. At the same time, financial professionals increased their representation in the top 0.1 percent by more than half to 18 percent and were responsible for roughly a quarter of the growth in national income concentrated in that rarified band.[78]

Without strict capital liquidity requirements for financial institutions as well as legal oversight of convoluted and exposed financial transactions, economic risk also expanded. Changes to the banking system abetted the process. Seeking to enhance the competitiveness of American banks, in 1999 the United States repealed the Glass-Steagall Act (1933), no longer separating the activities of commercial banks, which take deposits and make loans, from investment banks, which underwrite securities. Subsequently, banks played a critical role as traffickers in complex mortgage-backed securities—often based on "subprime" loans extended to low-income families at higher interest rates than normal. In 2007, such byzantine financial packages triggered the collapse of the American housing market, along with consumer spending, business investment, and employment. Given the US position as a global financial hub, much of the advanced industrial world accompanied it into the deepest recession since the 1920s. Canada was spared the worst, arguably because of a more centralized banking system—that is, fewer banks and stricter regulations. The Dodd–Frank Act (2010) has tried to rein in the most outrageous of American practices leading to the crisis, but the economic clout of finance and its contribution to income and wealth inequality have seemed not to suffer.[79] Over the last 30 years, finance's share of domestic corporate profits has steadily grown, from around 10 percent of the total to presently a quarter in the United States and fully a third in Canada.[80]

Computers also play a role. The transition to an economy driven by advances in information technology (IT) means that workers possessing desired knowledge-based skills are in high demand. We are now in a "race against the machine," as the title of a book by Erik Brynjolfsson and Andrew McAfee would have it, in which ever smaller, quicker, and computationally more powerful machines must win.[81] So, for instance, the finance sector has been revolutionized by high-frequency trading, in which brokerages with the best computers, most mathematically astute software, and fastest fiber-optic connectivity are able to pre-empt the investment decisions of potential rivals—and manipulate the stock market—in a matter of milliseconds. When workplaces are reconfigured to take advantage of developments in IT, capital equipment becomes more valuable to the production process. The share of labor income falls while returns to the owners of capital increase: Wealth begets even more wealth.[82]

In this hyper-digitized economy, individuals with the technological sophistication to race alongside the machine can be handsomely compensated. Accordingly, university education has become one of the more significant contemporary factors leading to income inequality within advanced economies, where a premium is placed on graduates who have the ability to deploy the new technologies and the informational resources they make possible. A sign is the income advantage paid to people who hold at least a bachelor's degree. In Canada such individuals make 53 percent more on average than do those with only a high school diploma; their American counterparts make 65 percent more.[83] This is not because savvy university graduates are swelling the ranks of uniformly well-salaried and high-skilled occupations.[84] Rather, within such occupations enormous pay differentials are bestowed on an elite subset of workers deemed truly exceptional. By expanding market reach, not only in the IT sector of the economy but also in business, finance, and entertainment, digital technologies magnify both the impact and the salaries of individuals at the very top of their professions. Such developments help explain why the ratio of the earnings of the average CEO to the average worker in Canada is now 206:1 and in the United States 345:1—four to five times where it stood in the 1990s.[85]

Gender has an effect, too. Increasing the number of women in the workforce tends to enhance economic growth and diminish household income inequality, especially with respect to women who are in full-time paid work. But a rise in the number of single female-headed households, presently a little more than a tenth of all Canadian and American families, has the opposite result: Earnings are reduced, and the financial risk of unemployment becomes more severe. An indication is the percentage of those households with children who are in poverty, around a third of the total in Canada and the United States, which is approximately three times the poverty rate of other families in each country.[86] Of equal note is that in the United States almost 30 percent of such families are headed by black women and more than 18 percent by Hispanic women, nearly half of whom are in poverty.[87] Alternatively, the growth of assortative marriage, whereby partners are of the same educational and occupational status, suggests that the earnings advantages for couples at the heights of the income scale are multiplied, as are the disadvantages of those who trail in their wake.[88] That is particularly the case as more women enter the ranks of professional, managerial, or technical workers. Among their advanced industrial peers, the United States (35 percent) and Canada (33 percent) place first and third for female employees who hold such highly skilled positions, an increase of 16 percent and 13 percent, respectively, from the mid-1980s to 2007.[89]

The genies of globalization, technological innovation, and family dynamics cannot be put back in the bottle—nor would one want to do so. But that does not mean the socioeconomic arrangements unleashed by these structural forces are inevitable. Public policy can make a difference. In the 1930s and 1940s, when income disparities in North America began to narrow, World War II and the American and Canadian governments' responses to it played a part. Labor scarcity during the war, when combined with wage and price controls and labor relations regulations, had the effect of driving up the earnings of blue-collar workers. After the war, wages continued to increase as demand for employment in manufacturing remained high. But that boost to the earnings of middle- and lower-income families was augmented, in fits and starts, by minimum-wage laws, political recognition of the right to collective bargaining, and the establishment of the central props of the welfare state: unemployment insurance, worker's compensation, old-age pensions, means-tested social assistance, and publicly funded health care. Personal income taxes were breathtakingly progressive. In 1950 the top marginal rate was 84 percent in Canada and 91 percent in the United States.

Much has changed. Since the beginning of the Great Divergence, the real value of the minimum wage has been in flux, more so in the United States than in Canada. After bottoming out in the mid-1980s, the average Canadian minimum wage (average since each province is constitutionally responsible for setting its own) has recovered 95 percent of its peak 1976 value and now stands at $10.13 an hour. But at $7.25 an hour, the US federal minimum wage has lost a third of what it was worth in 1968, when it was at an all-time high. Partly that is because, unlike the practice in most Canadian provinces, the minimum wage in the United States is not indexed to inflation but rather is recalibrated by sporadic federal legislation.[90] Economists disagree as to the precise effect this has on income dispersion, though the general consensus is that an increase in the minimum wage helps to reduce inequality among the bottom half of earners, particularly low-income women.[91] If so, Canadians have benefited more than Americans.

Organized labor is no longer so robust, its power diminished by shifts in global economic fundamentals as well as legal limits on the bargaining power of unions, especially the public sector unions that now constitute the greater part of the movement.[92] At its height in 1982, Canadian union density was 36.8 percent of the workforce but has since fallen to just above 27 percent. American unions now represent fewer than 11 percent of all workers, down from a high of 35 percent in the mid-1950s. Right-to-work laws, which are absent in Canada but affect half of all US states, are a factor. Collective bargaining coverage has likewise narrowed. Twenty-five years ago, 38 percent of full-time Canadian workers were covered by union-negotiated agreements, whether or not they were union members; by 2010, only 31.6 percent were. Organized labor in the United States has even less of a reach. In 1990, a little more than 18 percent of American workers were included under collective bargaining pacts, but by 2010 fewer than 14 percent were.[93] As wages and benefits suffer and the moral and political force of union demands for pay equity wanes, income equality is a casualty. Two sociologists of the labor movement, Bruce Western and Jake Rosenfeld, have found that among full-time US employees, a fifth of the growth in wage inequality for women and a third for men can be attributed to deunionization—as potent an explanation of wage inequality among men as differences in education.[94]

Fiscal policy now makes a smaller dent in income inequality, as governments have limited means-tested social spending and adjusted their tax codes. Twenty years ago taxes and transfers reduced inequality by 33 percent in Canada and 24 percent in the United States; most recently they do so by 28 and 23 percent—an impact that would be weaker still if not for the need to increase public benefits and extend tax credits in the wake of a recession.[95] Exemptions, exclusions, deductions, shelters, and in some cases drastic tax cuts—most famously with respect to corporate rates in Canada—have been to the advantage of high-income earners and to the detriment of greater economic equality.[96] And though social spending as a percentage of GDP has held steady (Canada) or increased (US) over the last two decades, the portion of that spending targeting middle- and low-income earners is modest.[97] Between a fifth and a quarter of public cash benefits are directed to the lowest earnings quintile in each country, but in Canada 12 percent and in the United States 16 percent go to the top quintile as well—most often for pensions or old-age security payments regardless of financial circumstances.[98] Income-tested cash benefits—largely for support in old age, survivors' benefits, and income supplements for the working-age population—comprise only 4.8 percent of Canadian GDP and 2.5 percent of US GDP. When it comes to government disbursements for social purposes, in both countries public services now have a role equal to or greater than direct cash transfers and are responsible, according to one estimate, for reducing income inequality by almost 20 percent.[99] Yet in light of the increasing strain that governments are under to pay for the largest part of these services—health and education—one wonders about their future redistributive role.

Finally, for the most vulnerable in the income sweepstakes, social assistance has been transformed—and not clearly for the better. In order to reduce central government expenditure on social programs, both Ottawa and Washington passed landmark welfare reform legislation in 1996. Conditional grants from the federal governments to states and provinces were replaced by block grants, ending automatic entitlements to federal cash assistance. In all provinces and states, means-tested benefits were de-emphasized in favor of work-tested benefits. Welfare as a social safety net for the poorest families has suffered. Since 1996, welfare caseloads in Canada have dropped by 14 percent, though it is hard to tell whether it is because demand has diminished or worthy recipients are being denied.[100] Controlling for inflation, incomes for families on social assistance have decreased in four of the ten provinces.[101] When one applies a more geographically fine-tuned index to assess welfare, the Canadian government's market basket measure of low-income need, all provinces fall short, covering only 61 to 79 percent of what is required.[102] The consequences of reform in the United States are even more dismal. Between 1996 and 2014, the number of social assistance caseloads dropped by 63 percent. So did the number of families with children in poverty receiving benefits—from 68 percent to 25 percent of the total—even though the number of families in poverty held steady.[103] It is easy to see why: The basic US block grant transfer for welfare, locked in at its original 1996 rate, has lost a third of its value to inflation. Few states have been inclined to make up the difference.[104]

Concluding Remarks

Canada and the United States are subject to many of the same structural forces that contribute to growing economic inequality in rich democratic countries. But as the evidence presented in this chapter suggests, the impact on each has not been quite the same. On all counts, Canada is more egalitarian than the United States, whether measured by the Gini coefficient, the distribution of income share and growth, the well-being of the middle class, the allocation of wealth, or the extent and depth of poverty. Part of the reason is that Canadian fiscal policy, and sometimes Canadian public policy more broadly (e.g., indexing the minimum wage to inflation, the absence of right-to-work laws, relatively more generous social assistance provisions), has a greater distributional effect. Canada may yet fall short of Nordic European social democratic ideals. But with respect to the North American distributional ladder, while it is very good to be rich in the United States, if one is just moderately well off or less, better to be in Canada.

That said, where economic opportunity is plentiful, concerns about distribution may be less pressing. From an economic point of view, material inequalities might actually serve as incentives to greater aspirations, productivity, and achievement, provided one is sufficiently confident of being able to move up the income and wealth scale by the force of one's effort. In the United States this self-assurance has a name: the American Dream. The steadfast belief in economic mobility it conveys is the subject of the next chapter.

Notes

1. Typically, Canadian and American government statistical agencies exclude income from capital gains from their basic calculations given that such earnings are most often irregular. Except where noted, I have done likewise.
2. For example, the *Current Population Survey* and its *Annual Social and Economic Supplement*, on which much US Census Bureau data concerning income is based, defines a *household* as "all the people who occupy a housing unit. ... A household includes the related family members and all the unrelated people, if any, such as lodgers, foster children, wards, or employees who share the housing unit. A person living alone in a housing unit, or a group of unrelated people sharing a housing unit such as partners or roomers, is also counted as a household" (US Census Bureau, "Current Population Survey"). Statistics Canada more often refers to an *economic family*: "a group of two or more persons who live in the same dwelling and are related to each other by blood, marriage, common-law or adoption. A couple may be of opposite or same sex. Foster children are included" (Statistics Canada, "Economic Family"). Statistics Canada treats unattached individuals—people living alone or with others to whom they are not related—as a separate category, though they often combine it with

economic families for income reporting purposes. My practice here, though, is to use the two terms, family and household, as synonyms.
3   OECD, "Focus on Inequality and Growth"; OECD, "OECD Income Distribution Database."
4   See Noah, *The Great Divergence*, 6. See also Fischer and Holt, *Century of Difference*.
5   See, for instance, Veall, "Top Income Shares in Canada"; Saez, "Striking It Richer."
6   Alvaredo et al., "The Top 1 Percent in International and Historical Perspective." As the creators of the database caution, their use of tax records to calculate the status of top income earners probably understates the true degree of inequality, since tax filers have an incentive to present their earnings in a way that reduces their tax liability.
7   Veall, "Top Income Shares in Canada," maintains that the gap between Canadian and American earners may be somewhat exaggerated by the way in which American business owners can claim S-corporation status for tax purposes. Under such provisions, instead of paying corporate tax, net revenues are funneled into the personal tax returns of business owners.
8   World Wealth and Income Database.
9   A caveat: Recent unpublished research by Thomas Piketty, Emmanuel Saez, and Gabriel Zucman suggests that once one takes into account the value of tax-exempt fringe benefits in the United States—most famously, perhaps, the tax deduction for mortgage interest payments—between 1980 and 2014, the pre-tax income of Americans between the 50th and 90th percentiles grew by 40 percent. Over the same period real income has been stagnant for the bottom half of US earners, and the greatest benefits of growth have flowed to individuals at the very top of the distributional ladder. In 1980 the average American among the leading 1 percent of earners accrued 27 times the income of his or her counterpart in the bottom half of the distribution; 34 years later the ratio was 81:1. See Piketty, Saez, and Zucman, "Distributional National Accounts."
10 Stiglitz, *The Price of Inequality*, 3; Saez, "Striking It Richer."
11 Krueger, "Land of Hope and Dreams."
12 As the World Bank defines it, the "purchasing power parity conversion factor is the number of units of a country's currency required to buy the same amount of goods and services in the domestic market as a U.S. dollar would buy in the United States." For 2011, the World Bank estimates the purchasing power parity of the Canadian dollar at 1.3 to the American dollar. World Bank, "Price Level Ratio of PPP Conversion Factor (GDP) to Market Exchange Rate."
13 OECD, "OECD Income Distribution Database"; Canadian data for 2011, US and OECD averages data for 2012.
14 A recent article by Janet C. Gornick and Branko Milanovic based on the Luxembourg Income Study Database cautions that it is the continued earnings of older workers, those 60 years of age and above, that is the main driver of market inequality in the United States, since workers in many other countries tend to retire at an earlier age. When considering income inequality for working people under 60, the United States is still one of the least egalitarian states among the 19 rich democratic countries that Gornick and Milanovic studied. But the authors hypothesize that the reason isn't a markedly less distributive tax

and transfer system (with respect to the difference between the Gini coefficients for market and disposable income, the United States is in the middle of the pack for the under 60 set), but rather a highly unequal distribution of wages and income from capital (market income). The finding is important when it comes to strategies for inequality reduction and whether it's more important, especially in the American context, to focus on factors making for large disparities in wages and salaries than after-market fiscal policy. In the same study, recalculating market and disposable income inequality for Canadian workers younger than 60 doesn't change Canada's place in the distributional rankings much—third lowest for all ages and fourth lowest for the under 60s. It does suggest, however, that American and Canadian taxes and transfers may have similar distributional effects on younger workers. The aggregate differences between them may be because Americans delay retirement longer than do Canadians, though in Canada the average working life span has been increasing, and Canadians tend to work for more years than do their peers in many other rich democratic countries.

All this said, it does seem that the disposable income available to residents of all ages is the most basic measure of inequality—after all, older people and children are citizens too—and by that criterion, Canada is a more egalitarian place than the United States. See Gornick and Milanovic, "Income Inequality in the United States in Cross-National Perspective."

15 Environics Institute, *Focus Canada 2012*, 14.
16 Morin and Motel, "A Third of Americans Now Say They Are in the Lower Classes." The title of the analysis is a bit misleading, since the authors merge the number of respondents who say they are lower middle class (25 percent) with those who simply say they are lower class (7 percent). Using slightly different markers—specifically, substituting the category "working class" for "lower middle class"—Gallup confirms that the number of Americans identifying as middle class has stayed fairly stable over time, at around 85–90 percent of their survey respondents. See Dugan, "Americans Most Likely to Say They Belong to the Middle Class."
17 The most recent Census Bureau data, for 2015, offer some hope. Median household income was up 5.2 percent from the previous year, the biggest annual increase since the Bureau began to record the measure in 1967. Nevertheless, in inflation-controlled terms, the median is still 2.4 percent lower than it was at the turn of the twenty-first century. Applebaum, "US Household Income Grew 5.2% in 2015."
18 See also Cross and Sheikh, "Caught in the Middle"; Atkinson and Brandolini, "On the Identification of the Middle Class"; Kenworthy, "Has Rising Inequality Reduced Middle Class Income Growth?"
19 See Congressional Budget Office, "Changes in the Distribution of Workers' Hourly Wages between 1979 and 2009"; Gould, "Wage Inequality Continued Its 35 Year Rise in 2015."
20 Leonhardt and Quealy, "The American Middle Class Is No Longer the World's Richest."
21 Thompson, "How Did Canada's Middle Class Get so Rich?"
22 McGee, "How America's Middle Class Fell Behind Its Canadian Neighbours."
23 Moffat, "Eight Charts Explain Why Canada's Middle Class Is Richer than America's."

24 Parlapiano, Gebeloff, and Carter, "The Shrinking American Middle Class"; Stabile and Jones, "The Shrinking Middle Class." Each newspaper set the definition of middle class from the US poverty line to 50 percent above it, roughly between US$35,000 and US$100,000 for a family of four. By that measure and holding constant for inflation, since 1967 the size of the American middle class has fallen from 53 percent to 43 percent of the population, while over the same period the Canadian middle class has remained stable at around 43 percent—broadly confirming the conventional academic wisdom.

25 That said, Cross and Sheikh argue that over the last 30 years changes in the Canadian transfer and tax system have actually been to the advantage of middle-income Canadians (in their analysis, the middle three quintiles of households by income), a by-product of higher taxes on high-income groups and lower taxes for the middle class, combined with smaller transfers to low-income groups and increased transfers to the middle class. Cross and Sheikh, "Caught in the Middle," 8.

26 By contrast, the difference in 2011 market and disposable income shares for the bottom quintile of Canadian and American households is 3.8 percent and 7.2 percent, respectively, but −8.0 percent and −10.8 percent for the top quintile. Statistics Canada, "Market, Total and After-Tax Income, Table 202-0701"; Congressional Budget Office, "The Distribution of Household Income and Federal Taxes, 2011."

27 According to the OECD, the P90/P50 ratio is "the ratio of the upper bound value of the ninth decile to the median income." In 2011, the ratio was 1.9 in Canada and 2.3 in the United States. The P50/P10 ratio is "the ratio of the median income to the upper bound value of the first decile." In 2011 it was 2.1 for Canada and 2.7 for the United States. OECD, "OECD Income Distribution Database."

28 For a similar perspective on US income distribution, see Reeves and Cuddy, "Stretchy Ends."

29 On the definition of wealth and capital, see Piketty, *Capital in the Twenty-First Century*, 18, 48.

30 Ibid, 25.

31 Ibid, 25–26.

32 For instance, Saez and Zucman estimate that from 2000–09, the wealthiest 1 percent of Americans on average saved 35 percent of their income, the next 9 percent saved 10 percent, and the bottom 90 percent in effect saved nothing. For the latter, that is consistent with historical norms. Since the 1920s the bottom 90 percent of families have rarely saved more than an average of 5 percent of their income, and they have seen their savings rate steeply decline since the 1970s. Saez and Zucman, "Wealth Inequality in the United States since 1913."

33 Piketty, *Capital in the Twenty-First Century*, 146–58.

34 Ibid, 315–21. Also see Stewart Lansley, *The Cost of Inequality*.

35 Shorrocks, Davies, and Lluberas explain the anomaly of Denmark: "(H)igher wealth concentration can … result from more benign influences. For example, strong social security programs—good public pensions, free higher education or generous student loans, unemployment and health insurance—can greatly reduce the need for personal financial assets. Public housing programs can do the same for real assets. This is one explanation for the high level of wealth inequality we identify in Denmark, Norway and Sweden: the top groups

continue to accumulate for business and investment purposes, while the middle and lower classes have no pressing need for personal saving." Shorrocks, Davies, and Lluberas, *Global Wealth Report, 2014*, 36.

36 "The wealth share of the top decile is our preferred measure of inequality because it is simple to understand and not over-sensitive to wealth changes at the bottom of the wealth distribution. It also correlates well with the value of the Gini coefficient and the share of the top percentile." Shorrocks, Davies, and Lluberas, *Global Wealth Report, 2014*, 117.

37 OECD, "Wealth Shares of the Top Percentiles of the Wealth Distribution." Based on estimates made in 2014, Credit Suisse puts the top 10 percent share for the United States at 75 percent but 57 percent for Canada; for the top 1 percent, the US share was 39 percent and 24 percent for Canada; and for the bottom 40 percent the comparables were 0 percent for the United States and 2.2 percent for Canada.

38 Saez and Zucman maintain that the true beneficiaries of wealth inequality are the top 0.1 percent of American families—the 167,000 households with more than US$20 million in net worth. From 1986–2012, according to Saez and Zucman, this hyper-affluent cohort enjoyed average rates of return on capital of 5.3 percent per year, in the process accumulating almost half of the growth in national wealth over the period. See Saez and Zucman, "Wealth Inequality in the United States since 1913," 1.

39 More precisely, according to the Fed, it is the top 3 percent of households that account for almost all of the growth in net worth over the period. Bricker et al., "Changes in U.S. Family Finances from 2010 to 2013," 10; see also Kennickell, "Ponds and Streams"; and Levine, "An Analysis of the Distribution of Wealth Across Households, 1989–2010," 4.

40 OECD Wealth Distribution Database (2015). Alternatively, the Federal Reserve maintains that the mean-to-median net worth ratio in the United States increased from 4.0 in 1989 to 6.5 by 2010, slightly less than OECD estimates. Cited in Levine, "An Analysis of the Distribution of Wealth," 3. Regarding the mean-to-median ratio, as Levine observes, if more than half of all wealth in a given distribution is owned by a minority of households, then the mean for wealth will be higher than the median (2).

41 OECD, *In It Together*, 253–54.

42 Uppal and LaRochelle-Côté, "Changes in Wealth across the Income Distribution, 1999 to 2012," 10.

43 Ibid., 2–5. The median net worth for the highest quintile was C$879,100; for the next highest, C$388,200. The poorest 20 percent of families according to income had a median net worth of C$8,700.

44 Changes in the US tax code in 2013 that increased the top income tax rates on capital gains and dividends by 9 percent may also play a role.

45 Shorrocks, Davies, and Lluberas, *Global Wealth Report, 2014*, 125–26. Note that the Credit Suisse figures for Canadian wealth shares are a bit higher than the OECD estimates, confirmation that despite the best efforts of statisticians, the accumulation of comparative data on wealth can be a highly imperfect business.

46 Analysis of Statistics Canada data by the Broadbent Institute, "Haves and Have Nots."

47 Figures for Canada are based on the author's calculations from *Statistics Canada*, "Survey of Financial Security (SFS), Table 205-0003" and Broadbent Institute,

"Haves and Have Nots." US figures from Bricker et al., "Changes in U.S. Family Finances from 2010 to 2013," 12.
48 Ibid.
49 Saez and Zucman, "Wealth Inequality in the United States since 1913"; Statistics Canada, "Survey of Financial Security, Table 205-0003."
50 Shorrocks, Davies, and Lluberas, *Global Wealth Report, 2014*, 147.
51 OECD, *In it Together*, 266–68. Figures are calculated for the 18 OECD member states for which there are reliable data.
52 Ibid., 270. The percent of households in the OECD member states that are dangerously indebted are as follows: for the bottom income quintile, 9.9 percent; the second, 10.4 percent; the middle, 10.9 percent; the fourth, 10.3 percent; the richest, 5.6 percent. The OECD also measures what it calls the "depth" of indebtedness—the percentage of indebted households plotted against the median debt-to-income ratio of indebted households, the idea being that debt is especially problematic for countries that have a large number of indebted households of which a significant number have a high median debt-to-income ratio. By that measure, Canada has a higher median debt-to-income ratio than the United States, at 161 to 133 (the third- and fifth-highest among OECD countries measured), but in the aggregate, US households are more vulnerable to swings in the value of assets, given that 75 percent of American families are in debt as opposed to 45 percent of families in Canada.
53 For instance, according to the US Federal Reserve's Survey of Consumer Finances (2013), 92 percent of the top 10 percent of households according to income held stock, as opposed to around a quarter held by the bottom 49.9 percent of earners. The mean value of the holdings of the top 10 percent was US$969,000, and of the bottom 49.9 percent, US$53,600. Board of Governors of the Federal Reserve System, *Report on the Economic Well-Being*, 18–19.
54 Edward Wolff, based on Federal Reserve data for 2010, states that the bottom three American income quintiles had 67 percent of their assets in their homes, though given large mortgage debt, home equity was equivalent to only 32 percent of total assets. See Wolff, "The Asset Price Meltdown," 338.
55 Estimated loss in net value for US homes is for 2008–13. See ibid., 333–42; Board of Governors of the Federal Reserve System, *Report on the Economic Well-Being*, 22–23; Veiga, "Economic Recovery"; Hartman, "Fewer Homes Are Now 'Underwater'"; Bennett, "The Aftermath of the Great Recession." The time period for reduction in median net worth is 2007–10; for underwater homes at or near 25 percent the time period is 2009–11; for foreclosure, it is 2007–11.
56 US Census Bureau, "Quarterly Homeownership Rates for the U.S. and Regions: 1965 to Present"; Joint Center for Housing Studies of Harvard University, "America's Rental Housing"; Searcey, "More Americans Are Renting and Paying More."
57 The latest estimate (for 2013) of the Canadian home-ownership rate is 67.6 percent. Statistics Canada, "Survey of Household Spending"; Statistics Canada, "Homeownership and Shelter Costs in Canada."
58 Lang and Graves, "Closer Reading of StatsCan Report Troubling for Middle Class"; Marr, "Canada Household Debt Ratio Hits New Record of 163.3%."
59 Environics Institute, *AmericasBarometer*, 66; Statistics Canada, "Canadian Financial Capability Survey, 2014"; also see Ipsos-Reid, "Half (48%) of Canadians Are Less than $200 Away Monthly from Being Financially Insolvent."

60 Board of Governors of the Federal Reserve System, *Report on the Economic Well-Being*, 18, 38.
61 Luxembourg Income Study, "Inequality and Poverty."
62 Presently, the average Canadian family spends 43 percent of its income on these basic items, meaning that a family meeting the LICO threshold has to spend 63 percent or more of its income on those same things.
63 Statistics Canada, "Persons in Low Income, by Economic Family Type."
64 DeNavas-Walt and Proctor, "Income and Poverty in the United States: 2014." The official US poverty rate does not vary according to geography and regards all people living under the same roof who are related by birth, marriage, or adoption as sharing income.
65 See, for example, Jencks, "The War on Poverty."
66 Short, "The Supplemental Poverty Measure: 2014."
67 Deaton, *The Great Escape*, 184; emphasis in original. Adam Smith had much the same view, maintaining that a life free of poverty included "necessaries," which he understood to be "not only the commodities which are indispensably necessary for the support of life, but whatever the custom of the country renders it indecent for creditable people, even of the lowest order, to be without." See Smith, *An Inquiry into the Nature and Causes of the Wealth of Nations*, vol. 2, bk. 5, chap. 2: 148.
68 Banting and Myles, "Framing the New Inequality."
69 Economic Policy Institute, *The State of Working America*, 443.
70 Banting and Myles, "Introduction," 31.
71 Among nonstandard workers in Canada, 35 percent are in poverty compared to an OECD average of 22 percent. OECD, "In It Together."
72 Cf. Statistics Canada, "Labour Force Survey Estimates"; US Department of Labor, Bureau of Labor Statistics, "Seasonal Unemployment Rate"; World Bank, "World Development Indicators."
73 US Census Bureau, "People in Poverty by Selected Characteristics."
74 Friedman, *The Lexus and the Olive Tree*, 83–92.
75 See, for instance, *The Economist*, "Poverty: Not Always With Us." Citing a World Bank study, the author of the article demurs, "Growth alone does not guarantee less poverty. Income distribution matters, too. One estimate found that two thirds of the fall in poverty was the result of growth; one-third came from greater equality. More equal countries cut poverty further and faster than unequal ones."
76 Lansley, *The Cost of Inequality*, 101, 103. See also Sayer, *Why We Can't Afford the Rich*, Chapters 4–8, 12–14. The phrase "paper chasing paper" is attributed to Paul Volcker, former chair of the US Federal Reserve.
77 Lemieux and Riddell, "Top Incomes in Canada"; Fortin et al., "Canadian Inequality."
78 Bakija, Cole, and Heim, "Jobs and Income Growth of Top Earners and the Causes of Changing Income Inequality."
79 Among the Dodd-Frank reforms are establishing federal watchdogs within the Federal Reserve to protect consumers against credit and mortgage market abuse; restricting banks from owning, investing, or sponsoring hedge funds, private equity funds, or any proprietary trading operations for their own profit (the Volcker rule); regulating the riskiest derivatives, like credit default swaps; and monitoring banks' reserve requirements.

80 Statistics Canada, "Quarterly Balance Sheet and Income Statement"; US Department of Commerce, "Corporate Profits by Industry, 2015."
81 Brynjolfsson and McAfee, *Race against the Machine*. See also Cowen, *Average Is Over*.
82 According to the OECD, between 1990 and 2009 the share of labor income to GDP in Canada dropped more than five points to 59.8 percent; in the United States between 1990 and 2012 it declined four and one-half points to 63.7 percent. OECD StatExtracts, Unit Labour Costs, Annual Indicators: Labour Income Share Ratios. See also Karabarbounis and Neiman, "The Global Decline of the Labor Share"; Giovannoni, "What Do We Know about the Labor Share and the Profit Share?"
83 OECD, *Education at a Glance 2015*, Table A6.1a, 116.
84 See Schmitt, Shierholz, and Mishel, "Don't Blame the Robots."
85 US CEO-to-worker pay ratio is based on AFL-CIO analysis of average CEO pay at 327 companies in the S&P 500 Index for 2012. US rank-and-file worker pay calculated from US Bureau of Labor Statistics, "Average Hours and Earnings of Production and Non-supervisory Employees on Private Non-farm Payrolls, 2012." Average Canadian CEO pay calculated from 2012 or later CEO pay levels for companies from the S&P TSX 60. CEO-to-worker pay ratios for Canada are calculated using 2011 average annual wages as reported by the OECD StatExtracts database. Gavett, "CEOs Get Paid Too Much"; Brynjolfsson and McAfee, *Race against the Machine*, 44; AFL-CIO, "CEO-to-Worker Pay Ratios Around the World"; Allaire, "Pay for Value."
86 Figures are for poverty/low-income status before tax. US Census Bureau, "Families in Poverty by Type of Family: 2012 and 2013"; Statistics Canada, "Persons in Low Income, Table 202-0804."
87 US Census Bureau, "People in Poverty by Selected Characteristics"; US Census Bureau, "Poverty Status, by Type of Family."
88 See OECD, *In It Together*, chap. 5; Alderson and Doran, "How Has Income Inequality Grown?"; Fortin and Schirle, "Gender Dimensions of Changes in Earnings Inequality in Canada"; Carbone and Cahn, *Marriage Markets*.
89 OECD, *In It Together*, 219–22.
90 Figures are for 2013 and are denominated in 2013 dollars. Galarneau and Fecteau, "The Ups and Downs of Minimum Wage." See also Battle, "Restoring Minimum Wages in Canada"; Elwell, "Inflation and the Real Minimum Wage." In the United States, states and municipalities can and have set minimum-wage rates considerably higher than the federal floor. For instance, by 2015 Seattle, San Francisco, and Los Angeles all had rates of $15 an hour.
91 See, for example, Card, Lemieux, and Riddell, "Unionization and Wage Inequality"; Autor, Manning, and Smith, "The Contribution of the Minimum Wage to U.S. Wage Inequality over Three Decades"; Mishel, "Declining Value of the Federal Minimum Wage Is a Major Factor Driving Inequality."
92 US Department of Labor, Bureau of Labor Statistics, "Union Members Summary"; Uppal, "Unionization 2011." See also Warner, *Protecting Fundamental Workers Rights*.
93 OECD Employment Database (2015).
94 Western and Rosenfeld, "Unions, Norms, and the Rise in U.S. Wage Inequality." The authors studied the period from 1973 to 2007.

95   The most recent Canadian data are for 2011; for the United States, 2012. OECD Income Distribution Database.
96   See Frenette, Green, and Milligan, "Taxes, Transfers, and Canadian Income Inequality." Frenette et al. argue that a tightening of unemployment benefits, changes from Family Assistance to the Canada Child Tax Benefit, and the introduction of the Canada Health and Social Transfer were especially important. See also Alvaredo et al., "The Top 1 Percent in International and Historical Perspective"; Linden, "The Federal Tax Code and Income Inequality."
97   For 2014, the OECD Social Expenditure Database reports that Canada spent 17 percent of its GDP on public social benefits and the United States 19.2 percent. The OECD average is 21.6 percent.
98   All figures are from the OECD Social Expenditure Database, 2015.
99   OECD, *Divided We Stand*, 39. Data are for 2007. According to the OECD Social Expenditure Database (2015), in 2012 the United States disbursed 9.1 percent of its GDP on public social benefits in cash but 9.4 percent in services; the Canadian comparables are 9.1 percent and 8.1 percent.
100 Author's calculations from data in the Caledon Institute of Social Policy, *Social Assistance Summaries 2014*. See also Human Resources and Skills Development Canada, *Social Assistance Statistical Report*.
101 Tweddle, Battle, and Torjman, *Welfare in Canada 2014*; National Council of Welfare, "Total Welfare Incomes." Figures are for one-parent, one-child families.
102 Ibid.
103 Falk, "The Temporary Assistance for Needy Families (TANF) Block Grant"; Office of Family Assistance, "TANF Financial Data"; US Census Bureau, "Poverty Status of People by Age, Race and Hispanic Origin, 1959–2013"; Floyd, Pavetti, and Schott, "TANF Continues to Weaken as a Safety Net."
104 Floyd and Schott, "TANF Cash Benefits Have Fallen by More Than 20 Percent in Most States and Continue to Erode."

2
Mobility

IF CITIZENS COULD BE CONVINCED that regardless of background they had an equal chance to ascend the economic ladder, that hard work and perseverance would be met with success, then large inequalities might be less unsettling. Even in a highly unequal society, provided no extraneous or artificial barriers stood in the way, individuals might be willing to wager on their own energies and skills to move up the income scale, at the risk that they might have a worse life if they proved less talented or ambitious than they had thought.[1] *Mobility* is the concept that social scientists use to signify this capacity to move between different levels of socioeconomic well-being, and for many observers it is mobility rather than inequality per se that is the most important measure of a community's economic and political health.[2]

Mobile societies aren't always more equal, though they often are. And inequality can make certain kinds of mobility more difficult, insofar as it pushes the rungs of the income and wealth ladder further apart. Yet even the belief in mobility, aside from its actual achievement, can take the edge off the frustration that builds when the resources of the haves and have-nots are wildly different.[3] This connection between social well-being and mobility, real and imagined, is well documented.[4] Among liberal-democratic countries, anchored by norms of equality and individual freedom, it serves an especially important ideological purpose. To maintain their integrity, such polities must reassure citizens that the promise of equality, in particular equality of opportunity, is not empty—that an accident of birth determines neither one's eventual social status nor material welfare. This is despite the fact that people's initial endowments—the intellectual, physical, psychological, and social assets conferred by family and community—will vary, placing them at different starting points in the race to economic security. Frontrunners will be inclined to believe that they or their forebears, from whose largesse they may benefit, deserve their good fortune, that in a society of expansive opportunities they have applied themselves in a way others have not and are rewarded for their efforts. But those not blessed with a large portfolio of early advantages must come to feel that they, too, can ascend the affluence scale.

American political dialogue is especially partial to this narrative of mobility. Among the US citizenry the norm of equal opportunity as a means to material advancement is so widely endorsed that pollsters rarely ask about it—and when they do, almost 100 percent of respondents approve.[5]

Moreover, there is considerable evidence that Americans significantly overestimate the actual likelihood of upward economic mobility, and that those of lower income are the most inclined to do so.[6] Politicians follow suit, encouraging the electorate that the chances of flourishing are high given the appropriate circumstances. Consider one of the leading memes of the 2012 US election: "You didn't build that." It comes from a July campaign speech given by President Obama in Roanoke, Virginia:

> Look, if you've been successful, you didn't get there on your own ... I'm always struck by people who think, well, it must be because I was just so smart. There are a lot of smart people out there. It must be because I worked harder than everybody else. Let me tell you something—there are a whole bunch of hardworking people out there ... If you were successful, somebody along the line gave you some help. There was a great teacher somewhere in your life. Somebody helped to create this unbelievable American system that we have that allowed you to thrive. Somebody invested in roads and bridges. If you've got a business—*you didn't build that*. Somebody else made that happen.[7]

Obama's political adversaries seized on the phrase as the antithesis of American individualism and entrepreneurship, evidence that he was out of touch with core US values. "Clearly, this President doesn't understand how our economy works," a Republican ad scolded. "Success is not the result of government, it is the result of hardworking people who take risks, create dreams, and build lives for themselves and for their families."[8] At one level, of course, the debate turned on whether the well-to-do merit their affluence, including the right to keep the great majority of it for private purposes. That the idea of merit is deeply contested and often used as a rationalization for morally arbitrary economic outcomes made it no less potent a political symbol. But partisanship aside, either reading of the economic record is easier to the degree one is persuaded of living in an open society where progress is possible for all. Whether you move up through your own devices or with the assistance of others, on the common American political wisdom you move up.

Unfortunately, as this chapter will suggest, such optimism is not entirely justified. In response to some of the highest levels of economic inequality among rich democratic states, Americans who console themselves with expectations of equally high levels of mobility may be disappointed. That is particularly the case when it comes to an ability to advance independent of the socioeconomic status of one's parents. By that criterion, Canada is a far more economically mobile place than the United States, though Canadians seem loath to recognize it.

Measuring Mobility

Capturing mobility is no easy thing. Occupation, education, income, wealth, and social status can each be a focus of analysis, though mobility tends to move in the same direction across all these dimensions.[9] Yet at least with respect to income, the mobility marker that is most often studied, four research emphases seem the most common:

- *Absolute intra-generational mobility* refers to the movement in one's overall economic position on the income scale when measured over a particular segment of time: Does a person have more or less income at the end of a given period than he or she did when he or she started?
- *Relative intra-generational mobility* points to a situation in which a person has changed rungs on an economic ladder typically divided into income quintiles or deciles. A key question here is whether one's position has gotten better or worse compared to other income recipients of similar socioeconomic and demographic circumstances.
- *Absolute intergenerational mobility* indicates how adult children have done on the income scale when compared to their parents: Controlling for inflation, do they have more income and, presumably, a higher material standard of living than their parents did at the same age?
- *Relative intergenerational mobility* considers how someone's income rank compares to that of their parents at a similar age. In this instance researchers want to know the degree to which mobility is a function of one's family background, whether parents' economic advantages or disadvantages are communicated over time to their children.

Absolute Intra-generational Mobility

Of all the measures of mobility that social scientists deploy, absolute intra-generational mobility is the most forgiving. It simply addresses the question of whether in the foreseeable future an average family can expect to have more income in real terms than it does at present. Short of a cataclysm such as a depression or a war (hosting it, not simply fighting it), in rich democracies typically the answer is yes, inasmuch as the effect is tied to a country's overall economic growth rate.

There are important caveats. First, estimates of mobility are retrospective rather than prospective.[10] They indicate how members of a household have fared economically over time, but they cannot guarantee earnings going forward. It's an obvious yet significant point. One may dismiss the importance of a more equal and reliable distribution of income and wealth, being content to gamble on imminent prosperity, but it always *is* a gamble.[11] Moreover, while the average household will do better income-wise over the long term, not all households will do equally well and many will do worse. And a family's initial position on the income distribution scale can be relevant to just how well or poorly. So can the age of its members and their gender, race, marital/family status, educational credentials, occupation, and place of residence.[12] The time period for which mobility is considered can influence one's earnings outlook as well, since macroeconomic realities and the public policy responses to them will punctuate the pursuit of sustained economic advancement. All things being equal, the average person in Canada and the United States has a fair hope of becoming richer. But things are never equal.

Consider household disposable income growth over the last generation, the amount of money a family has in its pocket after government transfers and taxes. Table 2.1 displays average income levels and growth rates by quintile for the 25 years between 1986 and 2011.[13] During that time, Canadian and American constant dollar GDP growth rates were broadly similar and, with the exception of recessions in 1990–91 and 2008–09, positive. From 1986 to 2011, if the average household that had started in a given quintile was still there by the end of the period, it had realized a healthy percentage increase in real earnings—more in each American than Canadian quintile and more for the top fifth of earners than others. The performance of the lowest fifth of Canadian earners is a surprise. An average American family in that income tier increased its earnings by 33 percent, but its Canadian equivalent did so by only 7 percent. Part of the explanation is that the recession of the early 1990s—deeper in Canada than in the United States—hit low-income Canadians especially hard, as did Ottawa's fiscal restructuring in the middle of the decade. And one must remember the sums involved. An income gain of a third for the lowest American quintile translates to barely more than US$2,500—welcome, though hardly a guarantee of economic security. More importantly, when one factors in purchasing power parities, across the period the average family in the poorest Canadian quintile is consistently better off than its American counterpart.[14] In that respect, at least, Canada's greater egalitarian credentials are not in jeopardy.

Shifting the time frame alters the picture. Table 2.1 also assesses income growth at 15-, 10-, and 5-year intervals. At every stage, the US experience of earnings mobility is more fragile and that of Canada more impressive than for the 25-year window. In fact, with one exception—the top 20 percent of earners between 2001 and 2011—in each of the shorter periods Canadian quintiles register higher average household income growth than do corresponding American tiers. Cross-national gaps in the lowest quintile's performance from 1986 to 2011 are reversed, so that the mean income growth of

Table 2.1 Average Disposable Household Income and Income Growth by Quintile, Selected Years, 1986–2011

	United States							
Income Growth	1986–2011		1996–2011		2001–2011		2006–2011	
Avg. Inc. 1986		1996		2001		2006		2011
Low 20%	$7,526	33%	$9,378	7.4%	$10,047	0.0%	$11,123	−9.4% $10,074
2nd 20%	21,285	27.0	23,230	17.2	25,401	7.2	29,396	−7.3 27,230
Mid 20%	37,229	22.3	40,602	12.2	43,326	5.1	48,869	−6.7 45,563
4th 20%	59,003	22.3	66,372	8.7	68,236	5.7	76,426	−5.5 72,169
Top 20%	112,586	36.0	132,645	15.5	135,987	12.7	158,146	−3.0 153,326
	Canada							
Income Growth	1986–2011		1996–2011		2001–2011		2006–2011	
Avg. Inc. 1986		1996		2001		2006		2011
Low 20%	$14,100	7.0%	$12,900	17.0%	$13,600	11.0%	$14,300	5.5% $15,100
2nd 20%	29,600	12.8	26,900	24.1	30,500	9.5	32,000	3.7 33,400
Mid 20%	45,500	12.5	41,700	22.7	46,600	9.8	49,200	4.0 51,200
4th 20%	64,100	18.4	60,500	25.4	68,100	11.4	71,900	5.5 75,900
Top 20%	105,700	31.8	103,200	35.0	124,700	11.7	131,100	6.3 139,400

Source: Author's calculations from US Bureau of Labor Statistics, Table 1101, Table 55, and Table 1. Tables include values for mean household after-tax as well as before-tax income. Statistics Canada, "Market, Total and After-Tax Income, by Economic Family Type and After-Tax Income Quintiles, 2011 Constant Dollars, Annual."

the poorest fifth of Canadians now outpaces that of the poorest Americans by a significant amount—most dramatically in 2001–11 and 2006–11, when earnings for the average family among the bottom 20 percent of Americans were stagnant or reduced. Once again a recession is responsible, this time in 2008–09, but with a greater impact on Americans than Canadians, as the negative growth for all US tiers in the five-year margin indicates. Finally, the longer the time period being considered, the greater is the likelihood of higher average income growth, hence the appearance of mobility. In each of the five American quintiles, growth rates progressively diminish from the widest to the narrowest of the four windows. What appears to be a highly upwardly mobile US citizenry in 1986–2011 is quite the reverse by 2006–11. Canada does better in the nearer term, registering its most impressive gains in 1996–2011, after which the general rule of diminishing returns in briefer intervals holds true. All of which is to say that if mobility is merely a matter of having more income today than a generation ago, the average North

American household for each income quintile can be said to be reasonably mobile, though this seriously elides shorter-term variations in fortune.

Income earners don't stay in the same position over the trajectory of their working lives, of course. Since it is highly unlikely that exactly the same household will occupy the average rank in a given income quintile from year to year, a truer picture of mobility requires that the movements of particular families across the income schedule be more precisely tracked. Fortunately, social scientists in the United States and Canada have recourse to longitudinal panel studies—samples of regular household surveys or tax-filing data allowing them to follow the economic fortunes of specific families and individuals over time. The Panel Study of Income Dynamics (PSID), a nationally representative survey of households administered by the University of Michigan since 1968 (annually before 1999, biennially afterwards), is the principal American data source for this purpose. A Canadian equivalent, Statistics Canada's Survey of Labour and Income Dynamics, operated annually between 1993 and 2011 but has since been succeeded by the agency's Intergenerational Income Database (IID), which gleans income statistics from a yearly sample of federal tax records starting in 1978.

Panel evidence affirms that the earnings mobility of North American publics is substantial if not always predictable. In the long term, individuals on the lower rungs of the income ladder typically display more absolute income mobility than those at the top, in part because many are young people just entering the workforce whose earnings potential is high.[15] But shorter frames of analysis present a more nuanced picture.[16] In a study of real disposable income growth rates, Wen-Hao Chen of Statistics Canada estimates that from 1990 to 2003 the boost in earnings at various five-year intervals averaged between 34 and 44 percent for the United States and between 29 and 33 percent for Canada, meaning that a typical family could expect to receive that much more income at the end of a given period than they had had its start.[17] Averages, however, can conceal downward changes in pay. According to Chen, from 1996 to 2000 two-thirds of Canadians realized income gains, but a third suffered declines; the fraction of Americans experiencing losses was greater still. Whereas American families who gained during the period accrued higher earnings than did their Canadian counterparts, Americans who lost also lost more. For that reason, Chen cautions that US income mobility, though greater in the aggregate than in Canada, is not clearly superior.[18] Katherine Bradbury, an economist with the Boston Federal Reserve, is similarly guarded. On her reckoning, since the early 1980s real earnings growth for any particular American household over a 10-year period has become more dependent on where it starts on the income distribution scale, and gains for families from the lowest income quintile have lagged.[19]

Wojciech Kopczuk, Emmanuel Saez, and Jae Song agree that at least since the Great Divergence the prospects for American income growth have been more tightly tethered to one's economic origins, but only for men. On their reading, from the 1950s to the mid-2000s, the long-term (11-year) average earnings mobility of US workers increased because of reductions in the gender earnings gap and thus the upward mobility of women. Among men, average income growth across the period actually declined.[20] The impact of the last recession is beyond the range of these analyses, though one expects it would temper future results. Even so, all three studies agree that since the late 1970s absolute earnings mobility in Canada and the United States has been insufficient to offset large increases in income inequality.[21] It is an important reminder that an economically dynamic society does not necessarily make for a more equitable one.

Relative Intra-generational Mobility

Income growth alone is no panacea for contemporary inequality. But what of mobility as measured by a family's capacity to move beyond the various income tiers in which it finds itself? In this case mobility is not assessed according to how well one has done in constant dollar earnings over time, but rather the headway one makes relative to others in ascending the rungs of a common income ladder.

The relevance of such comparative measures may not be immediately clear. Provided a household's material welfare steadily increases, why should it matter how it stacks up to others? The short answer is social status. In North America, the relative size of a person's bank account and investment portfolio is a major determinant of his or her place in the social and political hierarchy, as well as access to the different opportunities that come with it. There is little that is new in this. Students of politics have often commented on the fluidity of class distinctions in New World democracies like Canada and the United States, where money as much as lineage denotes social position and "class struggle ... is carried on within a framework of mobility and hope."[22] That is not to discount the historical reality of concentrated power informed by family connections, ethnicity, race, religion, or gender. Yet the fact of who governs is one thing, while public beliefs about social advancement and prestige are quite another. When it comes to the rich, Americans may not go in for envy, as *The Economist* once observed, but they certainly appreciate the honorifics attached to greater and lesser wealth; so do Canadians.[23] Consequently, while absolute gains in income and net worth are the necessary benchmarks of economic success, they may not be sufficient. For many people it will be important to have more of that success, hence greater status, than their neighbors. By comparing the material advancement of the members of a given household in the labor market with that of individuals who are like them—sometimes defined as the entire workforce, sometimes as a demographic subset—one begins to capture this more expansive view of mobility.

According to ranked indicators, there is little doubt that Canada and the United States are mobile societies. The transition matrix in Table 2.2 indicates in percentage terms where Canadian and American earners from each income quintile in a base year (the left-hand side of the table) find themselves at the end of the period under observation. An analysis of 10-year panel data by Vancouver's Fraser Institute (the top half of the table) maintains that when compared to the income trajectory of all Canadian workers, 83 percent of 25–40 year olds who were initially in the bottom quintile of Canadian wage and salary earners moved into higher tiers between 1990 and 2000, as did 65 percent of the same age group in the next quintile.[24]

Table 2.2 Relative Income Mobility by Quintile Movement

	Canada 1990–2000						
	2000 Income Quintile						
	Low 20%	2nd 20%	Mid 20%	4th 20%	Top 20%	Up	Down
1990 Income Quintile							
Low 20%	17	26	25	20	12	83	X
2nd 20%	10	25	31	22	12	65	10
Mid 20%	5	12	35	34	15	49	17
4th 20%	2	5	13	44	36	36	20
Top 20%	1	2	4	13	79	X	21
	United States 1996–2005						
	2005 Income Quintile						
	Low 20%	2nd 20%	Mid 20%	4th 20%	Top 20%	Up	Down
1996 Income Quintile							
Low 20%	42.4	28.6	13.9	9.9	5.3	58	X
2nd 20%	17.0	33.3	26.7	15.1	7.9	49	17
Mid 20%	7.1	17.5	33.3	29.6	12.5	42	25
4th 20%	4.1	7.3	18.3	40.2	30.2	30	30
Top 20%	2.6	3.2	7.1	17.8	69.4	X	31

Note: Canadian data are from Statistics Canada's Longitudinal Administrative Database and are for individuals from 20–45 years old in 1990. American data are also from a sample of US tax returns but represent individuals 25 years of age and older in 1996.

Source: US Department of the Treasury, "Income Mobility in the US from 1996 to 2005"; Lammam, Karabegović, and Veldhuis, "Measuring Income Mobility in Canada."

Focusing on lower-income bands is understandable, since upward mobility is the most pressing for those in the tightest economic circumstances. Yet the same study observes that of the highest fifth of Canadian earners in the observed age group, 21 percent descended the income ladder, while virtually the same number was relegated from the fourth quintile. Mobility at the bottom of the income distribution and an apparent lack of stability at its top may be interpreted as signs of social and economic dynamism, the natural churning of a market-centered system of material rewards. But in some ways it is a glass half full/glass half empty story. Although Canadians in the first two income quintiles have significant upward mobility, 43 percent of those in the lowest income tier either held fast or made a small move to the adjacent quintile, while 35 percent of those in the second quintile remained where they were or fell to the bottom. And while almost half of the middle 20 percent of earners moved up the income ladder in the Fraser Institute's calculations, a further half kept their position (35 percent) or fell into lower tiers (17 percent). Canada is not a static society by any means. Whether the relative intra-generational mobility it has is cause for celebration is harder to say.

A US Department of the Treasury investigation, again for panel data over a 10-year interval, leads to similarly nuanced conclusions.[25] Juxtaposed to the Fraser Institute analysis, it indicates that socioeconomic uplift according to quintile rank may be less likely south of the border.[26] As the bottom half of Table 2.2 allows, the United States doesn't seem to have as much positional flux as Canada, especially at the low end of the income distribution. According to the Treasury, 57.7 percent of earners in the lowest American quintile and 49.7 percent in the next lowest ascended to other rungs of the income ladder fewer than their Canadian counterparts. Alternatively, more Americans than Canadians in the highest tiers had downward mobility, as almost a third of US earners in the top and fourth quintiles were demoted.[27] Proportionately more Americans in the middle (57.9 percent) held fast or slipped into the bottom two tiers. And more occupants of the bottom two US quintiles remained there, with 71 percent from the lowest tier staying put or moving to the next closest one, and half of those in the second quintile holding rank or descending.[28] Rags to riches stories are rare, though the chance of going from the bottom to the top of the income distribution is greater in Canada. Admittedly, since income inequality is considerably higher in the United States, the distance required to travel between the bottom and top tiers of the American earnings distribution is longer than in Canada; the rungs of the income ladder are farther apart. But if relative mobility per se is at issue, at least on the evidence of Table 2.2 Canadians appear to have a greater chance of moving up the income scale and a lower one of moving down—a comparative benefit that connotes socioeconomic opportunity.

Two studies taken in isolation are a thin foundation on which to build comparative judgments. But parallel analyses of intra-generational mobility tend to confirm the Treasury and Fraser Institute insights about the dynamism of North American economies, if not always their precise standing.[29] Ron Haskins and Isabel Sawhill agree that since the late-1960s around half of American families originally in the lowest income quintile moved into a higher one within a decade—a finding endorsed by Gregory Acs and Seth Zimmerman in their research on US mobility from 1984 to 2004.[30] On the other hand, when it comes to the bottom of the income distribution, assessments of Canadian mobility tend to be more temperate than those of the Fraser Institute. According to Statistics Canada, slightly more than 40 percent of earners in the lowest two quintiles in 2005–10 and 1999–2004 ascended to other tiers—substantial movement, but about half and two-thirds, respectively, of what the 10-year Fraser Institute study contends.[31] Statistics Canada is also less persuaded about stickiness at the top, maintaining that 43 percent of the highest fifth of Canadian earners fell into other quintiles across the two shorter intervals, or roughly twice the proportion indicated in Table 2.2.[32] Bradbury offers a similar corrective for the US data, maintaining that 45 percent of the richest quintile of American earners between 1995 and 2005 were downwardly mobile—considerably more than the Treasury allows.[33] Still, in both countries the probability of remaining in the same income band over time increases with a household's level of earnings; the higher the income quintile, the lower the chance that a given household will leave it.[34] The vicissitudes of life—marriage, divorce, the birth of children, illness, the death of a partner, unemployment, career changes, promotions—can sometimes make for quick moves across the income scale. Yet overall rates of mobility have been remarkably stable for most of the post-war period in the United States and Canada, with a slight decrease in the recent past for low-income families who hope to make it into the top quintile.[35]

In short, it's not always easy to get a consistent reading of panel study tea leaves. But the weight of the scholarly evidence suggests that the prospects for upward relative intra-generational mobility are not clearly better in the United States than in Canada and may be worse, a circumstance that has not changed significantly in a long time.

Absolute Intergenerational Mobility

How mobile people are over the course of their working lives is one thing; how their standard of living compares to that of their parents' generation is another. When people think about mobility, part of what they are interested in is whether their children will have a more comfortable life than they do. That question is especially poignant in large immigrant-receiving societies like the United States and Canada, where the act of migration will often have been motivated by the prospect of bettering a family's economic future.

Evidence of absolute intergenerational mobility is often indirect. In conditions of steady economic growth, in the long term one would expect adult income earners to have a richer life materially than their parents—an outcome implied by the data on intra-generational mobility already cited. Over the last 30 years or so, in both the United States and Canada, real per capita GDP calculated in terms of purchasing power parities has grown—by an average of 1.6 percent a year in the United States and 1.4 percent a year in Canada.[36] Therefore, even if one is anchored at the same relative position in the income distribution scale as one's parents at an identical age, provided that the benefits of growth are broadly dispersed, in inflation-controlled terms the average earner should do better than the previous generation. Indeed, according to the United Nations Human Development Indicator (HDI)—an index that combines data on life expectancy, access to education, and per capita PPP—since 1980 in Canada and the United States citizen well-being has significantly increased, again indicating that in the aggregate standards of living are higher for the present population than its predecessors.[37]

It is not surprising, then, that in an analysis of PSID data on behalf of the Pew Economic Mobility Project, Julia B. Isaacs finds that 67 percent of US adults between 1995 and 2002 had an average household gross income exceeding that of their parents at the same age (roughly 40 years old).[38] Across all tiers of the income distribution the younger generation fares better than its predecessor, including 82 percent of families whose parents are in the bottom fifth of income earners. Predictably, given life-cycle effects, a follow-up study finds that those same Americans, now a few years older, experience generational mobility that is higher still. When household income is averaged across 2002–08, 84 percent of US families have more income than their parents did, as do 93 percent of children raised in the lowest fifth of the income distribution.[39]

Evidence gleaned from Statistics Canada's IID and drawn from the tax files of Canadian parents and their adult children express the same general tendency.[40] Since readings of mobility based on tax records are more comprehensive and typically return more reliable results than surveys like the PSID, the Statistics Canada and Pew analyses are imperfectly comparable, but the relative direction and magnitude of change is instructive (Table 2.3).[41] As in the United States, two-thirds of Canadian children have more real total family income, averaged across 2006–08, than their parents did, including 89 percent of those whose parents were in the bottom quintile.[42] Moreover, the

Table 2.3 Percentage of Children with Gross Family Income Exceeding that of Their Parents

Income Quintile of Parents	United States (1995–2002)	Canada (2006–2008)
Lowest	82%	89.4%
Second	74	77.7
Middle	66	68.5
Fourth	67	58.9
Top	43	37.4
Aggregate Upward Mobility	67	66.4

Sources: For the United States, Isaacs, "Economic Mobility of Families across Generations." For Canada, custom tabulations for the author by Statistics Canada based on tax records via the Intergenerational Income Database (November 2015).

percentage change in median family income between generations is progressively greater for North American children who have grown up in less well-off households.[43] Any difference in absolute intergenerational mobility between Canadians and Americans centers on the size of the upward gains in income. Miles Corak, Matthew J. Lindquist, and Bhashkar Mazumder find that, on average, Canadian sons of fathers in the bottom half of the income distribution earn around $4,000 more in constant US dollars than do American sons of fathers in the same position, a gap that increases as parental earnings decrease. In an absolute sense, adult children raised in less prosperous households are better off in Canada than in the United States.[44] Still, in both countries, the more modest one's parents' place on the income ladder, the more likely one is to have exceeded their earnings. In real terms, most Canadian and American children appear to be in better financial shape than their parents were at an equivalent age.

Unless, that is, one is a young American in the contemporary workforce. Millennials—someone born between the late 1970s and the late 1990s—don't seem to have the earning power of previous generations. According to the US Census, the real median income of individuals 34 years old and younger in 2013 was 5.5 percent less than for a cohort of the same age three decades earlier.[45] Canada's mobility record is better, but the margin is wafer thin. In 2011, real median income for Canadians between 25 and 34 years old was 1 percent greater—that is to say, just $500 more—than for individuals of the same age in 1986.[46] What truly distinguishes the two countries are household income and wealth. Partly because more young women are working and the number of dual-income households has grown, in Canada median family earnings for 24–35 year olds are 16 percent higher than they were for that age group 15 years ago. Given the same parameters, millennial American families earn *less* than their predecessors.[47] And while on average young US households have 11.5 percent more net worth, Canadian millennials have nearly twice the wealth of age-equivalent families in the late-1990s.[48] Much of the difference can be explained by the greater frequency and value of home ownership in Canada, but lower student debt and relatively higher levels of labor market participation north of the border, especially for women, also have an impact.

To be fair, the news for American millennials isn't all bad. Falling prices for consumer goods and more two-income families mean that many young adults in the United States have higher standards of living than their parents did at the same age.[49] And if the economic mobility of American millennials is presently unimpressive, that is not to say their future earning potential is equally dismal; for young Canadians, of course, the reverse is also true.[50] Yet a changing job market, including the greater incidence of temporary and contract work, as well as growing indebtedness caused by the rising cost of university education and housing, present challenges for 20- and 30-somethings, challenges that were largely unknown to their parents. Young Canadians have weathered those storms better than Americans.

Relative Intergenerational Mobility

Gains in absolute income mobility between parents and children are rarely sufficient to challenge the superior earning power of the well-born. Individuals whose parents are at the top rungs of the ladder still make progressively more on average than do contemporaries from less privileged origins. As Isaacs relates with respect to the United States (Figure 2.1), the higher the median family income of parents, the higher the median family income of their children. If the relationship between the earnings of parents and children were completely random, she observes, the median income of each income quintile would be the same as for the population as a whole—about US$72,000 for the period under her observation.[51] But in fact, whereas children brought up in top quintile households do not have a greater median income than their parents—indeed, absolute intergenerational mobility is more robust in all other income tiers—they are far more likely to have higher earnings than peers who grew up in lower quintile families. Moreover, inasmuch as adult American children are more likely than not to surpass their parents' earnings across all income quintiles, individuals raised in the top fifth do so by the biggest margin—and those from the bottom fifth by the least.[52]

This raises a further concern for students of mobility: How much does family background determine one's chance to move up the hierarchy of

Figure 2.1 Generational Change in Median Family Income (Matched Parent–Child Pairs)

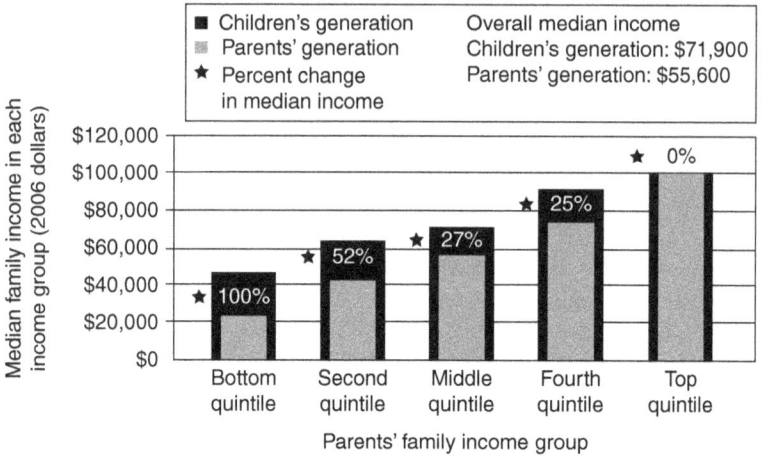

Note: PSID data on household earnings of adult workers between 1995 and 2002, who were between 0 and 18 years old in 1968, compared with matched sets of parents whose household earnings were logged between 1967 and 1971. Parents' household income is averaged across 1967–71; children's income is averaged for 1995–2002. Mean age of parents is 40.9; for children, 39.4 years old.

Source: Isaacs, "Economic Mobility of Families Across Generations," Figure 3.

economic success? The conventional approach is to compare the income ranks of children and parents across each generation's respective earnings distribution. Precise results vary across studies because of methodological differences between them, but the overall emphases are much the same.[53] Multiple analyses affirm that North American parents make the biggest difference to their children's prospects at the margins of the earnings ladder—a phenomenon sometimes called "stickiness at the ends." Using PSID data, the authors of *Pursuing the American Dream*, part of Pew's Economic Mobility Project, find that 43 percent of their 2002–08 cohort of children from families in the lowest quintile of the US income distribution remain there as adults, while 40 percent of individuals raised in the highest quintile also hold fast (Figure 2.2). Movement between ranks is far more likely for adult children whose parents at a similar age are positioned in one of the three middle-income quintiles. It's a tendency equally apparent in the distribution of American wealth, where 31 percent of individuals raised in the bottom quintile stay put, whereas 43 percent of children from families in the top quintile are still there as adults.[54] Drawing on tax records to produce a larger and more recent sample of earners, Raj Chetty and his colleagues at

Figure 2.2 US Adult Children Income Quintile Rank by Parents' Income Quintile Rank

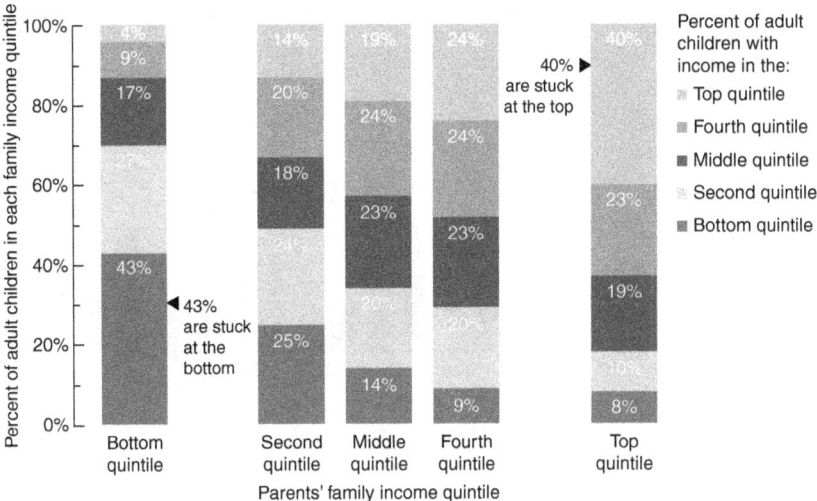

Source: Pew Charitable Trusts, "Pursuing the American Dream," Figure 3.

Harvard University's Equality of Opportunity Project find the ends of the income distribution in 2011–12 a little less sticky. On their reckoning, more than a third of Americans who grew up in bottom-quintile households have the same status as adults, whereas 36.5 percent of children from families among the top fifth of earners are themselves in the top fifth, though the authors caution that rates of mobility in the United States display considerable regional variation.[55]

Assessing American and Canadian intergenerational mobility for adult children during the mid-1990s, Miles Corak discovers the same basic pattern, though he notes that Canadians are not quite as tethered to the earnings status of their parents at the top and bottom of the distribution.[56] As Figure 2.3 indicates, the Canadian sons of fathers in the highest income decile are less likely than their American counterparts to stay there; only 18 percent of Canadians but 26 percent of Americans maintain their position. Alternatively, 40 percent of Americans raised in the bottom decile do not escape the lowest quintile of the US income distribution, whereas almost 30 percent of Canadians from similar circumstances remain.[57] For both countries, relative affluence and poverty are in large part a legacy from one's parents, but compared to Americans, Canadians are less vulnerable to the whims of the birth lottery.

Indeed, the citizens of most advanced industrial states are not as vulnerable.[58] *Income elasticity* is the single cross-national measure most often used

Figure 2.3 Earnings Deciles of US and Canadian Sons Compared to Fathers' Earning Deciles

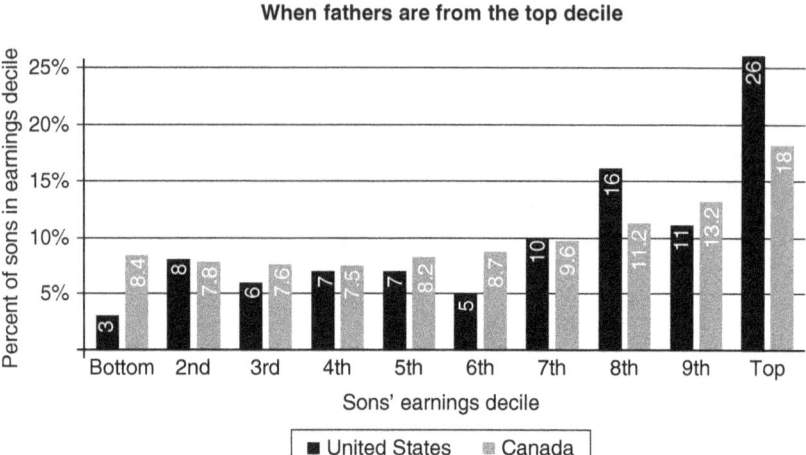

Source: Corak, "Chasing the Same Dream, Climbing Different Ladders," Figure 2 and Figure 3.

to describe relative intergenerational mobility, a way to indicate more precisely how much of the earnings advantages of parents are passed on to their children. The basic calculation is as follows: If between one set of fathers there is an earnings difference of, say, 20 percent, and the difference between their sons' incomes is 10 percent, then the income elasticity of father to son is 0.5—20 percent × 0.5 = 10 percent; that is, half of the difference between fathers is passed on to their sons.[59] Economists consider these variances across an entire population on the basis of how the income of linked parents and children compare to the averages for each generation over a particular period of time. On a scale of zero to one, where zero means that parents transmit none of their advantage to their children and one means they transmit all of it, multiple analyses place US income elasticity between 0.4 and 0.6 and that of Canada at 0.16 to 0.26.[60] In other words, presently as much as 60 percent of an American earner's income rank relative to others is a legacy from his or her parents; the assistance that Canadian parents give their children may be worth around a third of that. By this criterion, according to OECD estimates, Canada is one of the most mobile and the United States one of the least mobile of all rich democratic countries (Figure 2.4).[61]

Estimates of income elasticity, however, do not specify the direction—up or down—of the relative mobility that adult children experience. Corak, Lindquist, and Mazumder maintain that upward "transition probabilities"—the likelihood that an adult son's income rank will exceed a given percentile range in his generation's earnings distribution compared to an identical range for his father—are only slightly better for Canadians than Americans.[62] The larger difference concerns the potential for downward mobility from the upper rungs of the income ladder. When fathers are in the top income quintile of their generation's earnings distribution, Canadian sons have a 67.1-percent probability of falling below the same quintile in their own income rankings, whereas American sons have just a 62.2-percent chance. And should sons sink beneath their father's income status, on average Canadian sons are prone to drop a greater distance, especially when fathers are near the top of the income

Figure 2.4 Income Elasticities for OECD Countries

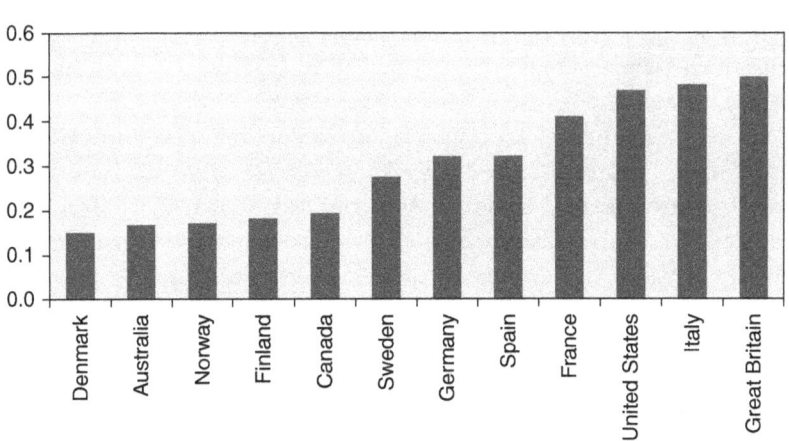

Note: The higher the elasticity, the more similar are sons' earnings to those of their fathers.

Source: D'Addio, "Intergenerational Transmission of Disadvantage."

distribution.[63] For parents in the ninety-first percentile and above, the average loss in percentile rank for sons compared to fathers is 37 points in Canada but 33 points in the United States. At a minimum, then, prosperous parents seem to offer more security to Americans than Canadians when the measure of security is the income rank of adult children.

Inequality and Mobility: The Great Gatsby Curve

For individuals of humble origins and means, upward mobility can take some of the edge off inequality. Large disparities in material well-being may be more palatable if greater income and wealth, and the social status and respect attached to them, are considered within reach of ordinary people. Mobility signifies opportunity, a fair chance to ascend the economic ladder regardless of who one's parents are. In that sense it functions as an independent variable, influencing popular perceptions of the acceptability of substantial disparities in economic outcomes and informing political deliberations about what should be done about them. But what if the direction of influence runs the other way, too, so that heightened inequality actually leads to lower intergenerational mobility?[64] This can have tangible economic consequences. As inequality increases and the prospects for socioeconomic advancement diminish, ultimately the investments in education and entrepreneurship that expand opportunity and foster economic growth are likely to contract as well, creating a vicious circle of lower expectations and provision. Public and private benefactors will be reluctant to waste their resources on people they suspect will never amount to anything in the first place. Indeed, when ancestry commands a higher market value than talent, not only are matters of fundamental equity placed in the balance, but the health of the entire economy is jeopardized by a misallocation of human resources as well.

Among economists, such possibilities are explored via the "Great Gatsby Curve," named for the F. Scott Fitzgerald protagonist who rises from abject poverty to extraordinary wealth.[65] As Figure 2.5 relates, the curve plots countries' intergenerational income elasticities on the vertical axis against income inequality as measured by the Gini coefficient on the horizontal axis.[66] States positioned nearer to the bottom left-hand corner of the diagram are comparatively mobile and egalitarian. Those located toward the upper right-hand corner—the United States prime among them—suffer from both high levels of inequality and low levels of mobility. Canadians occupy the middle ground as relatively unequal but fairly mobile members of the rich democratic club. For the curve's advocates, its statistical line of best fit suggests that mobility and inequality are correlated—that in less

Figure 2.5 The Great Gatsby Curve—the Correlation between High Inequality and Low Mobility

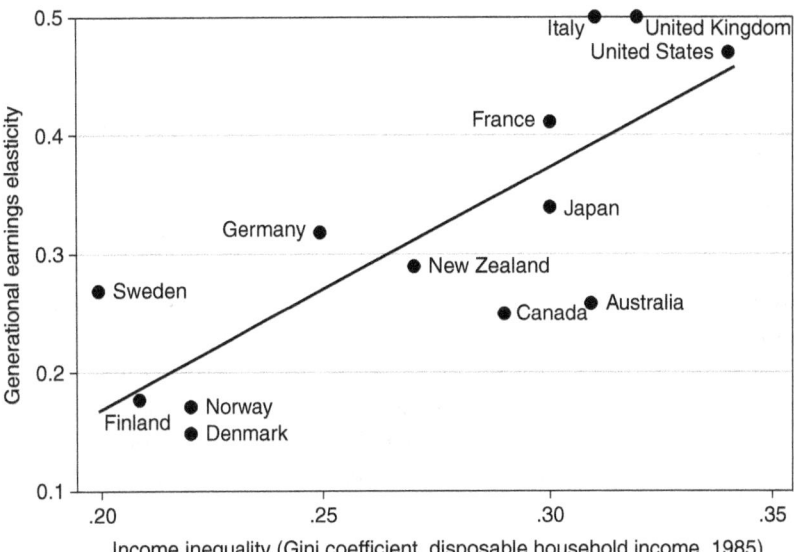

Source: Corak, "Inequality from Generation to Generation."

equal states the economic status that comes from an accident of birth is resilient. Poorer parents will be disposed to raise children who grow up to be poorer adults, while well-to-do families will have little to fear of their heirs falling very far down the income ladder.

Not all economists are persuaded. Correlation is not causation, which detractors are quick to point out. Questions are raised as well about the methodological difficulty of comparing states of different size, ethnic and racial composition, and political-economic structure—though treating each country as unique is not an extravagance that social scientists readily indulge.[67] But much of the skepticism centers on recent research indicating that American rates of relative intergenerational mobility have been fairly stable over the last 40 years, and this despite a progressively unequal distribution of income and wealth.[68]

The United States isn't the only country to be addressed by the Great Gatsby Curve, of course, which American critics are sometimes prone to forget. Even if the world's richest democracy isn't a perfect fit, that doesn't mean the curve on the whole is without merit. Still, the connection between American mobility and inequality is complex. Since the Great Divergence, income inequality in the United States has been driven largely by extraordinary growth in the earnings share of the richest decile—even more, the richest centile—of the population. Short of the lofty heights of the income distribution, it may be that Americans are still reasonably mobile. There is evidence of that in the transition matrices presented in this chapter; rags to riches stories are unusual, but rags to more-comfortable-than-my-parents-were stories, less so.[69] When inequality is high, states as well as private citizens may try to compensate for any constriction of opportunity by doubling down on support for education or expanding labor market access. Crucially, in the face of inequality they will need to do so, since markets are not self-regulating in this regard. So, over the last few decades, the integration of the American workforce through the removal of legal and de facto discrimination against women and racial minorities may have helped to stabilize aggregate mobility, income inequality notwithstanding.

But even if mobility in the United States has not changed much in the recent past, American income elasticity—up and down the scale—is more restricted than in virtually any other rich democratic country. Combined with historic levels of inequality that increasingly pry the rungs of the economic ladder further apart, one's level of material well-being is more than ever a birthright from one's parents. In the current environment, ascending and descending income ranks isn't just a matter of winning or losing social status but rather accruing constantly bigger monetary payoffs and penalties. For Americans from households at the top and bottom tiers of the income and wealth distribution, whose relative movement is the most confined, the stakes are especially high.[70]

Inequality and Mobility: Family and State

Mobility is a product of the interaction between individuals, states, and markets as resources are invested, opportunities extended, and rewards conferred on the next generation. Yet as financial and social barriers between the haves and have-nots thicken, so do differences in the kind of support North American families can give their children as a down payment on future success. This, too, is a point of intersection between inequality and mobility, an elaboration of the relationships behind the Great Gatsby Curve. Affluent families convert their superior resources into a decided opportunity edge for their children, an edge those children need if they wish to compete in an increasingly rarified economic world. Without sufficient public support, their not-so-fortunate peers find the route to the top far more difficult and their chances of arriving there more remote. Heirs of privilege flourish, and those born to privation flounder—a cycle of advantage and disadvantage compounded across generations.

In a powerful book, *Our Kids: The American Dream in Crisis*, the American political scientist Robert Putnam warns that something like this appears to be happening in the United States. Given profound inequalities in material circumstances, working-class and upper-class children increasingly lead separate lives with very different prospects for mobility.[71] Multiple influences are at work. Family structures have changed such that the percentage of children growing up in a stable home with two married birth parents has decreased.[72] Divorce, cohabitation, nonmarital births, and teenage pregnancies are far more frequent in low-income American households—a cultural transformation that is both effect and cause of changes in the economy as a whole.[73] As well-paid local manufacturing jobs disappear, many working-class men are forced to leave home to look for work—some never to return—with a predictable impact on family life. Trying to manage in communities that have been hollowed out economically and socially, and with a depleted store of human capital on which to draw, working-class children find it increasingly difficult to succeed, which aggravates existing inequalities and places additional stress on the family. Physical and psychological well-being is a casualty, including the potential for upward economic mobility.[74]

According to Putnam, differences in parenting styles are a contributing factor, since effective child development techniques are often tied to financial resources. Such assets may purchase the leisure to read and play with a toddler (or a suitable child care specialist to do so) and to buy travel opportunities to expand adolescent horizons. They can defray the cost of extracurricular activities in sports, the arts, even social services, all of which have intrinsic value but also look good on a resumé, as wealthier families appreciate.[75]

Homogenous neighborhoods reinforce the effect. When affluent children are surrounded by people like themselves, the social benefits of prosperity are enhanced, including the development of a dense network of well-connected friends to help navigate the challenges of higher education and career. In the absence of effective community institutions, including secure neighborhoods and well-functioning schools, the anxieties of working-class families are more grimly immediate. In a 2015 poll on parenting in the United States, almost half of low-income respondents—from households making $35,000 or less annually—worried that their children might get shot, more than half that they would be beaten up or attacked. This is a decidedly minor concern among families earning more than $75,000 a year.[76] Small wonder that social trust, a trait advantageous to mobility, is much stronger among upper- and middle-class families.[77]

When it comes to the social arrangements most favorable to a young person's economic advancement, on balance Canadian children are better equipped. Compared to Americans, they are more likely to live with their married birth parents and less likely to reside with a single mother—though if they do, on average that mother is older than her US equivalent and heads a smaller family. Teenage motherhood, strongly correlated with physical, emotional, and cognitive difficulties for children, is four times more frequent in the United States than in Canada.[78] Partly as a result, child poverty rates in the United States are significantly higher. Of Canadians under 17 years old, 14.4 percent reside in households whose income is below half the national median—the accepted international definition of poverty—as opposed to almost 20 percent of Americans.[79] The gap is even greater for young children. Twenty-five percent of Americans under six live below the US federal poverty threshold, roughly twice the proportion of Canadian peers whose families fail to meet Ottawa's low-income cut-off, though it's important to remember that national standards of hardship aren't precisely the same.[80] Young Canadian children are healthier, too. They are also less likely to have been delivered prematurely, fare better with respect to birthweight, are less prone to obesity or diabetes, and have a much lower chance of dying—either for medical or environmental reasons—than Americans of the same age.[81]

As registered by standardized achievement tests, Canadians are better prepared to enter and succeed at school than their American counterparts—a difference more pronounced when low-income children in each country are assessed.[82] Indeed, across a range of early childhood outcomes, parents' socioeconomic status matters less in Canada than in the United States.[83] Nor does it seem to matter much in adolescence. According to the OECD's Programme for International Student Assessment, which evaluates reading, science, and math ability among 15-year-olds—which are predictors of economic success, in the organization's view—the variance in scores between Canadians from the richest and poorest socioeconomic backgrounds is considerably below (i.e., is more equal than) the OECD mean, while the gap among Americans is bigger than average. Their conclusion is that whereas "the school system in Canada provides relatively equal access to high-quality education," in the United States it does not.[84]

Ottawa and the provinces have a hand in this, not least by providing universal public health insurance to Canadian children. By contrast, 7.6 percent of American youth under six are uninsured, as are almost 10 percent of all US children in poverty.[85] Targeted family-friendly policies receive marginally more budgetary emphasis in Canada than in the United States. Government support via cash payments, in-kind services, and tax benefits to families with children are equivalent to 1.4 percent of Canadian GDP versus 1.2 percent of the American, placing each near the bottom of the OECD table.[86] When one considers how that money is spent, however, national distinctions emerge. The US legal mandate for parental leave is Neanderthal: a maximum 12 weeks of unpaid leave for the parent of a newborn or adopted child, and only if one works for a company with more than 50 employees; this opposed to a potential 52 weeks of at least partly paid leave in Canada.[87] It's a difference that may be responsible for the higher labor participation rate of young Canadian women—for whom pregnancy does not connote the sacrifice of one's job—than their American peers, and hence the better economic outcomes for young families north of the border.[88] Moreover, public transfer payments in support of Canadian children have a broad ambit. Almost 90 percent of youth in Canada receive some form of government provision, as opposed to less than half of American children, and measured in purchasing power parities the per capita dollar amount Canadians receive is greater.[89]

Social scientists regularly point out that by leveling the playing field when it comes to school readiness, a sound preschool/daycare experience compensates for variations in the social and economic environment of families and may actually increase the wages one receives as an adult.[90] In both Canada and the United States, public provisions for early childhood education are piecemeal—subject to provincial, state, and local as well as federal interventions—and trail peer-country averages. Higher percentages of Canadians than Americans look after preschool children at home, meaning that until the beginning of kindergarten more US children are enrolled in daycare.[91] By age five, however, proportionately more Canadian than American children attend school, mainly because six US states do not require school districts to offer kindergarten. Similarly, low-income American families tend to be underserved when it comes to affordable child care. Head Start, the federally supported US daycare program for children in poverty, covers a little more than 40 percent of eligible 3- to 5-year-olds, whereas funding via the Child Care and Development Fund block grant, at the discretion of individual states, offers subsidies to less than a third of other low-income youth.[92] Canadian provinces, constitutionally tasked with responsibility for education, including child care, are more generous. Quebec is a leader in this regard, since it adopted a universal daycare program (presently at a cost of $7 a day per child) for preschool children in the late 1990s. But in the rest of Canada the number of subsidized students in regulated care as a percentage of the whole ranges from a high of 49 percent (Ontario) to a low of 17 percent (British Columbia).[93] Roughly half the cost of preschool in Canada is paid for privately; more than three-fifths of it is in the United States.[94]

For reasonably well-off American families this early advantage is magnified, since children of means are better able to cope with—or opt out of—a public education system of uneven capacity. In contrast to Canada, where the collection and disbursement of revenue for primary and secondary education is a province-wide matter, public schools in the United States are financed mainly through local property taxes, a practice that produces deep inequities in budget and quality. Nationally, the highest-poverty US school districts receive almost 10 percent less per student—around $1,200—in annual state and local funding than better-heeled schools, an amount that is smaller still if those poor districts have large numbers of non-white students. Supplementary federal government assistance is given to poorer school districts, though the impact varies significantly between states since it is they who distribute it. Consequently, it often does little to alleviate the fundamental imbalance in resources available to low-income American children and others.[95]

Inequality and Mobility: University Education

Higher education promises to advance the economic well-being of children relative to the families into which they are born. Certainly Americans and Canadians see things that way. Huge majorities in each country believe that a good university degree is crucial to one's chances for upward economic mobility.[96] Yet college can be expensive—and in the United States, more expensive than in any other rich democratic state.[97] Among OECD members, the United States vies with the United Kingdom for the distinction of the biggest tuition bill for a bachelor's degree at a public or government-supported university. What distinguishes the United States, though, is that about a third of American undergraduates matriculate at private colleges, whose tuition is two-and-a-half times higher. (As in most advanced industrial countries, Canada's independent private higher education sector is very small, too small as a proportion of the undergraduate population to be a factor in cross-border comparisons.) The difference in university fees between Canada and the United States is dramatic. In 2013–14, the average annual charge for a bachelor's program at a Canadian university was US$4,761; for an equivalent American public university it was $8,202; at a private US college it was $21,189.[98] In each country costs have escalated. Controlling for inflation, over the last decade undergraduate tuition, room, and board grew by 39 percent at American public universities and 27 percent at private nonprofit ones. During the same period the price of a Canadian degree increased by as much if not more.[99] Nevertheless, from an American point of view, at a 60-percent discount Canada's public universities are a bargain, one that's even greater when the cost of room and board in the United States is factored in, since few Canadian campuses are predominantly residential.

Figure 2.6 Relative Earnings of Tertiary-Educated Workers by Level of Education

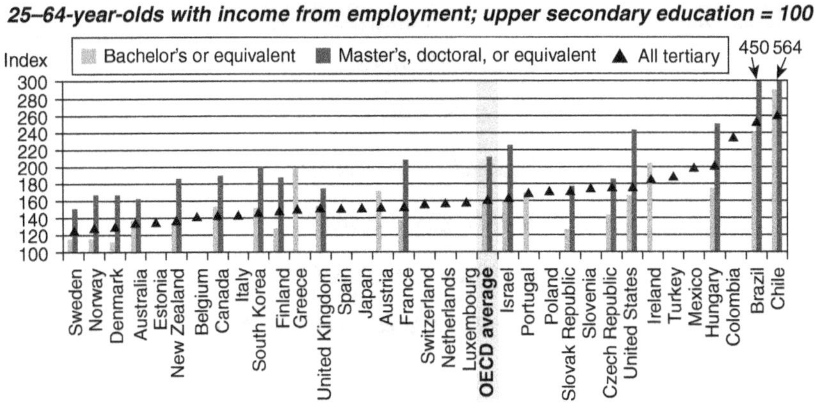

25–64-year-olds with income from employment; upper secondary education = 100

[Bar chart with Index axis 100–300, showing Bachelor's or equivalent, Master's/doctoral or equivalent, and All tertiary for countries: Sweden, Norway, Denmark, Australia, Estonia, New Zealand, Belgium, Canada, Italy, South Korea, Finland, Greece, United Kingdom, Spain, Japan, Austria, France, Switzerland, Netherlands, Luxembourg, OECD average, Israel, Portugal, Poland, Slovak Republic, Slovenia, Czech Republic, United States, Ireland, Turkey, Mexico, Hungary, Colombia, Brazil (450), Chile (564).]

Note: Tertiary education includes short-cycle tertiary, bachelor, master's, doctoral, or equivalent degrees. Neither Brazil nor Colombia are OECD members.

Source: OECD, *Education at a Glance 2015: OECD Indicators*, Table A6.1a.

Because income inequality is more pronounced in the United States, the prospective financial burden falls hardest on the poorest American households. The typical American family in the top income quintile needs to pay about 9 percent of its annual earnings to send a child to a four-year public university; a family in the bottom quintile pays 114 percent, a share that has nearly tripled over the last 40 years.[100] A majority of students receive public loans to defray the expense. Consequently, an estimated 50 percent of Canadians and 70 percent of Americans graduate with outstanding debt, at a per borrower average of around US$22,300 for the former and US$29,000 for the latter.[101] Total student debt has risen dramatically in the recent past, but in the United States the increase has been astonishing: From 2005 to 2012, Canadian student debt grew by a quarter; in the United States it more than doubled.[102]

Access to higher education is an important concern in all rich democratic countries given the sizable wage premium a bachelor's degree confers—the average boost in pay one gets with a university as opposed to a high school diploma (Figure 2.6). Yet in the United States, the magnitude of that gain, combined with the high price of a college education, makes the issue all the more poignant.[103] If below the OECD average, the Canadian premium is still a hefty 53 percent, although it has been flat for more than a decade. Partly that is because as a share of its population Canada has more post-secondary graduates than any other OECD member, and of late its supply of highly educated workers exceeds the demand.[104]

Figure 2.7 Absolute Family Income and Wealth Mobility by Education and Parents' Quintile

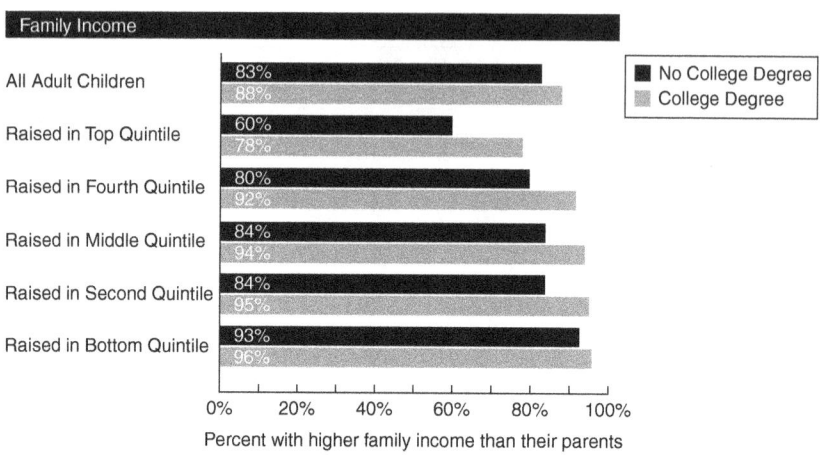
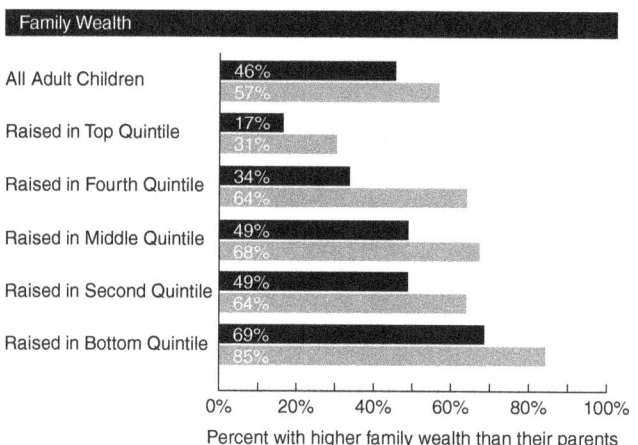

Source: Pew Charitable Trusts, "Pursuing the American Dream," Figure 17.

But at 65 percent, the return on a US degree is one of the largest among advanced industrial states and has grown steadily over the last 30 years. With respect to absolute mobility, the impact is especially marked regarding wealth (Figure 2.7). Depending on the quintile of the household in which one was raised, Americans who are college graduates are up to 30 percent more likely to exceed the net worth of their parents at roughly the same age than are nondegree peers. The benefit is even greater for relative intergenerational mobility. American children who complete university have a much better chance of escaping the bottom of the income

Figure 2.8 Relative Family Income and Wealth Mobility by Education and Parents' Quintile

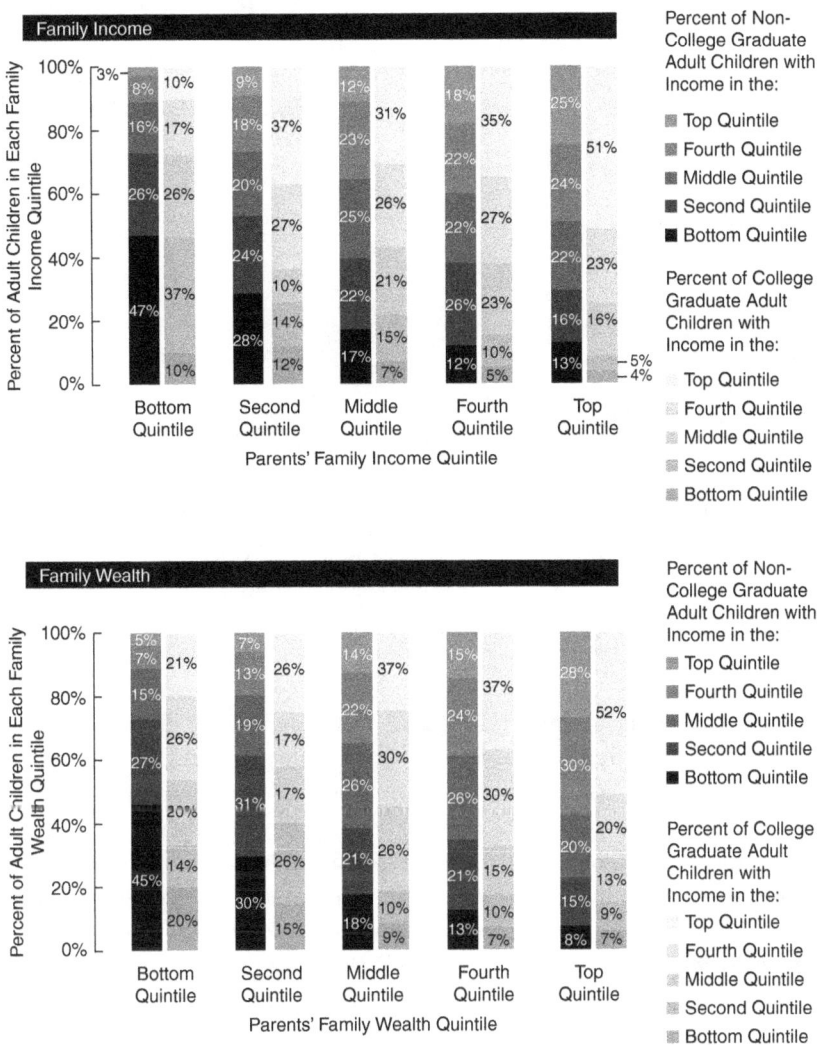

Source: Pew Charitable Trusts, "Pursuing the American Dream," Figure 18.

and wealth table and, if born to privilege, are far less likely to experience downward movement from the top (Figure 2.8).[105]

Before enjoying the full economic benefits of higher education, however, one must apply, attend, and graduate from a four-year institution. In the United States more than Canada—in fact, more than in most places—the

Figure 2.9 Percent Achieving a Bachelor's Degree by Age 24, per Family Income Quartile

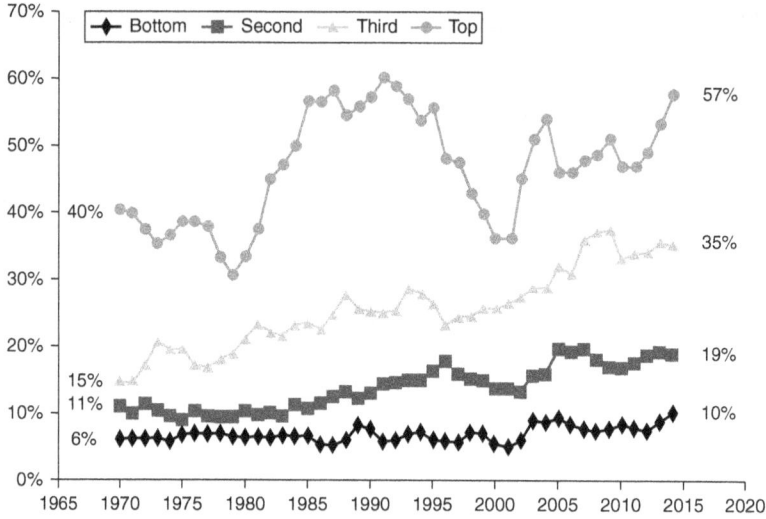

Note: Figures are for US students considered as family dependents, which may underestimate the total number of college graduates among families in lower income tiers.

Source: Pell Institute, "Indicators of Higher Education Equity in the United States," Equity Indicator 5a, p. 31.

prospects of doing so are firmly related to family income: The higher the earnings of one's parents, the greater the probability of pursuing a degree.[106] Research by the US Department of Education finds a 30-point gap in the percentage of American high school students from the highest and lowest family income quartiles who submit university applications; a similar study of Ontario youth puts the difference at 13 percent.[107] As opposed to their better-off classmates, low-income Americans who apply to college are less certain to matriculate, though in Canada the distinction between applying and registering for university is negligible across income categories.[108] And while rates of college attendance are 43 percent greater for US students from the highest family income quartile as opposed to the lowest, the discrepancy in Canada is less than half of that.[109] It is true that more Americans than Canadians enroll at a university. In the mid-2000s, nine in ten Americans from the top income quartile, but 46 percent of those from the bottom, matriculated within two years of receiving their high school diploma. At approximately the same time, about half of 19-year-olds from the top Canadian income quartile attended university, while 31 percent from the lowest quartile did.[110] Yet enrolling is one thing, graduating another. Figure 2.9

indicates the percentage of American students who by their early 20s attain a bachelor degree, sorted by the income of the households in which they were raised. Young adults from US families in the highest quartile of earners are almost six times more likely to be college graduates (57 percent) than contemporaries from the lowest quartile (10 percent).[111] Equivalent Canadian data are not available, though the chasm between low- and high-income graduates could hardly be wider.[112]

Not all four-year US universities are created equal. Compared to Canada, where undergraduate education is assumed to be of roughly the same standard across institutions, the great number and variety of American colleges ensure a significant diversity in academic quality. Americans from low-income backgrounds more often attend less competitive four-year and two-year community colleges that provide fewer economic gains upon graduation. Poorer students are also overrepresented in the private for-profit sector—the best known is the ubiquitous University of Phoenix—where graduation rates are lower and the median student debt load and default rate higher than at public and private nonprofit universities.[113] But at the most selective US institutions, only a few of which are public, 70 percent of students come from families in the highest income quartile and just 5 percent from the lowest, a ratio that hasn't changed much over the last 30 years.[114] The monetary value of a diploma from these elite colleges is substantial. By one estimate, graduates have entry-level job earnings up to 45 percent greater on average than individuals who attend less prestigious places—a matter of an affluent student body getting an early start on becoming all the more affluent.[115]

It's not simply that prosperous families alone can manage the spiraling cost of tuition, room, and board. If the sticker price is high, so are the resources such schools expend on each enrollee. That includes financial need, which many cover in full, though assistance goes to lower- and higher-income students alike.[116] The crucial question is who gains admission and with the support, financial and otherwise, to see a program of study through to its end. At highly competitive American institutions whose degrees are the most lucrative, the challenge is especially daunting. It's no coincidence that a child with a university diploma is likely to have a parent with one.[117] When charting the path to college acceptance, it's a plus to have a mentor who understands the culture of higher education, its complexities, and the standards of assessment. Typically, the academic qualifications of parents are parlayed into resources that smooth the path for their offspring.[118] Some of these are intangible and require the expenditure of human capital, including the vigilance and nurturing it takes to provide an aspirational academic environment for a child. But there can be no mistake: Deep pockets help. Money—and parents who are university graduates are likely to have more of it—shapes the physical and social environment in which young people are educated through the choice of neighborhoods, schools, and peer groups that affect the odds of student success. It also cushions any failures along the way if things don't go so well.

Then there is the hardware of the college preparation process, not just books and computers but the outlay required to take advantage of opportunities in sports, music, theater, travel, even service to others—ostensibly things that build resumés and indicate leadership, the *sine qua non* of university admissions committees. By one calculation, in the mid-2000s American families from the highest income quintile paid over $8,800 on average for such youth enrichment activities, almost seven times the amount spent by families from the lowest quintile.[119] Finally, there are expenses specific to the admissions industry. Standard review courses for the SAT and ACT, the entrance exams that most American university applicants are expected to take and which can cost $1,000 or more, may be the least of these. Far pricier are the independent education consultants (IEC) who shepherd students through the university search process, from resumés to exams to admissions essays, identifying the most auspicious institutions at which to hazard an application. For the half-year or so leading up to final submission of a candidate's dossier, the average fee for service is $4,000, though families wanting an earlier start may spend in the five figures. At an estimated value of over $400 million, IECs are a growing industry—and arguably an efficacious one. In a national survey of students who achieved high scores on their college boards, the gateway criterion for serious consideration by top US universities, more than a quarter said their families had hired professional academic minders.[120]

Canadians may not be completely immune to these forces, but given the nature of university education in Canada they are not as susceptible. To begin, the architecture of the admissions process is different. There are no mandatory standardized exams to be taken for entry to Canadian undergraduate programs, so there is no need for the additional investments in test preparation. Rather, the emphasis is placed on academic achievement as indicated in one's high school record. With the exception of a few specialized undergraduate programs, supplementary materials indicating extracurricular participation and achievement, responses to special essay prompts, or even letters of reference are rarely necessary.[121] There are more and less prestigious Canadian universities, but the perceived difference in academic rigor between them is not as great as for US institutions, and depending on the course of study the acceptance rates at even the best Canadian schools can be relatively high.[122] Both factors diminish the incentive for students to apply to multiple programs, thus limiting application and other fees.[123] To reiterate, tuition at a Canadian university is less expensive on average than at American institutions, and completing a bachelor's program in Canada usually takes three years rather than four, meaning that the cost of a Canadian degree is significantly lower as is the amount of debt the average student shoulders to afford it. Canadian students may have more stable academic foundations, too. Given that the secondary school system seems to produce better results than in the United States, it may be less important for families in Canada to undertake the additional expenditures to address deficiencies or make their children more appealing to admission committees.

None of this is to suggest the Canadian university system is superior—or the American one, for that matter. It is simply to say that money looms larger in American higher education because the payoff is greater. The income and wealth bounce that comes with a US degree is bigger, as is the economic return for an offer of admission—and all the more so at those highly competitive universities where students from relative prosperity are likely to be found. In the calculus of affluence, for many American families a university diploma is not enough; entry to the top schools is a must. Parents of means will pay—and US universities and the college prep machine that has developed around them will charge—for the privilege of putting their offspring in as favorable a position as possible.

Clearly this affects the economic mobility of young people. In the United States more than in Canada, the transmission of financial advantage across generations is mediated by parents' provision of a university education for sons and daughters. It's the mechanism whereby economically blessed American children pull themselves up by their parents' bootstraps. But it's also a reason why generational economic mobility—how far children progress beyond the socioeconomic status of their parents—is lower in the United States than in Canada. How much money American parents have in the bank matters more to their adult children's own economic well-being, partly because buying access to the university education that launches those children on their way is expensive. Whereas reasonably well-off Americans are equipped, willing, and able to do what is necessary to gain entry to those places offering the best yield on investment, less advantaged families can barely hope to compete. Indeed, the larger the income gain a college degree confers, the more tightly bound is an adult child's economic status to that of the household in which he or she was raised.[124]

It's not that American educators and policymakers don't recognize this. Federal and state governments regularly strategize over how to increase academic opportunity for low-income students.[125] But in the recent past, rarely has there been the collective political will to fundamentally change the economic structure of US colleges and universities.[126] It wasn't always so. On occasion American higher education has been seen as a democratizing force. Watershed legislation like the Morrill Acts of 1862 and 1890 establishing the public land grant universities, the GI Bills of the post-WWII period enabling veterans to pursue further education at state expense, and the Higher Education Act of 1965 expanding student loan programs and whose amendments initiated Pell Grants for undergraduates from low-income families all had this emphasis. Yet for young people seeking access to US colleges today, it's hard to escape family history. Far from diminishing economic inequality between generations, contemporary American higher education entrenches it.

Concluding Remarks

It's right to wonder about the fairness of social arrangements when equality of opportunity is compromised by family income and wealth. In a market economy, what a person is able to achieve should be independent of the special advantages that come from an accident of birth. Diligence, innovation, and perspicacity should carry the day, not the resources attached to one's pedigree. In some ways it's a severe standard, since part of what a parent gives a child—physically, emotionally, intellectually—is genetically endowed and can't be discarded even if one wished. Neither can markets be wholly indifferent to ability in the distribution of economic rewards, regardless of whether that ability is strictly of one's own making. Yet in the interest of maximizing opportunity, as many efforts as possible should be made to correct the deficit that comes from being raised in a household of limited means. The circumstances of an underprivileged childhood shouldn't be the decisive influence on one's chance for well-being as an adult.

Leveling the competitive playing field is complicated, given its financial, social, cultural, and spatial dimensions. And equal opportunity, like other forms of equality, is ambiguous. Even if all contestants can participate on even terms in a race to prosperity, the fact that some will win and others lose influences subsequent races—including those run by the next generation. Paradoxically, a meritocratic society can become self-sustaining, where the criteria of admission into its social, political, and economic elite grow static and unequal.[127] But where inequalities of outcome are especially large, as in the United States, not only is equal opportunity jeopardized, but so too is the economic mobility it facilitates.

As this chapter suggests, with respect to absolute mobility there is not much to choose from between the United States and Canada. Granting periodic churning in economic status, most Americans and Canadians move up the scale of income and wealth over time, though there is some evidence that Canadians from low-income households realize more gains in earnings than their American counterparts. US millennials, whose income and net worth lag previous generations at the same age, are not as well placed as their Canadian peers, though the difference may be short-lived. Bigger distinctions concern relative mobility. Canadians are less anchored to their parents' economic fortunes than are Americans. Possessing more of the resources that promote opportunity and increase the likelihood of mobility—healthy family dynamics, child-friendly public policies, sound academic preparation, school quality, access to higher education—Canadians are better equipped to make their own way across the income ladder. The economic mobility of Americans is narrower, especially at the ends of the distribution. North of the border, growing up in a low-income household is less of a barrier to positive economic outcomes; south of the border, a high-income pedigree more closely guarantees them.

To reprise the inquiry with which we began, is mobility in the United States sufficient to compensate for historic levels of economic inequality? Should Americans be willing to gamble on working their way up the ladder of material success regardless of socioeconomic origin? The answer is a resounding maybe, though given the vagaries of the data presented here it's a delicate wager. Canada offers an alternative—a country that in many ways is similar to the United States yet is less unequal and more mobile. With respect to absolute income growth, American chances for upward mobility aren't noticeably better than they are for Canadians, and in some cases they are worse, particularly for individuals at the bottom of the income table. But if one aspires to join the ranks of the well-to-do, or even just the reasonably comfortable, the evidence seems clear: In the United States far more than in Canada, it's important to choose your parents wisely.

Notes

1   See, for example, Benabou and Ok, "Social Mobility and the Demand for Redistribution." The authors argue that future expectations of upward income mobility, and thus limited support for redistributive policies, are not irrational, even among the poorest members of society.
2   See, for example, Gerson, "Economic Inequality Is the Wrong Issue"; Cowen, "It's Not the Inequality"; Saunders, "The Rich Do Get Richer."
3   A deep literature in social science warns about the consequences of "relative deprivation." The basic idea is that in conditions of increasing prosperity, citizens also have rising expectations of getting their fair share. Should those

economic gains be denied, social unrest and, at the limit, violence can result. See, for instance Davies, *When Men Revolt and Why*; Gurr, *Why Men Rebel*.

4   See, for instance, Fischer, "The Welfare Effects of Social Mobility."
5   Page and Jacobs, *Class War?* 57–58. That is not to say, of course, that a large majority of Americans believe opportunities for advancement are plentiful. In 2013, Gallup reported that only 52 percent of US respondents thought so, down from 81 percent a generation ago. Dugan and Newport, "In U.S., Fewer Believe 'Plenty of Opportunity' to Get Ahead."
6   Davidai and Gilovich, "Building a More Mobile America"; see also Alesina, Di Tella, and MacCulloch, "Inequality and Happiness."
7   "Remarks by the President at a Campaign Event in Roanoke, Virginia"; emphasis added.
8   Jacobson, "Putting Mitt Romney's Attacks on 'You Didn't Build That' to the Truth-O-Meter."
9   Gosta Esping-Anderson, for instance, maintains that income and occupational mobility are two sides of the same coin and highly correlated—linked, as they are, by common parental resources. See Esping-Anderson, "Unequal Opportunities and the Mechanisms of Social Inheritance." Katharine Bradbury, an economist at the Boston Federal Reserve, counts at least 20 ways in which researchers operationalize mobility. See Bradbury, "Trends in US Family Income Mobility."
10 See, for instance, the reservations voiced by Putnam in *Our Kids*. Putnam points out (pp. 42–44) that the most reliable economic mobility research pertains to income earners in their 40s and 50s—that is to say, at the peak of their earning potential. Consequently, he cautions, conventional readings of mobility are using a rearview mirror to interpret the past, since the factors that have led to present outcomes may be decades old.
11 Cf. Gordon, *The Rise and Fall of American Growth*, which argues that due to slowing technological progress most Americans (and by implication, Canadians) can anticipate a future of stagnating standards of living.
12 See, for example, Gill, Knowles, and Stewart-Patterson, *The Buck Stops Here*; Lafrance and LaRochelle-Côté, "The Evolution of Wealth over the Life Cycle"; Pew Charitable Trusts, "A New Financial Reality"; Norris, "Young Households Are Losing Ground."
13 These years (1986–2011) were chosen for analysis simply because 2011 is the most recent year for which Statistics Canada data are readily available.
14 For private consumption across the period, the OECD estimates purchasing power parities range between C$1.28 and C$1.30 per US dollar.
15 For instance, an analysis of Canadian absolute income mobility from Vancouver's Fraser Institute, one based on the Longitudinal Administrative Database (LAD), indicates that between 1990 and 2009 the average real income of individuals starting in the bottom Canadian income quintile increased by 635 percent, that of the top fifth by just 23 percent. Lammam, Karabegović, and Veldhuis, "Measuring Income Mobility in Canada." A US Department of the Treasury report based on a panel of tax records is only a little less optimistic: From 1996–2005 the average income of individuals beginning the period in the lowest American earnings quintile increased by 232.5 percent—and their median income by 90 percent—while that of families in the top quintile increased by 26.2 percent. US Department of the Treasury, "Income Mobility in the US from 1996 to 2005."

16 Percentage gains in absolute income can be sizable, but one must always remember what they actually represent. Consider the Fraser Institute study (see n.15), which is based on panel data logged by Statistics Canada. According to the authors, in 1990 the average wage and salary income for individuals between 20 and 45 years old in Canada's lowest income quintile was $6,000, denominated in 2009 dollars. In real terms, the real average income of those same individuals grew to $44,100 by 2009, a gain of 635 percent. Obviously it's a significant return in purchasing power, but at the same time it isn't exactly a princely sum on which to live.
17 Chen, "Cross-National Differences in Income Mobility." Chen draws on data from the SLID in Canada and PSID in the United States.
18 Ibid., 83–85.
19 Based on evidence from the PSID, Bradbury calculates that from 1995–2005, 55 percent of families in the bottom fifth of American earners were able to ascend, down from a high of 62 percent in 1982–92, according to her measure of "dollar-relative earnings mobility," where mobility means moving past the ceiling or floor of an income quintile as expressed in inflation-adjusted dollars across a 10-year period (i.e., not simply moving out of a quintile by doing better or worse than other families in that income tier, regardless of absolute gains or losses in earnings). As with Chen, Bradbury's calculations are based on equivalized household disposable income. Bradbury, "Trends in US Family Income Mobility," 14–16, 39.
20 Kopczuk, Saez, and Song, "Earnings Inequality and Mobility in the United States." Given their reliance on Social Security Administration records, Kopczuk et al. report individual-level data as opposed to the family mobility results of Chen and Bradbury.
21 Bradbury, "Trends in US Family Income Mobility," 16–18; Kopczuk, Saez, and Song, "Earnings Inequality and Mobility in the United States," 109–17; Chen, "Cross-National Differences in Income Mobility," 87.
22 Lerner, *America as a Civilization*, 539. See, for instance, Hartz, *The Founding of New Societies*; Lipset, *The First New Nation*.
23 *The Economist*, "The Rich, the Poor, and the Growing Gap between Them."
24 Lammam, Karabegović, and Veldhuis, "Measuring Income Mobility in Canada," 19–22. The Fraser Institute study draws on Statistics Canada's LAD, but considers only salaries and wages, not disposable or gross income and not self-employment or other market earnings like investment or retirement income. The age range for individuals in the base year of the 10-year period analyzed is 20–45 years old. This, plus the fact that the comparison group for mobility is all Canadians in the workforce rather than individuals of the same age group, is the subject of methodological controversy. Given life-cycle earnings patterns (that younger workers are more likely to start in lower income quintiles but typically have greater earnings potential than their older co-workers), it may have the effect of magnifying the relative mobility of earners from lower-income quintiles, as well as the staying power of their age-group peers at the top of the distribution. See Wolfson, "Income Mobility Is Still a Problem in Canada," and the response by Lammam, "Why Income Mobility Needs Closer Study."
25 There are a couple of important methodological differences between these two studies. Each compares the progress of a target group at the beginning of a 10-year period against the position of all income earners at its end. But the

US data are for all pre-tax cash income as indicated on individual tax returns and supplemented by Social Security benefits—not just wages and earnings—and are from taxpayers 25 years and older. The Canadian data are for wages and earnings alone and are confined to 20–45-year-olds at the beginning of a 10-year window. As already noted, the age parameters may have the effect of enhancing the upward mobility of the lower-income quintiles in the Canadian study. And, of course, the time periods considered aren't precisely the same, which means that the macroeconomic context may influence the results.

26 See Chen, "Cross-National Differences in Income Mobility," 80–81, for instance, who indicates that over the long term there is not much to choose between the United States and Canada when it comes to mobility in this sense.

27 US Department of the Treasury "Income Mobility in the US from 1996 to 2005."

28 A recent analysis of the Pew Charitable Trusts, Economic Mobility Project confirms the relatively low level of advancement from the bottom quintiles. According to Pew, 70 percent of Americans born in the lowest two income quintiles remain there as adults. Pew Charitable Trusts, "Moving on Up."

29 To be sure, comparisons can be messy given the wide variety of choices made in mobility methodologies: Are the data mined from tax records or household surveys? What is the time period considered, the definition of income, the age limits on the focus group? How are the rankings constructed according to quantile?

30 Haskins and Sawhill, *Creating an Opportunity Society*, 69; Acs and Zimmerman, "US Intragenerational Economic Mobility from 1984–2004," 12.

31 Statistics Canada, "Income in Canada: 2010." The difference is partly because of methodology. The data from Statistics Canada's Survey of Labour and Income Dynamics (SLID) on which the analysis is based are for post-tax, post-transfer income and are drawn from a sample of all Canadians 16 years of age and older. The Fraser Institute study also considers five-year relative mobility, drawing on the same SLID data as Statistics Canada, but again for wages and earnings alone and only for 20–59-year-olds in the initial year of the five-year interval. According to the Fraser Institute, from 1996–2001, 53 percent of individuals in the lowest income quintile moved into a higher group, as did 50 percent of earners in that quintile between 2002 and 2007. From 1996–2001, 47 percent of the observed age group in the lowest quintile remained there, while 66 percent of individuals in the second quintile either held or fell (31 percent) into the lowest quintile. In 2002–07, half of those in the lowest income quintile were still there at the end of the period, and 70 percent of the individuals tracked in the second quintile remained or fell (33 percent) to the bottom. Lammam et al., "Measuring Income Mobility in Canada," 14–17.

32 In each of the five-year Fraser Institute analyses, 31–32 percent of individuals in the top 20 percent of earners fell into lower quintiles. Lammam, Karabegović, and Veldhuis, "Measuring Income Mobility in Canada."

33 Bradbury, "Trends in US Family Income Mobility," 38.

34 Beach, "How Has Earnings Mobility in Canada Changed?" See also Murphy and Wolfson, "Income Trajectories of High Income Canadians." Murphy and Wolfson, who draw on Statistics Canada's LAD, discover a good deal of positional churning within the highest quintile of earners, as individuals within that tier scale and descend ever higher quantiles of the income distribution.

Alternatively, Quoctrung Bui points out that if one includes capital gains (e.g., from the sale of a house), in a given two-year cycle 61 percent of families make it into the top American income quintile, though a further 20 percent fall into poverty. Bui, "Most Americans Make It to the Top 20 Percent."

35 Sawhill, "Do We Face a Permanently Divided Society?"; Diaz-Gimenez, Rios-Bull, and Glover, "Facts on the Distribution of Earnings, Income and Wealth in the United States"; US Department of the Treasury, "Income Mobility in the US"; Bradbury, "Trends in US Family Income Mobility"; Chen, "Cross-National Differences in Income Mobility"; Murphy and Wolfson, "Income Trajectories of High Income Canadians."

36 Real GDP per capita growth for 1980–2012 as measured in 2012 purchasing power parities (US dollars). Conference Board, International Labor Comparisons Program, December 2013.

37 UN Development Programme, International Human Development Indicators, 2011 Report. Of course, estimates of average welfare don't take into account the unequal distribution of economic benefits, and based on what has already been established, large inequalities are very much part of Canadian and American economic life. So, for instance, the UN has an inequality-adjusted HDI, on the basis of which the United States falls from fourth to twenty-third place and Canada from sixth to thirteenth place among all UN members.

38 Controlling for family size, the percent of US adults with family income above their parents, by parents' income ranking, is, from lowest to highest quintile, 82, 74, 66, 67, 43. See Isaacs, "Economic Mobility of Families across Generations." The household earnings of adult workers between 1995 and 2002, who were between 0 and 18 years old in 1968 when the study began, are compared with matched sets of parents whose household earnings were logged between 1967 and 1971. Parents' household income is averaged across 1967–71; their children's income is averaged for 1995–2002. Mean age of parents is 40.9, and for children it is 39.4 years old. The sample for the parents' generation is taken from families whose head of household was directly responsible for raising a child who was under 18 years of age in 1968. Of the children's generation, 95 percent consisted of offspring of the head of household, with the remaining 5 percent coming from other related children (e.g., grandchildren).

39 Pew Charitable Trusts, "Pursuing the American Dream," 4–5. PSID data are from 1968 through 2009. Children's average age for 2002–08 is 45 years old. Parents' average age in 1967–1971 is 40.9 years old. Given that the parents' base year is the same as that used in the study by Isaacs, as expected, the upward mobility of older children has increased.

40 Most Canadian research on intergenerational mobility is based on the IID, which links children who were 16–19 in 1982, 1984, and 1986 to their parents. Using social insurance numbers, parent–child pairs are connected to individual tax returns—T1 files—to determine the income of each from 1978–2008. The IID continues to be updated.

41 For instance, the IID study cited here consists of over 203,000 observations, its PSID counterpart just over 2,300. Still, survey data like the PSID are sometimes said to better capture those at the lower end of the income scale. Note: For the United States, drawing on the PSID, the household earnings of adult workers between 1995 and 2002, who were between 0 and 18 years old in 1968 when

the study began, are compared with matched sets of parents whose household earnings were logged between 1967 and 1971. Parents' household income is averaged across 1967–71; children's income is averaged for 1995–2002. Mean age of parents is 41, for children, 39.4 years old. Values are expressed in constant 2006 US dollars. The sample is adjusted for the underrepresentation of low-income families. For Canada, parents and children were assessed at 40–43 years old in 2006 and 1982, respectively. Three-year household income averages for 1982–84 (parents) and 2006–08 (children) are used to reduce the impact of earnings volatility. All income is converted to constant Canadian 2014 dollars using the Consumer Price Index. The sample is adjusted for the underrepresentation of low-income families.

42 Custom tabulations for the author based on tax records. Children and parents were assessed at 40–43 years of age in 2006 and 1982, respectively. According to Statistics Canada, the percentage of children whose family income in 2006–08 was greater than that of their parents at the same age (40–43 years old) in 1982–84 by parents' quintile: lowest, 89.4 percent; second, 77.7 percent; middle, 68.5 percent; fourth, 58.9 percent; highest, 37.4 percent; aggregate upward mobility, 66.4 percent. All income converted to constant Canadian 2014 dollars using the Consumer Price Index. Three-year averages were used to reduce the impact of earnings volatility.

43 Again, given different methodological parameters, the available research on generational increases in median family income between Canada and the United States leads to highly provisional conclusions. But in each country the median household income of the child's generation seems to grow as one descends the income ladder. According to Isaacs, "Economic Mobility of Families across Generations," 18, the change in real US median family income from parents to children is, from lowest to highest income quintile (in percentages), 100, 52, 27, 25, 0. Unpublished custom tabulations by Statistics Canada indicate a difference between parents and children that is lower at the bottom end and higher at the top. The change in Canadian median family income is, from lowest to highest income quintile (in percentages), 36.9, 26.1, 22.3, 19.6, 13.5.

44 See Corak, Lindquist, and Mazumder, "A Comparison of Upward and Downward Intergenerational Mobility." Corak et al. find that Canadian sons whose fathers were in the bottom half of the income distribution on average earned $13,000 more than their forebearers; in the United States, the mean was $9,000 more. Insofar as there is downward mobility in father-to-son earnings, Canadians whose parents were in the top half of the income distribution were also likely to lose less in real terms as compared to their US peers. (For Canada, fathers' average income in the early 1980s was compared to that of their adult sons in the late 1990s; in the United States, fathers' average income from the late 1970s through the mid-1980s was compared with that of their adult sons in the mid-2000s. The average age for Canadian fathers was slightly higher—45.6 years old—than that of their US peers—40 years old. The mean age of Canadian sons was 34.7 years old; of American sons, 34.1 years old.)

45 US Census Bureau, American Community Survey, 2009–13 and decennial census 1980, 1990, 2000.

46 Statistics Canada, "Income of Individuals." See also Moos, "Generational Dimensions of Neoliberal and Post-Fordist Restructuring." In a study of the

Canadian labor market at the cusp of the recession, Moos focuses on Montreal, where in 2006 young adult earnings were 4 percent less than in 1981, and Vancouver, where relative income was 9.6 percent less. For virtually all job categories, young Canadians had lower earnings in 2006 than a generation earlier, even when differences in demographic profile—education, occupation, gender, marital status, and size of household—were held constant.

47   Caranci and Petramala, "Canadian and U.S. Millennials." The Federal Reserve Board's Survey of Consumer Finances relates that the median pre-tax income for US households headed by someone less than 35 years old in 2013 was 6 percent less than for similar families in 1989. US Federal Reserve, *2013 Survey of Consumer Finances Chartbook*, 10.

48   Caranci and Petramala, "Canadian and U.S. Millennials," 3; Lafrance and LaRochelle-Côté, "The Evolution of Wealth over the Life Cycle." See also Guatieri, "Household Finances." Guatieri relates that in real terms Canadian millennials have double the wealth their parents did at the same age.

49   See, for instance, Guateri, "Household Finances," 6–9. Pew confirms the relative wealth mobility among US workers, indicating that half of Americans exceed their parents' household net worth, and more do so when their parents are from the bottom of the income ladder than from higher rungs. Pew Charitable Trusts, "Pursuing the American Dream," 13–17.

50   For instance, Putnam warns that it is premature to draw conclusions about lifetime mobility for people in their 20s and 30s, since compared to their parents such individuals may delay entry into the job market to acquire higher educational and technical skills. Over the long run, that can lead to large earnings advantages in favor of the present generation. See Putnam, *Our Kids*, 294.

51   Isaacs, "Economic Mobility of Familes across Generations," 18.

52   Pew Charitable Trusts, "Pursuing the American Dream," 5.

53   Methodological issues include whether the data linking parents and children are based on tax records or panel surveys (the latter have smaller samples but generally are thought to better capture earners at the bottom of the distribution), the time frame across which income is averaged for parents and children, and the average age of the parent and child when earnings are logged for each.

54   Pew Charitable Trusts, "Pursuing the American Dream," 6, 15—Figure 3, Figure 11. On US wealth mobility, see also Keister, *Getting Rich*, 56–57. At the turn of the twenty-first century, Keister finds that the ranked intergenerational persistence of wealth is a little higher at the tails of the distribution: 45 percent for adult children from the bottom quintile and 55 percent for those from the top.

55   Chetty, Hendren, Kline, and Saez, "Where Is the Land of Opportunity?" Chetty et al.'s research draws on tax records and social security numbers to link parents with more than 9.8 million children in the core sample—children born between 1980 and 1982 and whose pre-tax adult household earnings are averaged for 2011–12 when they were 30 years old. Parent family income is averaged across 1996–2000, when parents were in their early 40s.

56   On the lack of upward mobility for Americans at the lowest tiers of the income distribution, see also Jäntti, Bratsberg, Røed, et al., "American Exceptionalism in a New Light."

57 Corak, "Chasing the Same Dream." Data for the United States are from Mazumder, "The Apple Falls Even Closer to the Tree than We Thought." Data for Canada are from Corak and Heisz, "The Intergenerational Earnings and Income Mobility of Canadian Men." The US data connect evidence from the Survey of Income and Program Participation to Social Security Administration earnings records and compares fathers' earnings from 1970–85 with that of adult sons from 1995–98 when sons were 27–35 years old. The Canadian data are drawn from tax records and social insurance numbers linking fathers' earnings between 1978–82 with the earnings of their adult sons between 1993–95. Sons were 27–32 years old when their income was assessed.

58 See Ermisch, Jäntti, and Smeeding, *From Parents to Children*; Corak, *Generational Income Mobility in North America and Europe*; OECD, *Economic Policy Reforms 2010*; Jantti et al., "American Exceptionalism in a New Light"; Solon, "Cross-Country Differences in Intergenerational Earnings Mobility."

59 Father–son pairings are the conventional way of calculating intergenerational elasticities. Given the far larger number of women in the contemporary paid workforce when compared to earlier generations, researchers fear that mobility results will be skewed by the greater likelihood of daughters' much higher earnings. That said, when one considers family household income, women do seem to have lower income elasticities—that is, they exhibit more income mobility—than do men. See Torche, "Analyses of Intergenerational Mobility."

60 See Corak, Lindquist, and Mazumder, "A Comparison of Upward and Downward Intergenerational Mobility"; D'Addio, "Intergenerational Transmission of Disadvantage"; Blanden, Gregg, and Machin, "Intergenerational Mobility in Europe and North America."

61 D'Addio, "Intergenerational Transmission of Disadvantage."

62 When fathers are from the bottom quintile of the income ladder, Canadian sons have a 69.4-percent probability of ascending beyond the lowest fifth of their own earnings scale; their American counterparts have a 67.8-percent chance. If the benchmark is the precise income standing of fathers within that bottom quintile, Canadian and American sons have even greater upward mobility—*directional rank mobility*, in the authors' idiom—though again there is little to choose between them; in this case, 84 percent of Canadians and 85.2 percent of Americans are likely to surpass the specific rank (rather than the percentile range) of their parents. Canadian data are taken from tax returns linked to social insurance numbers; US data are from the Survey of Income and Program Participation and matched to administrative records kept by the Social Security Administration. For Canada, fathers' earnings are taken from a five-year average in the early 1980s when sons were 15–19 years old; sons' earnings are defined as the three-year average from 1997–99 for individuals 33–36 years old. For the United States, fathers' earnings are calculated as a nine-year average between 1978 and 1986 when sons were no more than 20 years old; sons' average earnings are from 2003–07. The average age of sons in Canada was 34.7 in 1999; in the United States the average age was 34.1 in 2005. The average age of fathers in Canada was 45.6 in 1980; in the United States the average age was 39.9 in 1982. Corak, Lindquist, and Mazumder, "A Comparison of Upward and Downward Intergenerational Mobility," 187–90.

63 Ibid., Table 5.
64 According to Leslie McCall, an analysis of General Social Survey data since the late 1980s indicates that this is precisely what Americans fear about economic inequality—not that it is morally objectionable per se, but that by diminishing equal opportunity it makes it more difficult for hard-working and ambitious people to succeed. See McCall, *The Undeserving Rich*.
65 Alan B. Krueger, President Obama's chair of the Council of Economic Advisers, introduced the Great Gatsby Curve in a speech at the Center for American Progress in Washington DC in January 2012. Krueger and his staff credit the research of Miles Corak, Anders Bjorklund, and Markus Jäntti for the ideas the curve encapsulates.
66 For the methodology behind the curve see Corak, "Inequality from Generation to Generation"; also Corak, "Do Poor Children Become Poor Adults?"
67 See, for instance, Winship, "The Great Gatsby Curve"; Cross and Lee, "Why the Gatsby Curve Is a Poor Measure of Income Mobility."
68 Chetty, Hendren, Kline, Saez, and Turner, "Is the United States Still a Land of Opportunity?" Bloome, "Income Inequality and Intergenerational Income Mobility in the United States"; Lee and Solon, "Trends in Intergenerational Income Mobility"; Torche, "Analyses of Intergenerational Mobility." It should be noted, though, that Chetty and his colleagues find that intergenerational mobility and income equality are positively related at the subnational level in the United States—within the discrete aggregations of counties the authors call "commuting zones."
69 See Chetty et al., "Is the United States Still a Land of Opportunity?," 11; also Figure 2.2 in this chapter, drawn from the Pew Charitable Trusts, "Pursuing the American Dream," as well as Table III in Chetty et al., "Where Is the Land of Opportunity?"
70 Chetty et al., "Is the United States Still a Land of Opportunity?," 2–3.
71 In Putnam's conceptualization, families in which parents have not studied beyond high school are working or lower class; those in which at least one (but probably both) parents have at least a college degree are upper class.
72 In 2014, 62 percent of all US children were living with two married parents, with 26 percent living in one-parent families and 7 percent with cohabiting parents. In 1960 the respective figures were 87 percent, 9 percent, and 3 percent. Data are drawn from decennial US census data, 1960–2000; American Community Survey, 2010 and 2014; and Current Population Survey, 2014. Reported in Pew Research Center, "Parenting in America."
73 According to the National Center for Education Statistics (US), in 2013 21 percent of school-age children under 18 lived in poverty. Those living in a married couple household had the lowest poverty rate at 11 percent; those living in a mother-only household had the highest rate at 45 percent. This pattern holds true regardless of racial or ethnic cohort, though even controlling for differences in family status, black and Hispanic children still have higher rates of poverty than do whites and Asians. See Kena et al., "The Condition of Education 2015."
74 See, for example, Mood, Jonsson, and Bihagen, "Socio-economic Persistence across Generations"; also Bradbury, Corak, Waldfogel, and Washbrook, "Inequality in Early Childhood Outcomes."

75   Cf. Pew Research Center, "Parenting in America." Among the respondents in the Pew survey, student involvement in extracurricular activities—sports, the arts, volunteer work—diminishes in tandem with lower levels of family income. For instance, households making $30,000 or less a year have children who participate in such activities around half to a third as much as children from homes making more than $75,000 a year.
76   Among US parents whose household income was less than $30,000, 47 percent feared their child might be shot and 55 percent that he or she would be beaten up; among families making more than $75,000, the response was 22 percent and 38 percent, respectively. For both sets of parents, bullying was the leading concern. Pew Research Center, "Parenting in America."
77   Putnam, *Our Kids*, 219–20.
78   Based on Statistics Canada and Urban Institute (US) national surveys for the late 1990s, Corak et al. estimate that US teenage births accounted for 8.3 percent of the total, but Canadian teenage births just 2.1 percent. In the United States, just 65 percent of children younger than 13 years old lived with both biological parents, while in Canada 78 percent did. And while 77 percent of American children lived with their married mothers, 84 percent of children in Canada had that arrangement. See Table 3.1, p. 84, in Corak, Curtis, and Phipps, "Economic Mobility, Family Background, and the Well-Being of Children in the United States and Canada."
79   OECD, "OECD Income Distribution Database (IDD)".
80   Jiang, Ekono, and Skinner, "Basic Facts about Low Income Children"; Campaign 2000, "2013 Child Poverty Report Card," 4.
81   Woolf and Aron, *U.S. Health in International Perspective*, 57–77. On one indicator of early childhood health, however, infant mortality, the Canadian record, while marginally better than the United States, isn't especially distinguished. The latest OECD data for 2009–10 find Canada and the United States with two of the worst infant mortality rates among OECD countries, at 4.9 and 6.1 deaths per 1000 live births (for children under 1 year of age), respectively. MacDorman, Mathews, Mohangoo, Zeitlin, "International Comparisons of Infant Mortality and Related Factors."
82   Corak, Curtis, and Phipps, "Economic Mobility, Family Background, and the Well-Being of Children," 97–102.
83   See the summary of findings reported in Ermisch, Jäntti, Smeeding, and Wilson, "What Have We Learned?" 463–81.
84   OECD Better Life Index: Education. For the 2012 PISA, in the United States the average difference in results between the students with the highest and lowest socioeconomic status was 98 points, a little higher than the OECD norm of 96 points; in Canada it was 72 points, significantly lower than the average. In the PISA, "socioeconomic background" is a combined index reflecting parents' income, occupation, education, and possessions.
85   Smith and Medalia, "Health Insurance Coverage in the United States."
86   Presently (the most recent OECD data are for 2011), proportionately more family support in Canada comes in the form of cash benefits—equivalent to 1 percent of GDP in Canada versus 0.1 percent in the United States. In the United States, state support for in-kind services (0.6 percent of US GDP versus 0.2 percent in Canada) and family tax credits (0.5 percent

of US GDP versus 0.2 percent in Canada) is stronger. OECD, Family Database.

87 The Canadian government offers paid leave for parents through its employment insurance plan. A pregnant employee or new mother can take a paid maternity leave of up to 15 weeks. Either the mother or father can take a further 35 weeks of parental leave after a baby is born or adopted. The parents can share the leave however they choose. If eligible for the program, the benefits equal 55 percent of a parent's average weekly insurable wage (80 percent for low-income parents) up to a maximum of $485 per week.

88 Caranci and Petramala, "Canadian and U.S. Millennials."

89 Corak, Curtis, and Phipps, "Economic Mobility, Family Background, and the Well-Being of Children," 92.

90 Esping-Andersen, "Unequal Opportunities and the Mechanisms of Social Inheritance"; Dumas and Lefranc, "Early Schooling and Later Outcomes."

91 OECD Family Database, "Table PF 3.2: Enrolment in Childcare and Pre-school."

92 Walker, "Head Start Participants"; Glynn, "Fact Sheet: Child Care."

93 Beach, Friendly, Ferns, Prabhu, and Forer, "Early Childhood Education and Care in Canada."

94 Sutton Trust, "What Prospects for Mobility in the UK?"; Ermisch, Jäntti, Smeeding, and Wilson, "Advantage in Comparative Perspective"; Corak, Curtis, and Phipps, "Economic Mobility, Family Background, and the Well-Being of Children"; OECD, *Economic Policy Reforms 2010*.

95 Education Trust, "Funding Gaps 2015"; Baker and Corcoran, "The Stealth Inequities of School Funding." See also Heuer and Stullich, "Comparability of State and Local Expenditures among Schools within Districts."

96 For instance, in a 2009 Pew survey, 81 percent of Americans and 78 percent of Canadians did so. Corak, "Chasing the Same Dream," 15. See also Newport and Busteed, "Americans Still See College Education as Very Important"; and the 2010 Harris/Decima poll cited in CAUT, "Poll Shows Canadians Value Higher Education."

97 Unless otherwise noted, I am using "college" and "university" as synonyms, although I recognize that in Canada "college" most often indicates a tier of higher post-secondary education that is just below university and which in Quebec is required for admission to it.

98 Statistics are for national full-time students, in equivalent US dollars converted into purchasing power parities (academic year 2013–14). OECD, *Education at a Glance 2015*, Table B5.1a, p. 275; Table C1.4b, p. 320.

99 US Department of Education, National Center for Education Statistics, *Digest of Education Statistics*, Chapter 3. Statistics Canada, "Weighted Average Tuition Fees for Full-time Canadian Undergraduate Students."

100 Mettler, *Degrees of Inequality*, 121. Predictably, over the last 40 years families in the lowest three income quintiles have experienced the sharpest increases for public university education as a proportion of household to earnings: 123 percent for the middle income tier, and 142 percent for the next-to-lowest quintile. At the same time, Pell grants, the federal award for low-income US students, now covers much less of average public university tuition than it did in 1975, 27 percent compared to 67 percent. Pell Institute, "Indicators of Higher Education Equity in the United States: 45-Year Trend Report," 20.

101 It should also be noted that roughly 17 percent of Americans graduate with private loan debt, whose repayment terms are not as favorable as for public loans. For statistics on public loan and grant-in-aid coverage see OECD, *Education at Glance 2015*, 270–77. Data on student loan debt burden are for 2014 (US) and 2013 (Canada): Institute for College Access and Success, "Student Debt and the Class of 2014"; BMO Financial Group, "2013 BMO Student Survey."

102 Statistics Canada, "Survey of Financial Security (SFS), Composition of Assets (Including Employer Pension Plans Valued on a Termination Basis) and Debts Held by all Family Units, by Age Group, Canada and Provinces"; Lee, "Household Debt and Credit." Terms of debt repayment for public student loans seem somewhat more favorable in Canada, given that, in general, repayment of US debt may occur sooner and at a higher interest rate than in Canada. See OECD, *Education at a Glance, 2015*, Table B5.5, p. 280.

103 OECD, *Education at a Glance 2015*, Table A6.1a, p. 116. See also James, "The College Wage Premium"; Baum, "Higher Education Earnings Premium." The US Bureau of Labor Statistics reports that in 2014 the median annual wage for someone with a bachelor's degree was $69,260, versus $35,540 for a high school degree (http://www.bls.gov/emp/ep_table_education_summary.htm). Canada's National Household Survey (2011) indicates that in 2010 the median gross annual wage for bachelor degree holders *or higher* was C$50,886, versus C$23,912 for individuals whose highest qualification was a high school diploma. Statistics Canada, *2011 National Household Survey*.

104 Post-secondary graduates include those from Canada's extensive collegiate tier of institutions. See Frenette and Morisette, "Wages and Full-time Employment Rates of Young High School Graduates and Bachelor's Degree Holders, 1997 to 2012". See also Tal and Enenajor, "Degrees of Success."

105 PSID data is from 1968 through 2009. Adjustments are made for differences in family size. For parents, the reported mean value of total family income is for 1967–71; for children, the mean value of total family income reported is for 2000, 2002, 2004, 2006, and 2008. For income data, children's average age from 2002–08 was 45 years old; parents' average age from 1967–1971 is 40.9 years old. The value of parental wealth is measured only in 1984, when parents' average age was 55. For children, wealth is the mean value taken in 2001, 2003, 2005, 2007, and 2009. The average age of children across that period was 46. Consequently statistical age adjustments were made so that parent–child wealth data could be more comparable (at 40 years old for each). See Pew Charitable Trusts, "Pursuing the American Dream," 31–32.

106 See Belley, Frenette, and Lochner, "Post-secondary Attendance by Parental Income," 667: "Our results establish that family income is much more strongly related to (post-secondary) schooling in the U.S. than in Canada, even after controlling for adolescent cognitive achievement, family background, and local area of residence."

107 Lauff and Ingels, "Education Longitudinal Study of 2002," and also in Putnam, *Our Kids*, Figure 4.6, p. 189; Dooley, Payne, and Robb, "University Participation and Income Differences," 39. The latter research uses the average household income of the neighborhoods in which secondary schools are located as a

proxy for the family income of school students. College applications were submitted in 2004 for the US study and 2005 for the Canadian.

108 Lauff and Ingels put the attrition rate between applying and enrolling within a two-year period at 13 percent for low-income Americans. For the Canadian data, see Dooley, Payne, and Robb, "University Participation and Income Differences," 6.

109 Chetty et al. estimate the US "college attendance gradient" at 67.5 percent, the slope of the line representing differences in college participation rates according to family income—in effect, the gap in college attendance rates between students from the lowest and highest income families. Their cohort is 18–21 year olds who were enrolled at university in the late 1990s through the early 2000s. Parental income is average family income between 1996 and 2000. See "Where Is the Land of Opportunity?" Figure IV, Panel A: College Attendance and Teenage Birth by Parent Rank.

110 The well-developed Canadian college system is a likely factor in this. American data are from the Department of Education's *Education Longitudinal Study of 2002* and cited in Putnam, *Our Kids*, 189. Canadian data are from the Youth in Transition Survey, sponsored by Statistics Canada and Human Resources and Skills Development Canada, as reported in Frenette, "Why Are Youth from Lower-Income Families Less Likely to Attend University?" See also Zeman, "A First Look at Provincial Differences in Educational Pathways from High School to College and University."

111 Pell Institute, "Indicators of Higher Education Equity in the United States: 45 Year Trend Report," Table A-6, p. 112. The Pell Institute also relates information regarding the bachelor's degree completion rates of students already enrolled relative to family income quartile. Again, students from more prosperous homes do better. The six-year degree achievement for dependent students who entered college for the first time in 2003–04, by ascending income quartiles, is 26 percent, 36 percent, 46 percent, and 59 percent. Equity Indicator 5c(i), 65.

112 As the author's correspondence with Statistics Canada confirms, Canadian data on graduation rates by parents' income level are not collected.

113 Putnam, *Our Kids*, 186–87; Mettler, *Degrees of Inequality*, 29; Pell Institute, "Indicators of Higher Education Equity in the United States: 45 Year Trend Report," 17. According to the Pell Institute, 57 percent of students enrolled in four-year for-profit colleges in 2012 came from families earning less than $40,000 a year. Citing data from the College Board, Mettler relates that the six-year bachelor degree completion rate among for-profit institutions is 22 percent (versus 65 percent and 55 percent for private nonprofit and public universities); the median student debt load among 2007–08 graduates was $32,700, whereas the three-year default rate in 2009 was 23 percent (versus 7 percent and 8 percent for private nonprofits and public institutions).

114 Carnevale and Strohl, "How Increasing College Access Is Increasing Inequality," 136–37. Distinctions regarding competitiveness are drawn from *Barron's Profiles of American Colleges* and distinguishes between Barron's top two categories—most competitive/highly competitive plus—and the rest.

115 Ibid., 145. For a more recent and comprehensive treatment of the relationship between family income, university admissions, and post-graduation earnings— one that reaches many of the same conclusions—see Chetty, Friedman, Saez,

Turner, and Yagan, "Mobility Report Cards." The earnings advantages of highly selective colleges may be most apparent in non-STEM fields. See Eide and Hilmer, "Do Elite Colleges Lead to Higher Salaries?"

116 Snider, "Colleges That Report Meeting Full Financial Need"; Otani, "Ten Elite Schools Where Middle Class Kids Don't Pay Tuition." Actually, the United States may be more forthcoming than Canada when it comes to financial assistance for the most economically disadvantaged students. Belley, Frenette, and Lochner find that in the mid-2000s, American students from the poorest households had lower net tuition and living expenses—albeit at public universities—than their Canadian peers; Canada was comparatively more charitable toward middle-income students. Belley, Frenette, and Lochner, "Post-secondary Attendance by Parental Income."

117 OECD, *Education at a Glance 2015*, 81.

118 See, for instance, Corak, "How to Slide Down the 'Great Gatsby Curve.'" See also OECD, *Economic Policy Reforms 2010*, Chapter 5.

119 Duncan and Murnane, "Introduction." Expenditures include "books, computers, high quality child care, summer camps, private schooling, and other enrichment activities" (11). The authors found that the gap in spending between high- and low-income family spending tripled from 1972 to 2006.

120 Booth, "How Much Would You Pay to Get Your Kid into Harvard?"

121 Not all Canadians are satisfied with this status quo. See Coates, "Why Top Canadian Universities Should Add an Admission Test"

122 On the quality question, see Birchard, "Canada's Elite Universities Propose a National Strategy for Higher Education."

123 In the United States, the advent of the Common Application, the central online clearinghouse for applications to more than 500 American colleges and universities, has increased the propensity of high school students to apply to multiple schools. With the exception of Ontario, there is no equivalent service for Canadian universities. According to the National Association for College Admission Counseling, the percentage of US freshman who applied to seven or more colleges rose from 9 percent in 1990 to 28 percent in 2012, and while 61 percent submitted three or more college applications in 1990, 77 percent did so in 2012. Colleges waive fees for needy students, but the average charge per application is between $40 and $50. Weston, "How Many Applications Is Too Many?" In the United States, campus visits—highly recommended by colleges as an expression of student commitment and a help to the attractiveness of an applicant—are especially costly, and increasingly so as the number of institutions in which a candidate is interested grows. Based on one estimate, families who decide to explore the possibilities spend an average of $3,500 doing so. Scott, "Forget Tuition, Just Applying to College Can Cost Thousands."

124 See Chetty et al., "Is the United States Still a Land of Opportunity?," 7–8, who find that higher-earning college degrees are statistically correlated with family income rank. See also Corak, "How to Slide Down the 'Great Gatsby Curve'"; Solon, "A Model of Intergenerational Mobility Variation"; Esping-Anderson, "Unequal Opportunities and the Mechanisms of Social Inheritance"; Fortin, et al., "Canadian Inequality"; Frenette, "Why Are Youth"; and OECD, *Education at a Glance 2015*, 83–84.

125 For instance, see Executive Office of the President, "Increasing College Opportunity."
126 See the excellent discussion in Mettler, *Degrees of Inequality*.
127 See, for example, the provocative discussion in Hayes, *The Twilight of the Elites*.

3
Values

THE HERO OF *Flash Boys: A Wall Street Revolt*, Michael Lewis's book on predatory high-frequency trading, is Brad Katsuyama, a 35-year-old trader at the Royal Bank of Canada (RBC) in New York City. Born in Ontario, Katsuyama is the epitome of "RBC nice," a phrase he finds "embarrassingly Canadian" but which captures a workplace culture that insists on fair-mindedness and goodwill.[1] It is a different ethos from that of the American equity markets he confronts when he tries to execute large trades on behalf of his institutional clients, orders whose costs mysteriously rise once they are placed online. Gradually Katsuyama suspects the market is rigged. Traders with the most powerful computers and sophisticated algorithms, who pay to position their machines as close as possible to the servers of the public and private exchanges they wish to access, are milliseconds ahead in the buying and selling of shares. By pre-empting the orders of less-well-equipped competitors, these flash boys use superior speed to distort normal market pricing, forcing ordinary investors to pay more while realizing a tidy profit for themselves. Katsuyama and his colleagues' solution: create a public Investors Exchange (IEX Group Inc.) that neutralizes unfair trading advantages based on technology and the lack of transparency, a way to repair, not exploit, a vulnerable US financial system.

It's a cliché that Canadians are an especially decent people, but like most clichés it comes with an element of truth—as the story of Brad Katsuyama suggests. The Canadian novelist Mordecai Richler once wrote that there was no better definition of his compatriots than that they "are nice, very nice, and they expect everybody else to be very nice."[2] More than Canadians are inclined to believe it. American popular culture often uses Canada as a satiric foil, its good-humored civility juxtaposed to the sillier excesses of life in the republic, as *South Park* and the *Simpsons* regularly put to good effect. Or again, in 2013 the *New York Times* reported on the Bravo network's *Real Housewives* franchise, a series comic in its own way, as it appeared in countries outside the United States. Among the findings were that "the Real Housewives of Vancouver ... are slightly more polite than their American counterparts," presumably a reason why the program was short-lived north of the border.[3] More soberly, in *Bowling for Columbine*, Michael Moore's documentary about gun violence in the United States, disparate social norms are pointed to as the main reason why Canadians do not use firearms against fellow citizens with quite the same enthusiasm as their American neighbors, despite both countries having high rates of gun ownership.[4] Moore compares the easygoing urbanity of Toronto, many of whose residents don't bother to lock their front doors, to an anxious America, armed to the teeth to deter do-badders, both real and imagined. There is always the danger of caricature in this; one Toronto-based Canadian reviewer of the film said it made the city look so appealing he wished he lived there. Yet evidence of Canadian congeniality may be more than anecdotal. A recent analysis of over 3 million North American tweets conducted by two students of linguistics concludes that Canadians express themselves in ways that are more polite, cheerful, and less vulgar than Americans.[5]

All societies, including those defined by the legal boundaries of a state, are marked by elementary distinctions of culture—discrete sets of attitudes, beliefs, and behaviors.[6] Cultures matter for students of comparative politics. Consider the interaction between political institutions and values. If one were to filter the dominant American cultural ethos through the structures of Canadian government, the result would be neither the US nor the Canadian political system but a peculiar hybrid. That is because values, institutions, and the policies they produce are at once interdependent and autonomous. While cultures change, slowly, in response to the social, economic, and political environment in which they are embedded, they in turn influence that environment. So, when it comes to explaining variations in economic equality and mobility between Canada and the United States, it is reasonable to wonder if characteristic differences of outlook and standards of judgment are among the forces at work. If the majority of Canadians are considerate and kind in their personal and workplace interactions, why not in their political and economic convictions, too? It's not that Canadians are somehow intrinsically more virtuous than Americans. And the norms by which people conduct their private affairs don't always cohere with how they approach public life; liberality in one sphere doesn't guarantee it in another. Still, broad cultural attributes like niceness—or correlates of compassion, empathy, generosity of spirit, and fair-mindedness—may well translate into preferred political values and policies.[7] As the touchstone for a particular reading of social justice, Canada nice is not as fanciful as it seems.

At least that is a possibility the present chapter explores. Distributional outcomes are not inevitable; what Americans and Canadians think about economic inequality counts. In his classic book *Equality*, the British economist R.H. Tawney remarks that the allocation of wealth in a country depends on the nature of its institutions, and its institutions are determined "not by immutable economic laws but by the values, preferences, interests, and ideals that rule at any moment in a given society."[8] How one chooses to care for fellow citizens is among those ideals. Canada is a more egalitarian society than the United States, and arguably a more mobile one, in some measure because Canadians feel a greater sense of public responsibility to reduce the disadvantages of people at the bottom of the income and wealth ladder and are less indulgent of the privileges of those at the top.

In what follows, the evidence in favor of that claim is related in three parts. To begin, an examination of political values across history and constitutional practice indicates that Canadians have been more supportive than Americans of (1) collective well-being as opposed to individual autonomy; (2) the state as having an important redistributive role; and (3) equality in general and economic equality in particular. Pertinent public opinion poll data is related next, which tends to reinforce and elaborate on these basic cultural orientations in a more immediate way. Finally, a consideration of the institutions through which citizen preferences for equality are expressed suggests that Canadian government can be more accommodating, largely because the architecture of American politics is designed to limit change—including economic change—not facilitate it. These observations are offered more in the spirit of informed conjecture than sophisticated social scientific analysis, an effort simply to "sustain [an] interpretation by showing that there is a large body of confirmatory data in its favor."[9] But insofar as political values are at all influential, with respect to economic inequality and mobility it is not too much to say that Canadians and Americans may get the results they desire.

Before proceeding, two circumstances that qualify easy generalizations about political culture in North America merit a response. First, according to several recent analyses, in some respects American and Canadian values have been converging over time.[10] Given the cultural cross-fertilization implied by the forces of globalization, this is to be expected. Yet fine-grained national distinctions can still have a significant impact on public policies concerning equality and mobility. And as a comparison of the US and Canadian legislative record indicates—and the discussion of welfare reform in the next chapter confirms—policies can differ considerably even when the general contours of public opinion might not.

Second, regionally specific systems of belief may crosscut and overlap those defined by national boundaries.[11] Social scientists must be sensitive to spatial variations of culture within a single country, rooted in characteristic patterns of settlement, historical events, language, religious practice, economy, or political behavior. Inasmuch as Canada and the United States are both federal states, they concede the importance of such differences. Nevertheless, the content of regional cultures may not be any clearer or more resilient than national ones. Consider the ideological transformation of Quebec, a distinct culture to be sure, over the last 50 years. From being one of the most socially conservative provinces in Canada, arguably it has become the most progressive. One can never be quite certain when and where the lines of cultural fit should be drawn, hence the disagreement among scholars over just how many subnational North American societies there are.[12] The assumption here is that for students of politics the primary unit of analysis is still the nation-state, whose power takes concrete form in the laws and policies it enacts for its citizens, which are binding on all who live within its jurisdiction. It is these laws and policies that influence the attitudes of the North American publics for whom they are intended.

Political Culture

Over the last 40 years, Canada and the United States have not been the only countries to experience growing inequalities in income and wealth. A global economy is partly responsible, insofar as it highly remunerates certain kinds of skills and devalues others. Yet international economic pressures do not have uniform national effects. Governments make decisions that deflect the full impact of market forces. The range of options is not infinite or identical—better in the current climate to be, say, Germany than Greece. Neither is it trivial. It connotes the particular circumstances of a country, its history, its social and political structures, and the organization and health of its economy. But it is also influenced by the core principles of a citizenry about politics and government, including the criteria by which policy outcomes should be judged—in other words, by political culture.[13]

In the prolific literature of North American politics, the United States is characterized as a classically liberal or Lockean state, marked by commitments to individualism, freedom from government, participatory democracy, confidence in markets, and equality of opportunity.[14] By contrast, Canada's political values seem inspired as much by the communitarian traditions of European conservatism and social democracy as by the unmitigated liberalism of Locke. Canadians are typically portrayed as positively disposed toward political order and the traditional elites who preserve it, collective rights and the claims of community, and the appropriateness of using state power to achieve the public good, and are less inclined to defer to the market.[15] Granted, there are always intellectual cross-currents at play. In the historiography of American political thought, eighteenth-century liberalism and classical republicanism vie for dominance over the politics of the early United States, though the former has had the more lasting effect.[16] For Canada outside of Quebec, the major fault line runs between Anglo-American–style liberalism and British Toryism—a cultural dialectic that in one form or another seems to have endured.[17]

The truth is that all systems of political belief are amalgams in which particular tendencies happen to prevail. Students of political culture can only aspire to a fair if idealized reading of those tendencies.

Distinctions can be overdrawn. Canadians and Americans alike are committed to the procedural norms of liberal-democratic politics: political authority based on the consent of the governed as effectuated by elected representatives; equal political rights; an equal opportunity to influence political decision making; freedom of expression, conscience, and association. But such common denominators aside, it is not surprising that Canadians and Americans might maintain characteristic political outlooks. Different circumstances of development—geographic challenges, patterns of migration and settlement, natural resources and corresponding forms of political economy—have all played a defining role. Moreover, Canada was created as an alternative to the United States, a nation whose democratic passions the Fathers of Confederation thought dangerous. As a source of national identity, this desire not to be American continues to sustain many Canadians, especially members of the political class.[18]

In some ways it is more difficult to capture Canadian than American political culture. There is an explicitly creedal and universal quality about the sum of American beliefs for which there is no real Canadian counterpart. Instead of being expressed in stirring foundational documents like the Declaration of Independence or the US Constitution and Bill of Rights, Canadian political values are most often the product of compromises struck before and after Confederation in 1867 and implicit in the operation of public institutions and policies. The Constitution Act, 1982, which established Canada's Charter of Rights and Freedoms, has codified some of this. Yet the absence of a revolutionary break with the past, a defining moment for ideological stocktaking, when added to the diverse political ideas brought to Canada on waves of European (and most often British) immigration, informs a greater breadth of political perspective north of the border, where liberalism, conservativism, socialism, and populism have all had a formidable electoral presence. With respect to present concerns, such ideological diversity may itself be a sign of Canada's greater receptivity to the claims of economic equality. At the least, America's more thoroughgoing commitment to Enlightenment liberalism—including the priority of unfettered markets—makes for a less hospitable redistributive climate.

Individualism and the Community

The disposition of material resources is a collective concern. If Americans are more complacent than Canadians when it comes to economic inequality, perhaps it is simply because the United States is a less socially minded place. Writing in the late eighteenth century, J. Hector St. John de Crèvecoeur, a European observer of the early American scene, noted the individualist impulse in the "new man" of the United States: "Here the rewards of [his] industry follow with equal steps the progress of his labour … his labour is founded on the basis of nature, self-interest; can it want a stronger allurement?"[19] Scholars have argued ever since that the same motive informs the dominant American understanding of political community—the sum of the separate wills composing it, atomistic not organic. On a Lockean reading, the United States was manufactured by the voluntary consent of independent agents seeking to maximize their self-interest. Representatives who gathered at the Philadelphia Convention in 1787 conjured a country where there hadn't been one before—or in deference to the Articles of Confederation, not much of one. As the system of government they created allows, in the United States the public good is mainly another way of expressing the resolution of conflict among contending factions. It is no coincidence that American political science has pioneered an entire school of analysis, pluralism, whose point of departure is precisely this competition between interests for political influence and power.[20]

Numerous commentators take this "first language of individualism" to task for destroying the mutual obligations of public life.[21] Privatized standards of judgment are so persuasive, according to the critique, that they prevent Americans from developing a strong integrative sense of collective well-being, one that would provide the meaning and security they seek but have trouble finding. It is this very absence of connectedness that Robert Putnam famously laments in *Bowling Alone*, his seminal book on the hollowing out of American civil society.[22] Instead of a creative agency through which a common public life might be shared, the American state is more of a referee that promises judgment for the misdeeds of others. Thomas Paine draws the distinction in the opening lines of *Common Sense*: "Society is produced by our wants and government by our wickedness; the former promotes our happiness by positively uniting our affections, the latter negatively by restraining our vices."[23] Public opinion polls provide confirmatory data; Americans are far more inclined than citizens of other liberal-democratic countries to value an ability to pursue individual goals without the state's interference.[24]

Nowhere is it more evident than in the manner whereby the United States undertakes to protect its citizens' rights, including those entrenched in the first 10 amendments of the Constitution.[25] That these largely defend the individual against unwarranted societal and governmental intrusion may be chalked up to history. At its core, the US Constitution is an eighteenth-century document reflecting eighteenth-century concerns, not least of which was a revolution against a British colonial authority guilty of alleged overreach. Hence the Bill of Rights focuses on freedoms of religious and political expression, the inviolability of person and possessions, and fair judicial procedure and seeks to restrict the armed intervention of the state against its own people.

Contemporary American jurisprudence sides with the prerogatives of the individual as well. From criminal procedure to sexual behavior to the requirements of state security, landmark decisions over the last half-century have restricted the ability of government to short-circuit the due process of law or interfere with an individual's right to privacy and expression, even when benefits to the citizenry as a whole might be sacrificed.[26] So, by virtue of *Citizens United v. Federal Election Commission* (2010), *SpeechNow.org v. Federal Election Commission* (2010), and *McCutcheon et al. v. Federal Election Commission* (2014), money has been ruled an instrument of the right to free speech, thereby removing limits on third-party corporate and individual campaign spending and in the process unsettling the democratic character of elections.[27] The decision stands in sharp contrast to *Harper v. Canada (Attorney General)* (2004), where the Supreme Court of Canada upheld restrictions on third-party spending, the public being found to have an interest in "precluding the voices of the wealthy from dominating the political discourse."

Perhaps the most egregious recent example of American individualism, however, is the way in which the US judiciary has approached the Second Amendment right to keep and bear arms. In *District of Columbia v. Heller* (2008), the Supreme Court broke with almost 70 years of precedent in ruling that Americans have a right to carry a wide variety of firearms for substantially private purposes.[28] To be fair, the court had accomplices; public opinion on guns is mixed, and Congress has generally been unwilling to diminish their availability.[29] As a result, the American rate of gun ownership, at 89 firearms for every 100 residents, is the highest in the advanced industrial world. It's a principal reason why the United States also leads all rich democratic countries in the most antisocial behavior of all: murder—at 5.2 per 100,000 residents annually, of which 3.5 are firearm-related.[30] Not that the public fails to notice or lament this. But as Charles Taylor writes, "Americans have put a value on energetic, direct defence of rights and therefore are ready to mitigate their condemnation of violence."[31] By comparison, Canadians appear more peaceable and law-abiding. Guns are without constitutional protection in Canada, though it has the fifth-highest rate of gun ownership among OECD countries and ranks fifth in homicides as well. Still, at a rate of 1.5 killings per 100,000 residents, of which just 0.38 can be accounted for by firearms, deadly violence is much less frequent than in the United States. Further, the American incarceration rate, by far the highest of any advanced industrial country, is more than two-and-a-half times that for Canadians.[32] The tortured way in which the race issue plays out in the United States, and greater respect for the law and the police as well as more lenient sentencing for the possession of controlled substances in Canada, are contributing factors.[33]

Greater social awareness may be in Canada's DNA. At least a constitutional commitment to "peace, order, and good government" would seem to require more communal effort than America's revolutionary creed of "life, liberty, and the pursuit of happiness."[34] Some of this comes down to Canada's political lineage, which in good British fashion places less importance on a person's rights and more on the authority and cohesion of the state. But collective sensibilities also shape how Canada sees itself. Consider the Canadian creation myth. By the standard account, Canada was brought into existence by the nurture of three founding peoples—British, French, and Indigenous.[35] Even before Confederation, the resilience of French Canada and its early legal recognition from London—most famously via the Quebec Act (1774)—as well as its territorial concentration meant that at a minimum Canada was a culturally dualist country: Anglophone, Protestant, and of British origin on the one hand; Francophone, Catholic, and of French provenance on the other. Concessions to these two European "races" were at least weakly expressed in the initial provisions of the British North America (BNA) Act of 1867 concerning the rights of religious minorities to be taught in denominational schools (Section 93) as well as the equal accommodation of minority languages in Parliament, the federal courts, and the Quebec legislature and courts (Section 133). The Charter goes further. It confirms the collective rights of French and English linguistic communities, thus entrenching the emphases of Canada's Official Languages Act (1969); it reiterates the right of the children of French and English language minorities to be educated in their parents' language (albeit under certain conditions); it restates constitutional guarantees for publicly funded separate religious schools; and it affirms the rights, as yet ill-defined, of Indigenous groups under treaties and land claims agreements.

The historic priority of these communities—in truth the Indigenous contribution was late to be acknowledged—has not prevented other groups from being added to the national identity mix via Canada's policy of multiculturalism. Introduced by the Trudeau government in 1971, official multiculturalism grew out of a concern to coalesce, socially and politically, the ethnically diverse population introduced to Canada as a consequence of post–World War II immigration. At its most basic level, the policy intended to make immigrant-stock individuals of other than Anglo-Irish or French lineage feel that they, too, were an indispensable part of the Canadian polity. Thus Section 27 of the Charter pledges the federal government to interpret its provisions "in a manner consistent with the preservation and enhancement of the multicultural heritage of Canadians," an ethnic maintenance emphasis reiterated and amplified by guarantees against racial discrimination in the Employment Equity Act (1986) and the Canadian Multiculturalism Act (1988). Multiculturalism has been affirmed by the federal government and all provincial governments save one as a fundamental characteristic—perhaps *the* fundamental characteristic—of Canadian identity and an essential prop of the political order.[36]

The impact of this on Canada's political cohesion is a matter of controversy. Still, Canadians are eager to distinguish their country's ethnoracial mosaic, sanctioned by a multicultural policy solicitous of cultural difference, from what is imagined to be the great assimilative melting pot of the United States. This exaggerated American public policy does not lack for multicultural nuance, as legal protections for religious expression and the use of minority languages in schools, the workplace, and at polling stations attest, as well as constitutional guarantees of racial nondiscrimination.[37] But Canadian courts are sensitive to the principle of "substantive equality" as suggested by the equality rights provisions of the Charter, whereby the discriminatory effect on groups and on individual members of groups must be taken into account when determining a law's constitutionality.[38] The US Constitution does not explicitly acknowledge the kind of social prerogatives this implies, nor, given its emphasis on individual rights, is it clear how American jurisprudence could easily do so.

Recognizing that members of minority ethnic and racial communities, women, and the disabled may be subject to persistent economic discrimination, the Charter protects their ability to gain redress through programs of affirmative action (Section 15.2). The Employment Equity Act reinforces this commitment, charging employers to make "such reasonable accommodations as will ensure that persons in designated groups achieve a degree of representation commensurate with their representation in the Canadian workforce."[39] Part of the rationale is that a diverse job site in Canada is good in and of itself. In the United States, special legal and economic consideration for the claims of ethnicity and gender, largely through strategies of preferential hiring and university admissions, were passed into law even earlier than in Canada. But typically, promoting diversity in the American workplace or the classroom has been an insufficient rationale for the special treatment of minorities. By virtue of the Fifth and Fourteenth Amendments, constitutional provisions for due process and equal protection of the laws are invoked to prevent discrimination against individuals on the basis of race, religion, or gender, but no concession is made to the claims of the group per se. As a result, the primary justification for American affirmative action has been compensatory. An implicit assumption is that the effect of past discrimination must be put right only insofar as all individuals can take part in the race to prosperity and status on an even footing. Even then, recent US Supreme Court rulings have narrowed the rights of minorities to affirmative action, limiting it to instances where individual members of the white majority aren't clearly disadvantaged.[40] From a juridical point of view, in Canada employment equity has been less controversial, with the Canadian Supreme Court tending to find that positive measures of uplift for historically disadvantaged groups cannot be considered discrimination against individuals who are not from those groups.[41]

It is true that by introducing the principle of constitutional supremacy, the Charter has narrowed the difference between Canadian and American jurisprudence. Even so, the rights and freedoms the Charter enumerates are tentative, "subject only to such reasonable limits prescribed by law as can be demonstrably justified in a free and democratic society" (Section 1), a fillip to judicial restraint.[42] Such limitations are reaffirmed in the instance of mobility rights between provinces (Section 6) and by a notwithstanding clause (Section 33) permitting other rights, the fundamental freedoms of Section 2 and the legal and equality rights of Sections 7–15, to be overridden by federal and provincial legislatures.[43] To some degree this is a result of the political compromises necessary to the Charter's passage. But when judges rule in Charter cases their decisions are often modulated according to the impact they believe the granting of a right will have on the health of the community as a whole. So, for instance, in *R. v. Keegstra* (1990), which assessed restrictions on hate speech in Canada's Criminal Code (in this instance Holocaust denial and anti-Semitism), the Canadian Supreme Court upheld the prohibition on the basis that such speech undermines a pressing social concern to reduce racial, religious, and ethnic conflict and thus does not deserve constitutional protection. By contrast, in *Brandenburg v. Ohio* (1969), a landmark First Amendment case considering the Ku Klux Klan's advocacy for overthrowing the US government, a unanimous US Supreme Court found that constitutional guarantees of freedom of expression do not permit the state to ban speech unless not doing so would lead directly to episodes of violence. Short of inviting mayhem, in the United States an individual has the right to say in public what he or she wishes; in Canada, wider social interests confine that right.

Freedom, State, and Market

Freedom is nuanced in the United States in such a way as to diminish an overriding concern with economic inequality. In the American conception, freedom connotes autonomy from government and society rather than empowerment through collective effort. In part this is the legacy of a country born in rebellion, in part the consequence of being a settler society with an open interior beyond the grasp of established authority. Accordingly, Americans have restrained government with an impressive array of devices designed to fragment its power: a constitution assigning discrete competencies to the various branches of government, which, given an additional commitment to checks and balances, is functionally a system of separate institutions with shared powers; federalism, which imposes the countervailing power of individual states, themselves internally divided, against the national government; a bicameral Congress in which the two chambers are regarded as virtual equals, thereby inhibiting the cohesion of the central law-making process; and a bill of rights that protects against the full extent of state authority.

Lack of a single locus of political power also means that in the United States the concept of sovereignty, of ultimate decision-making authority, is fluid. At best, Americans entertain an amorphous belief in the finality of the law or the even more ambiguous sovereignty of the people, but they are made uncomfortable by any statement of government's conclusive power. Even political radicalism in the United States shares this anti-state cast. Historically, the most progressive parts of the American labor movement placed their confidence in worker voluntarism, not the state, as a vehicle of positive change. And while more needs to be said, one of the great comparative questions of American political development—why is there no European-style socialism/social democracy in the United States?—can be answered in much the same way. In the electorate's eyes, a major liability of the twentieth-century American socialist movement, and a reason for the meager support it received, was precisely its belief in the efficacy of state power.[44]

Canadians aren't quite as conflicted. Certainly there is no American equivalent to Canada's iconic symbol the Mountie (an officer of the Royal Canadian Mounted Police), who was originally an agent of government power deputized to bring order to the expanding frontier. Canadians may not be as deferential to established authority as political historians once claimed, yet there is a residue of comfort with the state that is lacking in the United States.[45] Canada's British political heritage, in particular its centralizing doctrine of parliamentary sovereignty, bears some responsibility, if grafted onto a federal system of government that disperses power. Nevertheless, as James Bryce, the British diplomat and academic, reasoned in the early twentieth century,

> The voters are in the United States more frequently summoned to act, but in Canada their power, when they do act at an election, is legally boundless, for their representatives are subject to no such restrictions as American

Constitutions impose. Were there any revolutionary spirit abroad in Canada, desiring to carry sweeping changes by a sudden stroke, these could be carried swiftly by Parliamentary legislation.[46]

By introducing the language of rights into the equation, the Charter has made the power of the legislature slightly less formidable than in Bryce's day, though when it comes to countermanding acts of Parliament such rights are far from absolute. What hasn't much changed, however, is the greater opportunity for electoral engagement in the United States. The sheer number of elective positions for all tiers of government—federal, state, and local—estimated at over half a million, is telling of the American compulsion to hold the state firmly accountable.[47] Parallel Canadian data are not available, but as a suggestive measure consider the number of seats in state and provincial legislatures. American assemblies are more than twice as large on average as their Canadian equivalents—at 147 elected members in state houses versus 70 in provincial chambers.[48] And public referenda and initiatives, populist measures to bring public officials to heel, are much rarer in Canada than in the United States. Since the turn of the twentieth century over 7,700 ballot measures have been considered by electorates in American states, but just 69 by their provincial Canadian counterparts.[49]

Compared to the United States, from the beginning Canadian economic development has relied more heavily on the power of the state. Given the physical challenges of Confederation, the BNA Act obligated the central government to construct a railroad uniting all four of Canada's original provinces. The Intercolonial Railway of Canada—expanded and renamed the Canadian National Railway in 1918—was owned and run by the federal authorities as one of Canada's first Crown corporations. Hydro Ontario (1906), Trans-Canada Airlines (1937), and Petro-Canada (1975) are among the well-known public entities that followed, though within the last 30 years all have been privatized or, in the instance of what remains of Ontario's electric utility, intended to become so. Still standing, however, is the Canadian Broadcasting Corporation, an instrument of national development in its own way, whose creation in 1936 was framed as "a choice between the state and the United States."[50] In Quebec, initiatives like Hydro-Québec (1962) and the Caisse de dépôt (1965), the public investment fund created by the National Assembly to manage provincial pension and insurance plans and provide capital to French Canadian businesses, have played an important role in a different kind of nation building. Both a cause and effect of Canada's greater willingness to intervene economically, Canadian trade unions have been more inclined than their American affiliates to pursue labor's objectives via direct political action.[51] In particular, there has been a close relationship between the union movement and Canada's largest social democratic party. The Co-operative Commonwealth Federation (CCF, est. 1932), rechristened the New Democratic Party (NDP) in 1961, has formed provincial governments and consistently been among the top three or four parties represented in the federal Parliament since the end of World War II. It is a crucial difference between socialism in the United States and Canada, even of the pale pink variety.

If Canadians have tended to view the government's role in the market pragmatically—frequently a matter of expanding citizen choice, not limiting it—Americans have insisted that the benefits of political freedom be extended to economic interaction so that the sphere of government authority over the market is diminished. As committed liberals in the classical sense, Americans are the archetypal "possessive individualists," in C.B. MacPherson's signature phrase, inclined to put minimal restrictions on the accumulation of wealth.[52] Indeed, in Federalist Paper #10 James Madison allows that the first object of government is the protection of faculties through which men are led to possess different amounts of property. Constitutional protection is a correlate: The Fourth Amendment secures private property against unreasonable search and seizure; the Fifth prohibits a person from being deprived of property without due process and insists that any taking of property by the state must serve a clear public purpose and be given just compensation; the Fourteenth reiterates the commitment to due process but in the context of an additional guarantee of the equal protection of the law. Not so in Canada, where the Constitution, defaulting to its common law roots, is silent on the matter of a citizen's right to property—with the exception of Indigenous peoples' land claims—including obligations of recompense for public expropriation. Although several attempts have been made to amend the Charter by making property rights explicit, all have failed in the face of objections that to recognize such a right would limit a government's ability to enact laws serving the general welfare.[53]

Capitalist principles—the voluntary exchange of goods and services, private ownership, unlimited appropriation, and the profit motive—have deep roots in American soil. On occasion this has had the effect of privatizing what in most rich democratic countries are considered public goods. Primary and secondary education is an example. Private school alternatives have always been available in the United States and Canada, but with the exception of Alberta no Canadian province has joined the burgeoning American movement for charter schools in the public system. Unlike Alberta, a growing number of US states allow those schools to be run by for-profit businesses, including private equity firms and hedge fund managers who see them as a lucrative investment opportunity.[54] Alternatively, and again contrary to American norms, for historical and constitutional reasons public funds in Canada can be used in support of sectarian schools, and in some cases private nonsectarian institutions, all of which are accountable to provincial governments.[55] So while most Canadian provinces authorize public financing and regulation of private education, several American states solicit private financing and regulation of public education.

On balance the Canadian state displays a greater willingness to mediate the market on behalf of the common good. Total tax revenue as a percentage of a country's GDP is one measure of the extent to which a government redirects its economic resources. By that criterion, the Canadian government has a more active economic presence than does the United States: In 2014, taxes represented a 31-percent portion of Canada's GDP but a 26-percent share in the United States.[56] Government expenditures are larger in Canada, too, accounting for 45 percent of the Canadian versus 39 percent of the American GDP.[57] So is spending on services that more directly affect economic equality and mobility. It is true that the United States now devotes slightly more of its GDP to social purposes (education, health, pensions, housing, family assistance, unemployment) than Canada. Partly this reflects the stronger impact of the 2008 recession south of the border as well as the high cost of American health care delivery.[58] But when one considers public spending on means-tested benefits, that is to say based on calculations of need, the American record is especially weak. Income-sensitive cash benefits constitute more than half of all public disbursements for social purposes in Canada, but in the United States they are just over a quarter. To be fair, means-testing existing benefits—a prospect mooted in the American debate over the long-term solvency of Social Security and Medicare—is sometimes seen as an attack on the social safety net, not a measure of its integrity. In European states, for instance, such tests are highly unusual. Then again, since Europeans rarely confront distributional inequalities on a North American scale there may be less incentive to use them.

Equality

Americans have an egalitarian pedigree. The Pulitzer Prize–winning American historian Gordon Wood writes that "Equality was in fact the most radical and most powerful ideological force let loose in the Revolution."[59] That all men are created equal, that they possess intrinsic worth and therefore are owed equal respect, is a first principle of the Declaration of Independence and reinforced by the philosophies of Thomas Jefferson and Andrew Jackson. It informs the fundamental American conviction that ordinary citizens must be allowed to share in the political decision-making process in equal measure. And it explains the recurrent strength of American populist movements, whose common denominator is the belief that a common person is as politically astute as an elected official, hence that public opinion should be translated directly into public policy—that is, minus the distorting effect of representatives.[60] Early US adoption of universal white male suffrage and the establishment of broad-based political parties to mobilize newly enfranchised voters were remarkably democratic gestures for their time, albeit imperfectly so.

What equality required in one aspect of American political, economic, and social life, however, didn't necessarily translate to another.[61] A newly independent United States affirmed the equal administration of the law, which is quite a different matter than recognizing the legal equality of all, as the history of black, Asian, Hispanic, and Indigenous peoples and women so clearly demonstrates. Even for white men, state-based property qualifications for suffrage were only removed in the 1850s. The Founding Fathers deployed institutional mechanisms that intentionally diminished the full force of democracy—for instance, by twinning a popularly elected House of Representatives with a Senate chosen by state legislatures (until the Seventeenth Amendment in 1913) and by interposing an electoral college between the voters and the presidency. Still, in comparative perspective the extent of social and political equality in the United States, even in its adolescence, was distinctive. European chroniclers of nineteenth-century America regularly contrasted the egalitarian emphases of the republic with the hidebound societies of the Old World. The most famous of them, Alexis de Tocqueville, wrote that the preeminent characteristic of the American social condition was democracy, Americans owning a greater equality in fortune and intellect than the nationals of any other country on Earth.[62] With respect to the white male population, for whom land ownership was relatively diffuse, he may have been right.[63]

For de Tocqueville, the promise of social mobility mitigated the threat of economic inequality of which the American founders were well aware.[64] Several early political elites accepted the connection drawn in classical republican thought between excessive inequalities of wealth and the corruption of a self-governing citizenry. Freedom, they feared, suffered when disparities in economic power led to imbalances of political power. Indeed, there is an inescapable tension between the American belief in social and political equality and an unfettered market economy that, by sanctioning enormous differences in material well-being, undermines that equality. That is especially so in a post-revolutionary society where ascribed status is diminished and the achievement of wealth is the major criterion of upward social mobility. Yet in the United States, status achieved in open economic competition does not appear to entail relations of social deference or jealousy. Even among Americans of modest means, wealth is generally regarded as a mark of individual distinction, applauded as a sign of personal industriousness and virtue.

This widespread belief that the affluent merit their good fortune has been a force for social cohesion across US history.[65] The British political scientist Harold Laski once remarked of the American working class that they didn't want to replace the upper classes; they wanted to join them. Perhaps that is why American television caters to a never-ending fascination with the lifestyles of the well-to-do—the "secret millionaires" with their "dream homes" and "million dollar listings." "I don't believe in a law to prevent a man from getting rich," Abraham Lincoln once said, "[but] we do wish to allow the humblest man an equal chance to get rich with everyone else."[66] Provided that minimum guarantees of equality of opportunity are assured and the reliability of market transactions are upheld by law, American justice is largely a matter of how one fares in impersonal economic competition, even if the outcome is grossly uneven.[67] In the United States, the freedom to accumulate trumps the material well-being of all.

Canadians are more inclined to temper the acquisitive impulse in the interest of collective provision. Unlike the American high court, in matters of constitutional interpretation the Canadian Supreme Court refuses to indulge the prerogatives of big business by granting corporations the legal status of persons.[68] Post-Charter jurisprudence is sensitive to the role that economic disparities have on the equality rights guaranteed by the Canadian Constitution and thus upholds the "ameliorative purpose" of programs designed to remedy systemic material disadvantage suffered by individuals or groups—the very type of programs that slowly but surely are being gutted in the United States.[69] And reflecting a concern for pan-Canadian integration, the Constitution Act (1982) also institutionalizes Ottawa's commitment to regional economic equalization, so that comparable levels of public service are made available regardless of province. Again, the contrast with the United States, where the public benefits and burdens of residence can and do vary wildly according to geography, couldn't be greater.

That is not to say that Canada has been consistently more egalitarian than the United States. Like colonial America, before Confederation Canada was a differentiated and class-aware society—from the seigneurs, habitants, and domestiques of New France, to the Family Compacts and Château Cliques of Upper and Lower Canada. For a long time the political institutions of the post-1867 state were wary of the commonality. Canada was a constitutional monarchy in which the authority of the Crown was used, via the power to reserve and disallow legislation, to deny the will of federal and provincial assemblies. It had, and still does have, an appointed upper chamber of the federal Parliament, where the legislative output of the popularly elected Commons was to be given "sober second thought." Suffrage, including the removal of property qualifications to vote, expanded at a leisurely pace. Consequently, the modern political parties necessary to structure a broadly enfranchised electorate were slow to develop.[70] Even after such practices were democratized, Canada remained a hierarchical if diverse society, as John Porter captured in his classic analysis *The Vertical Mosaic* (1965).[71] It is one of the reasons why the class-based approach to politics of the early CCF-NDP, supported by farmers as well as trade unionists, found purchase among a significant portion of the Canadian citizenry. American society may have been just as divided by class, but for the last hundred years or so political parties wishing to win elections have studiously avoided mentioning it.[72]

Whether from social democratic conviction or Tory *noblesse oblige*, for most of the post-war period Canadian parties from the left to the right of the political spectrum have endorsed a more substantial social safety net than their American counterparts.[73] It's worth remembering that as a response to the Great Depression, the American New Deal was the work of the liberal Democratic administration of Franklin Roosevelt, whereas the Canadian New Deal was initiated by the Conservative government of R.B. Bennett. While the right in the United States seems keen to dismantle what remains of the welfare state in the name of entrepreneurial autonomy and the virtues of the private sector, until recently Canadian conservatives have generally made peace with those public programs, health insurance first among them, since they promised a secure standard of living regardless of one's income or status. In *Continental Divide*, one of the most influential texts of comparative North American studies, Seymour Martin Lipset argued that this value distinction—Canada's concern for equality of economic condition versus US support for equal opportunity and meritocracy—was a principal line of cultural demarcation between the two countries. Less presciently, he maintained that Canada was a patrimonial and class-riven society when compared to the United States, that its tax code more actively concentrated income and wealth, and that its system of higher education was more elitist than among schools south of the border.[74] Lipset can be forgiven if these insights now appear quaint; *Continental Divide* was published in 1990. But as Chapters 1 and 2 of the present text take pains to demonstrate, on almost every economic measure, including the distribution of income and wealth, factually Canada is a significantly more equal place than the United States—and tertiary education in Canada is more accessible to students of modest means, too. Ultimately, the proof of contemporary Canada's greater egalitarian disposition is in the statistical pudding.

Public Opinion about Economic Equality

To get a sense of what a citizenry believes about issues of political economy, it's important to ask. Survey data are fundamental to observations about political culture, though interpretive caution is always in order, since questions on common political and economic themes are not always posed in the same way. Aggregate answers elide differences based on partisanship or ideological conviction, education, class, gender, ethnic or racial status, and region. Inquiries about mobility and equality are especially sensitive to the particulars of the immediate economic environment, respondents tending to give more optimistic answers when the economy is doing well. For that reason, explicitly comparative surveys are especially valuable, since identical questions can be asked of national publics at roughly the same time. Unfortunately, they are in shorter supply.

But as provisional as the results may be, it's worth the effort to sift through and find common patterns of belief from a variety of attitudinal evidence— in the present case from the survey marginals of questions about economic equality posed by leading American and Canadian polling organizations. Distinctions are often of degree rather than kind—unsurprising, since both Canada and the United States are liberal states where the government's mediation of the market is relatively modest.[75] They are not for that reason any less important. As the dean of US public opinion studies V.O. Key long ago advised, "Unless mass views have some place in the shaping of policy, all the talk about democracy is nonsense."[76] If democratic politics is about choice, including decisions about the distribution of material well-being, then at some level the value orientations of the public must influence the choices to be made.

Apprehensive and Aware (Sort Of)

According to a 2016 Gallup poll, slightly more than two-thirds of Americans are dissatisfied with the distribution of income and wealth.[77] It's not a new development. Over the last 35 years, the General Social Survey (GSS), a leading compendium of longitudinal data on social, economic, and political attitudes in the United States, consistently indicates strong to very strong support among Americans for the propositions that income differences are too high and that inequality benefits the rich and powerful.[78] If anything, Canadian anxieties may be more intense. In an Environics survey (2012) on behalf of Ottawa's Broadbent Institute, almost eight in ten respondents say inequality will have a long-term negative impact by reducing Canadians' standard of living, and seven in ten fear that the widening gap between the rich and the poor will undermine Canadian values—suggesting there is something profoundly un-Canadian about economic inequality itself.[79]

But if Canadians and Americans are not oblivious to economic inequality, neither are they especially informed about its magnitude. Environics (2011) relates that a significant majority of poll respondents in Canada and the United States—64 and 61 percent, respectively—recognize that disparities of income and wealth are at unprecedented levels.[80] Yet in each country there is a tendency to underestimate the true measure of inequality—and in the United States by a large margin. In a 2014 survey, Canadians surmised that the richest fifth of households held 56 percent of total wealth and the poorest fifth less than 6 percent; in 2011 the comparable American assessments were 59 percent and 4 percent.[81] The truth, of course, is much different. In both places the bottom quintile of the wealth distribution in effect has zero net worth, and while the top quintile in Canada has a 67 percent share, the richest fifth of households in the United States commands more than 84 percent.[82] Perceptions count, since what people think about economic inequality ultimately drives the kinds of policy prescriptions they endorse to deal with it. And while research in behavioral economics suggests that if citizens are carefully presented with relevant information about inequality, they can develop a more accurate assessment of its extent and significance, those same studies indicate that changing the policy preferences of even a well-informed citizenry is difficult.[83] The public's general sensitivity to economic inequality may be one thing; its support for redistributive political strategies quite another.

Economic Mobility

Confidence in one's economic prowess may be a reason why Americans seem less concerned to address material inequality than the citizens of many other advanced industrial democracies. According to Benjamin I. Page and Lawrence R. Jacobs in *Class War? What Americans Really Think about Economic Inequality*, US poll evidence regularly shows strong support for the idea that, regardless of circumstance, anyone can make their way up the ladder of economic success—a belief affirmed irrespective of income level, race, or partisanship.[84] Indeed, a majority of Americans in Page and Jacobs's inequality survey (2007) say that inequality is a useful incentive to achievement.[85] A Pew Economic Mobility poll (2011) reveals that 90 percent of Americans agree the two most important qualities making for advancement are hard work and ambition—each within a person's ability to control.[86] Large majorities over the last 20 years are persuaded that diligence is the prerequisite of material well-being, although in the recent past the proportion of those thinking so is somewhat diminished.[87] Nevertheless, compared to members of other rich democratic countries, Americans remain more disposed to believe that success in life is determined by one's own effort rather than outside forces or luck.[88]

A not-so-happy corollary is that in the United States low levels of economic mobility are not always viewed as a systemic malfunction but rather are attributed to lack of individual resolve. In a comparative assessment of longitudinal survey data in the United States and Europe, Alberto Alesina and Edward L. Glaeser contend that the American point of view about poverty is distinctive; US respondents are more likely to see low income as a personal failing than an accident of fortune.[89] Consider the World Values Survey (WVS), an initiative of social scientists who have conducted common public opinion polls in more than 80 countries, including Canada and the United States, over the last 30 years. When in 1995 the WVS asked Americans why people are in need—the only time the question has been asked—48 percent said that poverty was due to laziness and a lack of willpower on behalf of the poor; only 30 percent blamed an unfair society.[90] A recent Pew survey (2014) is more forgiving, with 35 percent of Americans blaming poverty on a lack of effort and 50 percent holding circumstances responsible—though it is still a significant result when over a third of respondents blame the poor for their own predicament.[91] Naïve optimism in the American Dream may reduce the need to confront the realities of persistent economic disadvantage. Research conducted by Shai Davidai and Thomas Gilovich, for instance, reveals that Americans are prone to overestimate the likelihood that individuals from the bottom income quintile are upwardly mobile, and poorer Americans are the most likely to do so.[92]

On the face of it Canadians aren't all that different, though they do appear less inclined to attribute poverty to lack of effort. Angus Reid (2011) reports that 63 percent of survey respondents allow that "poverty is a trap some Canadians just can't escape no matter how hard they try."[93] But with respect to keys for economic success, in a comparative Pew poll (2009) Canadians rank hard work and ambition just as highly as Americans—right at the top of the list of necessary attributes.[94] Expectations of mobility are broadly similar and optimistic, though by respective majorities of 64 percent and 56 percent Canadians more often than Americans say it is easier to move up the income ladder than it was in their parents' generation.[95] Opinion is evenly split as to whether their specific children will be able to do likewise, although by a margin of 62 percent to 47 percent considerably more Americans than Canadians think the next generation will go on to have a higher standard of living than its predecessor.[96] Ironically, one of the few other significant variances concerns the possibility that financial success is tied to parental income. Only 42 percent of Americans but 57 percent of Canadians maintain that it is—the reverse of what the hard data on income elasticity in each country show.[97] Thus Canadians may be more willing to consider a reallocation of economic resources because they imagine society to be less mobile than it actually is, whereas for Americans an enduring myth of mobility is a powerful disincentive to tackle issues of redistribution.[98]

Fairness and Opportunity

When Pew (2009) asked North American publics what is more important, "to reduce inequality, or to ensure that everyone has a fair chance of improving their economic standing," 71 percent of Americans and 68 percent of Canadians opted for fairness; only 21 percent of Americans though 26 percent of Canadians chose equality of result.[99] Fairness is an especially abstract concept, but the common denominator seems to be whether equal opportunities for upward economic mobility have been afforded and thus if inequalities of outcome are deserved. Gallup reports that between 1998 and 2013 the number of Americans saying that the US economic system is "basically fair, since all Americans have an equal opportunity to succeed" decreased from just over two-thirds to half of those polled.[100] And according to the 2015 American Values Survey (AVS), which includes an "Economic Inequity Index," a composite measure of answers to three questions touching on opportunity, almost 60 percent of US respondents fall into the very high/high category of individuals with serious reservations about the fairness of the US economy.[101]

Common to both countries is the idea that the rich have unwarranted advantages. In a 2015 poll, Gallup relates that 63 percent of Americans think the economic system is biased toward the wealthy, a figure that has fluctuated little over the last 30 years.[102] Respondents in a Pew poll (2011) concur, 77 percent elaborating that too much power is in the hands of "large corporations and a few rich people."[103] Canadians are just as worried. Ekos (2013) finds that two of the top four factors blamed for poor economic growth in Canada are "an excessive share of profits going to the wealthy" and "corporate greed and corruption."[104] This is not a simple matter of class resentment. In the United States, 58 percent of individuals surveyed by Gallup (2011) say they do not think of their country as divided between haves and have-nots, although that is a smaller majority than 20 years earlier.[105] Instead, North American publics are circumspect about the rich, believing them more likely than ordinary citizens to be greedy, dishonest, and tax cheats on the one hand, though intelligent, entrepreneurial, and hardworking on the other.[106]

Uneven access to opportunity is often cited to explain the fundamental difference between the well-to-do and everyone else. More than half of Americans in a YouGov survey (2014), for example, say people are wealthy simply because they have had more economic chances.[107] There may be no condemnation in this. Leslie McCall maintains it is only the "undeserving rich" who Americans find alarming, people whose wealth is acquired without having to exercise diligence on a level playing field and who feel little compunction to help others by building an economy in which all have an equal ability for advancement.[108] Based on a thorough examination of equality-related items in the GSS, McCall argues that Americans are concerned with growing inequalities of income and wealth primarily because of the negative impact on equal opportunity, not because they offend their distributional sensibilities per se. Gallup (2011) indicates that 70 percent of Americans are highly committed to increasing equal opportunity, but only 46 percent wish to reduce the gap between the rich and the poor. Canadians, too, seem sensitive to the connection between skewed outcomes and opportunities. A York University/*Toronto Star* poll (2014) allows that 70 percent of Canadians believe growth in income inequality makes Canada a less fair society—a distributional concern that crosscuts region, gender, age, and income level.[109]

A Problem Needing a Solution?

Fewer Americans than Canadians think economic inequality is a condition demanding a political remedy.[110] Less than half of US respondents in the AVS (2015) regard inequality as a critical issue, though its significance sharply divides Democratic and Republican voters.[111] And slightly more than half (52 percent) of Americans, according to Gallup (2011), say that notwithstanding growing inequality the fact that some people are rich and others poor is "an acceptable part of the economic system" rather than a "problem that needs to be fixed."[112] Canadians are not so sure. Ekos (2013) reports that only 28 percent believe "income inequality is a natural by-product of a strong economy," and 61 percent say it hinders economic growth.[113] Further, Canadian support for a more equitable distribution of income and wealth is barely affected by partisan affiliation.[114]

The WVS sheds a little more light on these varying outlooks, since in two waves of the survey (2005/2006 and 1999/2000) it poses the same question about economic inequality to American and Canadian publics. On a scale of one to ten, people were asked if incomes should be made more equal or whether income differentials are necessary as economic incentives; the strongest approval for the former option was ranked as one, the strongest support for the latter as ten. As Table 3.1 indicates, in each case the

Table 3.1 World Values Survey Questions on Income Equality

	Total	Country	
		Canada	United States
Incomes should be made more equal	6.6%	7.0%	6.1%
2	3.7%	4.7%	1.9%
3	6.3%	7.4%	4.2%
4	8.2%	8.9%	6.9%
5	16.3%	15.2%	18.4%
6	13.3%	10.5%	18.2%
7	18.6%	18.3%	19.2%
8	15.4%	17.1%	12.4%
9	5.2%	5.8%	4.2%
We need larger income differences as incentives	6.3%	5.1%	8.5%
(N)	(3,324)	(2,121)	(1,203)
Mean	5.91	5.82	6.08
Standard Deviation	2.36	2.42	2.26
Base mean	(3,324)	(2,121)	(1,203)

Selected samples: Canada 2005, United States 2006

	Total	Country	
		Canada	United States
Incomes should be made more equal	11.9%	13.2%	10.0%
2	4.4%	4.5%	4.2%
3	6.8%	7.2%	6.4%
4	8.6%	8.2%	9.2%
5	14.6%	14.7%	14.4%
6	12.2%	12.0%	12.4%
7	15.6%	15.6%	15.8%
8	14.8%	14.6%	15.2%
9	4.6%	4.1%	5.4%
We need larger income differences as incentives	6.4%	5.9%	7.2%
(N)	(3,107)	(1,911)	(1,196)
Mean	5.55	5.44	5.72
Standard Deviation	2.60	2.63	2.56
Base mean	(3,107)	(1,911)	(1,196)

Selected samples: Canada 2000, United States 1999

Source: World Values Survey, Wave 5, Question V116; Wave 4, Question V141.

mean response of Americans is higher than for Canadians—that is, Americans are less willing that incomes should be made equal. Whereas at the margins more Canadians than Americans support the most egalitarian response, the reverse is true for the least egalitarian answer.[115] Drawing on International Social Survey Programme data (1999), Lars Osberg and Timothy Smeeding again find Canadians more disposed than Americans to agree/strongly agree that income differences are too large—by 70.6 percent to 66.2 percent. Yet what truly distinguishes the United States from other countries, according to Osberg and Smeeding, is the degree to which Americans are unconcerned with bringing up the tail of the earnings distribution—an acceptance of inequality at the bottom that has grown over time.[116]

Markets and the State

State intervention on behalf of economically disadvantaged citizens rests less easily on the American than the Canadian political conscience. Environics (2012) finds that 67 percent of Americans versus 61 percent of Canadians agree that people are better off in a free market economy.[117] Relatedly, the WVS reveals a firmer US commitment to two of the essential props of the free enterprise system: private ownership of business and economic competition. When Americans and Canadians are asked by the WVS to indicate on a scale of one to ten their views about private as opposed to government ownership of business, the mean American answer is closer to the private end of the ranking (Table 3.2). And when the statements to be assessed are "Competition is good. It stimulates people to work hard and develop new ideas," or contrariwise "Competition is harmful," the average US preference is closer to the pro-competition end of the scale than is true of Canadians (Table 3.3). American reactions are echoed in polls drawing a specific connection between markets and income inequality. In a Pew survey (2014), 70 percent of Americans agreed that "most people are better off in a free market economy even though some people are rich and others are poor."[118] Probing the same relationship, the *New York Times* (2014) asked about the bigger problem in the United States, "overregulation that may interfere with economic growth or too little regulation that may create an unequal distribution of wealth." Overregulation was the larger worry among 54 percent of those polled, while just 38 percent were concerned about aggravating inequality by too little state intervention.[119]

Americans distinguish themselves in the degree to which they are wary of the state's economic activism. In 2010 and 2012 AmericasBarometer, a survey sponsored by the United States Agency for International Development, asked individuals across the western hemisphere to agree or disagree with

Table 3.2 World Values Survey Questions on Preference for Markets: Private versus Government Ownership of Business

	Total	Country	
		Canada	United States
Private ownership of business should be increased	14.4%	11.4%	19.4%
2	9.1%	9.1%	9.2%
3	17.9%	18.4%	17.0%
4	14.6%	13.5%	16.6%
5	21.4%	20.2%	23.4%
6	9.2%	9.7%	8.4%
7	5.6%	7.2%	2.8%
8	4.4%	6.2%	1.2%
9	1.6%	2.2%	0.6%
Government ownership of business should be increased	1.9%	2.1%	1.4%
(N)	(3,277)	(2,069)	(1,208)
Mean	4.14	4.39	3.71
Standard Deviation	2.16	2.23	1.97
Base mean	(3,277)	(2,069)	(1,208)

Selected samples. Canada 2005, United States 2006

	Total	Country	
		Canada	United States
Private ownership of business should be increased	21.4%	18.5%	26.2%
2	11.3%	11.2%	11.4%
3	17.0%	17.3%	16.5%
4	14.5%	14.5%	14.6%
5	16.5%	18.2%	13.9%
6	8.5%	9.2%	7.5%
7	4.2%	4.3%	4.0%
8	3.2%	3.3%	3.0%
9	1.3%	1.6%	0.8%
Government ownership of business should be increased	2.1%	2.0%	2.1%
(N)	(3,088)	(1,896)	(1,192)
Mean	3.74	3.88	3.52
Standard Deviation	2.22	2.21	2.24
Base mean	(3,088)	(1,896)	(1,192)

Selected samples. Canada 2000, United States 1999

Source: World Values Survey, Wave 5, Question V117; Wave 4, Question V142.

Values 127

Table 3.3 World Values Survey Questions on Preference for Markets: Economic Competition

	TOTAL	Country	
		Canada	United States
Competition is good	17.3%	15.0%	21.3%
2	15.5%	16.5%	13.6%
3	19.1%	18.8%	19.7%
4	15.9%	16.2%	15.4%
5	15.6%	14.8%	16.9%
6	5.5%	5.7%	5.2%
7	4.1%	4.8%	2.9%
8	3.8%	4.5%	2.5%
9	2.0%	2.4%	1.4%
Competition is harmful	1.2%	1.3%	1.0%
(N)	(3,335)	(2,132)	(1,202)
Mean	3.70	3.82	3.48
Standard Deviation	2.14	2.18	2.04
Base mean	(3,335)	(2,132)	(1,202)

Selected samples: Canada 2005, United States 2006

	Total	Country	
		Canada	United States
Competition is good	25.7%	23.8%	28.9%
2	15.9%	15.3%	16.9%
3	16.1%	17.6%	13.7%
4	12.7%	13.4%	11.5%
5	11.6%	12.6%	9.9%
6	6.5%	6.0%	7.4%
7	4.1%	4.0%	4.3%
8	3.2%	3.4%	2.9%
9	1.7%	1.4%	2.2%
Competition is harmful	2.4%	2.4%	2.4%
(N)	(3,112)	(1,913)	(1,199)
Mean	3.48	3.52	3.40
Standard Deviation	2.32	2.28	2.39
Base mean	(3,112)	(1,913)	(1,199)

Selected samples: Canada 2000, United States 1999

Source: World Values Survey, Wave 5, Question V119; Wave 4, Question V144.

the statement that their country's government "should implement strong policies to reduce income inequality between the rich and the poor." As the results in Figure 3.1 reveal, when answers are scaled from 0 (strongly disagree) to 100 (strongly agree), the United States is the only country whose

Figure 3.1 AmericasBarometer: Agreement That the State Should Reduce Inequality

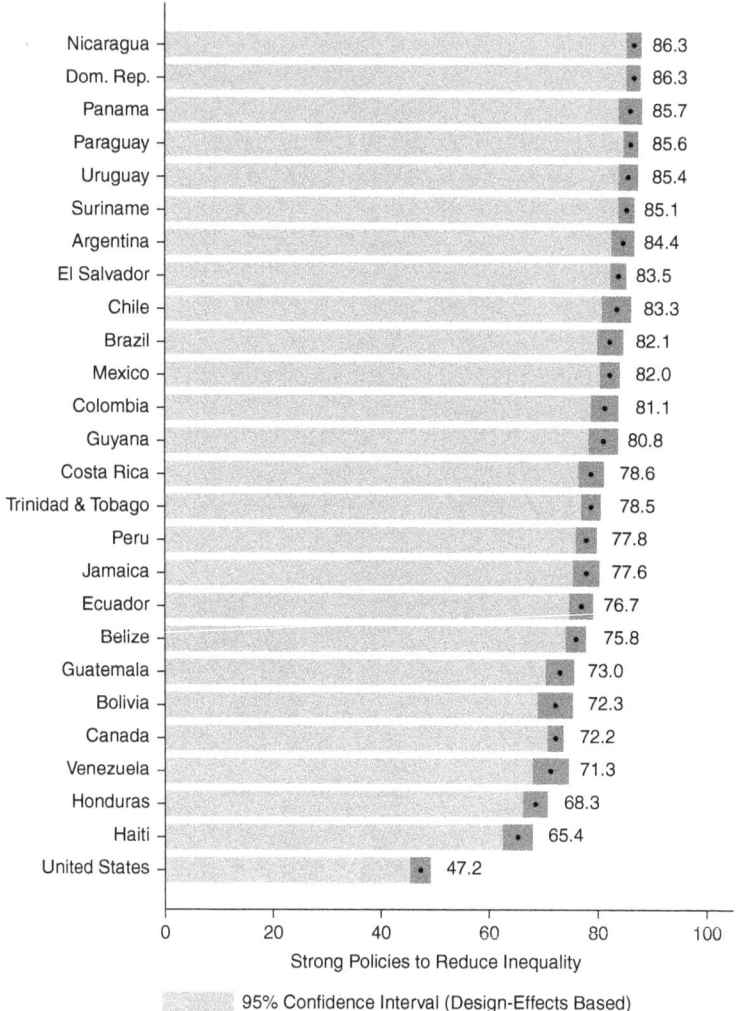

Source: Seligson, Smith, and Zechmeister, "The Political Culture of Democracy in the Americas, 2012."

average response is below the midpoint—that is to say, on the disagree side of the ranking. All other countries in the region, including Canada, are significantly above.[120] Moreover, in the same survey, whereas 51 percent of Canadians indicate strong agreement with the idea of the state redistributing economic resources, just 29 percent of Americans give that response. While only 6 percent of Canadians strongly disagree with the idea of an interventionist government, six times as many Americans do.[121]

In fact the great majority of studies confirm the reluctance of Americans to endorse state-sponsored redistribution. Over the last three-and-a-half decades, according to the GSS, support for the idea that the government should act to reduce inequality has remained fairly constant, with just under half of all Americans believing it is merited (Figure 3.2).[122] Neither is there great enthusiasm for the government to do all it can to improve the living standard of poor Americans. Since 1975, GSS data show that support for Washington to focus on helping the poor has decreased from 40 percent to less than 30 percent of those polled, though partisan polarization around the issue is at an all-time high.[123]

Figure 3.2 General Social Survey: Percent of Americans Saying That the Government Should Reduce Income Differences between the Rich and the Poor, 1978–2014

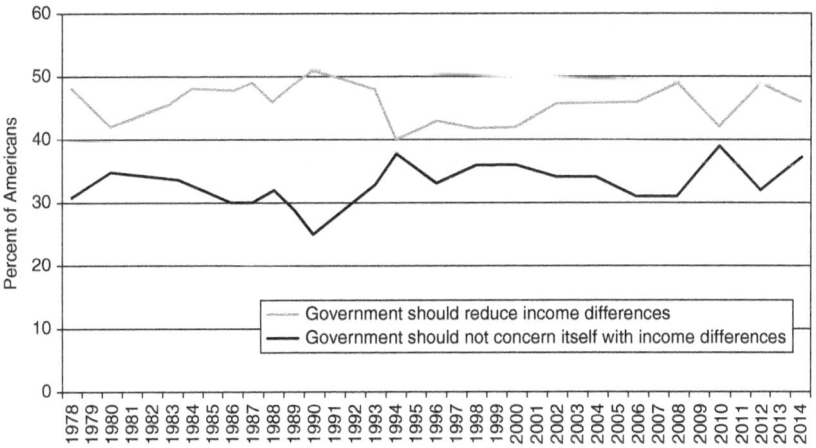

Question: "Some people think that the government in Washington ought to reduce the income differences between the rich and the poor, perhaps by raising the taxes of wealthy families or by giving income assistance to the poor. Others think that the government should not concern itself with reducing this income difference between the rich and the poor."

Source: AP/NORC, "Inequality Trends in American Attitudes."

Canadians are much more favorably inclined toward political efforts at redistribution. As Figure 3.3 indicates, from the mid-1980s to 2011, Environics surveys show that large majorities of Canadians—around 80 percent in most years—support government attempts to reduce the gap between rich and poor citizens.[124] And when each public is asked specifically what the government might do to reduce poverty and inequality, a majority of Americans (52 percent) but less than half of Canadians (40 percent) say it should improve the economy and create jobs—presumably a means of enhancing opportunity. By contrast, Canadians more often than Americans choose the overtly distributional response—increase taxes on the rich—by 31 percent to 22 percent.[125]

One can speculate as to the reasons for these discrete national responses. It may be that Americans endorse the kind of equity produced by an unencumbered market, or that optimism about their own mobility insulates them from wider distributional considerations. Alternatively, in good entrepreneurial fashion, in the United States even sharp inequalities of economic reward may be viewed as reasonable incentives to greater productivity. Survey evidence offers support for all these possibilities.[126] Similarly, equality of opportunity—and the role of the well-to-do in affording or subverting

Figure 3.3 Environics: Percent of Canadians Saying That the Government Should Reduce the Gap between the Rich and the Poor, 1986–2011

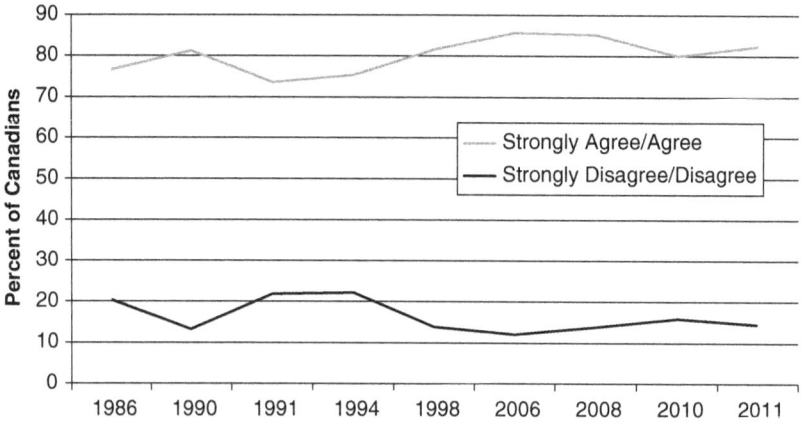

Question: "Do you strongly/somewhat agree/disagree that the government should reduce the gap between the rich and the poor?" In 2011 the wording was changed to "Do you strongly agree, somewhat agree, somewhat disagree, or strongly disagree that governments in Canada should actively find ways to reduce the gap between wealthy people and those less fortunate?"

Source: Canadian Opinion Research Archive.

that opportunity—may be of more compelling interest to US citizens than abstract calculations of economic fairness. McCall contends that Americans will not endure egregious inequalities of opportunity forever; eventually they turn to the government for remedial action.[127] In much the same way, Page and Jacobs observe that Americans are philosophically conservative but operationally liberal, willing to pay for programs affecting education or job training, as well as those that offer a hedge against unforeseen circumstances like illness or disability, in order to enhance opportunity.[128] Indeed, when Gallup (2011) inquired of Americans how important it is that the government acts to reduce income and wealth disparities between the rich and the poor, fewer than half of all respondents indicated it is extremely or very important to do so—far more (70 percent) opt for expanding the economy or increasing equality of opportunity.[129] Even then, Pew (2011) cautions that a little more than half of Americans believe government efforts to promote mobility are counterproductive.[130] When a parallel question is asked of Canadians, nearly 90 percent declare that Ottawa should make reducing income inequality a top- or medium-level policy priority.[131] Trust in government is an additional variable, inasmuch as approving state intervention in the market in support of greater economic equality assumes such intervention will be effective. International comparisons regularly indicate that confidence in political institutions is higher in Canada than in the United States—46 to 35 percent, according to Gallup in 2014—even if it has eroded in both places of late.[132]

Whatever the immediate causes of these differences of national opinion, they appear to reflect and reinforce deeply rooted value commitments specific to each country—about individual and collective responsibility, the role of markets and of states, and the substance of equality. At least American and Canadian responses to questions about such issues tend to track in the same direction across multiple surveys. In matters of economic justice, political culture is not destiny—public opinion and policy can move and be moved—but it does define the likely range of citizen attitudes about income and wealth inequality. In the United States, those attitudes are more privatized and protective of markets and less supportive of equal economic outcomes than in Canada.

Equality and Institutions

Rarely is there a one-to-one correspondence between the economic policies that citizens want and what they actually get. Before public initiatives that in some sense embody the value aspirations of Americans and Canadians can be successful, the organization of political power in each country must be confronted.

To be sure, the institutions through which that power is expressed are themselves the effect and cause of a political culture. Given its liberal heritage of limited government, in the United States power is fragmented, making cohesive and comprehensive policy change hard. It is difficult to overcome the multiple institutional barriers and mobilize the critical mass of citizen support necessary to move forward on those occasions when policies with egalitarian economic implications begin to develop democratic momentum. Influential elites, inside and outside of government, will try to move public opinion in the direction of their own less-than-progressive agendas—a promising strategy in light of the multiple access points at which blocking influence can be wielded in a decentralized US political system.[133]

It's not that American governments are completely hamstrung. One can cite all sorts of decisive legislative achievements, from the construction of transcontinental railway lines and public universities in the nineteenth century to the interstate highway system and the New Deal and Great Society programs of the twentieth. But most often change is slow in coming. Publicly mandated universal health insurance is a case in point. Proposed by the Truman administration in 1945, it was finally passed in a truncated form by the Obama administration in 2010—and upheld as constitutional by the Supreme Court only in 2012 (although, as of this writing, given the result of the 2016 US presidential election, its future is in jeopardy). Even when there is sustained majority support for a reshuffling of the economic deck, as there has been recently for the idea that the richest Americans pay too little in taxes, institutional gridlock and partisan polarization can thwart significant reform.[134] It's worth remembering that it took the threat of a fiscal cliff, draconian spending cuts, and across-the-board tax hikes to finally raise US income taxes in January 2013, from a top marginal rate of 35 percent to 39.6 percent, on the less than 1 percent of individuals who earn more than $400,000 a year. The point is that in a fundamental sense the American system of government is not designed to do things; instead it is designed *not* to do things. When change is so difficult, those who benefit under the political, economic, and social status quo tend to keep their advantages.

By comparison, the structure of Canadian politics would seem to hardwire citizen acceptance of what is a relatively centralized process of policymaking. Concentration of executive and legislative power in a Westminster style of governance—or more precisely, their fusion under norms of party responsibility and discipline—vests legal authority in government ministers acting on behalf of the Crown. Since the basic pattern of national parliamentary government is reproduced in all 10 provincial capitals, if power in Canada is dispersed across federal–provincial jurisdictions it is still centralized within them. Thus, when Canadian public sentiment moves in such a way as to endorse significant policy change, either of its own accord or due to concerted persuasion by opinion leaders, a purposeful federal or provincial Canadian government can more readily oblige provided that a sympathetic party is in office. In that respect, the Canadian experience jibes with the "power resource theory" of economic distribution, in which higher trade union density and the organizational strength of left-of-center parties are linked to more generous welfare provisions and less income inequality.[135] Specifically, one should not gainsay the role played by the NDP as well as the Parti Québécois in nudging Canada in a more egalitarian direction—social democratic parties of government for which there is no real US equivalent.

On the other hand, federalism can weigh against the extension of economic equality. In part that is because a federal state will encompass a variety of cultural perspectives, some of which are territorially specific. To the degree these outlooks find expression through the institutions of states and provinces, social policy may differ across jurisdictions. For instance, and to foreshadow the subject of the next chapter, an analysis of welfare spending among American states has found that, independent of a state's fiscal capacity or the needs of its most disadvantaged residents, policy choices about cash assistance levels are most influenced by the ideology of elected state officials.[136] Similarly, a study of Canadian welfare policy observes that whereas Quebec's more comprehensive public approach is like that of the Scandinavian states, Alberta departs from Canadian norms in pursuing a stingier US style of income assistance.[137] Given the political convictions of governing parties in Quebec City and Edmonton, magnified by the centralized power available under cabinet government, such provincial outliers are not remarkable. Yet, as Chapter 4 will relate, discrepancies in welfare benefits are consistently greater between American states than Canadian provinces. It's hard to know for sure, but Canada's broader egalitarian commitments may be part of the reason. Within a given country, a decentralized political system makes addressing economic equality in a uniform way more difficult, though depending on the public will, not inconceivable.

Finally, there is a further institutional explanation of the relationship between inequality and redistributive public policies that deserves consideration, one favored by advocates of a rational choice approach to political behavior. Centering on the logic of elections, it posits an idealized median voter whose desire for more egalitarian economic policies increases as the gap between the median and average income in a country widens. That occurs when the income gains of those at the top of the distribution pull significantly away from the rest, heightening the dissatisfaction of median earners who in an absolute sense are falling further behind. Insofar as political parties must court voters at the center to win elections in a majoritarian system, escalating inequalities in market income should meet with a redistributive political response—as long as those median voters turn out in sufficient numbers. And yet virtually alone among advanced industrial states, in the United States there is barely any positive statistical relationship between growing market inequality and redistribution through tax and transfer policies over the last 40 years.[138] Here again the independent impact of values on public policy preferences cannot be discounted. When there is a deep-seated cultural and institutional aversion to government activism, and equality signifies opportunity more than outcome, redistributive policy preferences are not always as rational as they seem.

Concluding Remarks

Cultural interpretations of politics, as have been offered here, are not without critics. A principal objection is reductionism, that culture is used as a causal catchall, appealed to without considering what explains the explanation—that is, what is behind the cultural norms themselves. Such criticism, however, does not so much discount the influence of public values on political and economic life as it calls for more work to be done, so that the sources of a given pattern of belief and behavior can be identified.

Culture always has multiple drivers. But as a way to distinguish the United States and Canada, one may be especially relevant: religion. Not only are Americans more devout than Canadians, but the dominant strain in American religious life is privatized.[139] There is an enduring poignancy in de Tocqueville's observation that US history was determined by the first Puritan who touched American soil.[140] Religious expression in the United States continues to be more evangelical than not: individualistic, in that it tends to emphasize a believer's experience of spiritual rebirth, unmediated access to God through prayer and the Bible, and congregational forms of church polity; pietistic, with an expectation of holiness in personal behavior; moralistic, in that it most often seeks to remake society and state in its own image.[141] Catholics comprise the largest single religious denomination in the United States, but the most significant groups among Protestants are Methodists and Baptists—nonconformist churches with evangelical inclinations, though people calling themselves evangelical span far more denominations than these. Conversely, Canada's religious demography and outlook were fixed by the semi-established Anglican and Catholic Churches, who along with the ecumenical United Church of Canada continue to constitute the majority of Canadians who declare a religious affiliation. It is these churches—hierarchical in governance, liturgical and sacramental in worship, corporate in their approach to matters of faith and practice—that set a decidedly different Canadian cultural tone, one less focused on the individual and more on the collective than their American brethren. Inasmuch as Canadian and American politics mirror the distinction, it is an unlikely coincidence.

Skeptics of culture's revelatory power make a further objection: To speak of a country's political culture is a historically contingent assessment, one unable to account for changes in belief. The error, from this view, is to treat cultural values as though they are eternal verities, when in fact they are attitudinal and behavioral snapshots of the moment. Yet at the limit this is a crude form of historicism. If everything is temporally conditioned, then one can never generalize about political life, a luxury social scientists do not have. More importantly, political cultures are neither hopelessly fluid nor wholly static. As Ronald Inglehart's work on the transition in advanced industrial democracies from materialist to post-materialist norms well documents, cultures shift over time, though they are simultaneously quite durable.[142] With respect to economic equality, deep structures of cultural belief mediate between the polity and the economy, a guidepost as countries choose how to react to increasingly skewed market outcomes. These public value preferences make certain national strategies more likely than others. But culture is no straitjacket, worn in perpetuity. Its values, and the way they are interpreted, can be reconstituted. Again, consider religion, in many places part of what feeds a national culture. Its importance to social science is not negated by the fact that across the centuries the beliefs of adherents have evolved in all sorts of ways, nor that some religious people completely forsake the sacred for the secular. Cultures have a disposition to preserve but an ability to change. That does not weaken their analytic relevance.

Doubters may not be persuaded. But the argument here is not that culture is the only reason why American and Canadian engagement with economic inequality is different, or even the principal reason, merely that it is a highly plausible and therefore important reason—as the weight of the present evidence suggests. Given an accelerating gap between the haves and have-nots, what constellation of values would one expect to find in a country attuned to the claims of economic redistribution? It should be more social and less individualistic; more open to the ameliorative role of the state and less convinced about the inherent fairness of the market; more agreeable to the case for equal outcomes, especially with respect to the requirements of the poor, and less inclined to believe that equal opportunity suffices. On all these counts Canadians are more disposed than Americans to endorse reductions in egregious disparities of income and wealth.

Does this mean Canadians are "nicer" than Americans? Perhaps. Yet it's not only what a public says but what it does that expresses the fullness of its political convictions. To see what political culture looks like on the ground, one must assess its embodiment in policy. Chapter 4 considers a policy with particular significance to those at the bottom of the distributional ladder: welfare.

Notes

1 Lewis, *Flash Boys*, 26–27.
2 Richler, "Canadian Identity," 55.
3 It seems they are not more polite than Parisian women, however, who the *Times* said are so insufficiently vulgar that no series could be based in France. Stanley, "It's a Small World of Real Housewives."
4 According to the United Nations Office on Drugs and Crime for 2011, the United States has a homicide rate by firearm that is seven times higher than Canada's—3.5 versus 0.5 deaths, respectively, per 100,000 residents.
5 Terry, "Canadians More Upbeat than US Neighbours."
6 Inglehart, *Culture Shift in Advanced Industrial Society*, 1.
7 See, for instance, Howard-Hassmann, *Compassionate Canadians*.
8 Tawney, *Equality*, 54.
9 Lipset, *Continental Divide*, xiv.
10 See Inglehart and Welzel, "WVS Cultural Map"; Inglehart and Welzel, *Modernization, Cultural Change, and Democracy*; Adams, "America Pivots toward Progressive Canada; Brooks, "Imagining Each Other."
11 Grabb and Curtis, *Regions Apart*; Garreau, *The Nine Nations of North America*; Woodward, *American Nations*.
12 Ibid.
13 Almond and Verba, *The Civic Culture*. See also Inkeles, *National Character*.
14 See, for instance, Hartz, *The Liberal Tradition in America*; Bellah, *The Habits of the Heart*; Diggins, *The Lost Soul of American Politics*; Hofstadter, *The American Political Tradition*; Laski, *The American Democracy*; Myrdal, *An American Dilemma*; Huntington, *American Politics*; Dworetz, *The Unvarnished Doctrine*; Lipset, *The First New Nation*; Abbott, "Still Louis Hartz After All These Years."
15 For example, Morton, *The Canadian Identity*; Bell, *The Roots of Disunity*; Verney, *Three Civilizations, Two Cultures, One State*; Cook, *The Maple Leaf Forever*; Stewart, *The Origins of Canadian Politics*; Resnick, *The European Roots of Canadian Political Identity*.
16 See, Harles, *Politics in the Lifeboat*, 43–45; Wood, *The Creation of the American Republic*, 562 ff., 594 ff.; MacDonald, *Novus Ordum Seclorum*, 7–10; Pangle, *The Spirit of Modern Republicanism*, 124 ff.; Norton, *Alternative Americas*.
17 See, for instance, McHugh, "Toward a Grand Theory of the Study of Canadian Political Thought"; Grabb and Curtis, *Regions Apart*; McRae, "The Structure of Canadian History"; Horowitz, "Conservatism, Liberalism, and Socialism in Canada."
18 See, for example, Brooks, "Imagining Each Other"; Resnick, *The Labyrinth of North American Identity*; Bashevkin, *True Patriot Love*; Harles, "Multiculturalism, National Identity, and National Integration."
19 de Crèvecouer, *Letters from an American Farmer*, 44.

20 Bentley, *The Process of Government*; Dahl, *Pluralist Democracy in the United States*; Lowi, *The End of Liberalism*; Truman, *The Governmental Process*.
21 Bellah, *Habits of the Heart*. See also Diggins, *The Lost Soul of American Politics*; Ketcham, *Individualism and Public Life*.
22 Putnam, *Bowling Alone*.
23 Paine, *Common Sense and Other Political Writings*, 3.
24 See, for instance, Pew Research Center, "The American-Western Values Gap."
25 For a comparative discussion of US–Canadian differences in the understanding of law and order, see Lipset, *Continental Divide*, Chapter 6.
26 For instance, refer to *Gideon v. Wainwright* (1963), *Miranda v. Arizona* (1966), *Griswold v. Connecticut* (1965), *Roe v. Wade* (1973), *Lawrence v. Texas* (2003), *Katz v. The United States* (1967), *ACLU v. Clapper* (2015—US Court of Appeals, Second Circuit), *SpeechNow.org v. FEC* (2010—US Court of Appeals for the District of Columbia Circuit).
27 Provided they are made by groups—the so-called super PACs—whose expenditures are independent from a candidate's own election organization.
28 That decision was reaffirmed and made incumbent on individual states in *McDonald v. Chicago* (2010). Since *United States v. Miller* (1939), the right to possess a gun had generally been affirmed only insofar as it might be necessary to participate in a "well-regulated Militia"—per the language of the Second Amendment.
29 Pew Research Center, "Public Views about Guns"; Pew Research Center, "Continued Bipartisan Support for Expanded Background Checks on Gun Sales."
30 Masters, "US Gun Policy"; OECD, Better Life Index: Safety, 2014.
31 Taylor, *Reconciling the Solitudes*, 158.
32 At 478 inmates per 100,000 American residents versus a Canadian rate of 188 per 100,000. Data from the Council of Europe's annual penal statistics for 2013, as cited in Lee, "Yes, US Locks Up People at a Higher Rate than Any Other Country."
33 See, for instance, Lipset, *Continental Divide*, 94–101; Taylor, *Reconciling the Solitudes*, 158–59. In Canada, mandatory minimum sentences for possession of controlled substances for the purpose of trafficking were only introduced in 2012 and at the time of writing are being reviewed by the Supreme Court of Canada.
34 The phrase "Peace, Order, and good Government" appears in Section 91 of Canada's Constitution Act, 1867.
35 For instance, see the pamphlet given to newcomers considering applying for Canadian citizenship: Immigration, Refugees and Citizenship Canada, *Discover Canada: The Rights and Responsibilities of Citizenship*.
36 Quebec is the outlier. Instead of multiculturalism, the province is committed to "interculturalism"—the legitimacy of cultural diversity within a context where French language and culture are normative. On multiculturalism and Canadian identity, see Harles, "Multiculturalism, National Identity, and National Integration."
37 Harles, "Immigrant Integration in Canada and the United States."
38 *Andrews v. Law Society of British Columbia* (1989).
39 Canada Human Rights Commission, http://www.chrc-ccdp.ca/discrimination/apfa_uppt/page1-eng.aspx.

40 For example, see the US Supreme Court rulings on affirmative action in employment in *City of Richmond v. JA Croson Co.* (1989) and on race-based admissions policies in *Texas v. Hopwood* (1996) and *Gratz v. Bollinger* (2003).
41 For instance, see *R v. Kapp* (2008), *Athabasca Tribal Council v. Amoco Canada Petroleum Co. Ltd. et al.* (1981), *Canadian National Railway Co. v. Canada (Human Rights Comm.) and Action travail des femmes* (1987).
42 In *R. v. Oakes* (1986), the Canadian Supreme Court articulated the two-pronged Oakes test for adjudicating Charter rights. The test asks whether (1) the rationale behind a law that infringes on a Charter right is "pressing and substantial," and (2) whether the harm done to that right is proportionate to the government's objective in passing the law that impairs it.
43 With respect to mobility rights, Canadians may not expect equal treatment when relocating to a different province vis-à-vis (1) the receipt of public social services benefits or (2) programs giving hiring preferences to long-term provincial residents, provided that province's rate of employment is below the national average. The notwithstanding clause does not affect constitutional provisions concerning Canada's two official languages or the rights of members of minority linguistic communities, English or French, to have their children taught in that language under certain conditions. It also does not impinge on the Charter's acknowledgement of the rights of Indigenous communities or of the equal application of rights and freedoms regardless of gender.
44 Lipset, *Continental Divide*, 27–30, 164–65. Lipset also notes the aversion to the state of the New Left movement of the 1960s, another indication, in his view, of the anarchist strain in American radicalism. See also Foner, "Why Is There No Socialism in the United States?" The question of American socialism was famously posed by the German sociologist Werner Sombart in *Warum gibt es in den Vereinigten Staaten keinen Sozialismus?*
45 See, for example, Nevitte, *The Decline of Deference*; also Adams, "America Pivots toward Progressive Canada."
46 Bryce, *Modern Democracies*, 495.
47 U.S. Department of Commerce, 1992 Census of Governments, Volume One, Government Organization, Number Two, Popularly Elected Officials, GC92 (1)-2, June 1995.
48 This has little to do with relative population size. The biggest state legislature in the United States is the General Court of New Hampshire, with 424 representatives.
49 US data through 2015 from National Conference of State Legislatures, Ballot Measures Database. Canadian data from Qvortrup, *Referendums around the World*, 37. Although the United States has never had a national referendum, Canada has had three—on prohibition (1898), conscription (1942), and the Charlottetown Accord (1992). Most provincial governments permit referenda, but only British Columbia allows citizen-led initiatives to put measures to a public vote; almost half of American states have provisions for both.
50 Graham Spry is responsible for the famous quote, delivering it in testimony to hearings convened by the House of Commons in Ottawa. House of Commons, *Special Committee on Radio Broadcasting*, 46.
51 Lipset, *Contintental Divide*, 167–68.

52 MacPherson, *The Political Theory of Possessive Individualism*.
53 Johansen, "Property Rights and the Constitution"; Kheiriddin, "Will Property Rights Finally Get Charter Protection?"
54 Ravitch, *Reign of Error*. In 2016, 40 US states permitted charter schools. The great majority of these do not permit charters to be run directly as for-profit concerns. Yet in Michigan and Florida the majority of charters are for profit. Ohio is a variation on the theme, where more than 30 percent of nonprofit charters are managed by for-profit corporations.
55 On one estimate, in the United States just 446,000 students out of a school-age population of 56 million receive some form of public support through vouchers or tax credits for private school attendance. Goldstein, "School Choice in Iowa May Preview the One Facing Trump."
56 OECD, *Revenue Statistics: 2015 Edition*.
57 Data are for 2014. OECD, "General Government Spending," 2016; International Monetary Fund, "Public Expenditure Reform."
58 For instance, as a segment of total disbursements by all levels of government, at the cusp of the recession in 2008, expenditures for social purposes consumed 17 percent of Canadian GDP versus 16 percent in the United States. Presently, Canada holds fast at 17 percent versus 19.2 percent in the United States. OECD Social Expenditure Database (SOCX).
59 Wood, *The Radicalism of the American Revolution*, 232.
60 On populism see Shafer, "'Exceptionalism' in American Politics?"
61 See, for instance, Hochschild, *What's Fair*.
62 de Tocqueville, *Democracy in America*, 45–49. See also Martineau, *Society in America*; Trollope, *Domestic Manners of the Americans*.
63 Allen, "Equality and American Democracy."
64 See, for instance, Fatovic, *America's Founding and the Struggle over Economic Inequality*.
65 See Lipset, *American Exceptionalism*, 72–73; also Lipset and Bendix, *Social Mobility in Industrial Society*, 17.
66 Cited in Morris, "Economic Injustice for Most."
67 A recent study of Norwegian and US distributional inclinations is illuminating. In an online experiment, 1,000 "spectators" from each country were asked to decide how workers recruited via the Internet should be paid for certain computer-based tasks they had completed (such as creating a website or translating text). Americans were far more likely to regard unequal compensation as fair even when based purely on luck, whereas Norwegians were much keener to equalize earnings regardless of whether doing so came at a financial cost. Representatives of each country looked favorably on merit-based income inequality, but US respondents did so with significantly greater enthusiasm. In short, Americans were not particularly troubled by economic inequality. Almås, Cappelen, and Tungodden, "Cutthroat Capitalism versus Cuddly Socialism."
68 In particular, *Irwin Toy Ltd. v. Quebec (Attorney General)* (1989), which explicitly denied corporations the status of persons, thus economic rights, under the Charter's Section 7 guarantees of the "right to life, liberty and security of the person." On the other hand, the *Irwin* decision suggests that, like persons, corporations do have freedom of (commercial) expression under Section 2 of

the Charter, a position reiterated in *Canada (Attorney General) v. JTI-Macdonald Corp* (2007).
69 The central principles of adjudication in such instances are laid out in *Law v. Canada (Minister of Employment and Immigration)* (1999).
70 The power of the governor-general of Canada to disallow or reserve federal legislation ended in 1931 by virtue of the Statute of Westminster; with one eccentric exception, the federal government's ability to do the same via provincial legislation was last used in the 1940s. A universal right to vote in federal elections without restrictions based on property ownership or gender was recognized by the Dominion Elections Act of 1920; Indigenous peoples as well as Canadians of certain Asian ancestry, however, had longer to wait (until 1960 and 1948, respectively). In several cases, the uniform right to vote in provincial elections was slower to be extended. Thankfully, and unlike in the United States, black Canadians have never been officially prohibited from voting.
71 Porter, *The Vertical Mosaic*.
72 The online political news site Politico reports that in 2011 President Obama asked a group of well-known American historians, who gather annually for a dinner hosted by the White House, to help him find a way to "discuss the issue of economic inequality in our society without being accused of class warfare." Dovere, "Obama: Historian–in–chief."
73 On the interplay between socialism and conservativism in Canada, including the phenomenon of the "Red Tory," see Horowitz, "Conservatism, Liberalism, and Socialism in Canada."
74 Lipset, *Continental Divide*, 130–31, 155–63.
75 Esping-Anderson, *The Three Worlds of Welfare Capitalism*.
76 Key, *Public Opinion and American Democracy*, 7.
77 Newport, "Americans' Satisfaction with Ability to Get Ahead Edges Up."
78 McCall, *The Undeserving Rich*, 102. See also Kohut, "Partisan Polarization Surges."
79 Broadbent Institute, "Majority Think Income Inequality Undermines Canadian Values." See also Environics Institute, *Focus Canada 2011*.
80 Environics Institute, *Focus Canada 2011*, 12. Canadian results are from Environics' own polling of Canadians; US results are from an ABC News/Washington Post poll from November 9, 2011.
81 Canadian data from the Broadbent Institute, "The Wealth Gap," 3–7. American data in Norton and Ariely, "Building a Better America," 9–12.
82 Ibid.
83 Kuziemko, Norton, Saez, and Stantcheva, "How Elastic Are Preferences for Redistribution?"; Gimpelson and Treisman, "Misperceiving Inequality."
84 Page and Jacobs, *Class War?*, 51.
85 Ibid., 32.
86 Pew Charitable Trusts, "Economic Mobility and the American Dream."
87 Admittedly these results can fluctuate over time. So, from a highpoint of 74 percent in 2000, 60 percent of Pew respondents in 2014 indicated that "most people who want to get ahead can make it if they're willing to work hard." In Pew Research Center, "Most See Inequality Growing," 4. From 2000–16, Gallup polls reveal the same confidence among Americans that

hard work leads to economic success, with confidence being highest at 77 percent in 2002, dipping during the Great Recession and its aftermath to 53 percent (2012), and recovering to 62 percent in 2016. Newport, "Americans' Satisfaction with Ability to Get ahead Edges Up." On the other hand, see Jones, Cox, Cooper, and Lienesch, "Anxiety, Nostalgia, and Mistrust." Jones et al. find that public confidence that hard work leads to economic success has eroded by 10 points since 2013; in 2015, 64 percent of Americans said that hard work was no guarantee, though this seems an outlier among US polls.

88 For instance, in a 2014 survey of publics in 44 countries, the Pew Research Center found that 57 percent of Americans disagreed with the statement "Success in life is pretty much determined by forces outside our control," a higher percentage than in most other places and considerably higher than the global median response of 38 percent. Gao, "How Do Americans Stand Out from the Rest of the World?"

89 Alesina and Glaeser, *Fighting Poverty in the US and Europe*, Chapter 7. Environics surveys of Canada and the United States offer further comparative evidence that firm belief in the "work ethic" is an American distinctive. See Adams, "Fire and Ice Revisited."

90 World Values Survey Wave 3: 1995–1999, WVS question V172.

91 Pew Research Center, "Most See Inequality Growing," 3.

92 Davidai and Gilovich, "Building a More Mobile America."

93 Salvation Army, "The Dignity Project," 6. Granted, deciphering respondent intentions can be a challenge. Whereas less than a quarter of respondents in the same survey thought "people are poor because they are lazy," 43 percent believed that "a good work ethic is all you need to escape poverty"—the latter in tension with the 63 percent who claimed that effort alone is not enough.

94 Eighty-nine percent of Canadians and Americans thought having ambition was essential or very important to upward mobility, while 88 percent of Canadians and 92 percent of Americans said the same about hard work. Corak, "Chasing the Same Dream," Figure 6, p. 15. A 2013 Ipsos-Reid poll suggests the same Canadian conviction about the link between hard work and economic success: Two-thirds of Canadian respondents disagreed with the statement "people mostly become wealthy because they are lucky, not because they work hard." Ipsos-Reid, "Nine in Ten Canadians Support Taxing the Rich More."

95 Corak, "Chasing the Same Dream," 13–15. Environics finds that Canadian confidence that they will do better economically than their parents' generation has dipped a little to 52 percent in 2012, though three-quarters of respondents believe they will either do better or at least as well as their parents—roughly the same proportion that said so in 1990. See Environics Institute, *Focus Canada 2012*, 15.

96 Corak, "Chasing the Same Dream." Responses can be fickle. In a 2014 Pew poll, 65 percent of Americans said that the next generation will be worse off than they are, a response roughly in the middle of the pack of the advanced industrial countries polled (Canadians were not included in the survey). Pew Research Center, "Emerging and Developing Economies Much More Optimistic than Rich Countries about the Future." Alternatively, a 2012 Environics poll found

that just 38 percent of Canadians thought their children's generation would be worse off than they were. Environics Institute, *Focus Canada 2012*, 15.
97 Corak, "Chasing the Same Dream," 16.
98 See, for example, the discussion in Lipset, *Political Man*, 267–69.
99 Corak, "Chasing the Same Dream," 16. It is fair to wonder whether the anti-equality results are inflated by posing the question in such a way that fairness and equality are opposed, with the implication that a focus on equality is somehow unfair. For the United States, see also the results from the National Election Studies from 1984–2004 as reported in Bartels, *Unequal Democracy*.
100 Dugan and Newport, "In U.S. Fewer Believe 'Plenty of Opportunity' to Get Ahead." In the same survey, only 42 percent of American respondents thought there was still "plenty of opportunity in the US."
101 The statements were as follows: (1) the economic system in this country unfairly favors the wealthy; (2) business corporations do not share enough of their success with their employees; and (3) hard work and determination are no guarantee of success for most people. In Jones et al., "Anxiety, Nostalgia, and Mistrust," 20–22.
102 Newport, "Americans Continue to Say US Wealth Distribution Is Unfair."
103 Pew Research Center, "For the Public, It's Not about Class Warfare, but Fairness."
104 Among Ekos survey respondents, 51 and 55 percent, respectively, expressed these grievances. Ekos Politics, "So What's Really Bothering You Canada?"
105 Morales, "Fewer Americans See US Divided into 'Haves,' 'Have Nots.'"
106 Ipsos-Reid, "Nine in Ten Canadians Support Taxing the Rich More"; Motel, "Five Facts on How Americans View Taxes"; Parker, "Yes, the Rich Are Different."
107 Moore, "Poll Results: Poverty."
108 McCall, *The Undeserving Rich*.
109 Northrup and Jacobs, "The Growing Income Inequality Gap in Canada," 3–4.
110 For instance, according to Gallup (2015), 63 percent of Americans think that wealth should be distributed more evenly, while in a 2012 Pew poll 57 percent of US respondents say that the growing gap between the rich and poor is a bad thing for society. Newport, "US Wealth Distribution Is Unfair"; Parker, "Yes, the Rich Are Different."
111 Jones et al., "Anxiety, Nostalgia, and Mistrust," 12–13. For 62 percent of Democrats, but only 29 percent of Republicans, the growing gap between the rich and the poor was considered a critical issue in the AVS.
112 Newport, "Americans Prioritize Economy over Reducing Wealth Gap." Also see Page and Jacobs, *Class War?*, 14–19, 43–45.
113 Ekos Politics, "So What's Really Bothering You Canada?" See also Osberg and Smeeding, "'Fair' Inequality?," whose survey research (1999) confirms that Americans are more likely than Canadians to agree that "large incomes are necessary for a country's prosperity."
114 Broadbent Institute, "The Wealth Gap," 4–5.
115 Americans alone were asked the same question in 2011 and 1995; their mean answers, respectively, were 5.58 and 5.49.
116 Osberg and Smeeding also note that American responses about equality are quite polarized compared to other countries. "'Fair' Inequality?," 452, 470.

117 Environics Institute, *Focus Canada 2012*, 12.
118 Pew Research Center, "Emerging and Developing Economies."
119 "Poll Finds a More Bleak View of American Dream."
120 Seligson, Smith, and Zechmeister, "The Political Culture of Democracy in the Americas," 63–64. The authors note that distrust of state intervention is a common theme among US responses to other questions in the survey, Americans strongly agreeing that "individuals should care for their own well-being, without government involvement" (p. 63).
121 Environics Institute, *AmericasBarometer: Canada 2012*, p.55.
122 AP/NORC, "Inequality Trends in American Attitudes." More sophisticated statistical analyses of the same data suggest that, if anything, American support for government action to reduce economic inequality has diminished over time. See Ashok, Kuziemko, and Washington, "Support for Redistribtution in an Age of Rising Inequality."
123 Ibid. Not all American polls are dismissive, just most. In 2014, a Pew survey found that 69 percent of Americans thought government should do "a lot" or "some" to reduce the gap between the rich and the poor. Pew Research Center, "Most See Inequality Growing."
124 Canadian Opinion Research Archive.
125 Environics Institute, *AmericasBarometer: Canada 2012*, 56.
126 See, for instance, the discussions and data in Bartels, *Unequal Democracy*; McCall, *The Undeserving Rich*; Page and Jacobs, *Class War?*
127 McCall, *The Undeserving Rich*, Chapters 4 and 5.
128 Page and Jacobs, *Class War?*, Chapter 3.
129 Newport, "Americans Prioritize Economy."
130 Fifty-two percent, to be exact. Pew Charitable Trusts, "*Economic Mobility and the American Dream*," 3.
131 Results reported in Broadbent Institute, "Equality Project 2012."
132 Gallup World Poll as reported in OECD, *Government at a Glance: 2015*. Alternatively, see the Edelman Trust Barometer, "Annual Global Study 2016," in which 53 percent of Canadians but 39 percent of Americans express trust in government.
133 See the argument in Bartels, *Unequal Democracy*, especially Chapters 6 and 7, and McCall, *The Undeserving Rich*.
134 For instance, Newport, "Americans Favor Jobs Plan Proposals"; "CNN Poll: 7 out of 10 Support 'Buffett Rule'"; Parker, "Yes, the Rich Are Different."
135 See Korpi, "Social Policy and Distributional Conflict in the Capitalist Democracies"; see also Kellermann, "Power Resources Theory and Inequality in the Canadian Provinces."
136 Toikka, Gais, Nikolov, and Billen, "Spending on Social Welfare Programs in Rich and Poor States."
137 Bernard and Saint-Arnaud, "Du Pareil au Meme?"
138 See Kenworthy and Pontusson, "Rising Inequality and the Politics of Redistribution in Affluent Countries." See also Figures 2.5 and 2.7 in Chapter 2 of the present volume.
139 Pew Research Center, "Canada's Changing Religious Landscape."
140 de Tocqueville, *Democracy in America*, 310–19.

141 According to the Pew Research Center, over a quarter of Americans consider themselves evangelical—the largest of the religious categories for which Pew polls. Pew Research Center, "America's Changing Religious Landscape."
142 Inglehart, *Culture Shift*.

4
Policy

SUBJECT TO GLOBAL ECONOMIC IMPERATIVES for market liberalization and fiscal restraint, during the last decade of the twentieth century Canada and the United States became ardently committed to lower taxes and balanced budgets. One method of achieving such ends was to cut central government expenditures on social programs—most dramatically welfare.

In North American parlance, welfare indicates help extended to the poor via income assistance, vocational training and job placement, health insurance benefits, child care subsidies, and food support.[1] By virtue of the Canada Health and Social Transfer (CHST) and the US Personal Responsibility and Work Opportunity Reconciliation Act (PRWORA), in 1996 the majority of administrative authority and much of the policymaking and financial responsibility for such measures was devolved to subcentral tiers of government. Conditional grants from Ottawa and Washington to provinces and states were replaced by block grants, ending automatic entitlement to federally funded support. At the same time, means-tested benefits were de-emphasized in favor of work-tested benefits. Consequently, in each country welfare is now disbursed largely on the basis of an individual's accommodation to the market rather than because it is an intrinsic right of what the British sociologist T.H. Marshall famously called "social citizenship."[2]

As a means of bringing value differences into sharper resolution, the present chapter offers an overview of the Canadian and American experience with welfare reform. In doing so, it tries to make concrete the way in which Canada and the United States understand the claims of equality— specifically, the extent of any obligation to enhance the well-being of individuals at the very bottom of the income distribution. Political scientists have often observed congruence between public values and policies, one that is mutually reinforcing since policies affect the popular beliefs that forge them.[3] The evidence presented here confirms that relationship. Given similar broad-brush changes to social policy, the distinct methods whereby the two countries have engaged their most economically vulnerable citizens highlights the priorities of each. Canadian public policy has the stronger egalitarian credentials, both in its particular approach to welfare reform and in the impact that reform has had on people in low income. It may be one reason why Canada is a more mobile place than the United States. Social assistance per se is not a strategy for upward mobility, though some might claim that the work provisions of welfare reform have that intent. But it does reduce the financial and psychological stress of a circumstance—falling into poverty—that prevents people from making their way up the economic ladder.[4] For individuals of modest means, Canada's deeper commitment to equality, tangibly manifested in a more comprehensive social safety net of which welfare is just one part, leads to public strategies offering greater economic protection and opportunities for advancement than is the case in the United States.

A caveat: In even the most vibrant democracy, public policy is never purely an expression of popular cultural preference. Political institutions trace the constitutional confines within which the policymaking process operates, structuring the participation of elected officials, civil servants, interest groups, and the general public as political demands are hammered into principle, regulation, and law. So, too, policy is shaped at the intersection of the economy and the state, where balance sheets can be just as confining. And time-honored ways of proceeding—"path dependency" in the idiom of policy analysis—play a formative role, at least as a braking mechanism against changes in administrative and legislative direction. What follows does not diminish the importance of any of these. Yet ultimately policy decisions are made by flesh-and-blood actors whose choices will, to some degree, reflect national sensibilities about what should be done and how it should be done. The probability of a policy proposal being placed on the political agenda, the moral authority it commands, the legitimacy of the means whereby it is implemented, and the criteria according to which it is judged are informed by the shared convictions of the people for whom it is intended.[5] At its root, as the contours and consequences of welfare reform in the United States and Canada advise, all politics is personal.

The Immediate Context of Reform

Until the mid-1990s, social assistance in Canada and the United States was offered on the basis of a shared-cost arrangement between central and subcentral governments. The major welfare program in Canada was the Canada Assistance Plan (CAP). Established in 1966, the CAP was a conditional grant arrangement whereby Ottawa agreed to pick up half of the cost of provincial and municipal spending on welfare. The American counterpart was Aid to Families with Dependent Children (AFDC), christened in 1950 though with roots in the Social Security Act of 1935. AFDC, too, was a conditional grant program to the states for which Washington set broad parameters for eligibility and covered, by the program's end, between 50 and 80 percent of benefit costs.[6] Over time, the escalating federal share of social assistance in both countries prompted a change in policy direction. Between 1980 and 1994, US federal grants-in-aid to state and local governments for welfare exclusive of health care more than doubled, from US$18.6 billion to US$43 billion.[7] Over the same period in Canada, federal transfers to the provinces—largely in support of social assistance and health—did the same, going from C$11.5 billion to C$26.3 billion.[8] Facing budget deficits, rising unemployment, and lower tax revenues, Washington and Ottawa determined to restructure public benefits for the poor.

Federal governments in Canada and the United States played the major role in charting a new course for welfare, but it was not the same role. The CHST resembled what James Rice and Michael Prince call "reform by stealth," whereby the federal government unilaterally and without significant provincial consultation recast the national budget to achieve desired policy ends.[9] Initial response was muted. Collectively the provincial premiers requested only that cuts in federal transfers not be greater than cuts to Ottawa's own operating expenses. By comparison, neither the White House nor the federal government in general exerted decisive influence over American welfare reform. Traditionally, representatives of US state and local government agencies relied on entrenched clientele relationships with counterparts in the federal government to protect their interests and stymie reform.[10] By 1996, however, many of these same potentially blocking forces crystallized in support of a change in policy. Given the wariness of the provinces to the CHST, even more remarkable is the virtually unanimous support of the American intergovernmental lobby for welfare reform—particularly the National Governors Association and the National Conference of State Legislators, who were persuaded by an opportunity to place more of their imprint on a policy that, given national political and economic realities, was going to be devolved to them in any event. Ironic, then, that whereas Canadian welfare policy in the post-CHST era bears few traces of Ottawa's influence, Washington has an abiding presence in post-PRWORA policymaking as the principal legislator, regulator, and paymaster behind American reform.

Many aspects of the post-PRWORA and -CHST reform agenda were elaborations of existing practice. AFDC, for instance, did not require that states provide any welfare benefits to their citizens in need. Neither did states have to meet their own welfare payment targets; at the program's end, a dozen did not. Benefit levels varied widely across jurisdictions. States often received waivers from federal AFDC guidelines concerning time limits and work expectations for receipt of cash assistance. Using such waivers, by 1996 20 states had prohibitions on payment of benefits to mothers for children conceived while on welfare, 22 had a time limit for receipt of cash benefits after which work was required or benefits reduced, and 32 had raised the threshold for the earnings and assets a family could possess while its members remained on welfare. For its part, CAP included no national minimum standard welfare rate; no nationally standard appeals process in cases where welfare benefits were denied, though all of the provinces adopted their own protocols; and provinces varied significantly in the way they could count earnings and asset exemptions against the receipt of benefits.[11] States and provinces operating under AFDC/CAP also implemented a variety of programs to speed the transition from welfare to work vis-à-vis job training, job search assistance, earnings supplements, and wage subsidies paid by employers to welfare recipients. The fundamental change heralded by PRWORA and the CHST consisted of ending the shared-cost arrangement between central and subcentral governments and giving even greater decision-making authority over welfare to the states and provinces.

American Reform

When PRWORA was signed into law by President Bill Clinton in 1996, it replaced the open-ended funding of the AFDC conditional grant with Temporary Assistance for Needy Families (TANF), a fixed-sum block transfer to the states of US$16.5 billion a year that removed automatic entitlements to federal cash assistance. The Act changed the criteria for access to welfare benefits in two principal ways: (1) welfare recipients now had to work in exchange for time-limited monetary support; (2) behavioral changes were encouraged among the beneficiaries of welfare, particularly with respect to child support enforcement and teen pregnancy prevention.[12]

In TANF's original incarnation, adult welfare recipients were required to work after a maximum of two years on cash assistance. Work was specified by the federal government as including subsidized or unsubsidized employment, on-the-job training, community service, a year of vocational training, or the provision of child care services to individuals participating in community service. Single parents were expected to participate in work-related activities for at least 30 hours by fiscal year 2000, 35 hours per week for two-parent families. Families who received cash assistance for five cumulative years, less if individual states desired, were ineligible for further monetary aid. States could exempt up to 20 percent of their welfare caseload from the time limit. They could also provide noncash assistance and vouchers to families who reached the five-year deadline by drawing on a separate PRWORA Social Services Block Grant, funds targeted at families and children in crisis because of poverty or physical and mental health. To access maximum TANF support, a state needed to move a sizable fraction of its welfare recipients into work—initially 25 percent of all families were to be employed or have left the welfare rolls by fiscal year 1997, a proportion rising to 50 percent by

2002. States were also subject to a "Maintenance of Effort" (MOE) clause, whereby they were required to continue their own spending on welfare at 80 percent or more of the level reached in fiscal year 1994. Those meeting the specified requirements for moving individuals off the welfare rolls could reduce their MOE to 75 percent of the 1994 threshold. Additional federal funds were available to defray the cost of welfare in states affected by high population growth or economic difficulty and for child care beyond an initial allotment, though in these instances states were expected to have a 100-percent MOE before such top-up funds could be accessed. One billion dollars was available as a performance bonus to states that might be especially successful at moving individuals from welfare into work.

Further provisions were aimed at promoting the integrity of the family unit. Both TANF and a Child Care and Development Block Grant (CCDBG) funded care for children in need, though the CCDBG was addressed to low-income families both on and off of welfare.[13] Stringent child support measures were established, including a nationwide system to track newly employed parents who were delinquent in their child support payments as well as seizing wages and assets for nonsupport. To be eligible for TANF block grants, states had to operate a child support enforcement program meeting these federal requirements. States were obliged to outline strategies for reducing out-of-wedlock pregnancies and could draw on a $250-million federal fund to implement programs of abstinence education. They were also given a performance bonus in the form of additional federal funds for reducing out-of-wedlock births without increasing abortions. Unwed teenage mothers were expected to live at home and participate in formal education or job-training activities.

TANF's initial authorization was for five years. Subsequent to the expiration of the enabling legislation and in the absence of agreement between the Senate and the House over how the existing policy might be reformed, Congress extended the act on a temporary basis, continuing its provisions in six-month increments. Finally, in February 2006, the law was reauthorized for a further five years as part of the Deficit Reduction Act of 2005; since 2010 it has been extended on several occasions, but only in the short term. The cumulative effect has been to make welfare provisions stingier. Still capped at $16.5 billion, the basic block grant has lost a third or more of its real value to inflation. Moreover, the amount that states must spend to access the federal grant in real terms (their MOE) is just half of what it was worth in 1995.[14] But revisions in the legislation have included terms more demanding than the original. In particular, stricter work provisions for welfare eligibility have been added, including financial penalties for failing to meet the federally mandated work participation rates of 50 percent for all families receiving assistance and 90 percent for two-parent families.[15] And though states can receive credits for reducing their welfare rolls or increasing their spending on welfare-related activities, thereby reducing some of the work participation expectations, since 2005 rule changes to TANF have made those credits harder to come by.[16] As for the family-building provisions of TANF, over the last decade a $100-million annual federal disbursement for healthy marriage promotion and a further $50 million earmarked specifically for "responsible fatherhood" initiatives have been available to the states to promote the benefits of stable two-parent families.

TANF codifies what had been the practice of federal–state relations concerning welfare under AFDC but goes further, transferring a measure of autonomy in the design and administration of welfare programs in return for an annual limit on the federal contribution for social assistance and introducing additional provisions for program waivers. States vary in the way they have used this policy freedom, but typically they have been more demanding and miserly than Washington requires. With regard to the "work-first" principles of welfare reform, in most places the emphasis has been on rapid labor force entry as opposed to longer-term development of job skills through vocational education. Although federal regulations permit a two-year grace period for welfare recipients before they must work to receive cash assistance, 19 states have imposed immediate work requirements. In the majority of states the work exemption for parents with young children has been reduced to 12 months from the federally stipulated three years, though a few have chosen even shorter periods, and 12 states have no exemption at all. Almost all impose sanction policies for noncompliance with work expectations that are harsher than the TANF minimum.[17] Most have adopted the 60-month lifetime federal limit on the receipt of welfare. But a quarter of all states have significantly shorter eligibility maximums—in four of them, just 24 months.[18] Though states are permitted to exempt 20 percent of welfare caseloads from the 60-month maximum limit on cash assistance, hardly any have done so.[19]

States also differ considerably in how they choose to spend their TANF grant. Largely this is because they are permitted to use TANF and MOE funds for purposes other than cash assistance. No state has been so bold as to do away entirely with monetary benefits, which, strictly speaking, is permitted. But on balance, cash support for welfare recipients has declined and noncash assistance has increased. In 2014, basic income assistance accounted for only 26.5 percent of combined federal and state TANF/MOE expenditures on welfare, and child care and work-related support accounted for another 25 percent.[20] Given the latitude that states have for spending on noncash benefits, state policy innovations have often come in welfare-to-work support programs: asset and earnings disregards in the determination of benefit eligibility, state supplements to the federal earned income tax credit (EITC) for low-income working families, the extension of Medicaid benefits, transitional child care, and pre-kindergarten programs. Yet TANF does not require states to report the nature of noncash assistance, nor how such activities improve the well-being of low-income families. Consequently, when states have experienced budgetary shortfalls, TANF/MOE money has sometimes been redirected for purposes not directly related to the needs of the poor.

Although the number of TANF caseloads has decreased by almost two-thirds since the program's inception, the poverty rate for US families has not kept pace. The number of Americans in poverty declined until 2000, after which it has gradually increased to almost 15 percent of the population—or 46.7 million people—at present.[21] Yet the share of American families in poverty receiving TANF cash assistance has decreased, from 68 percent in 1996 to 23 percent in 2014. Presently the median national benefit, at $429 a month, is just a quarter of the national poverty threshold, and in real terms it is worth 27 percent less than in 1996. But the variation across US states is extraordinary, so much so that in 10 states 10 percent or fewer of poor families receive income assistance under TANF.[22]

In-kind government transfers are designed to give low-income families additional relief—ideally housing subsidies, the EITC, and the Supplemental Nutrition Assistance Program (SNAP—food stamps) all do. But most TANF recipients do not receive housing support, and when they do it often falls short of what is needed according to fair market rents. And while EITC takes away the economic disincentive for families on welfare who are transitioning to work, it is of use only if employment can be secured, which for individuals of modest qualifications has been no sure thing since at least the turn of the present century.[23] SNAP benefits are critical; more than eight in ten TANF households receive food stamps, at a value of around $460 a month for a family of four.[24] Even then, in all but one state TANF and SNAP combined fail to bring households up to three-quarters of the poverty line.[25] Welfare reform may not be entirely responsible for persistent poverty, but in the severity of the measures that have been implemented, especially cuts made to the cash assistance part of the program, it must bear some of the blame.

Canadian Reform

The federal legislation that served as a spark to Canadian welfare reform is not quite as byzantine. The CHST consolidated and fixed existing federal transfers under the CAP and the block Established Programs Financing (EPF) grant for health and post-secondary education. It transferred federal cash to the provinces and territories for health, post-secondary education, and welfare spending. Tax points were also transferred, a process whereby Ottawa reduces federal taxes—13.5 percent in income tax and 1 percent in corporate tax—so that provinces can raise their own by the same margin to pick up the revenue slack. Few federal restrictions have accompanied the grant, only a ban on provincial and territorial legislation establishing residency requirements for welfare recipients, save for a three-month minimum, and the abiding principles of the Canada Health Act.

In what has been called an "exercise of the federal spending power in reverse," between 1995 and 1998 federal financial support for CHST social programs was reduced by 14 percent. Once Ottawa began to register annual budget surpluses—1998 was the watershed—the public coffers opened a bit wider. Though not fully compensating for early federal cuts to social assistance, between 1997–98 and 2003–04 the CHST transfer grew by roughly 50 percent. In 2004 Ottawa disaggregated the CHST and began to transfer money for health through a separate Canada Health Transfer (CHT). It was feared the change would not bode well for future spending on social services, given that the amount of federal cash in the remnant Canada Social Transfer (CST) declined from $8.5 billion in 2003–04 to $8.4 billion in 2005–06. But in the 2007 budget, the federal government committed to putting all transfers to the provinces and territories on a "long-term track," authorizing 3-percent annual increases in the CST through 2014, in the first instance, and then, by virtue of the 2012 Budget Implementation Act, through 2024. In 2015–16, the value of the CST was just shy of $13 billion. Even so, in light of comparatively greater federal financial spending on health via the CHT, the proportion devoted to welfare and post-secondary education in the CST has diminished, from 38 percent of the total when the two programs went their separate ways to 28 percent at present.[26]

Over the life of the transfer, the formula for allocating funds has been a matter of some controversy. Initially provinces varied in their per capita CHST entitlement—from 92 percent to 111 percent of the national average—because of historic patterns of cost sharing under the CAP and the EPF. Cash payments diverged given the fluctuating value of the tax points, which were worth more in those provinces whose economies performed better than the national average. Consequently, the federal government sought to smooth the differences via an annual "Associated Equalization" payment to the provinces. Beginning in 2001, the per capita value of the CHST tax points and cash combined was made equal across all provinces and territories. Persistent concerns over inequities in funding voiced by wealthier provinces, however, prompted Ottawa to provide CST cash on an equal per capita basis beginning in 2007; a similar arrangement was introduced in 2014 for the CHT. In order that no province or territory is penalized by the revised calculations and receives less money than in a previous year, Ottawa authorizes transition protection funds to compensate for any shortfall.[27]

Ottawa offers the provinces a further unconditional federal transfer under its Equalization Program (the territories are covered under a separate Territorial Formula Financing scheme). Entrenched in Section 32 of Canada's Constitution Act (1982), equalization is a means of ensuring that poorer provinces have sufficient revenue to offer comparable levels of social services—welfare, health, education—at similar levels of taxation as their more affluent counterparts. By measuring a province's fiscal capacity—its potential revenue yield from personal, business, property, consumption, and natural resource taxes—against a 10-province average, top-up funds are distributed to have-not provinces. Since 2009, growth in the total federal payout is pegged to a three-year rolling average of the national GDP. In effect this imposes a ceiling on provincial transfers but also a floor, inasmuch as the total value of the transfer increases in tandem with growth in Canada's GDP even when fiscal disparities between the provinces are reduced. The transfer is capped so that no province that is a recipient of an equalization payment can be placed in a better fiscal position than the average of all equalization-receiving provinces—a possibility, because of how the equalization formula calculates natural resource revenues.[28] In 2015–16, federal spending on equalization and the CHT/CST accounted for roughly a quarter of all federal program spending—and between a tenth and a third of the revenue of provincial governments—of which equalization comprised 27 percent and the CHT/CST 73 percent of the $68 billion disbursed.[29]

Removal of the CAP provision for a federally mandated and provincially administered needs test as the sole criterion for welfare eligibility gave provinces and territories substantial freedom in recasting their social assistance programs. Provinces vary considerably in their welfare mix. Compared to the United States, in real terms social assistance incomes in Canada have been fairly stable across jurisdictions, even though they are not indexed to inflation.[30] Still, the adequacy of contemporary welfare payments is a subject of concern. When all welfare entitlements are considered—the combined value of cash assistance, child and additional benefits, and tax credits—only Newfoundland and Labrador exceeds Canada's after-tax low-income cut-off for a single parent with one preschool child, and no province does so with respect to welfare support for a two-parent household with two school-age children. Indeed, in half of the provinces the sum is two-thirds or less of what is required.[31] Basic cash support diverges in benefit levels and qualifying criteria. For instance, in 2014 payouts for a single-parent/single-child family ranged from a high of $13,331 in Saskatchewan to a low of $7,314 in Manitoba, while for two-parent/two-child families, Prince Edward Island was the most generous province at $18,844 and Manitoba the least, at $11,231.[32] Provincial income supplements may subsidize housing, food, transportation, health (dental, optical, prescription drugs), disability services, child care, family allowances, and transitional in-work assistance programs. And certain income—the Canada Child Tax Benefit for low- and middle-income families, the National Child Benefit for children at risk of poverty, the former Universal Child Care Benefit, and various federal and provincial tax credits—is excluded from calculations of social assistance support. Beyond these, however, provincial assets and earnings disregards diverge considerably. For a one-parent/one-child family, exemptions range from a high of $8,000 in Manitoba to a low of $1,118 in Alberta, and from a high of $16,000 in Manitoba to a low of $1,599 in Alberta for two-parent/two-child families.[33]

As in the United States, welfare caseloads in Canada have plummeted. Since the mid-1990s they have been slashed in all but one province (Ontario)—and in seven provinces by between 25 percent and 40 percent.[34] The total number of social assistance recipients has declined everywhere—in half of the provinces by between 39 percent and 54 percent.[35] National social assistance rates—recipients expressed as a fraction of the Canadian labor force between 15 and 64 years old—confirm the provincial picture. From 1996 to 2012, the rate dropped by half, from 12 percent to a little more than 6 percent of the target population.[36] Robust provincial labor markets are part of the reason, combined with welfare-to-work programs and the proliferation of child care benefits making things easier for employed low-income parents. But there are punitive incentives, too. With the exception of Newfoundland and Labrador, all provinces expect labor force participation, including training and job searches, in return for basic assistance monies. British Columbia, Ontario, Alberta, and Nova Scotia are the places where welfare retrenchment has gone the furthest, insofar as work expectations are the most severe; in all of them benefits can be reduced or eliminated for noncompliance.[37] Still, there are limits to Canadian parsimony. In 2002 British Columbia became the first and only province to introduce US-style time restrictions on social assistance—a maximum of two years in any 60-month period. It was a short-lived experiment: Public outcry led to the measure being undone (in 2004) before it could be implemented.

Safety Nets, Values, and Outcomes

Welfare reform in Canada and the United States shares many features. In neither place is there a great affection for the idea of social assistance per se.

Each country has transitioned away from a strong social safety net, whose intent is to redistribute material resources to the most economically exposed citizens, in favor of a strategy of human capital investment, furnishing low-income families with the skills they need to become regular and productive members of the workforce.[38]

Yet if crafted according to common global economic imperatives and structured in broadly similar ways, Canadian and American approaches to welfare are informed by the public values specific to each. That is to be expected. Welfare states expanded among and within industrial democracies because the programs they instituted were a means of securing political legitimacy, citizens affirming the state's moral authority to rule as a quid pro quo for valued social benefits and norms. All the more reason, then, that to be considered equally legitimate the deconstruction of the welfare state should be defended in terms of a country's characteristic political ethos.

American welfare reform was cast explicitly as a values issue. During the policy debates of the early 1990s, leaders of the Democratic and Republican parties appealed to fundamental American ideals of freedom, in particular of "liberating the poor" from a cycle of welfare dependency—that is to say from government support.[39] In good populist fashion, US public officials championed the devolution of welfare responsibility to the states, an instance of bringing government closer to the people with accompanying strictures against laziness and promiscuity. The cumbersome title of the watershed legislation, the Personal Responsibility and Work Opportunity Reconciliation Act, drove home the message. Any help to households in want was to be decidedly brief, as the block grant portion of the bill—Temporary Assistance for Needy Families—denoted.

Ordinary citizens appear to have had the same understanding. Polling evidence confirms that Americans strongly support requiring able-bodied individuals to work in return for limited welfare benefits.[40] In a 1995 survey, two-thirds of US respondents said the most upsetting thing about welfare was that it encouraged people to adopt the wrong values and lifestyle; only 14 percent believed it cost too much in tax money.[41] It's not that Americans are uniquely cold hearted. But they seem to make a distinction between the poor—who should get help—and those on welfare who are most likely lazy and undeserving.[42] Hence the American citizenry's affirmation of things like improving schools in low-income areas, increased subsidies for daycare, subsidized housing, tax credits for low-income families, and special educational programs like Head Start, but their lack of enthusiasm for welfare. That Social Security is the most popular social assistance program in the United States is indicative—a universal old-age pension scheme not based on need or collective solidarity, but rather tied in the popular imagination to a person's work history and individual effort.

The reaction of the Canadian public is more difficult to gauge. According to Statistics Canada, there are no published polls on Canadian attitudes toward welfare reform. For the national government, however, it has always seemed a simple matter of fiscal and constitutional probity, of downloading federal resources to the provinces, which are constitutionally responsible for administering social assistance. When Liberal Finance Minister Paul Martin addressed the subject in his 1995 Budget Speech, his emphasis was on political pragmatism: "[We] believe that the restrictions attached by the federal government to transfer payments in areas of clear provincial responsibility should be minimized. ... [The] cost sharing approach of the past no longer helps the provinces, who have clear responsibility to design and deliver social assistance programs, to do so in a way that is as effective as possible and in tune with local needs."[43] What the minister did not say was that the CHST also signified the cascading of financial burdens, as subcentral governments have been expected to shoulder more of the weight of increasingly expensive social provision, especially health insurance.

The Privatization of Assistance

American reform is just as calculating if not so prosaic. It speaks to an explicit preference for bootstraps individualism and market-based justice. Consequently, the United States has enacted rules for social assistance that are more harsh and invasive than those found in Canada. Table 4.1 lists several of the key cross-national distinctions.

Eager to diminish the attractiveness of entitlements and to hasten the transition from welfare to work, Washington and most state governments have starved welfare programming of funds, especially the cash assistance part of that programming. Budgetary emphasis has been on work support measures, including tax credits, child care, and raising assets and earnings disregards, to smooth the entry of welfare recipients into the labor market—more precisely, to compel it. To reiterate, whereas the federal block grant for social services in Canada has increased in real terms since 1998, and will continue to grow by at least 3 percent per year through 2024, in the United States the annual federal transfer for social assistance to the states has been frozen since 1996 and has lost a third of its value. American states have been unable or unwilling to make up the difference.[44] A consequence is that the cash portion of welfare has been dramatically reduced to 26.5 percent of combined TANF and MOE outlays and constitutes less than 10 percent of benefits in 10 states. By contrast, monetary support remains the largest part of welfare assistance in every Canadian jurisdiction.[45] While a federally mandated 60-month time limit is placed on the receipt of US welfare,

Table 4.1 Key Differences in US/Canadian Welfare Reform Legislation

	United States	Canada
Title	Personal Responsibility and Work Opportunity Reconciliation Act, 1996 (PRWORA); Deficit Reduction Act of 2005 (DRA)	Canada Health and Social Transfer, 1996 (CHST); Canada Social Transfer, 2004 (CST)
Type and amount of transfer	Federal block grant, fixed at US$~6.5 billion per year for social assistance, including child care	Federal block grant, varies; in 2015–16, C$40 billion for welfare and secondary education; real value to increase by 3 percent per year from 2007–24
Time limits on receipt of benefits	Sixty-month federal maximum, less if states so determine; 24 months or less in 13 states	Legislated in British Columbia in 2002 (imposed 24-month maximum) but never implemented and overturned in 2004
Work requirements	Federal requirement that recipients must work after a maximum of two years on assistance; 19 states with immediate work requirements Three-year federal work exemption for parents with young children; reduced to 12 months in majority of states; 12 states with no exemption Fifty percent of families in state caseload must engage in "work activity" for at least 30 hours a week, 20 hours for families with young children Ninety percent of two-parent families in state caseload must be in work activity for 35 hours per week	Ontario is the only province to impose mandatory job expectations in exchange for benefits; four-month grace period before requirement takes effect No province refuses an exemption for parents with young children
State/provincial penalties for breaking work expectation	All states impose financial penalties; in 45 states, penalty means cessation of benefits; in six states, lifetime ban on benefits a possibility	Four provinces impose financial penalties, including cessation of benefits, for failure to meet work or work-seeking expectations; no province threatens lifetime ban on benefits
Behavioral changes	States must offer strategies to reduce out-of-wedlock pregnancy Federal funds available for state-based abstinence education Cash bonus for recipients of assistance to marry (PRWORA) Healthy Marriage Promotion and Responsible Fatherhood initiatives (DRA)	No equivalent
Equalization transfers or payments	No	Yes

22 American states have imposed shorter periods and 13 have limits of two years or less. In Canada, only British Columbia has attempted, unsuccessfully, to do the same.[46]

Unlike their provincial counterparts, US states are under threat of financial penalty for failing to meet federally mandated work participation rates in a given year. Nineteen states impose immediate work requirements for individuals on welfare, a standard more exacting than the federal expectation of work after a maximum two years of assistance and a provision shared by no Canadian province. Twelve states modify the three-year federal work exemption for parents with young children by substituting zero exemptions; no province has the temerity to do likewise. Should a welfare recipient not fulfill his or her expected work contract, all US states, though just four Canadian provinces, impose financial penalties for noncompliance. In all but five American states such violations require the complete cessation of cash benefits; in six states—though no province—a lifetime ban is a possibility.

Welfare in the United States has been privatized in another way. The willingness of government to wed political power to private ethics is a function of the moralism of American public discourse and speaks to the heightened place of religion in US politics. Compared to Canada, where cash is the greater part of the social assistance mix, there is at least a hint of paternalism in the inclination of American governments to severely cut the monetary portion of welfare, a reluctance to trust the spending choices of the neediest citizens. More importantly, cash bonuses to states for marriage promotion, reducing out-of-wedlock births without increasing the number of abortions, abstinence education, campaigns for responsible fatherhood, and stringent child support measures are all exclusively part of the American agenda. So is the involvement of religious organizations in the administration of welfare services. "Charitable Choice" provisions of PRWORA encourage federal and state governments to contract with faith-based organizations to deliver publicly funded welfare services—job training, transportation services, housing assistance, and child care, among others.[47] Churches in Canada rarely play this direct role in the provision of public social assistance, functioning instead as advocacy organizations for welfare-related objectives.

The most prominent religious voices in the American welfare debate have typically been conservative evangelicals who wish to reconfigure social policy in terms of a religious vision of individual conversion and decorum, one transforming personal behavior not socioeconomic structures.[48] There is precedent for this view. Organized religion's political efforts in the United States have often aimed at generalizing standards of righteous individual conduct—as Sabbatarian laws, prohibition, and more recently the anti-abortion and anti–same-sex marriage crusades suggest. Canadian social reform rarely elicits the same kind of moral enthusiasm. Religion does shape the perspective of many Canadian civic leaders about welfare, but in a way that tries to balance personal moral commitments against political and social awareness.[49] At least there is no Canadian equivalent to the pietistic political fervor of the contemporary American religious right. Quite the opposite: Outside of Quebec, perhaps, when religion has had an explicit political impact, in modern Canada it has often been manifested in movements of the left—the influence of the social gospel tradition on the founding of the CCF/NDP is a prime example.[50]

Religious people are often particularly disposed to use private charity as a means of addressing economic need. Americans, who indicate more formal religious commitment than the citizens of any other advanced industrial democracy, and who are typically suspicious of government's palliative role, seem particularly keen.[51] A quarter of Americans, though little more than a fifth of Canadians, donate to charity, whereas in the aggregate Americans direct 1.39 percent of their income to charitable causes and Canadians just 0.56 percent.[52] Canada's relative tightfistedness is not unusual; the citizens of most advanced industrial democracies tend to think of charity as a top-up to what should principally be a matter for government. Private economic largesse is not a function of one's material blessings, however. Individuals in the lowest fifth of US earners give proportionately more on average—3.09 percent of their pre-tax income—than do Americans in any other quintile, including those at the top who give just 1.33 percent.[53] Not all of this goes to individuals in economic want, of course. It is least likely to do so when its source is the wealthiest members of society, who prove more eager to fund arts centers and university lecture halls than soup kitchens.[54]

In all events, charitable means of redressing public privation are hardly adequate. Philanthropy that benefits the poor is not sufficiently countercyclical, to use the term favored by economists. It tends to diminish as the economy weakens, just when material needs are the greatest. And it is fair to ask whether citizens contribute out of compassion for their less fortunate compatriots or simply because they wish to take advantage of the revenue code. To be sure, the United States is a leader among advanced industrial countries in using its tax system, via deductions and credits, to achieve social purposes, such instruments being a third more powerful than similar measures in Canada.[55] But this comes at a cost. In engaging the material requirements of its citizens, relative to Canada the government in the United States is more often used to induce good behavior than require it, and social assistance that depends on the voluntary cooperation of the private sector cannot be secure in the long term. If the construction of the modern welfare state in Europe and North America has taught us anything, it is that.

Equality

Egalitarian sympathies in welfare reform are stronger north of the border. To begin with, equalization payments, which address the "federalism trap" in social programs—the acceptable range of variation in benefits, eligibility, and administration across jurisdictions—are not as forthcoming in the United States as they are in Canada. Since the intent of equalization is to underwrite the ability of subcentral governments to offer comparable levels of social services at similar rates of taxation, differences in public provision are narrower between provinces than states. With respect to the cash portion of welfare, for instance, consider the gap between the least and most generous Canadian and American jurisdictions: a single-parent/single-child family in Manitoba receives 54 percent of what it would in Saskatchewan, but a single-parent/two-child household in Mississippi receives just 18 percent of what the same family collects in Alaska (and only 21 percent of what it would receive in New York, the next runner-up).[56] Equalization is not without controversy. Canadian critics argue it encourages a "beggar thy neighbor" attitude, in which economic decisions in one province may reduce the size of the federal grant owed to another, and that it is a de facto subsidy from economically responsible provinces to those less conscientious. But if caseloads, cash assistance coverage, and poverty rates are any indication, equalization gives Canadian provinces the ability to more adequately address the circumstances of their neediest residents—an instrument, and arguably a disposition, that American states do not share.

American and Canadian beliefs about minority–majority group relations and the requirements of equality across them affect welfare policy too. More than 50 years ago the Swedish economist Gunnar Myrdal wrote that the fundamental dilemma of American society was a political creed that promised equality to all while delivering on the promise to all but African-Americans.[57] Clearly American welfare policy has shaped and been shaped by the uniquely difficult relationship between black and white Americans. One can make a good case that the landmark 1935 Social Security Act, the template of the American welfare state, was designed to accommodate the demands of southern politicians to keep poor relief for the aged, women, and blacks decentralized. Initially, agricultural and domestic workers, a large percentage of whom were African-American, were excluded from Social Security coverage. During the 1950s and 1960s, southern states and the senators who represented them fought federal welfare initiatives for fear of driving up the cost of cheap, largely black labor and thereby losing market advantage. Since then, the general trend has been toward a nationalization of US social policy, including welfare, in the interest of racial minorities. Policy devolution under PWRORA has threatened those interests. African-Americans are among the ethnoracial groups hardest hit by poverty, they are residentially concentrated in states with the harshest welfare provisions, and they are the group most likely to be cut off from income assistance.[58] Many of their fellow citizens are untroubled. Poll evidence indicates that Americans often "hate welfare" because they believe black recipients of cash assistance do not merit it.[59]

Canada's largest ethnocultural minority, Francophones, have been a force for the decentralization of social assistance but not its reduction. In recognition that Quebec is the primary place of residence of one of Canada's three founding peoples, and inasmuch as the Canadian political tradition is relatively solicitous of group identity and rights, Ottawa has devolved important aspects of social policy to the province. Unlike the situation in the United States, where no state can speak on behalf of black majority interests and African-Americans are susceptible to the actions of state governments beyond their control, in Canada provincial power with respect to Quebec can be understood as a means of securing Francophone well-being. In the name of provincial and cultural autonomy, Quebec has frequently resisted national programs regarding social policy, as decisions to opt out of Canadian pension and child benefit plans indicate. But in Canada, greater provincial responsibility for welfare programming as stipulated under the CHST and now the CST does not clearly discriminate against a particular minority group. Since dependence on social welfare benefits is not significantly higher in Quebec than elsewhere, there is no accompanying perception that Canada's changing welfare regime is especially disadvantageous to Francophones. If the situation were otherwise, in the interest of equality Ottawa would almost certainly be forced to respond.

Given that welfare seeks to improve the living conditions of the worst-off citizens, it is by nature an equality-affirming social policy. Although American scholars have been circumspect about the initial impact of TANF on poverty, since the Great Recession there is mounting evidence that it aggravates the difference between the haves and have-hardly-anything-at-alls.[60] Income support has been whittled away in all but two states, and with it the percent of the US poverty threshold it covers—from a high of 47.5 percent in Arizona to a low of 2 percent in Texas.[61] Expressed as a fraction of the low-income cut-off, the range of variation for cash assistance is smaller in Canada—from 64 percent of LICO in Saskatchewan to 30 percent in Manitoba—and the level of that assistance has more of an effect. Indeed, at 26 percent, the median American state cash benefit as a percentage of the poverty line is lower than in any Canadian province.[62] Provinces have just as much policy latitude to cut welfare as do American states—if anything they have more. It's simply that on most counts, they choose not to use it.

Risk of falling into poverty as the result of a dip in the US economy has grown as well. Under TANF, real cash support does not expand with a family's additional income needs—indeed, it often contracts.[63] Should employment rates be buoyant, strict market-based strategies of "ending welfare as we know it" can meet with success, but that success is fleeting if the economy sours. Thus, a growing proportion of unmarried American mothers with a high school education or less—prime candidates for welfare—entered the workforce during the first few years after PRWORA. However, early in the new millennium, once the US economy began to sputter, their participation in the labor market began steadily to decline—from about 76 percent in 2000 to 63 percent in 2013, or just a couple of points more than what it was when welfare reform first took effect.[64] Social assistance rates in Canada are strongly linked to labor markets too.[65] Yet Canadian welfare reform is not as draconian in its work provisions, leaving more room for public support, especially cash support, of individuals in jeopardy when markets fail—a cushion on which their American counterparts cannot rely.

US reform is not solely responsible for the intensification of poverty, of course, but neither is it well equipped to diminish it. In 1996, more than two-thirds of all households in poverty were enrolled in TANF; presently, less than a quarter are.[66] And while the number of American families with children in poverty has been rising, welfare caseloads have been falling. Caseloads and recipients have declined in Canada as well, though it's worth remarking by how much. Between 1996 and 2015, the number of US households receiving cash assistance dropped by 63 percent and individual recipients by 66 percent; from 1996 through 2014, Canada realized a decline of 14 percent in caseloads and 31 percent among recipients.[67] Discrete macroeconomic forces may explain some of the cross-border variance, but the gap is so large it can hardly explain all of it.

Monetary assistance does not exhaust a government's poverty-fighting arsenal. Welfare reform includes a host of initiatives—job training; child benefits; tax credits; and medical, housing, and transportation subsidies—designed to weaken the grip of poverty. Consequently, the official poverty rate in the United States can be misleading, since it is purely a cash-sensitive measure and exempts noncash public benefits from its calculations. Most importantly food support, which the United States offers under SNAP but which has no federal corollary in Canada, might be factored into the mix. Yet in no state is SNAP plus TANF enough to raise the value of assistance beyond the poverty mark.[68] And while over the long term the sum of welfare reform has not been sufficient to significantly dent the American poverty rate—whether by the official cash-exclusive or the supplemental noncash-inclusive US standard—individuals in the most desperate circumstances have been hit the hardest.[69] Progressive tightening of income assistance eligibility and benefit cuts have led to an increasing number of Americans in deep poverty—individuals whose household income is less than half of the threshold—as well as extreme poverty—those who live on $2 or less a day. Since the mid-1990s, there has been a 36 percent jump among Americans with the former status, to 21.6 million people in all, and a 160 percent increase in those in the latter situation, to 5.6 million.[70]

Welfare reform in Canada has not had the same deleterious effect. There is some evidence that for Canadians in low-income status the average distance beneath the LICO threshold at which they find themselves (the poverty gap) has increased since the mid-1990s; in that sense their hardship has grown, albeit modestly.[71] An analysis of reform at the regional level suggests that the overall impact has been mixed: In half of the provinces the percentage of people in poverty has gone down or stayed the same, while in the other half the poverty rate has gone up.[72] Yet over the same period, the total number of Canadians in low income has dropped by 42 percent.[73]

Given different official understandings of poverty in Canada and the United States—strictly speaking, LICO is not a poverty measure—it is difficult to get a common reading of the merits of their respective policies. When one draws the poverty line at half of the median income, the comparative standard adopted by many economists, Canadian welfare is estimated to reduce the number of individuals in poverty by about half, its US equivalent by roughly one-quarter.[74] As Chapter 1 relates, over the last 30 years, by international as well as national standards, poverty rates in Canada have been consistently lower than in the United States. And while the poverty rate in the United States has moved higher in the two decades since welfare reform, and the magnitude of that poverty has increased sharply for millions of Americans, over the same period in Canada the poverty rate—or at least its LICO proxy—has been cut and any deepening of low-income status has been relatively minimal. Acknowledging this north-of-the-border advantage does not discount the very real hardship suffered by Canadians in economic distress, a burden that falls more heavily on some communities than others—First Nations, in particular. But a tentative conclusion seems justified: With respect to welfare outcomes, Canada's greater public generosity makes a difference.

Beyond Welfare

On balance, the Canadian social safety net is more encompassing and better funded than its American counterpart—both for people in poverty and not. Canada's system of publicly financed universal health care, including widespread political recognition of a citizen's right to health care, is the most dramatic cross-border difference, but it is not the only one. Unemployment assistance, child care, child-centered tax benefits and monetary supplements, and sales tax refunds for people in low income are all part of a basic Canadian advantage, though the extent of it depends on the size and work status of the household at issue.[75] Pensions are the one area where social protection may not be clearly better in Canada. Yet according to OECD rubrics, proportionately fewer seniors are in poverty in Canada than in the United States—6.7 percent to 21.5 percent—and the safety net for retired low-income Canadian workers is more substantial.[76] Other differences between the two countries have a bearing as well. Levels of unionization and the bargaining power of organized labor, government-funded job-training programs, and mandated work protections and amenities—that is, provisions against unfair dismissal, paid family leave and sick leave, and vacation benefits—are all more favorable to income security in Canada than in the United States.[77]

This Canadian edge is largely a post–World War II development. There was little to choose between Canadian and American approaches to social policy until the combined effects of the Depression and the war caused their paths to diverge. As already noted, relative to many advanced industrial countries, particularly European ones, Canada and the United States remain welfare state laggards, more inclined to defer to the market than not. In 2014, public social expenditure was equivalent to 17 percent of the Canadian GDP as opposed to 19.2 percent in the United States—a difference due largely to the stronger impact of the Great Recession in the United States, though in both cases below the OECD average.[78] Heightened spending doesn't necessarily indicate the greater benevolence of a polity, of course, since part of the reason for it may have to do with the way in which social provision is structured. For instance, as a proportion of GDP the United States spends over 50 percent more on health care than does any other advanced industrial democracy; much of that is due to the administrative cost of running a decentralized and complicated mixed public–private system. It does not mean that the United States is more committed to public health than other countries, and certainly not that Americans are healthier.

But the raw data on expenditure do suggest policy priorities. They indicate that Canada is more distributionally sensitive and in an economic sense less solidly liberal than the United States. So, of all the social benefits paid out in the two countries, considerably more are directed to recipients in the lowest income quintile in Canada than in the United States. The bottom fifth of Canadian earners receive 26.4 percent of such disbursements, their American counterparts 21.8 percent. Conversely, the highest quintile takes a bigger share in the United States, 16.2 percent versus 12 percent in Canada.[79] As in the case of welfare, American governments are reluctant to disburse cash assistance as part of aggregate social spending; Canada puts nearly twice as much into the pockets of its working-age population.[80] Neither are such monetary benefits for working people or for pensioners likely to be means tested in the United States—roughly a quarter are, as opposed to a little more than half in Canada. Private spending for social purposes is weighted heavily south of the border. Around a third of total US expenditures for social protection come from nongovernmental actors, employers in particular, whereas around a fifth do in Canada.[81] Mainly that is because over half of American health care is privately funded, far higher than for any other OECD member.[82] The same market-based preferences are apparent when it comes to pensions; the United States spends significantly more privately funding them than does any rich democratic country, Canada included.[83]

Informed speculation to be sure, but it's hard not to detect in all this the enduring effect of cultural values on strategies of social protection. Canada's greater sensitivity to collective well-being and the ameliorative role of the state are expressed in public policies that engage poverty and low-income status more diligently than in the United States.[84] South of the border, private markets and the individual self-reliance they imply take precedence in the civic affections, less so the demands of economic equality.

Concluding Remarks

Do Canadians care more than Americans about their fellow citizens in economic distress? Yes, at least insofar as the specific measures used to confront it are a by-product of the values each public holds dear. When it comes to social policy, Canada is a more compassionate place than the United States. Compared to their social democratic European peers, it's true that differences in approach are not always marked. Yet among the Americans and Canadians for whom welfare policy is intended, even the slightest variations of outlook are important—an instance of the small, but sometimes not so small, differences that matter. South of the border, public values are more individualistic and market driven; north of it they are more communitarian and open to using the state to achieve desired social objectives. And while both countries pay homage to equality, economic and otherwise, in practice it is harder to square that commitment with an unbridled enthusiasm for the private sector, since markets are largely indifferent to distributional outcomes. No surprise, then, that poverty has responded better to welfare reform grounded in the Canadian than the American ethos.

Values are never the whole of the explanation for political outcomes. Economic realities; the momentum of public policies fashioned over time; political institutions; and underlying divisions of ethnicity, race, gender, and class will all have their say. Yet even when one or more of these factors are mooted to account for Canadian and American policy distinctions, as race often is with respect to the peculiar trajectory of welfare policy in the United States, it's difficult to escape the persistent influence of political culture. Indeed, discrimination against African-Americans, politically, socially, and economically, speaks volumes about the limits of US commitment to egalitarian principles. Moreover, as the characteristic development of welfare reform policies in Canada and the United States suggests, regardless of uniform transnational economic pressures—in this case, the neoliberal constraints of globalization—identikit social policy is not destiny. Deep citizen convictions about the nature of social and economic reform can yet find their way into public policy.[85]

There is no easy causality from political culture to policy outcomes. Public policies express the ideals of a given political community, but by reifying those ideals in law they also help shape them. The iconic status of public health insurance in Canada, now widely embraced as a defining feature of national identity and which in the Canadian view distinguishes a more humane Canada from the United States, is a good example. Things weren't always so clear.[86] Yet over time, the scope and generosity of Canadian medical provision has enhanced the public's commitment to redress the economic disadvantage of its less prosperous members—or to put it more starkly, to refuse to value some lives more highly than others. This relationship between public values and outcomes is always mutually reinforcing. But if Canadians are more attuned to the requirements of economic equality than Americans, in part it is because the greater egalitarian sensibilities embedded in Canadian social policy help make them that way. It's an important reminder, to borrow a litany intended for loftier purposes, that political values are expressed not only in thought and word but also in deed.

Notes

1 Unlike the United States, Canada has no separate federal supplemental nutrition assistance program for low-income families.
2 Marshall, *Citizenship and Social Class*.
3 For instance, Page and Shapiro, "Effects of Public Opinion on Policy"; Burstein, "The Impact of Public Opinion on Public Policy."
4 On the other hand, research does show that income support to the families of poor and young children has a positive effect on their earning potential and thus their upward economic mobility in adulthood. See Duncan and Magnusson, "The Long Reach of Early Childhood Poverty."

5   See the discussion in Béland, "Ideas and Social Policy"; Pal, *Beyond Policy Analysis*, 126 ff.
6   Weaver, *Ending Welfare as We Know It*, 19.
7   US Department of Commerce, National Income and Product Accounts Table, Table 3.17, "Selected Government Expenditures by Function."
8   Soucy and Wrobel, "Federal Spending."
9   Rice and Prince, *The Changing Politics of Canadian Social Policy*.
10 R. Kent Weaver offers an excellent account of how welfare reform was stymied in the 25 years before passage of the PRWORA. See Weaver, *Ending Welfare as We Know It*, Chapter 4.
11 Moscovitch, "The Canada Assistance Plan."
12 It should be noted that the PRWORA also changed eligibility requirements for Supplemental Security Income—a benefit for low-income seniors, individuals with certain disabilities, and children in medical distress—as well as food stamps, most importantly by limiting the access of recent immigrants. Most of the restrictions on immigrants have since been lifted.
13 Under the 1996 law, states might transfer up to 30 percent of their TANF funds to the CCDBG (the ceiling has since been raised), though 70 percent of that spending was required to go to welfare recipients. Child care subsidies counted as cash assistance and could trigger time limits. The CCDBG has continued to be funded on a successive short-term basis until 2014, when it was formally reauthorized and funded through fiscal year 2020 at between $5.26 billion (FY 2015) and $5.65 billion (FY 2020) per year.
14 In mid-2015, for instance, 17 states had the same nominal benefit level as they had in 1996, and in a further six states nominal benefit levels were actually lower than in 1996. Floyd and Schott, "TANF Cash Benefits Have Fallen by More than 20 Percent."
15 To date, financial penalties have been light, but strictly speaking they can be worth as much as 5 percent of the TANF transfer. To be able to access TANF funds, initially states had to increase minimum workforce participation rates by annual increments of 5 percent until they reached a ceiling of 70 percent in 2010. Presently work-rate expectations, which includes activities like vocational training that are outside of employment, are at 50 percent for all families receiving assistance (for at least 30 hours a week; 20 hours a week for single parents with one or more children under 6) and 90 percent for two-parent families (at a combined 35 hours per week; 55 percent if given child care subsidies). States can receive a caseload reduction credit, against which they can lower their workforce expectations, by decreasing the number of households on welfare or spending on welfare-related programs. Otherwise, about a third of all states fail to meet federal work expectations.
16 From 1998 to 2006, the law reduced work participation requirements by one percentage point for each 1 percent decline in caseloads, against a baseline of 1995. Since the Deficit Reduction Act of 2005, however, the baseline year was changed to 2005, beginning in 2007. According to the Congressional Budget Office, the change increased the required participation rate by more than 25 percentage points in almost half of the states. As a consequence, states have been more eager than ever to deny cash assistance to TANF recipients. Others have pursued alternative PRWORA provisions, which award caseload

credits reducing work participation mandates if states exceed MOE spending requirements on welfare. Due to an expansive federal interpretation of what counts as welfare, this spending can be funneled to programs attempting to reduce out-of-wedlock pregnancies or encouraging two-parent families, and not directed at low-income families per se. Even after caseload reduction credits, in 2012 13 states failed to meet the all-family work target. See Congressional Budget Office, "Temporary Assistance for Needy Families."

17 Six states have the potential for a permanent termination of benefits: Idaho, Indiana, Michigan, Mississippi, Pennsylvania, and Washington. In Huber, Cohen, Briggs, and Kassabian, "Welfare Rules Databook," 224–30.
18 Arkansas, Arizona, Idaho, and Indiana. Ibid., pp. 176–77.
19 See Jenson, "Redesigning the 'Welfare Mix' for Families," v; Weaver, *Ending Welfare as We Know It*, 344 ff; Shafer, "'Exceptionalism' in American Politics?," 16–19.
20 US Department of Health and Human Services data. https://www.acf.hhs.gov/sites/default/files/ofa/2014_tanf_moe_national_data.pdf?nocache=1447434621.
21 US Census Bureau, Current Population Survey, Annual Social and Economic Supplements.
22 Floyd, Pavetti, and Schott, "TANF Continues to Weaken as a Safety Net."
23 Center on Budget and Policy Priorities, "Chart Book: TANF at 19."
24 In order to be eligible for SNAP, a family's gross monthly income normally must be at or below 130 percent of the poverty line. After deductions for various expenses—for example, medical expenses, child support, child care, and housing—net income must be at or below the poverty line. Family assets must also fall below certain limits.
25 The exception is Alaska; see Floyd and Schott, "TANF Cash Benefits Have Fallen by More Than 20 Percent."
26 Gauthier, *The Canada Social Transfer*. At a little over $34 billion for 2015–16, the value of the CHT is now more than two-and-a-half times greater than the CST. The CHT will have grown by a federally stipulated 6 percent annually between 2004 and 2016–17, after which time it is guaranteed to increase by at least 3 percent per year through 2024.
27 Ibid.
28 "A province's actual fiscal capacity includes 100 percent of its resource revenues. However … [only] half of those revenues—at the most—count towards Equalization's measure of provincial fiscal capacity. Therefore, it is possible for a province to be entitled to an Equalization payment but, after receiving the payment, to have a higher actual fiscal capacity than a province that is not entitled to an Equalization payment. The purpose of the fiscal capacity cap is to eliminate this possibility." In Roy-César, "Canada's Equalization Formula."
29 Department of Finance Canada, "Federal Support to Provinces and Territories."
30 See Tweddle, Battle, and Torjman, *Welfare in Canada 2014*, Appendix B.
31 Ibid., Table 3, 41–42. Shortfalls with respect to the more geographically sensitive Market Basket Measure of low-income status are greater still; Table 4, 43–44. See also Kneebone and White, "An Overview of Social Assistance Trends in Canada," as well as Murphy, Heisz, and Zhang, "Low Income and Inequality Trends in Canada."

32 Figures are for a single-parent with a two-year-old child, and a two-parent household with two children, ages 10 and 15. Tweddle, Battle, and Torjman, *Welfare in Canada 2014*, 50–53.
33 Figures are for liquid asset exemptions; fixed assets tend to be exempt from the calculations. As for monthly earnings exemptions, deployed as a financial incentive to make the transition from welfare to work, for both single- and two-parent families PEI excludes all income up to $125 per month, plus 10 percent of any additional income, whereas in Ontario the comparables are $200 and 50 percent. Ibid., 7, 9–11.
34 In addition to Ontario, where caseloads have risen by 3.4 percent, the two other provinces where cuts haven't been quite as deep are Manitoba (a 9.2-percent reduction) and Alberta. Alberta is only a partial exception to the pattern, since the number of Albertans in the Alberta Works program has diminished (by 15 percent) but the number of disabled residents who are part of the province's Assured Income for the Severely Handicapped program has increased, leading to an overall increase in the number of Albertans on social assistance. In Caledon Institute of Social Policy, "Canada Social Report." Data are for 1996–97 through 2013–14.
35 The six provinces are Nova Scotia (54 percent), Newfoundland and Labrador (50.7 percent), British Columbia (46.8 percent), New Brunswick (42.6 percent), Saskatchewan (40 percent), and Quebec (39 percent). Ibid.
36 Kneebone and White, "An Overview of Social Assistance Trends in Canada."
37 As of 2016, the Government of Quebec is considering similar measures to reduce assistance for noncompliance with work expectations. The Ontario Works program, instituted in 1998, makes Ontario the sole province to impose mandatory employment stipulations, including unpaid community service work, in exchange for benefits.
38 See, for instance, Banting, "Dis-embedding Liberalism?," 417–52; Weaver, *Ending Welfare as We Know It*.
39 See the fascinating discussion in DeParle, *American Dream*, Chapter 7.
40 See the survey done for the Kaiser Family Foundation and the John F. Kennedy School of Government, "National Survey on Poverty in America," and more recently for the Rasmussen Report, in which only 7 percent of Americans say they oppose workfare requirements: "83% Favor Work Requirement for Welfare Recipients."
41 Ibid.
42 See, for instance, Gilens, *Why Americans Hate Welfare*. The stronger individualized orientation of the American public is well captured in a World Values Survey question last asked in 1990: "Why are there people in this country living in need?" "Laziness" was the first-choice answer of American respondents, with 38.5 percent of the poll; among Canadians "laziness" tied with "injustice," each answer receiving 31 percent support. WVS question E190.
43 "Budget Speech," the Honourable Paul Martin, PC, MP, Minister of Finance, February 27, 1995. Accessed at www.fin.gc.ca/budget95/speech/SPEECH6E.html.
44 States can have radically different priorities. So, for instance, in 2009, 80 percent of poor families in California received social assistance while in Texas only 8 percent did. Rogers, "New Welfare Reform Directive Creates Unlikely Political Issue for Obama."

45 Falk, "The Temporary Assistance for Needy Families (TANF) Block Grant," Appendix B; Tweddle, Battle and Torjman, *Welfare in Canada 2014*, Appendix A.
46 Lower-Basch, "Cash Assistance."
47 There are no aggregate data indicating the percentage of TANF activities for which faith-based organizations are responsible, though in a 2004 study, 78 percent of the 34 state TANF agencies analyzed awarded contracts to such groups. Montiel and Wright, "Getting a Piece of the Pie." In a separate study of four US cities—Philadelphia, Chicago, Dallas, and Los Angeles—faith-based organizations accounted for 24 percent of all welfare-to-work programs offered, whereas private, nonprofit, secular organizations were responsible for a further 46 percent. Monsma and Mounts, "Working Faith."
48 Martin Olasky's *The Tragedy of American Compassion* and *Renewing American Compassion* are cases in point—two volumes that have been described as the Old and New Testament of right-wing American welfare reform.
49 Howard-Hassmann, *Compassionate Canadians*, 186–91, 216–17.
50 Historically, of course, religion and progressivism have occasionally intersected in the United States, too, most famously in nineteenth-century abolitionism and the twentieth-century civil rights movement.
51 Gao, "How Do Americans Stand Out from the Rest of the World?"
52 McIntyre, Lammam, and Ren, "Generosity in Canada and the United States." Data are for 2013 tax filers. Statistics Canada confirms the number of individuals who donated in 2013, though places the median donation at 0.48 percent of pre-tax median income. Statistics Canada. "Summary of Charitable Donors."
53 Calculations for 2013 based on the US Consumer Expenditure Survey and communicated to the author independently by Veri Crane and Aaron Cobert of the US Bureau of Labor Statistics. Statistics Canada data suggest that the same discrepancy exists in Canada, though given the greater generosity of the Canadian welfare state, the implications may not be quite as severe. See Statistics Canada, "Donor Rate and Distribution of Donations."
54 Massing, "How to Cover the One Percent." See also Piff, Kraus, Côté, Hayden Cheng, and Keltner, "Having Less, Giving More." An Indiana University study relates that in a given year only 30 percent of charitable contributions are made for basic needs—including donations to health care institutions, for scholarships, and to outreach programs for the poor by religious groups. Center on Philanthropy at Indiana University, "Patterns of Household Charitable Giving by Income Group."
55 The OECD estimates that in the United States the use of tax breaks with social purposes is equivalent to roughly 2 percent of GDP versus 1.5 percent of GDP in Canada. Cited in Adema, Fron, and Ladaique, "Is the European Welfare State Really More Expensive?"
56 For 2013, cash assistance in Manitoba was C$7,314 versus C$13,331 in Saskatchewan; in that same year, cash assistance in Mississippi was US$2,040 versus US$11,076 in Alaska. To be sure, Alaska is an outlier, but compared to the second most generous state, New York (at US$9,468), Mississippians still receive only a small fraction as much in cash aid. US data in Falk, "The Temporary Assistance for Needy Families (TANF) Block Grant"; Canadian data in Tweddle, Battle and Torjman, *Welfare in Canada 2014*.
57 Myrdal, *An American Dilemma*.

58 Schram, Soss, and Fording, *Race and the Politics of Welfare Reform*; Pierson, "Fragmented Welfare States"; Fellowes and Rowe, "Politics and the New American Welfare States."
59 Gilens, *Why Americans Hate Welfare*.
60 For instance, Jencks, "What Happened to Welfare?"
61 Floyd and Schott, "TANF Cash Benefits Have Fallen by More Than 20 Percent."
62 Author's calculations from data in Tweddle, Battle, and Torjman, *Welfare in Canada 2014*.
63 Noncash safety net provisions, like food stamps, are more countercyclical—that is, they are more responsive to economic distress—after reform. See Bitler and Hoynes, "The State of the Safety Net in the Post-Welfare Reform Era."
64 Center on Budget and Policy Priorities, "Chart Book: TANF at 19." According to Jeffrey Grogger, an economist at the University of Chicago, the uptick in employment for single mothers from 1996–2000 was due largely to a robust American economy (statistically responsible for 21 percent of the increase) and the expansion of the EITC (responsible for 34 percent of the increase); in Grogger's calculations, welfare reform per se had far less (13 percent) of an impact. Grogger, "Welfare Transitions in the 1990s."
65 Between 1990 and 2012, for instance, Gerard Boychuk relates that statistically "the variation in median provincial employment rates can account for just under 90 percent of the variation in median social assistance recipiency rates." Boychuk, "Federal Policies, National Trends, and Provincial Systems."
66 Center on Budget and Policy Priorities, "Chart Book: TANF at 19."
67 Author's calculations based on data in Falk, "The Temporary Assistance for Needy Families (TANF) Block Grant"; Tweddle, Battle, and Torjman, *Welfare in Canada 2014*.
68 Floyd and Schott, "TANF Cash Benefits."
69 At the onset of welfare reform in 1996, the official poverty rate was 13.7 percent of the US population; at its nadir in 2000 it was 11.3 percent, but by 2014 it was 14.8 percent. US Census Bureau, Current Population Survey, Annual Social and Economic Supplements, "Poverty Status of People by Family Relationship, Race, and Hispanic Origin: 1959 to 2014." Estimates for the Supplemental Poverty Measure (for a definition, see Chapter 2) reveal much the same pattern—a decline in poverty from 1996 to 2000, then a gradual rise that has grown steeper since the Great Recession and now stands a half point higher than the official rate. See Wimer et al., "Trends in Poverty with an Anchored Supplemental Poverty Measure." This is not to say, of course, that US social assistance has been wholly ineffective at fighting poverty. Without welfare and other poverty reduction policies, things would be far worse. It may be that the scale of need is simply increasing at a higher pace than ameliorative measures can accommodate. Still, steep reductions in cash support and benefits and harsher eligibility rules cannot have helped.
70 Figures cited are for cash income. If SNAP benefits are included, between 1996 and 2014 the rise in extreme poverty was still 80 percent; if the total of all welfare benefits is included, extreme poverty grew by 50 percent. See Shaefer and Edin, "Rising Extreme Poverty in the United States and the Response of Federal Means-Tested Transfer Programs." Deep poverty data are from the Current Population Survey, 1990–2013, and the American Community Survey,

2009–2014, and cited in US Department of Agriculture Economic Research Service, "Rural Poverty and Well-being."

71 The low-income gap ratio—the average percentage difference between the incomes of low-income persons and their low-income thresholds—increased from 32.5 percent in 1996 to 33.3 percent in 2011. In Statistics Canada, "Persons in Low Income Families." LICO data are for after-tax income.

72 Weaver, Habibov, and Fan, "Devolution and the Poverty Reduction Effectiveness of Canada's Provincial Social Welfare Programs." For this study, poverty is stipulated as 60 percent of family median equivalized disposable income. By that criterion, the authors point out that the gap between the income level of people in poverty and the poverty threshold has grown across the provinces.

73 From 15.2 percent of the population with LICO status in 1996 to 8.8 percent in 2011. Ibid.

74 See Förster and d'Ercole, "Income Distribution and Poverty in OECD Countries in the Second Half of the 1990s"; UNICEF, "Child Poverty in Rich Countries, 2005." See also Picot and Myles, "Poverty and Exclusion."

75 Chen, *Cut Loose*, 140–43.

76 OECD, *Pensions at a Glance 2015*.

77 Ibid. See also the discussion in Zuberi, *Differences That Matter*.

78 For instance, in 2007, just before the Great Recession, as a percentage of GDP Canada's public social spending was slightly higher than that of the United States. OECD, "Social Spending Is Falling in Some Countries." The OECD defines *public social expenditure* as comprising "cash benefits, direct 'in-kind' provision of goods and services, and tax breaks with social purposes. ... Benefits may be targeted at low income households, but they may also be for the elderly, disabled, sick, unemployed, or young persons. ... Social benefits are regarded as public when general government (that is, central, state, and local governments, including social security funds) controls relevant financial flows."

79 Adema, Fron, and Ladaique, "Is the European Welfare State Really More Expensive?"

80 Ibid. In the United States, 2.4 percent of GDP is devoted to income support for the working-age population as opposed to 4.6 percent in Canada.

81 Ibid. Private disbursements for social purposes constitute 10.9 percent of GDP in the United States versus 4.6 percent of GDP in Canada.

82 American private health spending (exclusive of out-of-pocket costs) is equal to 8.5 percent of US GDP. In Canada such spending accounts for just 3 percent of GDP. Data are for 2013. In OECD, Health Statistics 2015.

83 Privately funded pensions account for 5 percent of US GDP but 3 percent of Canadian. The United States spends 6.7 percent of its GDP publicly funding pensions, whereas Canada spends 4.5 percent. Adema, Fron, and Ladaique, "Is the European Welfare State Really More Expensive?"

84 For example Chen, *Cut Loose*, 145: "Just as national trends in marriage and single-parenthood may reflect cross-border attitudes, the distinct ways that my families responded to unemployment can be chalked up to the culture divide between more individualistic and status-conscious America and more collectivist and egalitarian Canada."

85 The weight of scholarly evidence seems to agree. On continuing differences in Canada and US social policy, see Hoberg, Banting, and Simeon, "The Scope for

Domestic Policy Choice; Banting, "The Social Policy Divide"; Boychuk and Banting, "The Paradox of Convergence." For a good overview of the Canadian debate on globalization and social policy, see Skogstad, "Globalization and Public Policy"; Lewis, *In the Long Run We're All Dead*.

86 See, for example, Maoni, "Health Care in Canada and the United States." See also Boychuk, *National Health Insurance in the United States and Canada*.

5
Why It Matters

More than two millennia ago Aristotle wrote in *The Politics* about the merits of the "Middle Constitution," an ideal social and economic arrangement in which the largest number of citizens have moderate and sufficient property necessary to the good life. "In all states," he observed, "there are three state-sections: the very well off, the very badly off, and thirdly those in-between. Since therefore it is agreed that moderation and a middle position are best, it is clear that, in the matter of the goods of fortune also, to own a middling amount is best of all. … The state aims to consist as far as possible of those who are like and equal, a condition found chiefly among the middle people" (Book IV, Section XI). Since moral excellence is, in Aristotle's view, the mean between excessive behaviors, the most virtuous constitution, the one united by the strongest social and political bonds, is the one in which extremes of wealth are not allowed to flourish.

In the contemporary debate over inequality, that counsel is especially apt—an admonition that it's not only individuals at the bottom of the income and wealth distribution who deserve our attention, but also those at the top. Poverty, particularly when it implicates children, is a relatively uncontroversial object of public concern. While there are important differences of opinion about which policy levers should be used to reduce it, regardless of political persuasion few people will be bold, foolish, or callous enough to argue that hardly anything should be done at all. The same cannot be said about the fortunes of the very rich, whose extraordinary gains have been the immediate cause of accelerating inequality since the Great Divergence. Skeptics of redistribution often contend that as long as prosperity is realized legally, honestly, and in a way not clearly exploitive of others, its size should be of little consequence. Economic inequality, on this more forgiving view, is linked to material progress, the reward for market virtues like thrift, diligence, innovation, and responsiveness to public demands that make life better for everyone.[1] Provided the well-to-do achieve their affluence through free and fair economic competition, as the Canadian economist William Watson asks in a lively critique of the distributive impulse, "why should its growth be considered either a matter for regret or an offence against social justice?"[2] Under such circumstances it seems pointlessly punitive to deny people a right to see their bank accounts swell or to spend the great majority of their earnings as they wish. If Donald Trump, or David Thomson, or Galen Weston has staggering wealth and wants to flaunt it in a way that would make Solomon blush, what difference should it make to the rest of us?

Quite a lot of difference, actually. As the present chapter will relate, economic growth, public health, political and social solidarity, the integrity of democracy, and perhaps most importantly the obligations of justice, are all at issue as the distribution of income and wealth becomes increasingly skewed. Given a certain academic fashion for maintaining a firm separation between empirical and normative analyses, this merging of the practical and moral case in favor of economic equality will displease the strictest of social scientists. It cannot be avoided. The argument so far—that Canada is a more equal place than the United States when it comes to income, wealth, and economic mobility, and that a principal reason is because Canadians are more supportive of egalitarian ideals and policies than Americans—may indulge the curiosity of students of comparative politics and economics. But in the larger civic picture, to leave things there is irresponsible. The reason economic inequality has been a focus of such intense public discussion in the recent past is its relevance to the way in which people actually live, including the futures to which they and their children aspire. Requirements of human dignity are in play, the self-respect that comes from having sufficient resources to pursue a meaningful life of one's own choosing. When the stakes are this high, as Aristotle also advised, political inquiry necessarily turns to the requirements of a good life as well as the proper functioning of the state whose mandate is to secure it. At the heart of any thorough consideration of economic inequality, then, must be an assessment of the value—positive, negative, or indifferent—of equality itself.

Economic Growth

"To the extent that the system (of material rewards and penalties) succeeds, it generates an efficient economy. But the pursuit of efficiency necessarily creates inequalities. And hence society faces a tradeoff between equality and efficiency."[3] So wrote Arthur Okun in 1975, in a statement of the relationship between growth and inequality in developed countries that has become the received orthodoxy among his fellow economists. Economic growth suffers, in this perspective, when government interferes with the natural competitiveness of free markets. There might be good political reasons why inequalities in market outcomes should be corrected by state-enforced mechanisms of redistribution, but in constraining the role of material incentives as a spur to ever greater productivity—say, by imposing taxes to pay for redistributive programs—there is a cost to be paid in terms of aggregate economic output. And while growth isn't the only thing one should be interested in, insofar as it can improve citizen well-being across the income scale, it is certainly a very important thing.[4]

But that is not to say that the more inequality of income and wealth there is in a society, the more economic growth there will be, ad infinitum.[5] To the contrary, a strong case can be made that high levels of inequality lead to lower growth and stagnating incomes.[6] According to the Harvard economist Richard Freeman, the relationship between inequality and economic growth should be imagined as an inverted U, whereby increases in inequality incentivize economic growth up to a certain level—the threshold of "optimal inequality"—after which it will decline. Identifying the tipping point is no easy task and is best understood retrospectively in light of a country's economic history. Yet too much inequality is counterproductive, in Freeman's assessment, a symptom of competitive irregularities like monopolies, cronyism, rent seeking (securing special economic privileges and profits for a firm, typically via government regulation or subsidy, that do not produce economic benefits for society at large), and other financial misbehaviors that drag on economic performance.[7] One need only think of the deceptions uncovered by the banking crisis of the last decade to see his point.

There is a positive economic rationale for greater equality as well, one endorsed by Nobel laureates, the International Monetary Fund, and the OECD alike: More equitable distribution means higher aggregate demand and hence greater productivity over the long run.[8] In conditions of high inequality, the majority of a country's population is unable to support the consumer spending that drives economic growth. Whereas middle- and low-income households are inclined to spend much of what they receive in earnings, partly because their material needs are pressing, those commanding the heights of the economic ladder will save more. Since savings can be a source of investment and ultimately growth, this does not seem bad in itself. But in conditions of great inequality, the "abstinence of the rich," as John Maynard Keynes once called it, has the effect of reducing total consumption and perpetuating an economy that favors the few at the expense of the many.[9] Troubling, then, that in the United States (though not Canada) since the 1970s workers' wages have not kept pace with the overall productivity of the economy. The real output per hour of the average American worker rose by 65 percent between 1979 and 2013, but the real compensation per hour of that worker increased by just 8 percent.[10] The gap isn't unusual—around the globe, labor's share of national income is diminishing and that of capital is rising, with the implication that increases in worker productivity no longer result in general increases in pay. Households of modest means may try to maintain consumption—or even raise it—by overborrowing.[11] Governments are often complicit, easing the flow of credit to stimulate demand.

But the strategy is unsustainable. Eventually the weight of personal debt takes its toll, sometimes dramatically so, as in the bursting of the US housing bubble and the financial catastrophe it helped precipitate.[12]

When economic inequality increases, mobility tends to decrease, with unhappy consequences of its own. A lack of opportunity makes for discouraged, sullen, and less productive employees.[13] But low mobility also misallocates human resources by wasting the economic capacity of much of the citizenry. As Chapter 2 relates, one way is by limiting the access of able students from humble origins to the higher education required for an innovative workforce. Opportunities for a broader constituency are similarly at risk. Rich democracies, Canada and the United States prime among them, are in a global labor market for talent. Highly skilled immigrants will not be as attracted to places where their chances for advancement—and those for their children—are uncertain. Lower skilled immigrants can have a salutary effect on a country's economic dynamism, too.[14] For them, a family's future prospects may be an even more important concern, and the lack of mobility in a potential host society a severe disincentive to relocate.

To be fair, among economists these are contested insights. Scholars of a less progressive outlook warn that redistribution winds up rewarding people of modest means for being unproductive—that reducing their economic discomfort gives them little reason for diligence. By the same logic, if inequality is too low and economic elites fail to be sufficiently compensated for their superior creative talent and investment acumen, they may be inclined to redirect their energies or take their gifts elsewhere, in which case the economy as a whole will suffer, including its less well-off members.[15] Both possibilities raise empirical questions that remain unsettled. Yet they evoke a time-honored defense of economic privilege for which a healthy skepticism is warranted: Far be it incumbent on the wealthy to forgo well-deserved riches on behalf of the less fortunate, who are lucky to bask in their glow; if lesser lights wish to get anywhere, they must simply work harder. As the evidence on labor productivity suggests, however, people of middle and low income have been working harder. The problem is they have not seen a proportionate return on their investment. A sensible redistribution of income and wealth in the interest of greater equality and growth may not solve all such ills, but it would help.[16]

Public Health

Among advanced industrial democracies, more equal societies are healthier. In *The Spirit Level*, perhaps the seminal book on the subject, two British physicians, Richard Wilkinson and Kate Pickett, painstakingly marshal the relevant epidemiological evidence in support of their contention that in the richest states, "reducing inequality is the best way of improving the quality of the social environment, and so the real quality of life, for all of us."[17] On a range of health and social issues, including mental illness, life expectancy, obesity, infant mortality, homicide, and imprisonment, the authors demonstrate that reducing inequality leads to better outcomes not only for the least-advantaged citizens in a given economic distribution, but for the most advantaged as well. Within a given country, social, mental, and physical pathologies will more often afflict people who are lower on the income scale than those who are better off—in other words, the marks of health are on a social gradient. Yet between advanced industrial democracies, this pattern is not at all related to a country's relative economic well-being, at least as measured by per capita national income. Instead, the likelihood of being healthier is often higher in less prosperous states. As Figure 5.1 allows, it is the distribution of income *within* a country that makes it fare better or worse

Figure 5.1 Health and Social Problems and Inequality

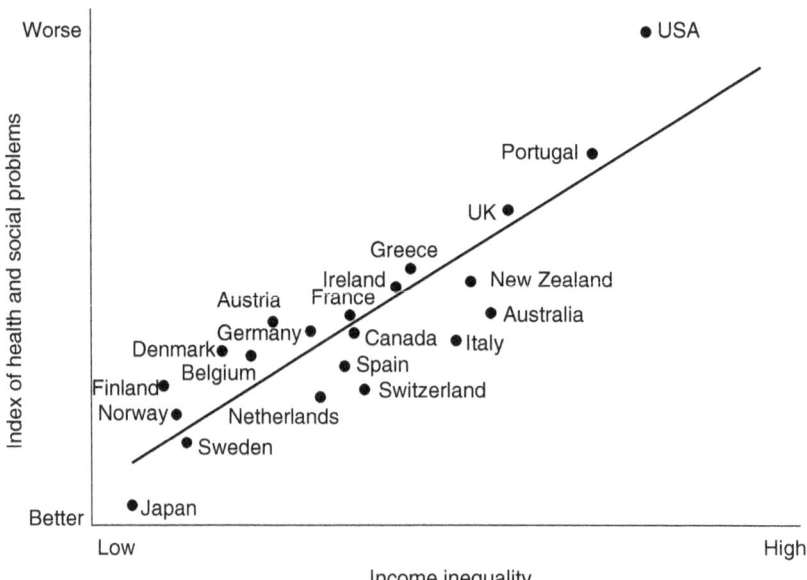

Note: Income inequality is calculated according to the ratio between the top and bottom 20 percent of post-tax income earners in a country.
The index of health and social problems combines levels of social trust, mental illness (including drug and alcohol addiction), life expectancy and infant mortality, obesity, children's educational performance, teenage births, homicides, imprisonment rates, and social mobility.

Source: Wilkinson and Pickett, *The Spirit Level*, Figure 2.2, p. 20.

than its peers on Wilkinson and Pickett's scale of well-being. That is equally true across American states: Those states where income is more equitably allocated also have superior health outcomes. Across the income and wealth ladder, for children as well as adults, greater distributional equality promises a better life.[18]

The Spirit Level is not without critics. Standard academic questions are raised about the choice of a particular set of countries to be examined, how the key variables of inequality and individual and social health are operationalized, the intensity and precise nature of the relationship between these variables, and whether the observed associations have alternative or supplementary explanations—say, of culture, ethnicity and race, or education, though the latter two factors are typically linked to underlying economic inequalities.[19] Yet the weight of scholarly evidence seems increasingly on Wilkinson and Pickett's side: In the words of the Cambridge sociologist Göran Therborn, "inequality kills."[20] *The Spirit Level*'s findings on life expectancy and infant mortality (Figures 5.2 and 5.3) have been confirmed by dozens of studies whose focus is inequality across and within countries.[21] Thus, in the United States the longevity gap between high- and low-income Americans has dramatically widened. Men born into the top 10 percent of households on the income scale in 1920 lived six years longer on average than men who were born into the bottom 10 percent (the advantage to high-income women was a little less than five years); for men born in 1950, the anticipated gap between the top and bottom 10 percent is 14 years (and for women, 13 years).[22] Moreover, since the Great Divergence, while the average longevity of men and women in the top US income quintile has grown by about five years, the longevity of those in the bottom quintile has decreased by the same amount.[23] Some of this is connected to the economic circumstances of the particular community in which one lives. As might be expected, average income is an issue, since poorer counties in the United States have a lower average longevity for their residents than richer ones. But so is the distribution of income within those counties; places where household earnings are more skewed are correlated with lower average life expectancy.[24] Canada is sensitive to differences between income, geography, and health outcomes as well, though the impact is not as acute. Arguably that is because economic inequalities are not as deep or decisive given Canada's public provision of universal health care.[25]

The precise nature of the link between inequality and health is a source of scholarly dispute. Among the most cited intervening factors are income-generated differences in education, especially when it comes to knowledge about the consequences of engaging in risky behaviors like smoking or a having a poor diet, the absence of social amenities and services in a given

Figure 5.2 Life Expectancy and Income Inequality

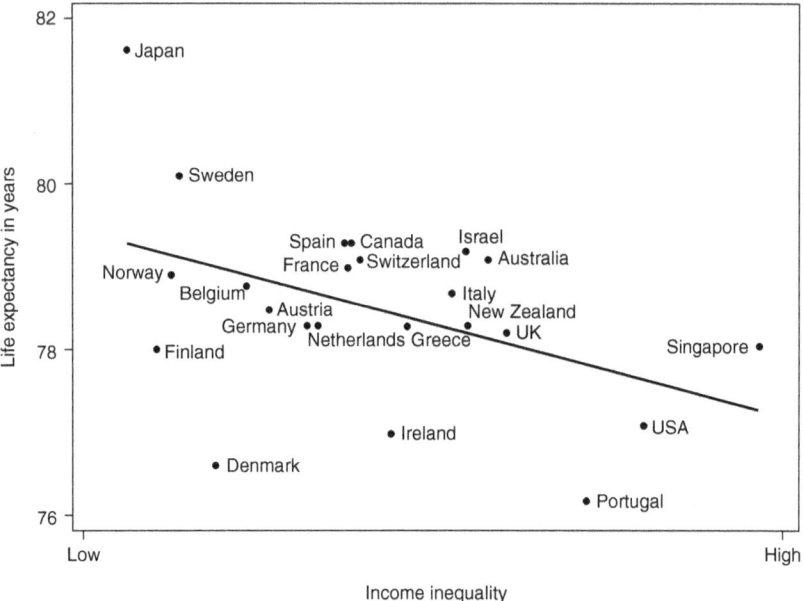

Source: Wilkinson and Pickett, *The Spirit Level*, Figure 6.3, p. 82.

Figure 5.3 Infant Mortality and Income Inequality

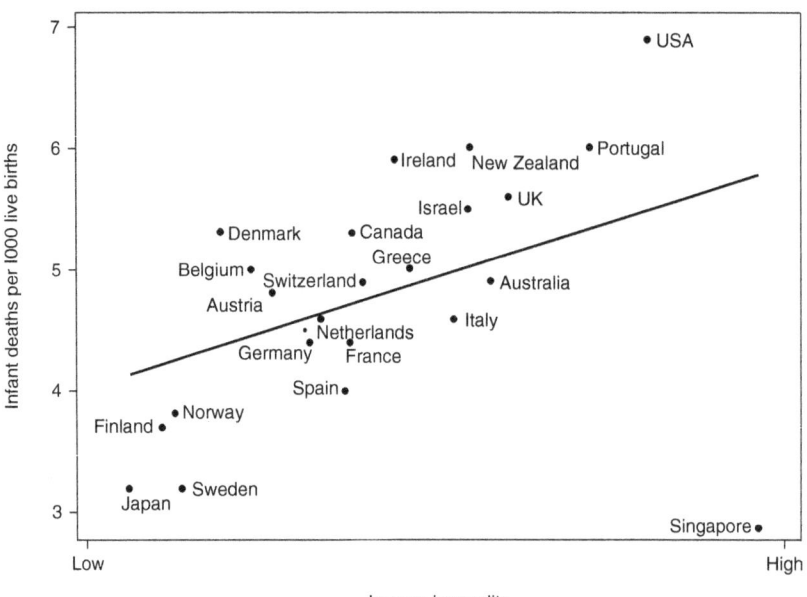

Source: Wilkinson Pickett, *The Spirit Level*, Figure 6.4, p. 82.

community, including easy access to health care facilities, and the prevalence of intact families. Yet many analysts, Wilkinson and Pickett among them, emphasize the role of psychosocial stress, which can compromise immune systems and trigger disease.[26] How much control one is able to exert over the immediate environment—at home, work, or elsewhere—is partly a function of the absolute level of economic resources on which one can draw. Almost by definition, people in lower income tiers will struggle to make their way. But in deeply unequal societies the strain can be aggravated by pressure to imitate the consumption patterns of those in higher economic strata— an indicator of status, social acceptance, and self-worth whose benchmarks grow more daunting as inequality expands. There is a psychological claim here, one backed up by considerable experimental evidence, that once people of modest means see the consumer goods at the disposal of a better-off reference group whose social norms and standing they wish to emulate, they will feel relatively deprived without such goods. In *Falling Behind: How Rising Inequality Harms the Middle Class*, Robert Frank describes how the logic works in the volatile US housing market. Attracted by the social cachet—and debatably better schools—that a premium property might bring, American families seek homes on the order of the next highest social stratum to which they aspire—inflating prices, swelling mortgages, and increasing work rates beyond reason to pay for it all.[27] It is not unequal income as such that produces stress and ill health in this instance, but rather the position in the social hierarchy that money confers.[28] As that hierarchy becomes increasingly elongated, the perceived inadequacy of those who fail to ascend it becomes all the more severe.

If fellow citizens are viewed as rivals in a great race to the top for power, prestige, and wealth, networks of communal interdependence and the sentiments of social trust that undergird them will be compromised as well— further ratcheting up the pressure and potential for illness.[29] Cultural norms regarding social comparison may temper some of this.[30] National outlooks vary as to the acceptability of economic inequality, whether it connotes an appropriate reward for effort and ingenuity or a fundamental unfairness in the operation of the market. Research in the economics of happiness is suggestive of such differences. According to Alberto Alesina, Rafael Di Tella, and Robert MacCulloch, unequal economic distribution has more of a negative effect on how citizens report their sense of well-being in Europe than in the United States. Whereas the bottom half of earners in Europe are made particularly unhappy by inequality, statistically there is no relationship between the two for their US counterparts; the only Americans aggrieved by inequality are political progressives in the upper half of the income distribution.[31] Therefore, in the United States a "happy peasant, miserable millionaire" way of looking at economic inequality may have something to recommend it, at least for millionaires of the left.[32]

In general, however, rich individuals are likely to be happier than their fellow citizens not so blessed. On the other hand, rich *countries* aren't necessarily any happier than those less rich—a circumstance called the "Easterlin paradox" after Richard Easterlin, the American economist whose work most famously explores it.[33] Social scientists regularly observe that the overall growth of a state's economy is no guarantee of corresponding increases in the sense of well-being of its members. Again, this is contested academic terrain, but consideration of the inequalities created by economic growth may be a key to the paradox's resolution.[34] So, in a study by Shigehiro Oishi, Sele Kesebir, and Ed Diener, based on responses to General Social Survey questions from 1972 to 2008, American happiness fell during the years when income inequality increased, even though economic growth as measured by US per capita GDP rose steadily over the same period. The authors believe that intervening variables of fairness and social trust are responsible; statistically, the values for each went down when inequality went up, if mainly for lower-income households.[35] It is not just an American phenomenon. The same connection between diminished happiness and economic inequality holds across advanced industrial states, regardless of relative advances in GDP.[36] Even in good times, it seems, money may not buy you happiness unless everyone shares in the proceeds.

Inasmuch as greater income and wealth inequality generally lead to lower economic mobility, citizens from highly unequal states are doubly cursed. Independent of a country's level of economic development, mobility has been found to contribute to a citizen's sense of social well-being, though even a false perception of mobility can mitigate the negative psychological effect of income inequality—an insight with particular relevance to the United States.[37] One wonders, though, how long the good feeling that comes from living in a fantasy world of economic advancement can last. Surely democratic stability turns on whether citizens are confident that the promise of equal opportunity is real, that through a diligent application of their own efforts and the deployment of their talents they and their children have a chance for a better life. If the gap between what individuals expect and what they actually receive becomes too great, social unrest can't be too far behind.[38]

Solidarity

Bloody revolution is hardly imminent among today's rich democracies. But rising economic disparities threaten to compromise the functioning of any state. A reason is their impact on the sense of belonging to a country and solidarity with one's fellow citizens—what Émile Durkheim called the "collective consciousness" of a people.[39] Modern democracies are in particular need of these mutual sympathies. If the democratic ideal of popular sovereignty is to be approximated, the cohesion of the citizenry must be especially high. It will be realized by a willingness to trust in the good intentions of one's fellows, even those with whom one profoundly disagrees, on the basis that they are partners in a political process whose end is the common good. Yet there is considerable evidence that social trust is diminished in conditions of significant inequality, expressed in the not unpopular view that civic participation is futile because political outcomes are scripted in favor of the rich and powerful.[40]

As a practical matter, all states periodically require their members to make sacrifices for the good of the whole. Without belief in a joint destiny, individuals will find it difficult to subordinate private interest to public wellbeing. Take taxation, for instance. Not even the most doctrinaire capitalist will readily argue that the market can provide all desired social goods and services; the state must undertake some of the required functions that the market cannot or will not do. At the very least, provision must be made for security, though the public catalog of services will be far more extensive. And all of these will be funded in large measure by revenues collected from individuals whose remittances may be quite disproportional to the personal benefits they bring. If self-interest alone is the motivation, short of fear of punishment why should I pay my taxes at all or support public policies that do not immediately benefit me? Belief in a common national identity and consequently an acceptance of mutual civic obligations is one answer—the faith that I share a future with other members of my political community and have a stake in the public interest.[41]

When economic conditions are polarized, it is easier to imagine that we have little in common with less (or more) fortunate others. From the ancient Greeks through the Christian Scholastics to modern theorists like Rousseau, Mill, and Marx, leading philosophers of the western political tradition consistently warn about the tendency of economic inequality to increase the psychological distance between the rich and not so rich, with toxic social and political consequences.[42] In some instances the remedy is moral, to bend the hearts of the affluent more decisively to the poor. In other cases structural changes in the economy and government are advised, either by keeping material inequality within limits or by completely reconfiguring the relationship between society, economy, and polity. Marx, of course, advocated for the wholesale transformation of public and private life. Advanced industrial states have not taken the majority of his counsel, but even in the least receptive democracies it's hard to miss hints of the class struggle. Pundits from both the left and the right of the American political spectrum warn that over the last few decades the working and upper classes have become more divided than ever.[43] For some analysts it is basic cultural shifts that are the culprit; for others it is the loss of well-paying manufacturing jobs. But as Chapter 2 relates, the result is that children from better-off families are living in a significantly different world than their peers from more modest households. Superior parental resources buy enhanced extracurricular involvement for sons and daughters, expanding their educational and economic opportunities as young adults and giving them the means to do the same for the next generation. Without satisfactory schools, stable neighborhoods, and adequate social services, low-income kids cannot keep up. And when the marks of economic inequality are acute, meritocracy—the supposed solvent of American class distinction—is anything but.

Economic inequality falls harder on certain members of the political community than others. In some instances it is the latest manifestation of a pattern of disadvantage with deep historical roots; in others discrimination is of a more recent vintage. But the effect is to entrench preexisting social disparities, further fracturing the sense of common purpose necessary to a polity. In Canada, Indigenous peoples, visible minorities, and recent immigrants are among the most vulnerable populations.[44] Median employment income for Indigenous individuals regularly lags that of other Canadians—by a little over 30 percent according to the latest available government data—a discrepancy that persists whether an Indigenous person lives on or off reserve or in a rural or urban area. Indigenous unemployment rates are consistently twice as high as for non-Indigenous, higher still if a First Nations member lives on reserve.[45] Although the percentage of off-reserve Indigenous individuals with low-income status has decreased somewhat in the recent past, 20 percent remain below Canada's low-income cut-off, considerably more than the population at large. Conditions are far worse on reserve, where perhaps 60 percent of children are in poverty.[46]

Visible minorities endure their own disadvantages.[47] According to the most current official estimates, the median income of non-white Canadians is a third less than that of white Canadians, and the unemployment rate is a third higher.[48] Recent immigrants, the majority of whom are visible minorities, typically have higher-than-average joblessness too, though presently the unemployment gap between non-whites and whites expands even when only Canadian-born individuals are considered.[49] Low income is also more likely to afflict people of color.[50] Over 40 percent of Canadians who live in low-income neighborhoods belong to non-white groups—almost as many are recent immigrants.[51] And while low-income status is transitory for most

Canadians, including recent immigrants, visible minorities have a greater likelihood of being in poverty for several years in succession.[52]

The deep American data on ethnicity, race, and socioeconomic disadvantage is even more telling. Over the last 40 years, real household income has increased for all major ethnoracial and linguistic groups tracked by the US Census. Yet during that period, black Americans have regularly received just 60 percent of the median household income of non-Hispanic whites. At the same time, the Hispanic–white gap has increased, such that the median earnings of the former have now dropped to around 70 percent of the latter.[53] Unemployment figures are stubborn. For as long as the US Bureau of Labor Statistics has been collecting the relevant information, joblessness among Hispanics has been around one-and-a-half times the white rate, and among African-Americans twice as high as for whites.[54] Poverty follows suit: Two-and-a-half times as many African-Americans live in poverty as whites, and almost as many Hispanics.[55] Physiognomy drives differences in health and longevity, family dynamics, education, crime, and incarceration—all of which influence participation in labor markets and impact earnings.

Making the picture grimmer, economic mobility discriminates by race— at least when it comes to African-Americans. According to a Brookings analysis based on the Panel Study of Income Dynamics, at every point on the American income scale white children are more likely than black children to exceed their parents' earnings.[56] Compared to the earnings tier of the households into which they were born, white children also have a considerably greater chance of moving up, and black children of falling down, the income ladder. In the Brookings study, only 16 percent of whites born to parents in the middle-income quintile fell to the bottom fifth of the distribution as adults, though 45 percent of African-Americans did. And while 37 percent of middle-income whites moved to the highest two rungs of the ladder, just 17 percent of their black peers joined them.[57] In short, the American Dream of equal opportunity and success has a decidedly pale cast.

Variances are especially pronounced when it comes to wealth. The median net worth of white US households is now 13 times greater than for African-Americans and 10 times greater than for Hispanics.[58] Contrary to popular perception, debt is not the reason. On average, whites are more indebted than non-whites, though the majority of that debt consists of mortgages and student loans that, ideally, underwrite the production of wealth in the long term. Instead, white households possess considerably more assets—seven times more than black households and three times more than Hispanics. Minorities lag whites in the tenure of home ownership, family income, inheritance, and the holding of securities and retirement accounts—the absence of which limits wealth accumulation.[59] And although the Hispanic–white median wealth ratio has held roughly constant over the last 30 years, African-Americans have ceded ground to whites, with the result that the gap between the two groups is now wider than at any time since 1989.[60] Within a specific minority cohort, the burden of any net reduction in wealth is not evenly distributed. Members of the bottom three wealth quintiles bear all of the losses, while the top two tiers receive all of the gains. Consequently, the US wealth distribution is pulling apart not only across demographic differences but also inside of them. Since 2000, the richest fifth of African-Americans and Hispanics have put far more distance between themselves and their less-well-off co-ethnics than have the wealthiest whites. All of which is to say that in the United States, while in the aggregate whites are still far better off than non-whites, sharp socioeconomic distinctions crosscut ethnic and racial ones.[61]

There is a spatial dimension to economic inequality that further complicates the requirements of democratic cohesion. Research in the United States suggests that social networks tend to be racially homogenous, especially for whites. When the PRRI American Values Survey (2013) asked respondents to indicate the racial composition of their immediate social circle (to a maximum of seven people), whites named a group that was 91 percent white, African-Americans a group that was 83 percent black, and Hispanics a group that was 64 percent Hispanic; three-quarters of whites named an exclusively white network.[62] This lack of diversity—that we tend to talk to people who are most like us—is predictable. It is foreshadowed by evidence about the segregation of American schools and neighborhoods of residence, not only by race but by economic status. These are among the places where social interactions are most likely to congeal. Yet four-fifths of Hispanic students and three-quarters of black students attend majority non-white public schools in the United States—and around 40 percent of each is in an "intensely minority school" where whites constitute less than 10 percent of enrollment. Alternatively, the average white student attends a public school where three-quarters of the student body are white.

Economics play an overlapping role. The typical Hispanic and black student attends a school where almost two-thirds of their classmates are from low-income households, double the share in schools attended by the average white or Asian student. The higher the percentage of African-Americans and Hispanics in the mix, the more likely a school is to be poor.[63] To make matters worse, in both instances, by race and by income, over the last 25 years schools have become resegregated after Supreme Court decisions that permitted federal court–ordered desegregation provisions to lapse.[64] Public education has historically been seen as a training ground for a civically educated population, a means to nurture unifying public values across a diverse constituency. That the *civitas* is so fragmented at an early age comes at a political cost.

A family's place of residence is most often related to the schools its children attend. While the racial segregation of US metropolitan areas has modestly diminished over the last few decades, their economic segregation has increased.[65] According to Sean F. Reardon and Kendra Bischoff, since 1970 the proportion of American families living in either poor or affluent neighborhoods has more than doubled, from 15 percent to 33 percent, while the share of families living in middle-income neighborhoods has declined, from 65 percent to 42 percent.[66] The authors observe that this middle-class squeeze, and consequently the growth of residential pockets of wealth and destitution, is statistically correlated with income inequality.[67] They also indicate that income sorting by neighborhood is most likely among black and Hispanic households, so poorer families are less apt to have middle-income neighbors of the same race or ethnicity than they did 40 years ago.[68] Prosperous white and Asian families are already long gone, and wealthier black and Hispanic families move away, leaving urban public schools that remain racially segregated as well as poor.

Academic quality—and low-income schools have less of it—helps determine whether the American promise of opportunity is real. But mobility is also a function of the geographic expression of income inequality, which in turn has an impact on education. In the United States, the chance that a child exceeds parental earnings as an adult is strongly affected by the place where he or she grew up. Once again, the intensity of income inequality and the degree of residential segregation by earnings are contributing factors. Municipalities with less of each are encouraging of mobility; those with more of each are strongly limiting.[69] Doubtless the well-established connection between income inequality, crime, and violence is an additional part of the explanation.[70] Through no fault of their own, children from modest backgrounds are subject to a double whammy: born into the wrong neighborhood and fated to attend the wrong school, with economic marginalization and political exclusion as their probable reward.

Residential segregation rooted in economic inequality may strain democratic solidarity in another way. In the United States, housing associations— for single-family home owners, condominiums, townhouses, neighborhoods, and so on—have been rising in popularity over the last 50 years; by one estimate more than 60 million Americans live in them.[71] At their most autonomous, such community-interest developments signify the substitution of private government and amenities for public ones. Local governments have often welcomed the trend, in part because members pay local taxes without expectation of full public services in return. Residents are not always rich by any means. But the de facto emphasis of such arrangements is often on housing homogeneity, including economic and racial uniformity. For the truly affluent, the implications for democracy are just as serious. Public space itself begins to shrink, as the well-to-do pay to segregate themselves in exclusive neighborhoods, schools, and places of recreation—what the American economist and former US Secretary of Labor Robert Reich has called "the secession of the successful."[72] When private security forces patrol gated communities, supplanting the local police, it is a sign that even the most basic tasks of government have been commodified. So, one fears, has civicmindedness.

Democratic Integrity

Equality is at the heart of the democratic ethos, the aspiration that all adult citizens should have an equal ability to influence collective decisions about the kind of life they wish to share. As large inequalities of income and wealth are translated into corresponding inequalities of political power, democracy suffers. Differences in economic resources produce unequal access to influence, to the ability to campaign for office, to articulate an effective political message via the media, to lobby persuasively and successfully. Money counts in democratic politics, as the political bagmen and bundlers who dot the North American electoral landscape attest. And the bigger the economic inequalities there are in a country, the more it counts.

In the process of political decision making, long gone are the days of convening the *ecclesia* to ask for a show of hands. Contemporary democracy is an expensive business, inevitable in representative systems of governance whose national electorates number in the tens of millions. But the American brand is more costly than any other. In the 2012 election cycle, the priciest in US history, over $2.6 billion was spent on the race for the White House—over $7 billion if Congressional campaigns are added in—and this excludes the thousands of state and local offices that were up for grabs as well.[73] There are multiple explanations. The scale of American democracy—the size of its population, the geographic expanse of the country, the number of political offices to be contested—inflates the price of the vote. Without publicly subsidized and dedicated advertising time for a party's candidates, access to US media markets can be especially expensive. Most rich democratic countries have laws specifying the campaign period—typically just a few weeks—thus reducing the amount of money to be spent on it, but the duration of American campaigns is limited mainly by a candidate's inclination and the money available to fund them. Moreover, changes in campaign finance law, in particular the intervention of the judiciary in the *Citizens United* (2010),

SpeechNow.org (2010), and *McCutcheon* (2014) cases, gives legal protection to an endless supply of money that can be expended on behalf of contestants for public office, provided the political action committees aggregating such funds don't coordinate with a candidate's own election organization. In 2012, the most famous of these groups, the super PACs, spent $609 million supporting candidates and causes.[74] Canada offers a sharp counterpoint. In the 2015 federal election, third-party spending on political advertising—that is, expenditures made independent of any established party organization and which have a per-group contribution cap during the official campaign period—totaled C$6 million, six times greater than in any previous Canadian election but less than 1 percent of what similar groups spend in the United States.[75]

The amount of money at play in elections, inasmuch as it is diverted from other more productive public purposes, is an issue in itself. From the viewpoint of democratic equality, however, questions must also be asked about the uses to which campaign funds are put. One aim, obviously, is to choose people for office. Candidates rarely share the typical economic profile of their constituents, but in the United States differences are conspicuous. In 2013, for the first time in American history the median annual net worth of members of Congress was over a million dollars, a sum that would put its possessor in the top 10 percent of the US wealth distribution.[76] Presidential hopefuls are better heeled. According to *Forbes* magazine, of the 20 Republican and Democratic candidates who contested their party's primary in 2016, only three had a net worth of less than a million dollars and eight had wealth valued at over $10 million (including a former first lady and a well-known real-estate developer, who were among the top three).[77] None of this is to say it is impossible for less affluent electors to gain fair and favorable representation from candidates more moneyed than they are. And there is evidence that ordinary voters sometimes welcome the idea of their socioeconomic "betters" representing them, seeing the latter's success as aspirational.[78] Yet if democracy functions on the basis that voters know and express their own interests better than anyone else, interests that ideally should be equally weighted in the collective decision-making process, then the absence of representatives who have shared in the economic circumstances in which those views are forged is problematic.[79] Harder to walk in another's shoes without having ever known what they feel like.

Just as troubling, though, is the source of campaign finance. Optional public funding for American presidential campaigns has been available since 1976, though of late major party candidates have refused to accept it, not wanting to be bound by the spending limits it imposes. The majority of US election spending, then, comes in relatively small dollops from private donors. But individually these can barely compare to the impact of a massive injection of campaign cash from a well-connected benefactor. In the 2012 presidential election, 5.6 million small donors—people contributing $200 or less—gave $370 million to the Romney and Obama campaigns; in the same year, just 100 mega-donors funneled $470 million to super PACs who spent $600 million on behalf of those same candidates.[80] The most generous contributor was the Las Vegas hotelier Sheldon Adelson, who gave a staggering $93 million to the Republican cause.[81]

Additional largesse—almost $300 million in all—was directed to "social welfare" organizations, known in the US tax code as 501(c)(4) nonprofit groups, which are permitted to spend up to half of their resources on political causes parallel to though not strictly part of a candidate's campaign, and which are legally exempt from the need to reveal the names of their donors to the public.[82] The most famous "dark money" exemplars are David and Charles Koch, the Kansas-based industrialists who have used private foundations—largely free of tax and political transparency—to create a network of wealthy like-minded others to fund campaigns, lobbyists, think tanks, and university departments in support of a ferociously conservative agenda.[83] Big donors span the ideological spectrum. Arguably, the hedge fund billionaires Tom Steyer and George Soros are progressive counterparts of the Kochs, though the way in which they fund political projects is not as convoluted. Super PACs—to which Steyer and Soros but rarely the Kochs openly contribute—benefit from roughly equal financial support by liberals and conservatives. But by a margin of almost 8 to 1, nondisclosing/dark-money groups are overwhelmingly on the right flank of the partisan divide.[84]

Political scientists disagree as to whether all this spending is efficacious. Across American political history, progressive critics of the role of private money in the election process have argued that in effect it is an investment strategy to secure the political and economic prerogatives of wealth.[85] Yet throwing cash around doesn't always produce the desired results, especially when both candidates are reasonably well financed.[86] The *New York Times* columnist David Brooks relates that in 2012, American Crossroads, the Karl Rove–led 501(c)(4) group, spent $117 million for political purposes, 90 percent of which went to candidates who lost.[87] Not all contributors give money in the expectation of receiving a tangible legislative or regulatory benefit—many solicit the good feeling that comes from supporting a cause.[88] And among the handful of extremely wealthy mega-donors are some who simply enjoy the celebrity that comes from being courted by politicians—egos that candidates in need of funds are happy to stroke.[89] Nor can money substitute for an effective campaign message, tactics, or an agreeable candidate. For all these reasons, the direct link between money and a winning candidacy may appear tenuous. Yet without deep pockets—including one's own, as the 2016 Trump campaign vividly demonstrated—no national candidate in the United States can hope to compete. Indeed, if money is not overly important to American political outcomes, one is entitled to wonder why contestants for office spend an inordinate amount of time raising so much of it. And if doing so is essential, then in circumstances of high income and wealth inequality, individuals at the top of the distributional ladder are better positioned to provide more of the desired economic resources, giving them political access and potential influence that ordinary citizens cannot rival. Only the bravest or most naïve observer will conclude that the relationship between economic and political power, and thus economic and political inequality, is inconsequential.

It's not just in the electoral system that low- and middle-income voters have less muscle, but in the policymaking process too. In quantitative research linking US senators' voting records over a 20-year period to their constituents' preferences, Larry Bartels estimates that people in the top third of the income distribution get the lion's share of policy attention, the middle third 50 percent less, and the bottom third none at all.[90] That said, according to Bartels, in any given policy debate it is the ideological convictions of elected politicians—who are typically well off themselves—that usually carry the day; the views of the affluent are only intermittently influential.[91] Equally distressing, in his opinion, is that people of modest means seem to endorse policies (like upwardly redistributive tax cuts) and parties (the Republicans) that do not reflect their economic interests. A majority of Americans want a more equitable allocation of income and wealth, argues Bartels. But the greater resources of the affluent, including their superior political knowledge and higher voter turnout, when combined with skilled partisan messaging and the insulation of elected officials from broad popular pressure, means the requirements of those lower on the economic ladder go wanting.[92] There may be supplementary explanations. Voters typically underestimate the true degree of income and wealth inequality in a country, giving governments less incentive to do something about it.[93] Americans are prone to exaggerate their likelihood of upward economic mobility as well, making the need for a political response to economic disadvantage seem less immediate. And the limited government/free market nexus of US political culture can dull demands for government-engineered redistribution, as Bartels himself suggests. Then there are the institutional blocking mechanisms of American politics that make change of any sort difficult. Policy drift, in this instance the inability to respond adequately to the social strains created by growing economic inequality, is frequently the result.[94]

Politically inclined individuals aren't the only ones spreading the money around. Among collective bodies like corporations, professional associations, or labor unions, lobbying is an even more important way of intervening in the political process, an effort priced at well over $3 billion a year.[95] As opposed to focusing on the selection of candidates, pressure groups petition all individuals involved in the policymaking process. To take an extreme example, in 2012 the US Chamber of Commerce—in terms of expenditures the richest single American lobbying client—contributed $222,500 via its PAC to federal candidates who supported its pro-business outlook; in the same year it spent over $136 million on lobbying activities.[96] Superior funding doesn't guarantee interest group success—elected officials and bureaucratic administrators with a given policy focus will also have a say—but it helps.

Certain interests are helped more than others. When industry sectors are ranked by lobbying expenditures, business interests lead the way with over half a billion dollars disbursed, followed by health, finance/insurance/real estate, communications/electronics, and energy/natural resources; labor comes twelfth at $46.7 million.[97] The order is much the same with respect to the contributions made to candidates and parties: Finance/insurance/real estate is in first place, disbursing contributions totaling $264 million, with lawyers' associations and single-issue groups joining business and health in the top five; in this instance labor comes ninth, at $30.7 million.[98] The United States is not alone. Interest group activity is a regular feature of all democratic countries, enabled by liberal guarantees of freedom of association and expression. And typically the interests of business and finance are more strongly articulated than those of labor, save in countries where historically the union movement is formally or informally part of the policymaking process. But in the United States the scale of such activity is unparalleled, a function of America's size, a highly decentralized political system, and a lack of strict party discipline—elected representatives are more capable of being persuaded by outside interests—that afford multiple entry points at which to wield group influence.[99]

Competition by interest groups over public goods and services, including political power, is the defining feature of pluralism, perhaps the most famous school of American political interpretation.[100] On the pluralist perspective, the interplay of interests is democratic if for any given issue area different but equally powerful sets of political contestants mobilize to compete for influence. Democracy, then, is understood as a system of "minorities rule" or "polyarchy."[101] Yet in light of the forgoing, as E.E. Schattschneider trenchantly observed, "The flaw in the pluralist heaven is that the heavenly chorus sings with a strong upper-class accent."[102] Empirical political analysis confirms the insight. Mining a data set of nearly 2,000 survey questions about prospective public policy, and comparing popular preferences with the content of the policies actually adopted, Martin Gilens carefully demonstrates that individuals in the highest decile of the US income distribution have considerably more clout over legislative outcomes than their middle- or low-income compatriots. Partly this is a function of private money's importance in electoral politics.[103] But interest groups, themselves more or less wealthy, play a complementary role in expressing the preferences of the well-to-do according to Gilens. He notes that in a few circumstances—with respect to social welfare issues, for instance—sympathetic groups have been able to produce benefits for those less privileged.[104] Still, in a further multivariate study by Gilens and Benjamin Page, it is moneyed individuals and pro-business–oriented pressure groups working in tandem that are held to account for the failings of pluralist democracy.[105] "When a majority of citizens disagrees with economic elites or with organized interests," the authors conclude, "they generally lose."[106]

The dominance of business and financial interests in the policymaking process compounds economic inequalities among the citizenry at large. Whether what's good for General Motors or Goldman Sachs is good for America may be debatable, but it cannot be said that the captains of industry enthusiastically advocate for the welfare of the least advantaged. Democratically responsive states must do that, and not only by designing sympathetic tax and transfer policies that help level the enormous economic imbalances markets can create. As Robert Reich crucially observes, "Few ideas have more profoundly poisoned the minds of more people than the notion of a 'free market' existing somewhere in the universe, into which government 'intrudes.'"[107] Governments necessarily establish the fundamental rules of markets with respect to property rights, monopolies, contracts, bankruptcy, and regulatory oversight.[108] The pressing question is not whether such rules should be subject to the political process, but rather who wields the greatest influence in setting them—and to what end? That same question is germane to the multiple policy areas that shape how markets operate: directly in fields like employment, trade, banking, investment, and monetary policy, and indirectly in matters of education, environment, crime, health, family, civil rights, and gender. Then there are those state responsibilities that affect the distribution of political power with economic implications of their own— citizenship, enfranchisement, representation, the scope of money in politics, even the proper operation of the central institutions of government. It's a particularly long laundry list; political consensus on what might reasonably be achieved would help. Yet one of the discouraging social science findings about growing economic inequalities in the United States is that they move in step with partisan polarization, making more remote the joint solutions that address the needs of the less fortunate.[109]

So tightly bound are politics and economics that virtually any policy concern will be of consequence. In that respect, as is often remarked, politics shapes markets.[110] Just as importantly, the reverse is also true. All rich democracies have market-centered economies in which the majority of economic activity is registered through the voluntary exchange of goods and services between buyers and sellers. Consequently, as Charles Lindblom notes, governments are compelled to be attuned to the desires of businesspeople, in whose hands "jobs, prices, production, growth, the standard of living, and the economic security of everyone" rests—the very things that define the tenure of elected officials.[111] Yet the power this gives to the prerogatives of private business—which are exaggerated in the United States, where corporate wealth may freely buy political influence—fits oddly with the norms of democratic equality. "Indeed," Lindblom warns, "it does not fit."[112]

Left to its own devices, the free market system, for all its unquestioned productive power and pretensions to affluence, politically disappoints. Alone it cannot guarantee the integrity of the democratic state, and in conditions of growing income and wealth inequality it may serve to undermine it. This is no essentialist claim. Democracy comes in many different shapes and sizes, but at its core it is a mode of governance that aspires to the equal influence of all individuals in the collective decision-making process, anchored by a further belief in their equal moral worth. Markets, of course, are an essential component of liberal democracy, the freedoms of economic exchange they embody a bulwark against the concentration of state power. Nevertheless, as Bernard Crick has advised, democracy has no necessary relationship with freedom—indeed, democratic methods of decision making are able to make free regimes freer and unfree regimes more unfree.[113] By the same token, depending on the nature and intensity of the private power that markets unleash, they can make democratic regimes more or less democratic. In short, the market's promise of freedom must be continually weighed against democracy's egalitarian emphases.

Conceptually, one might imagine democracy on a sliding scale. The more each person's point of view is given equal consideration in civic deliberations, and the more equal their chances of achieving a desired political outcome, the more the process of decision-making passes democratic muster. So, while expanding economic inequalities per se are not enough to rescind a country's democratic credentials, should the political advantages of wealth be increasingly evident in the political process, they will make it less democratic. If they do so by a significant margin, questions can be raised about that state's political legitimacy. That is why the expense of elections, the economic status of candidates, and the influence of money, disbursed individually and collectively, on the electoral and policymaking process are more than an idle curiosity. Ultimately they speak to a democratic government's moral authority to rule and be obeyed.

Justice

Justice is a further gauge of democratic legitimacy, the guiding principle whereby the benefits and liabilities of life in a political community should be allocated—including income, wealth, and the well-being they afford. By nature, it is an egalitarian concept. Amartya Sen, the Nobel Prize–winning economist, points out that every normative theory of social arrangements (i.e., justice) demands the equality of something.[114] Even when critics, in the name of alternative principles, complain that a certain distribution of social, political, or economic goods on egalitarian grounds is arbitrary or unfair, what they are really saying is that they disagree with the specific way in which equality is applied. Aristotle famously taught that at its core, justice is a matter of treating equals equally. Ever since, the difficulty for social and political theorists has been to specify the precise nature of the equality that is required: Equality for whom and with respect to what?

Consideration of those questions should begin with an affirmation of the common humanity of all. Despite differences in genetic inheritance or how we are socially situated, there is an irreducible quality that unites us, the source of our dignity and the register of our intrinsic value. That acknowledgment, too often observed in the breach, is front and center in the great civil liturgies of modern politics: "We hold these truths to be self-evident, that all men are created equal," asserts the American Declaration of Independence; "Men are born and remain free and equal," insists the French Declaration of the Rights of Man and of the Citizen; "Recognition of the inherent dignity and of the equal and inalienable rights of all members of the human family is the foundation of freedom, justice and peace in the world," echoes the United Nations Universal Declaration of Human Rights.[115] But the origins of the idea are more distant, an inheritance from the spiritual equality fundamental to the world's great religious traditions as well as the ancient philosophers' belief that self-reflection is the definitive human quality. Almost a century ago, the English liberal and sociologist L.T. Hobhouse wrote,

> there is something peculiar to human beings without distinctions of class, race or sex, which lies far deeper than all the differences between them. Call it what we may, soul, reason, the abysmal capacity for suffering, or just

> human nature, it is something generic, of which there may be many specific, as well as quantitative differences, but which underlies and embraces them all.[116]

If the sentiment seems axiomatic, it's only because left unqualified the alternative is monstrous. That one should be treated as a mere means to a desired end as opposed to an end in oneself, in violation of the equal moral worth of all, is the ethic of holocaust.

This essential equality is the moral basis of a person's claim to be treated equally in some relevant way. On the Aristotelean view, but not only that view, the purpose or *telos* of a person is to develop fully the attributes with which he or she is endowed, to become all one is meant to be.[117] A political society, properly constructed, is the context within which each individual has what is necessary to achieve this best possible end. Certainly the successful pursuit of a good life depends on effort, so people who are industrious and sagacious as they apply their talents and abilities are more likely to flourish. But the political community also has a role in nurturing the aptitudes of its members, helping them gain access to the resources they need to achieve the lives to which they aspire. For Aristotle, to provide for the common good in this way is to fulfill the *telos* of the state itself.

As attractive as this initial depiction of a commonwealth may be, justice requires more. In its Aristotelean form the idea leaves slight room for choice about the kind of person one wishes to be. Instead, the *telos* is predestined, like the genetic code that transforms a seedling into a specific kind of plant. Individuals cannot chart an alternative destiny, only corrupt the one toward which they are already traveling. In the name of social stability, their aspirations cannot be affirmed if contrary to the ends for which they are best suited. And most individuals are not fully aware of who they are meant to be or the civic distinctions to which they are entitled. It takes perspicacious elites, in Aristotle's assessment well-to-do and highly educated men, Athenian citizens all, to deliberate about and allocate the social and political rewards, the "honorifics," appropriate to a person's qualities. They must ensure not only that equals are treated equally but also that unequals are treated unequally, applying the appropriate criteria of discrimination and exclusion. Ultimately this leads to a justification of servitude—that by nature certain people can achieve only an imperfect kind of human flourishing, since they lack the reasoning abilities necessary to self-government and hence require direction from enlightened others. Indeed, in Aristotle's world only a small minority of the population, those fit for citizenship, escape this subordinate status.

An enriched understanding of justice, then, requires at least three improvements to the Aristotelean template. First and most obviously, ascriptive political hierarchies, those based on related advantages of birth and wealth, have no place in contemporary democratic politics. Elites cannot be permitted to make a priori judgments about the aptitudes and life ambitions of their compatriots, assessments used to deny people a right to full and equal participation in the exercise of citizenship. Instead, and second, justice must be inclusive, insisting that by virtue of their shared humanity and capacity to reason about their own interests, all people merit equal political consideration and respect, including the freedom to pursue meaningful lives of their own choosing. Third, justice must be needs-centered. Through civic engagement and public debate the question must persistently be raised as to whether people have the basic material requirements essential to their health in the broadest sense, as well as the social, economic, and political instruments to make a satisfying life a reality. In the interest of the common good, the provision of each should be regarded as a collective responsibility of the political community, insofar as its resources reasonably permit.

A Capabilities Approach to Justice

A full-blown examination of justice on these terms is beyond the scope of this book, but the capabilities approach of Amartya Sen and Martha C. Nussbaum, among others, suggests what is necessary. From their perspective, people's ability to achieve the "functionings" they value—things they would like to do or to be—is the litmus test for assessing whether social and economic arrangements are just. It is a concept of justice that respects the equal dignity of all people, insofar as they are encouraged to choose life plans that are personally satisfying and given equal public regard.[118] Nussbaum observes that a capabilities approach to justice is "evaluative and ethical from the start: it asks, among the many things that human beings might develop the capacity to do, which ones are the really valuable ones, which are the ones that a minimally just society will endeavor to nurture and support?"[119] If politics is about "who gets what, when, how," then on Sen's and Nussbaum's view justice depends in large part on whether the goods and relationships people secure through the political process enhance their ability to lead fulfilling lives.[120]

One can appreciate the moral force of the capabilities argument, which attempts to reconcile ideals of equality and freedom by offering a liberal interpretation of the golden rule. As D.D. Raphael reasons, "because every man also has the capacity for imaginative sympathy, for putting himself in other people's shoes, he can understand that other people, like himself, want to live their lives in their own way."[121] This is not to say that there is nothing to choose between rival conceptions of a good life. Clearly some aspirations may not be worthy of public support, especially if they are hazardous to the community or to the individuals who suggest them. To use David Miller's pointed example, the pyromaniac's wish to set the world ablaze doesn't entail a political obligation to provide the matches, though it might require an offer of psychological assistance.[122] Since in a well-functioning democracy the particulars of any proposal are a matter for vigorous civic discussion, it seems a sensible requirement that one's reasoning about a prospective life plan should be intelligible from the viewpoint of others who are being asked to endorse it.[123]

Any list of essential capabilities will be hotly contested, but Nussbaum's top 10 are a good starting point: longevity; bodily health; bodily integrity (to move freely and without fear of physical harm); senses, imagination, and thought (to think and reason in a "truly human" way, informed by a sound education); emotions (psychological health); practical reason (being able to form an idea of the good life and reflect on how best to achieve it); affiliation (positive community interaction and social belonging); other species (ensuring the well-being of the natural environment); play (leisure); and control over one's environment (political participation and economic welfare).[124] Justice, in her reading, requires that an "ample" threshold of all 10 capabilities be achieved across a given distribution—ample being a quantity determined by the discursive processes of government. Nussbaum is less immediately concerned with inequality at the top of the income and wealth scale than at the bottom. She notes, however, that the security of a capability's enjoyment, how far in the future it can be counted on, is a relevant consideration for justice, and consequently that "for each capability we must ask how far it has been protected from the whims of the market or power politics."[125] Given the influence of economic elites over both, the capabilities approach certainly has something to say about individuals at the heights of the distributional ladder.

Granted, this understanding of justice will be a bit "squishy" for some tastes, though perhaps intentionally so. In *The Idea of Justice*, Sen criticizes theorists, John Rawls in particular, for trying to outline how institutions must function in an ideally just world. For Sen, justice is more appropriately a comparative idea, in that one may not be able to say that a certain distribution of social, economic, and political goods is just, rather that this one is more just than that one. Still, the determination of capabilities is no small challenge. The intent becomes clearer when the question is put in the negative: What are the factors that clearly impede people from becoming all they are meant to be? According to Sen, a minimal criterion is the degree to which all people have what they need to be relieved from hunger, ill health, humiliation, prejudice, insecurity, and all the other things that interrupt a person's ability to live a self-directed life.[126] In his calculations, the redistribution of monetary resources through collective political action is of secondary, though not negligible, importance to such requirements. That is because what a person can and can't do depends not only on income and wealth but also on a variety of physical and social characteristics specific to that individual. Consequently, an equal allocation of monetary resources does not always lead to an equal outcome. An infant and an adult will both need food, but they will not need the same amount of food, nor will they require the same sum of money to acquire it; in this example, an equality of consideration demands an inequality of provision. Whether justice has been done depends on whether that provision leads to a result enhancing the basic capabilities at issue.[127]

Inequality and Capability

The markers laid down in the present chapter strongly suggest that high inequalities of income and wealth have the effect of reducing the capabilities of a citizenry—of making a political community less just. Long-term economic growth is jeopardized by a maldistribution of economic resources. As wages drop and with them consumer demand, the economy slows, personal debt and pecuniary misbehaviors rise, and the competencies of the majority of the population are diminished.[128] Capabilities suffer too when inequality produces worse health outcomes for the rich and poor alike, increasing stress, reducing physical and mental well-being, and making citizens more vulnerable to the crime and violence that signify social dysfunction. Inasmuch as gross disparities in income and wealth have a corrosive effect on social and political cohesion, the ability of the political process to provide a range of public goods instrumental to a person's life plan—a sound education, transportation, safety, health, a clean natural environment—is hindered. Empathy wanes and with it sentiments of social belonging, except perhaps for those whose identity is imprisoned in entrenched disadvantages of class, ethnicity, race, or geography. When big money asserts itself politically, democracy is hollowed out as well, making all citizens equal but some more equal than others. Representatives who faithfully and effectively speak on behalf of the interests of ordinary citizens are in perilously short supply, cowed by the power of personal and corporate wealth. And in what may be the most damning capability outcome of all, in conditions of high inequality the upward economic mobility of children lags. Winning the cosmic birth lottery increasingly has everything to do with one's chances for a good life.

There is a decided bias in this cautionary tale in favor of a concept of justice prioritizing community well-being. For that there are no apologies.

Strictly speaking, in a capabilities approach the totality of individual capabilities is a measure of the justness of the political society at large, so that individual and social considerations merge.[129] But society is more than the sum of free personal choices or the maximization of private utilities, perspectives that begin with the individual and regard the common good as an afterthought. Rather, the capabilities analysis runs in the opposite direction, whereby the collective welfare of a political community requires and promotes the equal development and life prospects of each of its members. In *Ill Fares the Land*, Tony Judt offers a reminder of why considerations of community must be at the center of a citizenry's moral and political compass:

> If we remain grotesquely unequal, we shall lose all sense of fraternity: and fraternity, for all its fatuity as a political objective, turns out to be the necessary condition of politics itself. The inculcation of a sense of common purpose and mutual dependence has long been regarded as the linchpin of any community. Acting together for a common purpose is the source of enormous satisfaction, in everything from amateur sports to professional armies. In this sense we have always known that inequality is not just morally troubling: it is *inefficient*.[130]

Social justice, the kind whose ambit is the distribution of material resources, opportunities, and privileges within a community, must above all things be social. In political deliberations about the allocation of such goods, raw calculations of self-interest have to defer to assessments of what is required for the benefit of everyone. Inevitably those discussions will be messy; moral reasoning about what should be done and who should get what always is. That is especially so when civic discourse is inclusive, so that a variety of perspectives about what constitutes a good life are expressed and carefully considered, as the equal dignity of all persons demands. Selflessness may be a lot to ask in these circumstances, though even the great free-marketer Adam Smith knew that beneficial economic outcomes depend on the moral sentiments of persons of goodwill.[131] But by definition society is interdependent. In tending to the needs of others, we enhance the freedom—that is to say the capability—to pursue meaningful and secure lives of our own.

Politics is an indispensable part of the process. Many capabilities are afforded through public goods and services, state-provided benefits that people enjoy in common—for defense, police, education, public health, transport, communications, and so on. Practically speaking, governments are the only institutions that have the capacity to implement changes in the allocation of resources and opportunities on the scale that justice demands.

But more than this, the legitimacy of a state, expressed through democratic means, provides the moral authority for any coordinated effort at redistribution. It is through open and tireless collective reasoning about the fundamentals of a good life that a public chooses how best to arrange its resources to meet the claims of justice. This requires, or at least encourages, active citizens, whose capacity for sound judgment, one hopes, improves the more they participate in the process of discernment about the common good. The state must strive to facilitate their equal influence as they deliberate. Its guardianship is compromised when large economic inequalities are transformed into inequalities of political power and concern.

Why Markets Are Not Enough

Markets are no substitute. Along with government, they are the principal means of social coordination in the modern world, but alone they cannot ensure just economic outcomes. Where markets are dominant—as they are in one form or another across all advanced industrial democracies—many of the resources required for a satisfying life will be purchased privately. A consequence is that individuals with superior financial means are able to pay for more of these goods than are those without, giving the former a greater opportunity to realize their potential than the latter. C.B. MacPherson notes that a market economy "by its very nature compels a continual net transfer of part of the power of some men to others, thus diminishing rather than maximizing the equal individual freedom to use and develop one's natural capacities."[132] In this way, the central norms of justice are constantly recalibrated as people's needs are more and less satisfied. Yet if one person has as much innate value as another, on principle they should have equal access to the things they require to lead a rewarding life. When inequalities of income and wealth are severe, people at the top of the distributional ladder have far more of that access. That is not to say that from the viewpoint of justice markets are fatally flawed. It cannot be doubted that market-oriented economies have proved the most productive among alternatives. Abolishing them as an affront to justice is not a serious option; historically the equal penury of command economies has little to recommend it. But markets must be tamed to maximize the chances of all people to fulfill their destinies. When inequalities of income and wealth are exaggerated, it is harder to do so.

There are, of course, theories of justice in which markets feature prominently, offering justifications for the privileges of wealth.[133] According to such conceptions, markets are reliable indexes of economic value and properly determine what rewards people deserve for their efforts at enhancing the general prosperity. Libertarians, for instance, who prize individual autonomy and strong rights to private property above all, hold that what a person deserves should be determined by how talent and entrepreneurship are compensated in a system of noncoercive economic exchange. Markets are to be appreciated, from this perspective, because they uphold the freedom to dispose of private property as an individual sees fit, dispassionately allocating the economic benefits that result from buying and selling in conditions of fair competition.[134] Utilitarians, on the other hand, frequently maintain that markets generate the greatest level of economic satisfaction for the greatest number of people—the defining principle of utility—inasmuch as any fairly constructed and voluntary economic transaction will advantage both parties to it. On occasion this approach is refined in terms of "Pareto optimality," named after the Italian statistician who popularized the idea that as long as a deal makes one party to it better off without hurting anyone else, the total utility of buyers and sellers grows. If such criteria are met, even though the absolute inequality between the two agents has increased, *ipso facto* the distribution of benefits via the market is held to be just.

There is good reason to doubt that market-based rules are impartial in the strictest sense. As already noted, markets do not descend from the heavens fully formed; rather, they are subject to a political decision-making process in which the interests of wealth will have a major say. But even if this objection could be overcome, a further weakness of markets is that they are morally arbitrary with respect to economic outcomes, and outcomes, not merely the procedural fairness of economic transactions, should be central to assessments of justice.[135] Imagine two equally resourced players betting on a roulette wheel that is not rigged in any way. Say that via dumb luck one of them consistently wins on every spin of the wheel while the other does not. After a while the earnings of the first player balloon, as do the losses of the second, affecting the ability of each to pursue a way of life that is personally rewarding and condemning the latter to a future far more bleak than is likely to have been anticipated. In such circumstances it seems cruel to tell the second player that no injustice has been done because the terms and execution of the betting game were fair, even when, as a consequence, the possibility of a worthwhile life is diminished. In fact, the ordinary language people often use to describe this predicament suggests otherwise. It is a common refrain of individuals in economic hardship that they have been playing by the economic rules without getting ahead. For them, justice is ultimately about their chances for economic well-being, not whether legal niceties concerning fair economic transactions have been observed.

Further, and contra Pareto, commercial deals which on the face of it make no one worse off but make those who benefit extremely well off are not justice neutral. Even if there is no chicanery involved, a widening gap between the haves and have-nots can have negative consequences on the well-being of all, on how needs are met and capabilities fostered. Markets per se are largely indifferent to the social, economic, and political strains this creates. And this puts aside the distinct possibility that the big winners in the market sweepstakes do not play by the same rules. Indeed, on some accounts markets are inclined to reward bad behavior, by encouraging deception and the manipulation of consumer attitudes in the name of competitive advantage—*Phishing for Phools*, as the title of a recent book would have it.[136]

Examine, as well, the alleged connection between fair market competition and economic freedom. While people may engage in economic transactions that are procedurally fair, depending on their economic circumstances they may not do so with equal willingness or advantages. An employed software developer can leisurely entertain offers from the highest corporate bidder, but an unemployed machinist may be forced to take a pay cut in the hope of securing a new position. In any economic interaction there are power relationships that compromise the easy exercise of property rights. When commercial redevelopment of a low-income neighborhood is being debated, the bargaining chips of the modest home owner and the real-estate tycoon will not be the same, nor is the chance of reaching an equally agreeable economic result. Economic freedom, moreover, is subject to opposing interpretations. It can mean the freedom to hold property, to buy and sell, to enter into contracts, to save and invest, and to bequeath wealth without external impediment. It can also mean freedom from want or the removal of material barriers that prevent one from achieving a satisfying life—freedom as empowerment, it might be called. But surely it cannot mean to do whatever one wishes, even within the boundaries of the law, regardless of the economic consequences on others. There is a difference between freedom and license.

Alternatively, ideas of merit are regularly invoked to justify wide discrepancies in the distribution of economic resources produced by markets. One argument centers on process: We deserve what we receive in fair conditions of market competition in which opportunities for advancement are equally open to all. Yet the connection between economic opportunities and just outcomes is invidious. Inevitably, equal opportunity leads to unequal results, and it is results that should be of primary interest to students of justice. To use the hackneyed but instructive example of a foot race, even if opportunities to win are made sufficiently equal so that all contestants approach the starting line in unison and are kitted out with the same equipment, their chances for victory will not be the same. Runners do not possess the same qualities. There will be winners and there will be losers, and the fate of each will influence subsequent races—including competitions in which their heirs will participate, inasmuch as parents leave legacies of success or failure. Conditions would have to be continually and radically reconfigured for each new competition to preserve even a rough equality of opportunity. And while political intervention can help correct for many arbitrary social and economic disadvantages, such as those of race, ethnicity, gender, sexual orientation, disability, or the handicaps that come from who one's parents happen to be, it cannot and should not correct for all. Physical prowess, mental agility, and emotional fortitude are partly matters of biology, intrinsic to the person who possesses and cultivates them. They are properly beyond the reach of well-intentioned governments, though inevitably they prejudice the great race to affluence.

Markets may also be romanticized as a way to register the contributions an individual makes to the well-being of the community at large. On this view, in a market economy what one merits in terms of income or wealth is held to be roughly proportionate to the utility of the goods and services produced—the enjoyment or satisfaction received by the consumers for whom the items are intended. Yet at best what markets choose to reward are the subjective assessments of what consumers seem to desire at any point in time. The political theorist Michael Sandel wryly observes that in the United States this produces a situation in which the reality television star Judge Judy earns 10 times more than Supreme Court Chief Justice John Roberts.[137] Compensation that markets apportion in no way discriminates between competing standards of public excellence, as we might expect justice to do. If pornographers make far more than school teachers or social workers, so be it. Even in more reputable enterprises, for those at the very top of the pay scale compensation has been decoupled from the value one adds to an organization, as stock options and guaranteed annual bonuses supplant remuneration in wages. It would be hard to argue that such individuals are being rewarded proportionately for contributions made to their own firm let alone the general welfare, especially when wages lag the productivity of the average worker. Moreover, it should be remembered that hefty incomes are often the product of economic rents. Wealth cannot easily pass the test of moral desert when it is the result of manipulating complex financial instruments—paper chasing paper— rather than producing goods or services that more clearly enhance the common good.

Finally, consider the idea that markets aim fairly to compensate effort, a staple of many libertarian and utilitarian understandings of justice. Again, people whose riches derive principally from rent accrued on the ownership of assets or resources, whose value, say, simply increases in tandem with a robust stock market, can hardly be said to merit their takings on the basis of effort. In the near term at least, the same is true for the increasing number of the super-rich whose wealth comes from inheritance.[138] But if effort is taken to mean purely the measure of one's diligence—that one deserves compensation on the basis of how much blood, sweat, and tears one exerts at a certain task—it is clear that markets cannot reward effort any more than a teacher grades a student according to the energy expended in the writing of a research paper and not the thoroughness of evidence or persuasiveness of argument. Ultimately it is the final product that counts, less so the circumstances whereby it is created. Further, according to many social psychologists and biologists the disposition for effort and the favorable economic outcomes it often does produce are frequently linked to extraneous factors like birth order or genetic inheritance—attributes for which an individual cannot, on the grounds of justice, claim independent credit.[139] Some of us may simply be wired to be conscientious and with a high work rate. In that respect, markets aspire to honor achievements for which at best we can claim only partial responsibility.

We are not entirely our own creation. Instead we are the evolving sum of the forces at work upon us—of parents and children, spouses and partners, neighbors and friends, teachers and coaches, co-workers and co-religionists, and a host of others who intersect with our lives at various points. We are situated spatially and historically, subject to governments, economic systems, physical environments, and social networks, for good and for ill. Markets cannot engage us as if we were completely self-determined, falsely personalizing the rewards we are deemed to deserve for the economic contributions we make.[140] To be sure, it would be impossible to untangle the attributes for which people are directly responsible from those for which they are not. And in no way is this to dismiss the importance of our own determination or how we cultivate the talents we have been given. Fair compensation will account for both. But we should not be fooled into thinking that what the market prizes—or justice demands—is down to us alone. Whatever our income or wealth, we did not earn it in a vacuum. And if we are blessed to have a lot of it, the debt we owe to the society in which it was accrued may be just that much greater.

Concluding Remarks

Are present levels of income and wealth inequality in the United States and Canada unjust? That question may be wrongly put. What can be said is that rising levels of inequality make the two countries less just than they might be, insofar as inequality diminishes the ability of Americans and Canadians to achieve the kinds of lives that are very much worth living. If economic growth, public health, social solidarity, and the integrity of the democratic process are all diminished in conditions of high inequality, and this chapter argues that they are, justice suffers.

How much it suffers is ultimately a political question. The answer depends on the way in which a citizenry articulates its aspirations and needs and how a government chooses to respond. States do not have inexhaustible resources, so tough decisions will have to be made. Justice does not demand, for example, that everyone be given a Muskoka cottage or a chalet in Aspen, even if they would like one.[141] Neither does it insist that the economic elites who own such positional goods should have them taken away. Justice is not principally about leveling down, unless leveling down includes the well-to-do paying a share of taxes proportionate to the benefits of living in a country that makes their earnings possible. Rather it is about figuring out ways to give as many people as possible good things too—in this instance, by promoting the development and availability of satisfying recreational opportunities. Democratic polities must carefully consider what basket of collective goods citizens require to pursue equally meaningful plans of life, ones they have a reasonable possibility of achieving. Appeals to intuition can be fraught. But the moral case for meeting the equal needs of the citizenry—at a minimum for nourishment, clothing, shelter, medical care, education, work, and leisure, all indispensable to enhanced capabilities—seems difficult to deny. Without such fundamentals of well-being, other life ambitions, including those leading to greater economic innovation and productivity, will be far harder to accomplish.

Recognition of our interdependence—socially, economically, and politically—underscores a theory of justice that privileges the capabilities of all. Such a theory insists that accidents of birth should not be permitted to decisively affect a person's chances for a healthy and fulfilling life. Markets will play a crucial role in providing what is necessary to that life, but their proper operation is not justice. Even when insulated from economic behaviors that are "anti-competitive, corrupt, coercive, or criminal," markets must not be fetishized, impervious to critique and regulation.[142] Instead, it is up to the democratic state to harness the market's unrivalled productivity by turning it into economic security for all. In public deliberations about justice, the first item on the agenda should not be whether markets are proceeding according to free and fair standards of economic competition—as important as that is. Instead, the central question must be whether all members of the polity have what they need to live in ways they find gratifying—needs more difficult to meet in conditions of escalating inequality. Like all political ideals it is aspirational, one whose importance is in the striving.

Notes

1. On the distinction between good and bad inequality see Milanovic, *The Haves and the Have Nots*, 12 ff.
2. Watson, *The Inequality Trap*, 46.
3. Okun, *Equality and Efficiency*, 1.
4. See, for instance, Deaton, *The Great Escape*, 172–79.
5. See Therborn, *The Killing Fields of Inequality*, 47 f.
6. See, for example, Perrsson and Tabellini, "Is Inequality Harmful for Growth?"; Berg and Ostry, "Inequality and Unsustainable Growth"; Berg and Ostry, "Equality and Efficiency."
7. Freeman, "Optimal Inequality for Economic Growth."
8. Stiglitz, *The Price of Inequality*, Chapter 4; Krugman, "Inequality Is a Drag"; Ostry, Berg, and Tsangarides, "Redistribution, Inequality and Growth"; Cingano, "Trends in Income Inequality."
9. John Maynard Keynes, *The General Theory of Employment, Interest, and Money*, 372–74. See also Reich, *Aftershock*.
10. For production/nonsupervisory workers in the private sector, who constitute more than 80 percent of the private sector workforce. Calculations by Economic Policy Institute and based on US Bureau of Labor Statistics data, in Gould, "Why America's Workers Need Faster Wage Growth," 11. In part because of healthy prices for Canada's commodity exports, Canadian wage growth has outrun its workers' productivity—a problem of a different kind. See, for instance, Shufelt, "Canada's Productivity Gap Looking Worse than Ever."
11. Frank, *Falling Behind*; Rajan, *Fault Lines*; Ostry, Berg, and Tsangarides, "Redistribution, Inequality and Growth."
12. Drennan, *Income Inequality*.
13. OECD, *Economic Policy Reforms 2010*.
14. See, for instance, Shierholz, "Immigration and Wages."
15. For instance, see Mankiw, "Defending the One Percent"; Barro, "Inequality and Growth Reconsidered."
16. Ostry, Berg, and Tsangarides, "Redistribution, Inequality and Growth."
17. Wilkinson and Pickett, *The Spirit Level*, 29. See also Daly, Wilson, and Vasdev, "Income Inequality and Homicide Rates."
18. Wilkinson and Pickett, *The Spirit Level*, 20–24. Wilkinson and Pickett insist that the relationship between inequality and social, mental, and physical health is causal—from the equality of income distribution to the index of well-being. They point to the firmness of the statistical relationships they observe between equality and health, achieved across so many separate dimensions of the latter, as well as the confirmatory evidence found in around 200 tests of the same hypothesis by other scholars. In *The Spirit Level*, 187–93.
19. For a good summary of these objections as well as the research response to them, see Rowlingson, "Does Inequality Cause Health and Social Problems?"
20. Therborn, *The Killing Fields of Inequality*, 7. In addition to the surveys of the research landscape offered by Wilkinson and Pickett and Rowlingson, see Kondo, Sembajwe, Kawachi, van Dam, Subramanian, and Yamagata, "Income Inequality, Mortality and Self-Rated Health"; Evans, Wolfe, and Adler, "The SES and the Health Gradient."

21　For the United States, for instance, see National Academies of Sciences, Engineering, and Medicine, *The Growing Gap in Life Expectancy by Income*. For Canada, see Canadian Institute for Health Information, *Trends in Income Related Health Inequalities in Canada*; Greenberg and Normandin, "Disparities in Life Expectancy at Birth."
22　Bosworth, Burtless, and Zhang, "Later Retirement, Inequality in Old Age," Chapter 4.
23　National Academies of Sciences, *The Growing Gap*.
24　Catlin, Jovaag, and Willems van Dijk, *County Health Rankings*.
25　See the data in Wilkinson and Pickett, *The Spirit Level*; also, Wilmoth, Boe, and Barbieri, "Geographic Differences in Life Expectancy"; Greenberg and Normandin, "Disparities."
26　Wilkinson and Pickett, *The Spirit Level*, 36–45, 81–85; Verhaege, *What about Me?*; World Health Organization and Calouste Gulbenkian Foundation, *Social Determinants of Mental Health*.
27　Frank, *Falling Behind*.
28　Marmot, *The Status Syndrome*.
29　Wilkinson and Pickett, *The Spirit Level*, 49–58; Marmot, *The Status Syndrome*, 158–63. See also Putnam, *Our Kids*; Rothstein and Uslaner, "All for All"; and Holt-Lunstad, Smith, Layton, "Social Relationships and Mortality Risk."
30　Goldthorpe, "Analysing Social Inequality."
31　Alesina, Di Tella, and MacCulloch, "Inequality and Happiness." In the United States, the survey data on happiness are taken from questions in the General Social Survey (1972–97), in Europe from the Eurobarometer survey (1975–92). In each case inequality is measured by the Gini coefficient for countries and US states.
32　Graham, *Happiness around the World*.
33　Easterlin, "Does Economic Growth Improve the Human Lot?"
34　For an alternative view see Stevenson and Wolfers, "Economic Growth and Subjective Well-Being"; Deaton, "Income, Health, and Well-Being around the World."
35　Oishi, Kesebir, and Diener, "Income Inequality and Happiness."
36　Oishi and Keseber, "Income Inequality Explains Why Economic Growth Does Not Always Translate to an Increase in Happiness."
37　Fischer, "The Welfare Effects of Social Mobility"; Graham, *The Pursuit of Happiness*, 14 f.; Alesina, Di Tella, and MacCulloch, "Inequality and Happiness."
38　Two of the foundational works on this theme are Davies, "Toward a Theory of Revolution"; and Gurr, *Why Men Rebel*.
39　Durkheim, *The Division of Labor in Society*.
40　Wilkinson and Pickett, *The Spirit Level,* 51–58; Uslaner and Brown, "Inequality, Trust, and Civic Engagement."
41　For a similar analysis see Taylor, "Democratic Exclusion"; Etzioni, *The New Golden Rule*, 12–14; Anderson, *Imagined Communities*; Miller, "In Defence of Nationality."
42　See, for instance, the discussion in Thompson, *The Politics of Inequality*, Chapter 1.
43　See, for instance, the comments of Putnam, *Our Kids*, as well as Murray, *Coming Apart*.

44 Gee, Kobayashi, and Prus, "Ethnic Inequality in Canada."
45 National Aboriginal Economic Development Board, "The Aboriginal Economic Progress Report 2015"; Wilson and Macdonald, "The Income Gap between Aboriginals and the Rest of Canada." According to Canada's National Household Survey (2011), a voluntary survey instrument that replaced the compulsory long-form census that had preceded it, the median income for Indigenous Canadians was $20,701 versus $30,195 for non-Indigenous Canadians; the unemployment rate for Indigenous peoples was 15 percent versus 7.5 percent for other Canadians.
46 Murphy, Zhang and Dionne, "Low Income in Canada"; Kirkup, "60% of First Nation Children on Reserve Live in Poverty." Statistics Canada does not collect data on low income among First Nations who live on reserve, nor for Indigenous peoples who live in the territories (e.g., the Inuit in Nunavut).
47 Canada's Employment Equity Act (1995) defines visible minorities as "persons, other than Aboriginal peoples, who are non-Caucasian in race or non-white in colour."
48 In 2010 the median total income of non-whites was $20,153 versus $29,649 for whites. The unemployment rate for visible minorities was 9.9 percent versus 7.4 percent for whites. Data are from the 2011 National Household Survey of Canada.
49 Ibid.
50 Ren and Xu, "Low-Income Dynamics and Determinants under Different Thresholds."
51 Statistics Canada, "Persons Living in Low Income Neighborhoods." A low-income neighborhood is defined by at least 30 percent of its residents being in low-income status according to Canada's low-income cut-off.
52 Ren and Xu, "Low-Income Dynamics." See also Palameta, "Low Income among Immigrants and Visible Minorities"; Lammam and MacIntyre, "An Introduction to the State of Poverty in Canada."
53 DeNavas-Walt and Proctor, "Income and Poverty in the United States," Table A-1.
54 US Bureau of Labor Statistics, "Unemployment Rates by Age, Sex, Race, and Hispanic or Latino Ethnicity."
55 In 2014, the official US poverty rate was 10.1 percent for whites, 23.6 percent for Hispanics, and 26.2 percent for blacks. US Census Bureau, "Poverty Status of People by Family Relationship, Race, and Hispanic Origin." Race-based gaps in low income do not relent as people retire. The poverty rate among whites 65 years of age and older is 7.8 percent, less than half that for blacks and Hispanics. US Census Bureau, "Poverty Status of People by Age, Race, and Hispanic Origin."
56 In order to smooth annual income fluctuations, parents' earnings were determined by using five-year averages of income between 1967 and 1971; five-year average income for their grown children was determined for 1995, 1996, 1998, and 2002. Isaacs, "The Economic Mobility of Black and White Families." As Isaacs indicates, parallel studies of Hispanic intergenerational mobility are precluded by the data limitations of the PSID.
57 Ibid. See also Mazumder, "Black-White Differences in Intergenerational Economic Mobility in the US."

58 Figures are based on US Federal Reserve's Survey of Consumer Finances; the latest available data are for 2013. Cited in Kochar and Fry, "Wealth Inequality Has Widened." US Census Bureau data based on the Survey of Income and Program Participation puts the ratio of white to non-white median net worth even higher—at 17.5:1 for whites and blacks, and 14.4:1 for whites and Hispanics (in 2011); in each case the gap has grown by more than 70 percent since 2000. In Vornovitsky, Gottschalk, and Smith, "Distribution of Household Wealth in the US."
59 Shapiro, Meschede, and Osoro, "The Roots of the Widening Racial Wealth Gap"; Kochar and Fry, "Wealth Inequality."
60 A contributing factor was the loss of equity in black homes during the Great Recession, homes that were especially vulnerable to the high-risk predatory loans that targeted minority communities. According to the US Federal Reserve, between 2010 and 2013 the home-ownership rate for non-Hispanic whites fell 2 percent versus 6.5 percent for minority households. In Kochar and Fry, "Wealth Inequality."
61 According to the Census Bureau, between 2000 and 2011 the ratio of the median net worth of the highest quintile to that of the second quintile for whites grew from 21.8:1 to 31.5:1; for Hispanics from 158.4:1 to 220.9:1; and for African-Americans from 139.9:1 to 328.1:1. Vornovitsky, Gottschalk, and Smith, "Distribution of Household Wealth."
62 Public Religion Research Institute, "Race and America's Social Networks."
63 Orfield, Kucsera, and Siegel-Hawley, "E Pluribus." Low income in the Orfield et al. study is measured according to a student's free and reduced-price lunch eligibility.
64 The watershed Supreme Court case was *Board of Education of Oklahoma City Public Schools v. Dowell* (1991).
65 That said, whites continue to live in neighborhoods that are 75-percent white, whereas African-Americans typically live in areas that are 35-percent white—about the same as in 1940. The spatial diversity of American life has increased, but that does not mean black–white residential integration has done likewise. Logan and Stults, "The Persistence of Segregation in the Metropolis."
66 See, for instance, Reardon and Bischoff, "Growth in the Residential Segregation of Families by Income." Poverty is defined as being at less than 67 percent of a metropolitan area's median income; affluence is defined as being at 150 percent of the median. Neighborhoods are synonymous with census tract areas occurring within census designated metropolitan areas. For a Canadian perspective, see Bolton and Breau, "Growing Unequal?
67 Ibid, 3.
68 Ibid, 15.
69 Chetty et al., "Where Is the Land of Opportunity?" See also Graham and Sharkey, "Mobility and the Metropolis."
70 Fajnzylber, Lederman, and Loayza, "Inequality and Violent Crime."
71 McKenzie, *Beyond Privatopia*, 2.
72 Reich, *Aftershock*, 39.
73 Federal Election Committee, "FEC Summarizes Campaign Activity of the 2011–2012 Election Cycle"; Choma, "The 2012 Election."
74 Center for Responsive Politics, "2012 Outside Spending, by Super Pac."
75 Elections Canada, "Third Party Election Advertising Reports for the 42nd General Election."

76 There is little difference between Democrats and Republicans on this score, though on the whole senators are better off than their House colleagues. Choma, "Millionaires' Club."
77 According to *Forbes*, Hillary Clinton has an estimated net worth of $45 million; Donald Trump, $4.5 billion. The three paupers? Democrats Bernie Sanders and Martin O'Malley and Republican Marco Rubio. *Forbes*, "The Candidates and Their Net Worth."
78 Gelman, *Red State, Blue State, Rich State, Poor State*.
79 Dahl, *Democracy and Its Critics*.
80 Vogel, *Big Money*, 181. All this said, the funding approach of the 2016 Sanders campaign suggests there might be another way.
81 Center for Responsive Politics, "Top Individual Contributors."
82 Center for Responsive Politics, "Outside Spending by Group."
83 Mayer, *Dark Money*. The Kochs also take advantage of 501(c)(6) nonprofits that regulate trade associations' election activities and that do not need to disclose donors to the public.
84 Center for Responsive Politics, "Outside Spending by Group."
85 See for instance, Ferguson, *Golden Rule*. This perspective has deep roots in the work of early-twentieth-century scholars like James Allen Smith, Charles A. Beard, and Vernon Parrington.
86 Levitt, "Using Repeat Challengers to Estimate the Effect of Campaign Spending on Election Outcomes in the US House."
87 Brooks, "Money Matters Less." For a similar Canadian perspective, see Press and Bryden, "Money No Guarantee of Success in 2015 Federal Election."
88 Ansolabehere, de Figueiredo, and Snyder, "Why Is There So Little Money in US Politics?"
89 Vogel, *Big Money*.
90 Bartels, *Unequal Democracy*, 254.
91 Ibid., 289.
92 Ibid., Chapters 4 and 5.
93 Engelhardt and Wagener, "Biased Perceptions of Income Inequality and Redistribution."
94 See, for instance, Hacker and Pierson, *Winner-Take-All Politics*, 83 f.
95 Center for Responsive Politics, "Lobbying Database." https://www.opensecrets.org/lobby/
96 Ibid.
97 Ibid.
98 Ibid.
99 Comparisons with Canada are difficult since Canadian regulations don't require organizations to reveal how much money is spent on lobbying activities. But according to the annual general reports of the Canadian Medical Association—the most active lobbying organization in Ottawa, on the evidence of official lobbying registration figures—and the American Medical Association, in the former C$5.6 million was set aside for advocacy and public affairs (in 2013), while the latter reserved over US$37 million for similar purposes (in 2014). Controlling for population size, the sums aren't so different. Then again, the AMA is typically in the lower half of the top 10 spending on US lobbying concerns.

100 See, for example, Bentley, *The Process of Government*; Truman, *The Governmental Process*; Dahl, *Pluralist Democracy in the United States*.
101 Dahl, *A Preface to Democratic Theory*, 128–32.
102 Schattschneider, *The Semi-Sovereign People*, 35.
103 Gilens, *Affluence and Influence*.
104 Ibid., Chapters 4 and 5.
105 Gilens and Page, "Testing Theories of American Politics."
106 Ibid., 576.
107 Reich, *Saving Capitalism*, 3.
108 Ibid., Chapters 2–9.
109 McCarty, Poole, and Rosenthal, *Polarized America*; Voorheis, McCarty, and Shor, "Unequal Incomes, Ideology and Gridlock."
110 See, for example, Polanyi, *The Great Transformation*.
111 Lindblom, *Politics and Markets*, 172.
112 Ibid., 356.
113 Crick, *In Defense of Politics*.
114 Sen, *Inequality Reexamined*, 12. See also Raphael, *Problems of Political Philosophy*, 183–85.
115 United States, Declaration of Independence (1776); France, Declaration of the Rights of Man and of the Citizen (1789); United Nations, The Universal Declaration of Human Rights (1948).
116 Hobhouse, *The Elements of Social Justice*, 95, as cited in Benn and Peters, *Social Principles and the Democratic State*, 109.
117 MacPherson, *Democratic Theory*, 5–6; Sandel, *Justice*, Chapters 8–10; Skidelsky and Skidelsky, *How Much Is Enough?*.
118 Sen, *Inequality Reexamined*, Chapter 3.
119 Nussbaum, *Creating Capabilities*, 28.
120 Lasswell, *Politics*.
121 Raphael, *Problems of Political Philosophy*, 186.
122 Miller, *Social Justice*, 135.
123 Sen, *Inequality Reexamined*, 17–18.
124 Nussbaum, *Creating Capabilities*, 33–34.
125 Ibid., 43.
126 Sen, *The Idea of Justice*.
127 Sen, *Inequality Reexamined*, 28–30.
128 See, for instance, Reich, *Saving Capitalism*, 163 ff.
129 Sen, *The Idea of Justice*, Chapter 4.
130 Judt, *Ill Fares the Land*, 185; emphasis in original.
131 Smith, *The Theory of Moral Sentiments*.
132 MacPherson, *Democratic Theory*, 10–11.
133 I rely on the excellent discussion in Sandel, *Justice*.
134 See, for instance, Nozick, *Anarchy, State, and Utopia*; Tomasi, *Free Market Fairness*.
135 For a recent defence of justice as fair economic procedure, see Watson, *The Inequality Trap*.
136 Akerlof and Shiller, *Phishing for Phools*.
137 Sandel, *Justice*, 162.
138 For instance, see Reich, *Saving Capitalism*, 92 ff.

139 Hartshorn, "How Birth Order Affects Your Personality."
140 Sandel, *Justice*.
141 Contra Watson, *The Inequality Trap*, 88 ff.
142 The phrase is Watson's, ibid., 11.

Conclusion

> "Would you tell me, please, which way I ought to walk from here?"
> "That depends a good deal on where you want to get to," said the Cat
> "I don't much care where—" said Alice.
> "Then it doesn't matter which way you walk," said the Cat.
> Lewis Carroll, *Alice's Adventures in Wonderland*, 1865[1]

Like Alice navigating Wonderland, in matters of economic equality Canadians and Americans must decide which way they wish to go. If the prospect of a healthier, more productive, cohesive, democratic, and just society has any purchase, then where the path leads should be clear: a future in which outlandish disparities in economic well-being are greatly reduced and the material needs of the citizenry, those required for a meaningful and self-determined life, are readily and equally available.

Over the last several decades Canadians have been more consistent than Americans in moving toward that future, where the privileges of wealth are not indulged at the expense of the common good. As the forgoing chapters have indicated, Canada does better on almost every standard measure of economic equality and mobility than does the United States. Partly this is down to distinctions of national attitude and belief. Canadians place a higher value than Americans on the norms of collective well-being, the importance of a broad parity in economic outcomes, and the redistributive role of the state. Public policies with greater egalitarian effect, including a more generous social safety net, are a consequence, produced by institutions of Canadian government more able than their American counterparts to deliver decisive socioeconomic change. Compared to other rich democratic countries, Canada may not be a paragon of social democratic virtue. But if distributive justice aspires equally to meet the needs of individuals for vigorous and satisfying lives regardless of who their parents happen to be, it's fair to say that Canada comes closer to the ideal than the United States. At least the Canadian advantage across basic indicators of well-being like longevity, children's health, the absence of poverty, crime and violence, educational preparedness and achievement, and the relative prosperity of the middle class strongly suggests so.

Americans of more egalitarian sensibilities need not despair. Although presently the United States leads almost all of its rich democratic rivals in income and wealth inequality, things weren't always that way. The 1930s through the mid-1970s was the era of the "Great Compression," when the benefits of a rapidly growing American economy were more widely and equitably shared. Granted, the economic circumstances of the immediate post-war period were different. Yet the policy framework that contributed to the broad prosperity of the period has been whittled away over time, and if there is one thing a comparative perspective on economic inequality reveals, it is that policy choices make a difference. Globalization and rapid advances in information technology are drivers of economic inequality common to all rich democracies. But whereas disparities of income and wealth have risen across virtually all the advanced industrial states, they have not increased to the same degree. A host of discrete political decisions—about taxes and transfers, collective bargaining, the minimum wage, financial regulation, health, education, and the integrity of the family—aggravate or diminish the impact. Politics matters, whether in the policy initiatives taken to reduce economic inequality or the policy drift that defers to it.

What Can Be Done?

Economists have no shortage of proposals promising greater income and wealth equality. Perhaps the most comprehensive single set of suggestions, principally designed for a European and North American audience, is outlined in a recent book by Sir Anthony B. Atkinson, *Inequality: What Can Be Done?*[2] Atkinson offers 15 initiatives to reduce the extent of inequality, including the following:

1. *Democratize the workplace*: Ensure that trade union rights to bargain collectively on behalf of their members are respected; establish a social and economic council to institutionalize the participation of labor, employer, and government representatives in the setting of economic competition policy as well as that of consumer and relevant nongovernmental organizations so that the distributional effects of markets are consistently assessed.
2. *Reduce unemployment and affect fair wages*: Lower unemployment should be a national priority, and the offer of guaranteed public sector employment at a minimum wage must be part of the strategy; the minimum wage should be set at a level that guarantees a decent standard of living; executive pay should be capped. (Atkinson speaks favorably of the practice of the British department store John Lewis, whose highest

paid director is not permitted to be paid more than 75 times an employee's average salary.)
3. *Promote savings and the accumulation of wealth*: Introduce a national savings bond with a guaranteed positive inflation-controlled rate of return and a maximum holding limit per person; establish a minimum inheritance (capital endowment) to be paid out to all members of the political community at adulthood; create a public investment authority to administer a state-owned/sovereign wealth fund, the revenue from which would be used to foster a more equal society.
4. *Impose equitable taxation*: Introduce a more progressive structure for personal income tax, including marginal rates capped at 65 percent; broaden the tax base by reconsidering current exemptions or deductions that benefit the well-to-do; establish an earned income discount similar to the earned income tax credit in the United States, but to be deducted, not refunded, from the taxable income of individuals in the lowest earnings band; make grants of inheritance and gifts between living persons subject to a progressive lifetime capital receipts tax; levy a progressive property tax based on up-to-date assessments and ability to pay.
5. *Thicken publicly provided social benefits*: Offer child benefits to all families at a "substantial" level, taxing their value as income; pay a basic "participant income" to all contributing members of the political community, whereby social contribution is considered as employment, education, training, an active job search, home care for children or the elderly, or regular efforts on behalf of a registered voluntary association, with exemptions for the ill or disabled; alternatively, increase social insurance benefits—for sickness, unemployment, disability, or old age—and make coverage more comprehensive.[3]

Atkinson considers all of these within the context of an economic debate over their effect on revenue, including the impact on investment, incentives to work, and productivity. Yet he concludes that among rich democratic countries there seems to be no necessary connection between more economic equality and lower economic growth—quite the opposite.[4] He advances other talking points as well, including a proposal most vigorously advocated by Thomas Piketty: a progressive global tax on capital to address the tax havens and lack of transparency that permit individuals to shield domestic liabilities by shifting assets to other countries.[5] To be sure, the transnational emphasis is ambitious, even in Piketty's wistful judgment. Individual nation-states are the more likely targets for reform.

What Can Be Done in the United States?

Changes to the tax code are a favored remedy of proponents of equality. That is particularly so with respect to the United States, since it is among the most lightly taxed of all advanced industrial countries. In 2015, taxes were equivalent to just over 26 percent of the American GDP; among OECD countries, only Ireland and South Korea accrued proportionately less.[6] Since income taxes on corporations have diminished as a major source of US government revenue—from almost 40 percent in 1943 to around 10 percent at present—business-specific measures are often on the American reform agenda. Among policy analysts, there is considerable disagreement over whether at 35 percent the statutory US federal tax on corporate profits is too high, or at 27 percent the effective rate—what corporations actually pay on average, given deductions and credits for health insurance, pensions, and investment returns—is too low.[7] But that debate aside, ending the process of tax inversion, whereby American companies register their headquarters in out-of-country subsidiaries to avoid higher US domestic tax rates, stopping tax deferrals on corporate profits made in foreign states, and imposing a financial transaction tax on Wall Street speculation would produce tens of billions of dollars of additional revenue, making it easier to fund the kind of spending that Atkinson and others recommend.[8]

Taxes imposed on individuals come in for greater scrutiny. Personal income taxes are progressive in the United States, meaning that earners in the higher income bands pay proportionately more than those in the lower. In fact, the US pioneered the use of graduated income and inheritance taxes for the purposes of wealth distribution in the second decade of the twentieth century, long before European countries did so.[9] According to the Internal Revenue Service, in 2014 Americans with adjusted gross incomes over $250,000 a year paid 51.6 percent of all individual taxes at an average rate of 25.7 percent; those making less than $50,000 accounted for 5.7 percent of the total at an average rate of 4.3 percent.[10] Yet after a half century of cuts to the effective rate of tax paid by the highest American income earners, compared to other rich democratic countries the current US fiscal imposition is relatively gentle, as is its effect on reducing economic inequality.[11] Several economists suggest that ratcheting up the top marginal rates for ordinary income would be a step in the right direction, a proposal which—in theory—a majority of Americans seem to endorse.[12] On the other hand, given the enormous amount of political capital that had to be expended the last time the top American income tax band was successfully raised—in 2013, from 35 percent to 39.6 percent for individual earnings over $400,000—a more viable strategy may be to make future marginal rates increase automatically only when income disparities worsen.[13]

There are, however, other kinds of personal taxes with a regressive effect. At a maximum rate of 23.8 percent, capital gains taxes are a popular target of reformers. A joint analysis by economists from the US Federal Reserve and the Brookings Institution suggests that the long-term reduction of the capital gains rate is the major explanation for the inability of the US income tax schedule to significantly reduce economic inequality.[14] Since the richest Americans can parlay their monetary resources into investments and eventually dividends—70 percent of which accrue to the top 1 percent of earners—they are able to pay far less tax than they would on the realization of regular income. "Flow-through taxes" are a related issue, the practice whereby owners of certain types of businesses can have their profits taxed at a single personal rate of income, thereby avoiding higher corporate levies (which would require a business owner to pay one tax under the corporate rate and another as capital gains on individual dividend income or retained earnings); these now account for just over a third of business profits, on which the average federal income tax rate, given available deductions and deferrals, is just 19 percent.[15] Inheritance taxes are a concern as well, whether it's the ability to avoid paying capital gains taxes on assets bequeathed at death, which have increased in value during the lifetime of the owner, or the tax exemption on estates worth less than $5.43 million per benefactor. So, too, the deductions, credits, and exclusions that riddle the tax code and are typically to the advantage of the well-to-do, in effect a public subsidy for private expenditures on things like higher education, retirement, savings, and most of all housing. According to the Congressional Budget Office, the 10 largest of these fiscal indulgences are worth over $900 billion. More than half the benefit goes to households in the top income quintile versus just 11.7 percent to the lowest fifth of earners—unsurprising since it is the wealthiest households who can afford to spend more on the goods and activities that receive favorable tax treatment.[16] Thus, while it is true that the richest Americans pay the lion's share of taxes—they are rich, after all—it is also true that they receive the far greater portion of the revenue code's forbearance.

For all the inequities, though, given an American political climate that typically emphasizes tax cuts, not redistributive enhancements, egalitarian reformers may look elsewhere to make a difference. Expanding the social safety net is one stratagem, notably by delivering comprehensive and publicly funded health care to the more than 35 million Americans under 65 years old who remain without it.[17] Though the Obama administration was wary of advertising the redistributive aspects of the Affordable Care Act, the law mediates income inequality by subsidizing the purchase of health insurance for low-income Americans, reducing out-of-pocket costs that poorer Americans pay for medical services, and taxing high-income earners and wealthy investors to help pay for it.[18] In addition, there is little doubt that programs of income security—food stamps, Temporary Assistance for Needy Families, federal housing subsidies—have not kept pace with the burden of families flirting with poverty, though except in times of recession there seems to be little political enthusiasm for making them more generous.[19] A promising suggestion, insofar as it incentivizes moving from welfare to work, may be the expansion of the earned income tax credit, particularly for single individuals who presently are eligible to receive only a small fraction of the benefit available to low-income families with children.[20] Momentum for significantly raising the minimum wage to a "living" wage—$15 seems to be the progressive benchmark—has been growing as well, the evidence that it does not cut business profits or increase unemployment having gained considerable traction.[21]

Individual opportunity and economic equality can also be promoted by making investments in human capital. Generous policies of family leave are in this category. The United States is the only rich democratic country to offer no national entitlement to paid leave to care for a newborn child or a sick relative; 12 weeks per year of job-protected unpaid leave is available, but only for individuals who work at a company with at least 50 employees. Paid family leave would have a double benefit. It helps to keep women in the workforce, 40 percent of whom are the principal breadwinners in US households, thereby raising their lifetime earnings, and it is a way to nurture children at the very beginning of their lives, a commitment that pays off in their future material welfare.[22]

The same logic is behind proposals to fund more extensive programs of early childhood education, giving young people from modest backgrounds the kind of advantages that better-heeled families can afford.[23] Equitable access to quality higher education is part of the mix, too, though it is difficult to compensate fully for the extracurricular advantages that upper-middle-class parents can provide. Vigilance over the funding formulas for public elementary and secondary schools could help, as present allocations often work to the disadvantage of districts with poorer socioeconomic profiles, including their ability to recruit and maintain accomplished teachers.[24] More public attention has been generated for proposals reducing the indebtedness of students upon completion of tertiary education, or even making tuition at public universities free, though there is considerable disagreement over whether equality is better served when such assistance is means tested or universally available.[25] Public investment in thoroughgoing apprenticeship programs would be complementary, leading to well-paying and stable jobs for individuals not interested in or suited to a four-year college program.

Finally, market reforms can have egalitarian overtones. For Americans believing that the Dodd–Frank Wall Street Reform and Consumer Protection Act (2010) did not go far enough in tightening the rules governing the US financial system—whose collapse in 2007 was disastrous for low- and middle-income home owners—banks remain undercapitalized and overleveraged, regulators are given too much latitude to interpret the law's provisions, commercial and investment activities need to be separated, and leading financial institutions are still too big to fail. Reductions in outrageous CEO-to-median-worker pay differentials, which have played a large part in the steady enrichment of the top 1 percent at the expense of households further down the income ladder, are merited as well.[26] Short of legislative remedies, this requires stricter oversight by company boards and watchful shareholders to establish a closer connection between company performance and executive pay and to avoid the practice of interlocking directorates. A change in the tax code, making it more difficult to convert CEO compensation rendered in stocks into capital gains income for tax purposes, where it is assessed at a lower rate than regular earnings, is another move in the right direction. And although the task is formidable, given the current state of organized labor, a reinvigorated American union movement would be to the advantage of low- and middle-income workers. Currently the median wage bump for union members is around 9 percent, with such individuals being far more likely than their nonunion peers to have access to employer-provided health insurance, retirement benefits, life insurance, and paid sick leave.[27] An increase in the number of union members, of workers covered by union-negotiated collective bargaining agreements, or, per Atkinson, experiments in workplace democracy whereby labor is formally represented promises to spread the benefits of economic growth more widely.[28]

Why Canada Counts

On almost every one of these suggested measures, from the perspective of greater economic equality Canada is better situated than the United States. Admittedly, it is difficult to say which country has the more progressive tax regime, since the ways in which taxes are assessed vary considerably.[29] Canada's total tax haul as a percentage of GDP (30.8 percent) is higher than that of the United States, as is its top marginal personal income tax rate when central and subcentral levies are combined.[30] On the other hand, at 33 percent the top marginal federal rate in Canada is actually lower than in the United States, as are Canadian corporate tax rates and, more arguably given the complexities of the calculations, taxes on capital gains and dividends.[31] That said, Canada's egalitarian edge is clearly apparent in the following:

- Provision of universal health insurance
- Programs of income security that are more generous and less skewed to the advantage of seniors
- Paid maternity leave as well as paid family leave for men and women, with the dollar value of the benefit increased for low-income families
- Subsidized and extensive programs of early childhood education
- A more equitable funding formula for public education
- A system of higher education that is more accessible and affordable for students of modest means
- A schedule of working income tax credits that follows the EITC lead of the United States but expands it significantly for single individuals without children
- Public oversight of financial institutions, which helped Canada avoid the worst of the Great Recession
- A healthier labor movement, as measured by enrolled union members and the number of individuals covered by collective bargaining arrangements
- CEO-to-average-worker pay ratios that, while rising in the recent past, are much lower than those in the United States

No country has a monopoly on virtue or vice, of course, and compared to some other rich democratic countries the Canadian record isn't sterling. As Chapter 1 relates, the average income as well as the income share of households in the top fifth and above of earners, especially the top 1 percent, has accelerated in Canada as in the United States—just not by as much. Nor do taxes and transfers make as big a dent in Canadian inequality as they did 20 years ago. None of the initiatives listed above are eternally secure. And what Canada's more centralized system of parliamentary government has wrought it can also take away, depending on the ideological complexion of the party in power. Alarmingly, the polarization of the Canadian party system and electorate has intensified in the recent past; as Keith Banting and John Myles observe, north of the border "redistributive politics has been stuck for more than a decade."[32] So the judgment offered here is inescapably nuanced. But given the strong historical, cultural, social, political, and economic bonds between two countries that share the majority of a continent, for advocates of greater economic equality Canada is America's better self.

The Habits of a Democratic Heart

Economic policy prescriptions do not exhaust the roster of reform. Ultimately inequality is a political question. States are essential to the operation of economic markets, including those given wide latitude to operate independent of the redistributive hand of government. Even in laissez-faire economies, as Adam Smith long ago observed, states create and stabilize the currency, regulate financial institutions, enforce contracts, uphold the security of property by employing the police and armed forces, facilitate and regulate internal and external trade, and impose taxes to fund necessary public goods and services that the private sector finds difficult to provide.[33] But markets are also influenced by decisions in policy fields only tangentially economic—those touching on gender, race, education, immigration, or environmental and urban planning, among many others. Contemporary governments are entrepreneurial too, investing in infrastructure and basic research, or incentivizing it through a creative use of the tax code, and thereby impacting the kinds of goods and services that are eventually brought to market. Transportation and communication networks—including the Internet, smartphones, and global positioning systems—biotech, and green energy initiatives are all among the by-products of such efforts.[34]

Consequently, a government's redistributive role is inescapable. The state constantly makes choices about expending economic resources on or collecting revenue from this group and that one. Indeed, while redistribution is typically imagined as a transfer from the haves to the have-nots, it is just as likely to work in the opposite direction—from the haves to the have-mores. Eccentricities of the US tax code that cater to the interests of the well-to-do have already been cited. But tax credits that underwrite the living standards of low-income earners, in effect giving employers the latitude to underpay workers while their own compensation packages balloon, might be mentioned as well. Then there are the contracts tendered to big-money private interests for public service delivery programs—for health, education, social assistance, and most notably in the United States prisons. Or again, in the recent past there are the hundreds of billions of dollars—or pounds or euros—that bailed out financial institutions, reimbursement for the avarice and malfeasance of their leaders, the prelude to the Great Recession. All are examples of "socialism for the rich," as the British journalist Owen Jones has called it.[35] And it's not only what governments do but what they don't do that bears on economic inequality. If a state fails to maintain programs devised to blunt the sharper edges of the market economy or bring to justice individuals who scam the system, then that too is a redistributive decision.

So the issue is not whether governments should be involved in redirecting the operation of markets—they already are, and in a big way. Rather it is whether the decisions they make will be more or less democratically informed and sensitive to the economic requirements of justice. Political and economic equality are two sides of the same coin. When economic elites are permitted to drive the greater part of the policy agenda, the democratic ideal of the equal political influence of all is corrupted. No country is immune from the threat of big money—certainly not Canada.[36] But the United States, whose decentralized political structure offers multiple access points for exerting private influence, and where spending cash for political purposes is given constitutional protection as a right of free speech, is susceptible like no other. Overturning *Citizens United* and related court cases would help to rid elections of super PACs and dark money, which is hugely important in its own right. But it would not directly address the way in which well-financed lobbyists wield power in the policymaking process. Part of the response should be to create or reinvigorate progressive civic organizations, interest groups, and parties—progressive in the sense of being focused on issues of economic inequality—as counterweights in the same political game.[37] But nothing can substitute for the sustained vigilance of an engaged democratic electorate prepared to hold their representatives to account.

Ultimately it is the convictions of the citizenry that must carry the day. In the early nineteenth century, Alexis de Tocqueville, the great French chronicler of North America, a comparativist by nationality and nature, wrote that the intellectual and moral condition of the American people, the character of their mind and the habits of their heart, was a sustaining cause of the republic.[38] The same cultural influences can be ventured to explain why Americans are saddled with less economic equality and lower rates of economic mobility than peers from other rich democratic countries. What people believe about the political and economic world in which they live, and the moral compass with which they negotiate it, makes a difference. How do they understand their prospects for advancement, what freedom requires, the obligations they owe to the less fortunate, their willingness to use the auspices of the government to help meet those obligations? Unbridled individualism, reflexive anti-statism, and a reading of equality emphasizing economic opportunities at the expense of outcomes do Americans no favors if the goal is a broadly shared prosperity that tends to the material needs of everyone.

All is not lost. Political values, beliefs, and attitudes are not etched in stone; they can and do change, if slowly, over time. In the United States there is an egalitarian lineage on which to draw, one insisting that people are created equal, possess equal value, and are owed equal consideration. Across the American experience, ideological cross-currents emerge periodically—republican, populist, progressive—that are critical of the easy relationship between economic and political power that America's liberal orthodoxy rarely confronts. Neither are Americans hopelessly individualistic. Sacred and secular communitarian experiments dot US history, and for many people the social ties of parish, neighborhood, workplace, or voluntary association remain firm. There can even be, if intermittently and largely in times of crisis, a reservoir of goodwill for the decisive actions of the state. It is the first place that citizens and otherwise antagonistic politicians look to for relief when localities are stricken by acts of violence, natural disasters, or economic crises.[39] Moreover, young Americans seem far less reticent than older peers about government's importance to their well-being. Recent polling (2016) finds that large majorities of 18–29 year olds believe basic necessities like food and shelter should be publicly provided if individuals are unable to afford them, that health insurance is a basic right for all people, that the federal government should play a significant role in reducing income inequality and poverty, and that it should regulate the economy as well.[40] It remains to be seen whether such perspectives will be sustained. But economic inequality on the scale the United States is now experiencing is not inevitable, as the lessons of American history and the example of other rich democratic countries suggest. Neither is it random. Over the last few decades, in the context of economic forces common to all advanced industrial states, political choices have been made, in some cases deflecting the full effect of inequality, in others embracing it.

For an active and attentive democratic electorate there are still choices to be made. The political process is not hostage to impersonal global economic forces, institutional inertia, or deterministic historical trajectories. What people believe about the kind of life they wish to share and how they desire to distribute the collective benefits of life in community is crucial. If, as this book has argued, cultural orientations are among the factors responsible for the way in which particular states address economic inequality, then for advocates of greater equality shifting those perspectives offers hope—ideally, of a world in which each citizen's potential is maximized by the equal provision of his or her basic material needs. Granted, given the prevailing American reticence about state-sponsored redistribution, it may not be easy to turn the tide of public opinion.[41] Since November 2016 it will have become harder. The election of Donald Trump heralds an administration whose agenda promises regressive changes to the tax code, the stripping of financial regulation, and the end of the Affordable Care Act—all of which are likely to aggravate inequalities of income and wealth.[42] A majority of Americans did not vote for Trump, but it's unclear whether they care enough about equality to pressure him to change his priorities once in office. And while civic education is a noble idea, when it comes to differences over public values our fellow citizens are not always as persuaded by reasoned arguments as we might wish—even good ones about economic growth, physical and mental health, social solidarity and stability, democratic integrity, and distributive justice.[43]

Better, then, to make an additional appeal to the heart. There is a moral effrontery, an intuitive unfairness, when an accident of birth is so influential in determining a child's future. Yet in the second decade of the twenty-first century, in the United States who one's parents happen to be has a disproportionate impact on the kind of life one is likely to lead—in youth and adulthood, materially and otherwise. Things do not have to be this way. If they are to change, however, Americans must care more about the circumstances of those at the bottom of the economic scale and be less enamored of the perks of those at the top. And they should be willing to use political instruments and the auspices of the state to effect a greater equality in economic outcomes. Americans, that is to say, must become more Canadian.

Notes

1 Carroll, *Alice's Adventures in Wonderland*, 89.
2 Atkinson, *Inequality*.
3 Ibid., Chapters 5–8.
4 Ibid., Chapters 9–11. See also Cingano, "Trends in Income Inequality and Its Impact on Economic Growth."
5 Piketty, *Capital in the Twenty-First Century*, Chapter 15. See also Zucman, *The Hidden Wealth of Nations*. Unilaterally the United States has tried to achieve a similar goal by passing the Foreign Account Tax Compliance Act (2010), which compels foreign banks and financial institutions to turn over information on American clients to the US Internal Revenue Service or else suffer a 30-percent surcharge on all payments that originate in the United States.
6 OECD, *Revenue Statistics, 2016 Edition*.
7 The United States has the highest basic rate of corporate taxation levied by central governments among OECD states, but its effective rate is below the OECD average. Gravelle, "International Corporate Tax Rate Comparisons and Policy Implications." The statutory corporate rate levied by the Canadian federal government is just 15 percent.
8 Stiglitz, "Reforming Taxation to Promote Growth and Equity"; Baker, Pollin, McArthur, and Sherman, "The Potential Revenue from Financial Transaction Taxes"; Gravelle, "Tax Havens."
9 Piketty writes that Americans "invented the confiscatory tax on 'excessive' incomes and fortunes." *Capital in the Twenty-First Century*, 505.
10 DeSilver, "High Income Americans Pay Most Income Taxes."
11 For instance, Piketty and Saez find that the top 0.01 percent of US earners paid more than 70 percent of their income in federal taxes in 1960, but only about 35 percent in 2005. They also observe that it is the tax treatment of the top 1 percent of earners that drives American inequality, and that favorable capital gains and estate tax treatment accounts for more of the effect than the top marginal rates on ordinary income. In Piketty and Saez, "How Progressive Is

the US Federal Tax System?"; Thompson, "How Low Are US Taxes Compared to Other Countries?"

12 Saez and Piketty, "Why the 1% Should Pay Tax at 80%"; Pew Research Center for the People and the Press, "Raising Taxes on the Rich Seen as Good for Economy, Fairness."

13 Shiller, "Better Insurance against Inequality."

14 Looney and Moore, "Changes in the Distribution of After-Tax Wealth." More broadly, Piketty observes that cuts in the top marginal tax rate since 1980 have been a principal driver of economic inequality in advanced industrial states, with no statistically detectable increase in economic productivity, as tax cutting advocates maintain. Piketty, *Capital in the Twenty-First Century*, 509–10.

15 Sole proprietorships, partnerships, and S corporations are the kinds of eligible ownership arrangements. According to the Tax Policy Center of the Brookings Institution and the Urban Institute, half of all business profits are now earned by flow-through entities. See Tax Policy Center, "Tax Policy Center Briefing Book."

16 Harris and Shakin, "The Distribution of Major Tax Expenditures in the Individual Income Tax System."

17 Centers for Disease Control and Prevention, "Early Release of Selected Estimates."

18 Harwood, "Don't Dare Call the Health Law 'Redistribution.'" For the purpose of the Affordable Care Act, households reporting a single annual income of $200,000 or a married couple having a joint income of $250,000 are considered "high-income" earners.

19 Federal entitlement spending, it should be said, is not neutral in matters of economic need. In the United States, the majority of it is directed to senior citizens via Social Security and Medicare, regardless of economic circumstances. And the payroll tax on Social Security is leveled at a single rate (6.2 percent) with a ceiling of $118,000, meaning that individuals earning more than that in wages do not pay as much proportionately as those earning less. Both may deserve a rethink, though reconfiguring spending on seniors is widely regarded as a third rail of American politics.

20 See, for instance, Sawhill and Karpilow, "Raising the Minimum Wage and Redesigning the EITC."

21 See, for example, *The Economist*, "The Logical Floor"; Editorial Board, "Business and the Minimum Wage"; Simon, "Raising the Minimum Wage Doesn't Affect Employment."

22 Wang, Parker, and Taylor, "Breadwinner Moms"; Esping-Andersen, "Unequal Opportunities and the Mechanisms of Social Inheritance."

23 Heckman, "Skill Formation and the Economics of Investing in Disadvantaged Children." See also Chetty et al., "How Does Your Kindergarten Classroom Affect Your Earnings?"

24 See the speech made by the chair of the US Federal Reserve, Janet Yellen, "Perspectives on Inequality and Opportunity from the Survey of Consumer Finances."

25 With respect to the effect of wider access to university education on income distribution in the United States, there is evidence that at the very least it reduces inequality in the bottom half of the earnings distribution. See Hershbein, Kearney, and Summers, "Increasing Education."

26 Bivens and Mishel, "The Pay of Corporate Executives and Financial Professionals as Evidence of Rents in Top 1 Percent Incomes"; Bebchuk and Fried, *Pay without Performance*.
27 Graham, Hahn, Poirier, and Powell, "Quantile Regression with 12 Panel Data"; US Department of Labor, Bureau of Labor Statistics, "Employee Benefits in the United States—March 2015."
28 See, for instance, the discussion in The White House, "Worker Voice in a Time of Rising Inequality." Graham et al., "Quantile Regression with 12 Panel Data."
29 Schlesinger, "A Taxing Question: How Does Canada Stack Up?"
30 The most recent OECD figures, for 2014, show that the combined marginal rates of personal income tax were a maximum 49.5 percent in Canada versus 46.3 percent in the United States. The Trudeau government (elected in 2015), however, has raised the federal rate so that for most of Canada the top marginal level of taxation is now over 50 percent. OECD, *Revenue Statistics, 2016*; OECD, "Top Statutory Personal Income Tax Rate."
31 Capital gains are taxed at a slightly lower personal rate in Canada than in the United States, though in Canada only half of any gain is taxed. Dividends are taxed at a higher rate in Canada—to a maximum of 39.3 percent versus 28.5 percent in the United States, according to the OECD. Canadian dividend tax credits significantly reduce the liabilities, however. OECD, "Overall Statutory Tax Rates on Dividend Income." Canada has no inheritance tax. Rather, capital gains are due on the transfer of an asset at death, which the estate of the deceased is responsible to pay. Unlike the United States, Canada also has a national sales tax—the goods and services tax, levied at 5 percent on most purchases. Though federal and provincial sales tax credits are available to low-income households, consumption taxes are notoriously regressive in that they are imposed regardless of the economic status of the consumer.
32 Banting and Myles, "Framing the New Inequality."
33 See, for instance, the more equality-friendly interpretation of Smith in Boucoyannis, "The Equalizing Hand."
34 See, for instance, Mazzucato, *The Entrepreneurial State*.
35 Jones, "It's Socialism for the Rich and Capitalism for the Rest of Us in Britain."
36 Conacher, "How to Stop Big Money from Influencing Elections."
37 See, for instance, Alperovitz, *America beyond Capitalism*; Hacker, "The Institutional Foundations of Middle-Class Democracy."
38 "I have previously remarked that the manners of the people may be considered as one of the great general causes to which the maintenance of a democratic republic in the United States is attributable. I here use the word customs with the meaning which the ancients attached to the word mores; for I apply it not only to manners properly so called—that is, to what might be termed the habits of the heart—but to the various notions and opinions current among men and to the mass of those ideas which constitute their character of mind. I comprise under this term, therefore, the whole moral and intellectual condition of a people." De Tocqueville, *Democracy in America*, Chapter XVII.
39 On the importance of the American state, see also Hacker and Pierson, *American Amnesia*.
40 For instance, Sargent, "The Bernie Effect?"

41 Kelly and Enns, "Inequality and the Dynamics of Public Opinion"; Luttig, "The Structure of Inequality and American Attitudes toward Redistribution"; Kuziemko et al., "How Elastic Are Preferences for Redistribution?" These studies suggest that as economic inequality has increased in the United States, general public support for redistribution has dropped, especially in terms of support for transfers to individuals at the bottom of the income ladder.

42 As of this writing (early 2017) the proposed Trump income tax reform plan would give the top 1 percent of American earners half of all the tax cuts anticipated, whereas the bottom four-fifths would receive just 17 percent of any reduction. Corporate taxes are to be dramatically cut as well, seemingly regardless of distributional effect. Rattner, "2016 in Charts"; also Neate, "Trump's Tax Plan."

43 On the limits of reason in politics, see Haidt, *The Righteous Mind*.

Bibliography

Abbott, Phillip. "Still Louis Hartz after All These Years: A Defense of the Liberal Society Thesis." *American Political Science Review* 3, no. 1 (March 2005): 93–120. https://doi.org/10.1017/S1537592705050085.

Acs, Gregory, and Seth Zimmerman. "US Intragenerational Economic Mobility from 1984 to 2004: Trends and Implications." Pew Charitable Trusts, Economic Mobility Project, October 2008. http://www.urban.org/sites/default/files/alfresco/publication-pdfs/1001226-U-S-Intragenerational-Economic-Mobility-From-to--.PDF.

Adams, Michael. "America Pivots toward Progressive Canada: Recent Trajectories of Social Change in North America." In *Canada and the United States: Differences that Count*, 4th ed., edited by David M. Thomas and David N. Biette, 46–60. Toronto: University of Toronto Press, 2014.

Adams, Michael. "Fire and Ice Revisited: American and Canadian Social Values in the Age of Obama and Harper." Presentation to the Woodrow Wilson Center, Washington DC, March 24, 2014. https://www.wilsoncenter.org/sites/default/files/Michael%20Adams%20Fire%20and%20Ice%20Revisited%20-%20Canada%20Institute%20-%20Washington%20March%202014%202014.pdf.

Adema, Willem, Pauline Fron, and Maxime Ladaique. "Is the European Welfare State Really More Expensive? Indicators on Social Spending, 1980–2012." Manual to the OECD Social Expenditure Database (SOCX), OECD Social, Employment and Migration Working Papers, No. 124, 2011. https://doi.org/10.1787/1815199X.

AFL-CIO. "CEO-to-Worker Pay Ratios around the World." April 1, 2013. http://www.aflcio.org/Corporate-Watch/Paywatch-Archive/CEO-Pay-and-You/CEO-to-Worker-Pay-Gap-in-the-United-States/Pay-Gaps-in-the-World.

Akerlof, George A., and Robert J. Shiller. *Phishing for Phools: The Economics of Manipulation and Deception*. Princeton: Princeton University Press, 2015. https://doi.org/10.1515/9781400873265.

Alderson, Arthur S., and Kevin Doran. "How Has Income Inequality Grown? The Shaping of the Income Distribution in LIS Countries." In *Income Inequality: Economic Disparities in the Middle Class and Affluent Countries*, edited by Janet C. Gornick and Markus Jäntti, 51–74. Stanford, CA: Stanford University Press, 2013. https://doi.org/10.11126/stanford/9780804778244.003.0002.

Alesina, Alberto, Rafael Di Tella, and Robert MacCulloch. "Inequality and Happiness: Are Europeans and Americans Different?" *Journal of Public Economics* 88, no. 9-10 (2004): 2009–42. https://doi.org/10.1016/j.jpubeco.2003.07.006.

Alesina, Alberto, and Edward Glaeser. *Fighting Poverty in the US and Europe: A World of Difference*. Cambridge, MA: Harvard University Press, 2006.

Allaire, Yvan. "Pay for Value: Cutting the Gordian Knot of Executive Compensation." Institute for Governance of Private and Public Organizations, 2012. http://igopp.org/wp-content/uploads/2014/04/pp_payforvalue_allaire_en_v4.pdf.

Allen, Danielle. "Equality and American Democracy: Why Politics Trumps Economics." *Foreign Affairs*, January/February 2016: 23–33.

Almås, Ingvild, Alexander Cappelen, and Bertil Tungodden. "Cutthroat Capitalism versus Cuddly Socialism: Are Americans More Meritocratic and Efficiency-Seeking than Scandinavians?" NHH Deptartment of Economics Discussion Paper No. 18/2016, November 15, 2016. https://brage.bibsys.no/xmlui/bitstream/handle/11250/2423528/DP18.pdf?sequence=1&isAllowed=y.

Almond, Gabriel, and Sidney Verba. *The Civic Culture: Political Attitudes and Democracy in Five Nations*. Boston: Little Brown, and Co, 1965.

Alperovitz, Gar. *America beyond Capitalism: Reclaiming Our Wealth, Our Liberty, and Our Democracy*. New York: John Wiley and Sons, 2005.

Alvaredo, Facundo, Anthony B. Atkinson, Thomas Piketty, and Emmanual Saez. "The Top 1 Percent in International and Historical Perspective." *Journal of Economic Perspectives* 27 (2013): 3–20. https://eml.berkeley.edu/~saez/alvaredo-atkinson-piketty-saezJEP13top1percent.pdf; https://doi.org/10.1257/jep.27.3.3.

Anderson, Benedict. *Imagined Communities: Reflections on the Origins and Spread of Nationalism*. London: Verso, 1983.

Ansolabehere, Stephen, John M. de Figueiredo, and James M. Snyder Jr. "Why Is There So Little Money in US Politics?" NBER Working Paper No. 9409, January 2003. http://www.nber.org/papers/w9409.pdf.

AP/NORC. "Inequality: Trends in American Attitudes: Issue Brief." Center for Public Affairs Research, 2015. http://www.apnorc.org/PDFs/Inequality/InequalityFinalToDTP-FINAL.pdf.

Applebaum, Binyamin. "US Household Income Grew 5.2 Percent in 2015, Breaking Pattern of Stagnation." *New York Times*, September 13, 2016. https://www.nytimes.com/2016/09/14/business/economy/us-census-household-income-poverty-wealth-2015.html.

Ashok, Vivekinan, Ilyana Kuziemko, and Ebonya Washington. "Support for Redistribution in an Age of Rising Inequality: New Stylized Facts and Some Tentative Explanations." *Brookings Papers on Economic Activity*, March 9, 2015. http://www.brookings.edu/~/media/projects/bpea/spring-2015/2015a_ashok.pdf.

Atkinson, Anthony B. *Inequality: What Can Be Done?* Cambridge, MA: Harvard University Press, 2015. https://doi.org/10.4159/9780674287013.

Atkinson, Anthony B., and Andrea Brandolini. "On the Identification of the Middle Class." In *Income Inequality: Economic Disparities and the Middle Class in Affluent Countries*, edited by Janet C. Gornick and Markus Jäntti, 77–100. Stanford, CA: Stanford University Press, 2013. https://doi.org/10.11126/stanford/9780804778244.003.0003.

Autor, David, Alan Manning, and Christopher L. Smith. "The Contribution of the Minimum Wage to U.S. Wage Inequality over Three Decades: A Reassessment." Unpublished paper, February 2015. http://economics.mit.edu/files/3279.

Baker, Bruce D., and Sean P. Corcoran. "The Stealth Inequities of School Funding: How State and Local School Finance Systems Perpetuate Inequitable Student Spending." Center for American Progress, September 2012. https://cdn.americanprogress.org/wp-content/uploads/2012/09/StealthInequities.pdf.

Baker, Dean, Robert, Pollin, Travis McArthur, and Matt Sherman. "The Potential Revenue from Financial Transactions Taxes." Center for Economic and Policy Research Issue Brief, December 2009. http://cepr.net/documents/publications/ftt-revenue-2009-12.pdf.

Bakija, Jon, Adam Cole, and Bradley T. Heim. "Jobs and Income Growth of Top Earners and the Causes of Changing Income Inequality: Evidence from U.S.

Tax Return Data." Unpublished paper, April 2012. http://web.williams.edu/Economics/wp/BakijaColeHeimJobsIncomeGrowthTopEarners.pdf.

Banting, Keith G. "Dis-embedding Liberalism? The New Social Policy Paradigm in Canada." In *Dimensions of Inequality in Canada*, edited by David A. Green and Jonathan R. Kesselman, 417–52. Vancouver: UBC Press, 2006.

Banting, Keith. "The Social Policy Divide: The Welfare State in Canada and the United States." In *Degrees of Freedom: Canada and the United States in a Changing World*, edited by George Hoberg, Keith Banting, and Richard Simeon, 267–309. Montreal, Kingston: McGill-Queen's University Press, 1997.

Banting, Keith, and John Myles. "Framing the New Inequality: The Politics of Income Redistribution in Canada." In *Income Inequality: The Canadian Story*, edited by David A. Green, W. Craig Riddell, and Francis St-Hilaire, 509–40. Montreal: Institute for Research on Public Policy, 2015.

Banting, Keith, and John Myles. "Introduction: Inequality and the Fading of Redistributive Politics." In *Inequality and the Fading of Redistributive Politics*, edited by Keith Banting and John Myles, 1–42. Vancouver: UBC Press, 2013.

Barro, Robert J. "Inequality and Growth Revisited." Working Paper Series on Regional Economic Integration No. 11, Asian Development Bank, January 2008. https://aric.adb.org/pdf/workingpaper/WP11_%20Inequality_and_Growth_Revisited.pdf.

Bartels, Larry. *Unequal Democracy: The Political Economy of the New Gilded Age*. Princeton: Princeton University Press, 2008.

Barton, John, and John Muddiman, eds. *The Oxford Bible Commentary*. Oxford: Oxford University Press, 2007.

Bashevkin, Sylvia. *True Patriot Love: The Politics of Canadian Nationalism*. Toronto: Oxford University Press, 1991.

Battle, Ken. "Restoring Minimum Wages in Canada." Caledon Institute for Social Policy, April 2011. http://www.caledoninst.org/publications/pdf/931eng.pdf.

Baum, Sandy. "Higher Education Earnings Premium: Value, Variation, and Trends." Urban Institute, February 2014. http://www.urban.org/sites/default/files/publication/22316/413033-Higher-Education-Earnings-Premium-Value-Variation-and-Trends.PDF.

Beach, Charles M. "How Has Earnings Mobility in Canada Changed?" In *Dimensions of Inequality in Canada*, edited by David A. Green and Jonathan R. Kesselman, 101–26. Vancouver: UBC Press, 2006.

Beach, Jane, Martha Friendly, Carolyn Ferns, Nina Prabhu, and Barry Forer. "Early Childhood Education and Care in Canada, 2008." Childcare Research and Resource Unit, University of Toronto, 2009. http://www.childcarecanada.org/sites/default/files/ECEC08_Frontmatter.pdf.

Bebchuk, Lucian, and Jesse Fried. *Pay without Performance: The Unfulfilled Promise of Executive Compensation*. Cambridge, MA: Harvard University Press, 2004.

Béland, Daniel. "Ideas and Social Policy: An Institutionalist Perspective." *Social Policy and Administration* 39, no. 1 (February 2005): 1–18. https://doi.org/10.1111/j.1467-9515.2005.00421.x.

Bell, David V.J. *The Roots of Disunity: A Study of Canadian Political Culture*. 2nd ed. Toronto: Oxford University Press, 1992.

Bellah, Robert N. *The Habits of the Heart: Individualism in American Life*. Berkeley: University of California Press, 1985.

Belley, Philippe, Marc Frenette, and Lance Lochner. "Post-secondary Attendance by Parental Income in the U.S. and Canada: Do Financial Aid Policies Explain the Differences?" *Canadian Journal of Economics* 47, no. 2 (May 2014): 664–96. https://doi.org/10.1111/caje.12088.

Benabou, Roland, and Efe A. Ok. "Social Mobility and the Demand for Redistribution: The Poum Hypothesis." *Quarterly Journal of Economics* 116, no. 2 (May 2001): 447–87. https://doi.org/10.1162/00335530151144078.

Benn, S.I., and R.S. Peters. *Social Principles and the Democratic State.* London: George Allen and Unwin, 1959.

Bennett, Pam. "The Aftermath of the Great Recession: Financially Fragile Families and How Professionals Can Help." *The Forum for Family and Consumer Issues* 17, no. 1 (Spring/Summer 2012): http://ncsu.edu/ffci/publications/2012/v17-n1-2012-spring/index-v17-n1-may-2012.php.

Bentley, Arthur F. *The Process of Government: A Study of Social Pressures.* 1908. Bloomington: Principia, 1935.

Berg, Andrew G., and Jonathan D. Ostry. "Equality and Efficiency." *Finance & Development* 48, no. 3 (September 2011). http://www.imf.org/external/pubs/ft/fandd/2011/09/Berg.htm.

Berg, Andrew G., and Jonathan D. Ostry. "Inequality and Unsustainable Growth: Two Sides of the Same Coin?" IMF Staff Discussion Note, International Monetary Fund, April 8, 2011. https://www.imf.org/external/pubs/ft/sdn/2011/sdn1108.pdf.

Bernard, Paul, and Sébastien Saint-Arnaud. "Du pareil au même? La position des quatre principales provinces canadiennes dans l'univers des régimes providentiels." *Canadian Journal of Sociology* 29, no. 2 (Spring 2004): 209–39. https://doi.org/10.2307/3654694.

Birchard, Karen. "Canada's Elite Universities Propose a National Strategy for Higher Education." *Chronicle of Higher Education*, August 17, 2009. http://chronicle.com/article/Canadas-Elite-Universities/48013/.

Bitler, Marianne, and Hilary W. Hoynes. "The State of the Safety Net in the Post-Welfare Reform Era." National Bureau of Economic Research, Working Paper 16504, October 2010. http://www.nber.org/papers/w16504.pdf. https://doi.org/10.3386/w16504.

Bivens, Josh, and Lawrence Mishel. "The Pay of Corporate Executives and Financial Professionals as Evidence of Rents in Top 1 Percent Incomes." *Journal of Economic Perspectives* 27, no. 3 (Summer 2013): 57–78. https://doi.org/10.1257/jep.27.3.57.

Blanden, Jo, Paul Gregg, and Stephen Machin. "Intergenerational Mobility in Europe and North America: A Report Supported by the Sutton Trust." Centre for Economic Performance, April 2005. http://cep.lse.ac.uk/about/news/IntergenerationalMobility.pdf.

Bloome, Deirdre. "Income Inequality and Intergenerational Income Mobility in the United States." Working Paper, Russell Sage Foundation, 2013. http://www.russellsage.org/sites/all/files/Bloome%20Inequality%20&%20mobility%20April%202013.pdf.

BMO Financial Group. "2013 BMO Student Survey: Canadian Students Relying Less on Family to Finance Higher Education." August 13, 2013. https://newsroom.bmo.com/press-releases/2013-bmo-student-survey-canadian-students-relying-tsx-bmo-201308130891837001.

Board of Governors of the Federal Reserve System. *Report on the Economic Well-Being of US Households in 2014*. US Federal Reserve, May 2015. https://www.federalreserve.gov/econresdata/2014-report-economic-well-being-us-households-201505.pdf.

Bolton, Kenyon, and Sébastien Breau. "Growing Unequal? Changes in the Distribution of Earnings across Canadian Cities." *Urban Studies* 49, no. 6 (2012): 1377–96. https://doi.org/10.1177/0042098011410335.

Booth, Barbara. "How Much Would You Pay to Get Your Kid into Harvard?" CNBC, November 12, 2014. http://www.cnbc.com/2014/11/10/is-a-college-planner-really-worth-it.html.

Bosworth, Barry, Gary Burtless, and Kan Zhang. "Later Retirement, Inequality in Old Age, and the Growing Gap in Longevity between Rich and Poor." Brookings Institution, Research Program, 2016. https://www.brookings.edu/wp-content/uploads/2016/02/BosworthBurtlessZhang_retirementinequalitylongevity_012815.pdf.

Boucoyannis, Deborah. "The Equalizing Hand: Why Adam Smith Thought the Market Should Produce Wealth without Steep Inequality." *Perspectives on Politics* 11, no. 4 (December 2013): 1051–70. https://doi.org/10.1017/S153759271300282X.

Boychuk, Gerard W. "Federal Policies, National Trends, and Provincial Systems." In *Welfare Reform in Canada: Provincial Social Assistance in Comparative Perspective*, edited by Daniel Béland and Pierre-Marc Daigneault, 35–51. Toronto: University of Toronto Press, 2015.

Boychuk, Gerard W. *National Health Insurance in the United States and Canada: Race, Territory, and the Roots of Difference*. Washington, DC: Georgetown University Press, 2008.

Boychuk, Gerard W., and Keith Banting. "The Paradox of Convergence: National versus Subnational Patterns of Convergence in Canadian and US Income Maintenance Policy." In *North American Linkages: Opportunities and Challenges for Canada*, edited by Richard G. Harris, 533–74. Calgary: University of Calgary Press, 2003.

Bradbury, Bruce, Miles Corak, Jane Waldfogel, and Elizabeth Washbrook. "Inequality in Early Childhood Outcomes." In *From Parents to Children: The Intergenerational Transmission of Advantage*, edited by John Ermisch, Markus Jäntti, and Timothy Smeeding, 87–119. New York: Russell Sage Foundation, 2012.

Bradbury, Katharine. "Trends in US Family Income Mobility, 1969–2006." Federal Reserve Bank of Boston, October 20, 2011. http://www.bostonfed.org/economic/wp/wp2011/wp1110.pdf.

Bricker, Jesse, et al. "Changes in U.S. Family Finances from 2010 to 2013: Evidence from the Survey of Consumer Finances." *Federal Reserve Bulletin* 100, no. 4 (September 2014): 10.

Broadbent Institute. "Equality Project 2012." http://www.broadbentinstitute.ca/sites/default/files/documents/equality-project_0.pdf.

Broadbent Institute. "Haves and Have Nots: Deep and Persistent Wealth Inequality in Canada." September 2014. http://d3n8a8pro7vhmx.cloudfront.net/broadbent/legacy_url/310/have-havenots.pdf?1431294012.

Broadbent Institute. "Majority Think Income Inequality Undermines Canadian Values: New Poll." April 9, 2012. http://www.broadbentinstitute.ca/majority_think_income_inequality_undermines_canadian_values_new_poll.

Broadbent Institute. "The Wealth Gap: Perceptions and Misconceptions in Canada." December 2014. https://d3n8a8pro7vhmx.cloudfront.net/broadbent/pages/31/attachments/original/1430002077/The_Wealth_Gap.pdf?1430002077.

Brooks, David. "Money Matters Less." *New York Times*, October 19, 2014. http://www.nytimes.com/2014/10/10/opinion/david-brooks-money-matters-less.html.

Brooks, Stephen. "Imagining Each Other." In *Canada and the United States: Differences that Count*, 4th ed., edited by David M. Thomas and David N. Biette, 23–45. Toronto: University of Toronto Press, 2014.

Bryce, James. *Modern Democracies*. Vol. 1. New York: Macmillan, 1921.

Brynjolfsson, Erik, and Andrew McAfee. *Race against the Machine: How the Digital Revolution Is Accelerating Innovation, Driving Productivity, and Irreversibly Transforming Employment and the Economy*. Lexington, MA: Digital Frontier Press, 2012.

"Budget Speech," the Honourable Paul Martin, PC, MP, Minister of Finance, February 27, 1995. www.fin.gc.ca/budget95/speech/speech.pdf.

Bui, Quoctrung. "Most Americans Make It to the Top 20 Percent (At Least for a While)." NPR, *Planet Money*, May 5, 2014. http://www.npr.org/sections/money/2014/05/05/308380342/most-americans-make-it-to-the-top-20-percent-at-least-for-a-while.

Burstein, Paul. "The Impact of Public Opinion on Public Policy: A Review and an Agenda." *Political Research Quarterly* 56, no. 1 (2003): 29–40. https://doi.org/10.1177/106591290305600103.

Caledon Institute of Social Policy. "Canada Social Report: Social Assistance, Combined Summaries, 2014." March 2015. http://www.caledoninst.org/Publications/PDF/1062ENG.pdf.

Campaign 2000. "2013 Child Poverty Report Card: British Columbia." November 2013. http://www.campaign2000.ca/wp-content/uploads/2016/03/BCRC2013.pdf.

Canada Human Rights Commission, "Discrimination." http://www.chrc.ccdp.ca/discrimination/apfa_uppt/pagel-eng.aspx.

Canadian Institute for Health Information. *Trends in Income Related Health Inequalities in Canada*. Ottawa: Author, 2015.

"Capitalism and Its Critics: A Modern Marx." *The Economist*, May 3, 2014. http://www.economist.com/news/leaders/21601512-thomas-pikettys-blockbuster-book-great-piece-scholarship-poor-guide-policy.

Caranci, Beata, and Diana Petramala. "Canadian and U.S. Millennials: One of These Things Is Not Like the Other." TD Economics, December 1, 2015. http://www.td.com/document/PDF/economics/special/Canadian_US_Millennials.pdf.

Carbone, June, and Naomi Cahn. *Marriage Markets: How Inequality Is Remaking the American Family*. Oxford: Oxford University Press, 2014.

Card, David, Thomas Lemieux, and W. Craig Riddell. "Unionization and Wage Inequality: A Comparative Study of the US, the UK, and Canada." National Bureau of Economic Research, Working Paper 9473, January 2003. http://www.nber.org/papers/w9473.pdf. https://doi.org/10.3386/w9473.

Carnevale, Anthony P., and Jeff Strohl. "How Increasing College Access Is Increasing Inequality and What to Do about It." In *Rewarding Strivers: Helping Low Income Students Succeed in College*, edited by Richard D. Kahlenberg, 71–190. New York: New Century Foundation, 2010.

Carney, Mark. "Inclusive Capitalism: Creating a Sense of the Systemic." Speech by Governor of the Bank of England, May 27, 2014. http://www.bankofengland.co.uk/publications/Documents/speeches/2014/speech731.pdf.

Carroll, Lewis. *Alice's Adventures in Wonderland*. 1865. Chicago: Volume One Publishing, 1998.

Catlin, Bridget, Amanda Jovaag, and Julie Willems van Dijk. 2015 County Health Rankings: Key Findings Report. Robert Wood Johnson Foundation, University of Wisconsin Population Health Institute, 2015. http://www.rwjf.org/en/library/research/2015/03/2015-county-health-rankings-key-findings-report.html.

CAUT. "Poll Shows Canadians Value Higher Education." *CAUT/ACPPU Bulletin* 57, No. 5 (May 2010). https://www.cautbulletin.ca/staging/en_article.asp?ArticleID=3074.

Center for Responsive Politics. "Outside Spending by Group; Non-Disclosing Groups, 2012." http://www.opensecrets.org/outsidespending/summ.php?cycle=2012&chrt=V&disp=O&type=U.

Center for Responsive Politics. "Top Individual Contributors: All Federal Contributions, 2012." https://www.opensecrets.org/overview/topindivs.php?cycle=2012&view=fc.

Center for Responsive Politics. "2012 Outside Spending, by Super PAC." https://www.opensecrets.org/outsidespending/summ.php?cycle=2012&chrt=V&disp=O&type=S.

Center on Budget and Policy Priorities. "Chart Book: TANF at 19." March 29, 2016. http://www.cbpp.org/research/family-income-support/chart-book-tanf-at-19.

Center on Philanthropy at Indiana University. "Patterns of Household Charitable Giving by Income Group, 2005." Summer 2007. https://philanthropy.iupui.edu/files/research/giving_focused_on_meeting_needs_of_the_poor_july_2007.pdf.

Centers for Disease Control and Prevention. "Early Release of Selected Estimates Based on Data from the 2014 National Health Interview Survey" http://www.cdc.gov/nchs/data/nhis/earlyrelease/earlyrelease201506.pdf.

Charvet, John. "The Idea of Equality as a Substantive Principle of Society." In *Contemporary Political Theory*, edited by Anthony de Crespigny and Alan Wertheimer, 154–69. New York: Atherton Press, 1970.

Chen, Victor Tan. *Cut Loose: Jobless and Hopeless in an Unfair Economy*. Berkeley: University of California Press, 2015.

Chen, Wen-Hao. "Cross-National Differences in Income Mobility: Evidence from Canada, the United States, Great Britain and Germany." *Review of Income and Wealth* 55, no. 1 (March 2009): 75–100. https://doi.org/10.1111/j.1475-4991.2008.00307.x.

Chetty, Raj, et al. "How Does Your Kindergarten Classroom Affect Your Earnings? Evidence from Project STAR." *Quarterly Journal of Economics* 126, no. 4 (2011): 1593–660. https://doi.org/10.1093/qje/qjr041.

Chetty, Raj, John N. Friedman, Emmanuel Saez, Nicholas Turner, and Danny Yagan. "Mobility Report Cards: The Role of Colleges in Intergenerational Mobility." The Equality of Opportunity Project, January 2017. http://www.equality-of-opportunity.org/assets/documents/coll_mrc_paper.pdf.

Chetty, Raj, Nathaniel Hendren, Patrick Kline, and Emmanuel Saez. "Where Is the Land of Opportunity? The Geography of Intergenerational Mobility in the United States." *Quarterly Journal of Economics* 129, no. 4 (2014): 1553–623. https://doi.org/10.1093/qje/qju022.

Chetty, Raj, Nathaniel Hendren, Patrick Kline, Emmanuel Saez, and Nicholas Turner. "Is the United States Still a Land of Opportunity? Recent Trends in Intergenerational Mobility." NBER Working Paper 19844, January 2014. http://www.nber.org/papers/w19844.pdf. https://doi.org/10.3386/w19844.

Choma, Russ. "Millionaires' Club: For First Time, Most Lawmakers Are Worth $1 Million-Plus." Center for Responsible Politics, January 9, 2014. http://www.opensecrets.org/news/2014/01/millionaires-club-for-first-time-most-lawmakers-are-worth-1-million-plus/.

Choma, Russ. "The 2012 Election: Our Price Tag (Finally) for the Whole Ball of Wax." Center for Responsible Politics, March 13, 2013. http://www.opensecrets.org/news/2013/03/the-2012-election-our-price-tag-fin/.

Cingano, Federico. "Trends in Income Inequality and Its Impact on Economic Growth." OECD Social, Employment and Migration Working Papers, No. 163. Paris: OECD Publishing, 2014. https://doi.org/10.1787/1815199X.

"The CNN Democratic Debate Transcript, Annotated." *Washington Post*, October 13, 2015. https://www.washingtonpost.com/news/the-fix/wp/2015/10/13/the-oct-13-democratic-debate-who-said-what-and-what-it-means/.

"CNN Poll: 7 out of 10 Support 'Buffett Rule.'" CNN.com, April 16, 2012. http://politicalticker.blogs.cnn.com/2012/04/16/cnn-poll-7-out-of-10-support-buffett-rule/.

Coates, Ken. "Why Top Canadian Universities Should Add an Admission Test." *Globe and Mail*, March 6, 2014. http://www.theglobeandmail.com/news/national/education/do-canadian-universities-need-an-admissions-test/article17342171/.

Cohn, Nate. "Why Trump Won: Working Class Whites." *New York Times*, November 9, 2016. https://www.nytimes.com/2016/11/10/upshot/why-trump-won-working-class-whites.html?emc=eta1.

Conacher, Duff. "How to Stop Big Money from Influencing Elections." *National Observer*, July 28, 2015. http://www.nationalobserver.com/2015/07/28/opinion/how-stop-big-money-influencing-elections.

Congressional Budget Office. "Changes in the Distribution of Workers' Hourly Wages between 1979 and 2009." February 2011. https://www.cbo.gov/sites/default/files/112th-congress-2011-2012/reports/02-16-wagedispersion.pdf.

Congressional Budget Office. "The Distribution of Household Income and Federal Taxes, 2011." November 2014. https://www.cbo.gov/publication/49440.

Congressional Budget Office. "Temporary Assistance for Needy Families: Spending and Policy Options." January 2015. https://www.cbo.gov/sites/default/files/114th-congress-2015-2016/reports/49887-TANF.pdf.

Cook, Ramsay. *The Maple Leaf Forever: Essays on Nationalism and Politics in Canada*. Toronto: MacMillan of Canada, 1977.

Corak, Miles. "Chasing the Same Dream, Climbing Different Ladders: Economic Mobility in the United States and Canada." Pew Charitable Trusts, Economic Mobility Project, January 2009. www.pewtrusts.org/~/media/legacy/uploadedfiles/pcs_assets/2010/pewempuscanadapdf.pdf.

Corak, Miles. "Do Poor Children Become Poor Adults? Lessons from a Cross Country Comparison of Generational Earnings Mobility." IZA DPf No. 1993, March 2006. http://ftp.iza.org/dp1993.pdf.

Corak, Miles, ed. *Generational Income Mobility in North America and Europe*. Cambridge: Cambridge University Press, 2011.

Corak, Miles. "How to Slide Down the 'Great Gatsby Curve': Inequality, Life Chances, and Public Policy in the United States." Center for American Progress, December 2012. https://milescorak.files.wordpress.com/2012/12/corakmiddleclass.pdf.

Corak, Miles. "Inequality from Generation to Generation: The United States in Comparison." In *The Economics of Inequality, Poverty, and Discrimination in the 21st Century*, edited by Robert Rycroft, 107–25. Santa Barbara: ABC-CLIO, 2013.

Corak, Miles, Lori J. Curtis, and Shelley Phipps. "Economic Mobility, Family Background, and the Well-Being of Children in the United States and Canada." In *Persistence, Privilege, and Parenting: The Comparative Study of Intergenerational Mobility*, edited by Timothy M. Smeeding, Robert Erikson, and Markus Jäntti, 73–108. New York: Russell Sage Foundation, 2011.

Corak, Miles, and Andrew Heisz. "The Intergenerational Earnings and Income Mobility of Canadian Men: Evidence from Longitudinal Income Tax Data." *Journal of Human Resources* 34, no. 3 (1999): 504–33. https://doi.org/10.2307/146378.

Corak, Miles, Matthew J. Lindquist, and Bhashkar Mazumder. "A Comparison of Upward and Downward Intergenerational Mobility in Canada, Sweden and the United States." *Labour Economics* 30 (2014): 185–200. https://doi.org/10.1016/j.labeco.2014.03.013.

Cowen, Tyler. *Average Is Over: Powering America beyond the Age of the Great Stagnation*. New York: Plume, 2014.

Cowen, Tyler. "Capital Punishment: Why a Global Tax on Wealth Won't End Inequality." *Foreign Affairs*, May/June 2014. https://www.foreignaffairs.com/reviews/review-essay/capital-punishment.

Cowen, Tyler. "It's Not the Inequality; It's the Immobility." *New York Times*, April 4, 2015. https://www.nytimes.com/2015/04/05/upshot/its-not-the-inequality-its-the-immobility.html.

Crick, Bernard. *In Defense of Politics*. Chicago: University of Chicago Press, 1962.

Cross, Philip, and Ian Lee. "Why the Gatsby Curve Is a Poor Measure of Income Mobility." *Globe and Mail*, November 11, 2013. http://www.theglobeandmail.com/opinion/why-the-gatsby-curve-is-a-poor-measure-of-income-mobility/article15372824.

Cross, Philip, and Munir A. Sheikh. "Caught in the Middle: Some in Canada's Middle Class Are Doing Well; Others Have Good Reason to Worry." SPP Research Paper 8, no. 12 (2015): 1–29. https://www.policyschool.ca/wp-content/uploads/2016/03/middle-class-cross-sheikh.pdf.

D'Addio, Anna Cristina. "Intergenerational Transmission of Disadvantage: Mobility or Immobility across Generations? A Review of the Evidence for OECD Countries." OECD Social, Employment and Migration Working Papers, no. 52, 2007. http://www.oecd.org/els/38335410.pdf. https://doi.org/10.1787/1815199x.

Dahl, Robert A. *Democracy and Its Critics*. New Haven, CT: Yale University Press, 1989.

Dahl, Robert A. *Pluralist Democracy in the United States: Conflict and Consent*. Chicago: Rand McNally, 1967.

Dahl, Robert A. *A Preface to Democratic Theory*. Chicago: University of Chicago Press, 1956.

Daly, Martin, Margo Wilson, and Shawn Vasdev. "Income Inequality and Homicide Rates in Canada and the United States." *Canadian Journal of Criminology* 43, no. 2 (2001): 219–36.

Davidai, Shai, and Thomas Gilovich. "Building a More Mobile America—One Income Quintile at a Time." *Perspectives on Psychological Science* 10, no. 1 (2015): 60–71. https://doi.org/10.1177/1745691614562005.

Davies, James C. "Toward a Theory of Revolution." *American Sociological Review* 27, no. 1 (1962): 5–19. https://doi.org/10.2307/2089714.

Davies, James C. *When Men Revolt and Why*. New York: The Free Press, 1971.

Deaton, Angus. *The Great Escape: Health, Wealth, and the Origins of Inequality*. Princeton: Princeton University Press, 2013.

Deaton, Angus. "Income, Health, and Well-Being around the World: Evidence from the Gallup World Poll." *Journal of Economic Perspectives* 22, no. 2 (Spring 2008): 53–72. https://doi.org/10.1257/jep.22.2.53.

de Crèvecouer, J. Hector St. John. *Letters from an American Farmer*. 1782. London: J.M. Dent, 1912.

DeNavas-Walt, Carmen, and Bernadette D. Proctor. "Income and Poverty in the United States: 2014." In *Current Population Reports*, 60–252. Washington, DC: US Government Printing Office, 2015.

DeParle, Jason. *American Dream: Three Women, Ten Kids, and a National Drive to End Welfare*. New York: Viking Press, 2004.

Department of Finance Canada. "Federal Support to Provinces and Territories, 2007–08 through 2016–17." https://www.fin.gc.ca/fedprov/mtp-eng.asp.

DeSilver, Drew. "High Income Americans Pay Most Income Taxes, but Enough to Be 'Fair'?" Pew Research Center, April 13, 2016. http://www.pewresearch.org/fact-tank/2016/04/13/high-income-americans-pay-most-income-taxes-but-enough-to-be-fair/.

de Tocqueville, Alexis. *Democracy in America*. Vol 1. Translated by Henry Reeve, revised by Francis Bowen, edited by Phillips Bradley. New York: Vintage Press, 1945.

Diaz-Gimenez, Javier, Jose-Victor Rios-Bull, and Andy Glover. "Facts on the Distribution of Earnings, Income and Wealth in the United States: 2007 Update." *Federal Reserve Bank of Minneapolis Quarterly Review* 34, no. 1 (February 2011): 2–31.

Diggins, John Patrick. *The Lost Soul of American Politics: Virtue, Self-Interest, and the Foundations of Liberalism*. New York: Basic Books, 1984.

Dooley, Martin D., A. Abigail Payne, and A. Leslie Robb. "University Participation and Income Differences: An Analysis of Applications by Ontario Secondary School Students." Higher Education Quality Council of Ontario, 2009. http://www.heqco.ca/SiteCollectionDocuments/University%20Participation%20and%20Income%20Differences2.pdf.

Dovere, Edward-Isaac. "Obama: Historian-in-chief." *Politico*, July 4, 2012. http://www.politico.com/story/2012/07/obama-historian-in-chief-078110.

Drennan, Matthew P. *Income Inequality: Why It Matters and Why Most Economists Didn't Notice*. New Haven, CT: Yale University Press, 2015. https://doi.org/10.12987/yale/9780300209587.001.0001.

Dugan, Andrew. "Americans Most Likely to Say They Belong to the Middle Class." Gallup, November 30, 2012. http://www.gallup.com/poll/159029/americans-likely-say-belong-middle-class.aspx.

Dugan, Andrew, and Frank Newport. "In U.S., Fewer Believe 'Plenty of Opportunity' to Get Ahead." Gallup, October 25, 2013. http://www.gallup.com/poll/165584/fewer-believe-plenty-opportunity-ahead.aspx.

Dumas, Christelle, and Arnaud Lefranc. "Early Schooling and Later Outcomes." In *From Parents to Children: The Intergenerational Transmission of Advantage*, edited by John Ermisch, Markus Jäntti, and Timothy Smeeding, 164–89. New York: Russell Sage Foundation, 2012.

Duncan, Greg J., and Katherine Magnusson. "The Long Reach of Early Childhood Poverty." *Pathways: A Magazine on Poverty, Inequality, and Social Policy*, Winter 2011: 23–7.

Duncan, Greg J., and Richard J. Murnane. "Introduction: The American Dream, Then and Now." In *Whither Opportunity*, edited by Greg J. Duncan and Richard J. Murnane, 1–23. New York: Russell Sage Foundation, 2011. https://www.rusellsage.org/sites/all/files/Duncan_Murnane_Chap1.pdf

Durkheim, Émile. *The Division of Labor in Society*. 1897. New York: The Free Press, 1997.

Dworetz, Stephen M. *The Unvarnished Doctrine: Locke, Liberalism, and the American Revolution*. Durham, NC: Duke University Press, 1990.

Dworkin, Ronald. *Sovereign Virtue: The Theory and Practice of Equality*. Cambridge, MA: Harvard University Press, 2000.

Easterlin, Richard. A. "Does Economic Growth Improve the Human Lot? Some Empirical Evidence." In *Nations and Households in Economic Growth: Essays in Honor of Moses Abramovitz*, edited by Paul A. David and Melvin W. Reder, 89–125. New York: Academic Press, 1974. https://doi.org/10.1016/B978-0-12-205050-3.50008-7.

Economic Policy Institute. *The State of Working America*. 12th ed. Ithaca: Cornell University Press, 2012.

The Economist. "The Logical Floor." December 14, 2013, 18–21.

The Economist. "Poverty: Not Always With Us." June 1, 2013. http://www.economist.com/news/briefing/21578643-world-has-astonishing-chance-take-billion-people-out-extreme-poverty-2030-not.

The Economist. "The Rich, the Poor, and the Growing Gap between Them." June 17, 2006, 26–29.

Edelman Trust Barometer. "Annual Global Study, 2016." http://www.edelman.com/insights/intellectual-property/2016-edelman-trust-barometer/.

Editorial Board. "Business and the Minimum Wage." *New York Times*, February 27, 2014. http://www.nytimes.com/2014/02/28/opinion/business-and-the-minimum-wage.html.

Edsall, Thomas B. "Why Can't America Be Sweden?" *New York Times*, May 29, 2013. http://opinionator.blogs.nytimes.com/2013/05/29/why-cant-america-be-sweden/?_r=0.

Education Trust. "Funding Gaps 2015: Too Many States Still Spend Less on Educating Students Who Need the Most." March 2015. http://edtrust.org/wp-content/uploads/2014/09/FundingGaps2015_TheEducationTrust1.pdf.

Eide, Eric R., and Michael J. Hilmer. "Do Elite Colleges Lead to Higher Salaries? Only for Some Professions." *Wall Street Journal*, January 31, 2016. https://www.wsj.com/articles/do-elite-colleges-lead-to-higher-salaries-only-for-some-professions-1454295674.

Ekos Politics. "So What's Really Bothering You Canada?" October 17, 2013. http://www.ekospolitics.com/index.php/2013/10/so-whats-really-bothering-you-canada/.

Elections Canada. "Third Party Election Advertising Reports for the 42nd General Election." http://www.elections.ca/content.aspx?section=fin&document=index&dir=thi/advert/tp42&lang=e.

Elwell, Craig K. "Inflation and the Real Minimum Wage: A Fact Sheet." Congressional Research Service, 7–5700, R42973, January 8, 2014. https://fas.org/sgp/crs/misc/R42973.pdf.

Engelhardt, Carina, and Andreas Wagener. "Biased Perceptions of Income Inequality and Redistribution." CESifo Working Paper Series No. 4838, June 12, 2014. http://ssrn.com/abstract=2463129.

Environics Institute. *AmericasBarometer: Canada 2012, Final Report*. http://www.environicsinstitute.org/uploads/institute-projects/environicsinstitute%20-%20americasbarometer%20canada%202012%20final%20report.pdf.

Environics Institute. *AmericasBarometer: Citizens across the Americas Speak on Democracy and Governance: Canada 2014: Final Report*. http://www.environicsinstitute.org/uploads/institute-projects/environics-iog%20-%20americasbarometer%202014%20final%20report.pdf.

Environics Institute. *Focus Canada 2011*. http://www.environicsinstitute.org/uploads/institute-projects/pdf-focuscanada-2011-final.pdf.

Environics Institute. *Focus Canada 2012*. http://www.environicsinstitute.org/uploads/institute-projects/environics%20institute%20-%20focus%20canada%202012%20final%20report.pdf.

Ermisch, John, Markus Jäntti, and Timothy Smeeding, eds. *From Parents to Children: The Intergenerational Transmission of Advantage*. New York: Russell Sage Foundation, 2012.

Ermisch, John, Markus Jäntti, Timothy Smeeding, and James A. Wilson. "Advantage in Comparative Perspective." In *From Parents to Children: The Intergenerational Transmission of Advantage*, edited by John Ermisch, Markus Jäntti, and Timothy Smeeding, 3–31. New York: Russell Sage Foundation, 2012.

Ermisch, John, Markus Jäntti, Timothy Smeeding, and James A. Wilson. "What Have We Learned?" In *From Parents to Children: The Intergenerational Transmission of Advantage*, edited by John Ermisch, Markus Jäntti, and Timothy Smeeding, 463–81. New York: Russell Sage Foundation, 2012.

Esping-Anderson, Gosta. *The Three Worlds of Welfare Capitalism*. Princeton: Princeton University Press, 1990.

Esping-Anderson, Gosta. "Unequal Opportunities and the Mechanisms of Social Inheritance." In *Generational Income Mobility in North America and Europe*, edited by Miles Corak, 289–315. Cambridge: Cambridge University Press, 2011.

Etzioni, Amitai. *The New Golden Rule: Community and Morality in a Democratic Society*. New York: Basic Books, 1996.

Evans, William N., Barbara Wolfe, and Nancy Adler. "The SES and the Health Gradient: A Brief Review of the Literature." In *The Biological Consequences of Socioeconomic Inequalities*, edited by Barbara Wolfe, William N. Evans, and Teresa E. Seeman, 1–37. New York: Russell Sage Foundation, 2012.

Executive Office of the President. "Increasing College Opportunity for Low-Income Students: Promising Models and a Call to Action." January 2014. https://obamawhitehouse.archives.gov/sites/default/files/docs/increasing_college_opportunity_for_low-income_students_report.pdf.

Fajnzylber, Pablo, Daniel Lederman, and Norman Loayza. "Inequality and Violent Crime." *Journal of Law & Economics* 45, no. 1 (April 2002): 1–39. https://doi.org/10.1086/338347.

Falk, Gene. "The Temporary Assistance for Needy Families (TANF) Block Grant: Responses to Frequently Asked Questions." Congressional Research Service, March 18, 2016. https://fas.org/sgp/crs/misc/RL32760.pdf.

Fatovic, Clement. *America's Founding and the Struggle over Economic Inequality*. Lawrence: University Press of Kansas, 2015.

Federal Election Committee. "FEC Summarizes Campaign Activity of the 2011–2012 Election Cycle." March 27, 2014.

Fellowes, Matthew C., and Gretchen Rowe. "Politics and the New American Welfare States." *American Journal of Political Science* 48, no. 2 (2004): 362–73. https://doi.org/10.1111/j.0092-5853.2004.00075.x.

Ferguson, Thomas. *Golden Rule: The Investment Theory of Party Competition and the Logic of Money-Driven Political Systems*. Chicago: University of Chicago Press, 1995.

Fischer, Claude S., and Michael Holt. *Century of Difference: How America Changed in the Last 100 Years*. New York: Russell Sage Foundation, 2006.

Fischer, Justina A. "The Welfare Effects of Social Mobility." OECD Social, Employment and Migration Working Papers, no. 93. Paris: OECD Publishing, 2009. http://www.oecd-ilibrary.org/social-issues-migration-health/the-welfare-effects-of-social-mobility_221272634852;jsessionid=3apo36gf90o10.x-oecd-live-02.

Fleury, Michelle. "Davos: Income Inequality on World Economic Forum Agenda." *BBC News*. January 20, 2015. http://www.bbc.com/news/business-30908234.

Floyd, Ife, and Liz Schott. "TANF Cash Benefits Have Fallen by More Than 20 Percent in Most States and Continue to Erode." Center on Budget and Policy Priorities, October 30, 2014. http://www.cbpp.org/research/tanf-cash-benefits-have-fallen-by-more-than-20-percent-in-most-states-and-continue-to-erode.

Floyd, Ife, LaDonna Pavetti, and Liz Schott. "TANF Continues to Weaken as a Safety Net." Center on Budget and Policy Priorities, June 16, 2015. http://www.cbpp.org/research/family-income-support/tanf-continues-to-weaken-as-a-safety-net.

Flyvberg, Bent. *Making Social Science Matter*. Cambridge: Cambridge University Press, 2001. https://doi.org/10.1017/CBO9780511810503.

Foner, Eric. "Why Is There No Socialism in the United States?" *History Workshop* 17, no. 1 (1984): 57–80. https://doi.org/10.1093/hwj/17.1.57.

Forbes. "The Candidates and Their Net Worth." http://www.forbes.com/election-2016/#699402937eb8.

Förster, Michael and Marco Mira d'Ercole. "Income Distribution and Poverty in OECD Countries in the Second Half of the 1990s." OECD Social, Employment and Migration Working Paper No. 22, February 18, 2005. http://search.oecd.org/els/soc/34483698.pdf.

Fortin, Nicole, David A. Green, Thomas Lemieux, Kevin Milligan, and W. Craig Riddell. "Canadian Inequality: Recent Developments and Policy Options." *Canadian Public Policy* 38, no. 2 (June 2012): 121–45. https://doi.org/10.3138/cpp.38.2.121.

Fortin, Nicole M., and Tammy Schirle. "Gender Dimensions of Changes in Earnings Inequality in Canada." In *Dimensions of Inequality in Canada*, edited by David A. Green and Jonathan Kesselman, 307–46. Vancouver: UBC Press, 2007.

Frank, Robert. *Falling Behind: How Rising Inequality Harms the Middle Class*. 2nd ed. Berkeley: University of California Press, 2013.

Freeman, Richard. "Optimal Inequality for Economic Growth, Stability, and Shared Prosperity: The Economics Behind the Wall Street Occupiers' Protest?" *Insights: Melbourne Business and Economics* 11, no. 2 (2012): 5–11.

Frenette, Marc. "Why Are Youth from Lower-Income Families Less Likely to Attend University? Evidence from Academic Abilities, Parental Influences, and Financial Constraints." Statistics Canada, February 2007. http://citeseerx.ist.psu.edu/viewdoc/download?doi=10.1.1.531.6041&rep=rep1&type=pdf.

Frenette, Marc, David A. Green, and Keith Milligan. "Taxes, Transfers, and Canadian Income Inequality." *Canadian Public Policy* 35, no. 4 (2009): 389–411. https://doi.org/10.3138/cpp.35.4.389.

Frenette, Marc, and Rene Morisette. "Wages and Full-time Employment Rates of Young High School Graduates and Bachelor's Degree Holders, 1997 to 2012." Analytical Studies Branch Research Series Paper no. 360, Statistics Canada. Ottawa: Statistics Canada, April 2014.

Friedman, Thomas L. *The Lexus and the Olive Tree*. New York: Farrar, Straus, Giroux, 1999.

Galarneau, Diane, and Éric Fecteau. "The Ups and Downs of Minimum Wage." *Insights on Canadian Society*. Statistics Canada Catalogue no. 75-006-X, July 2014. http://www.statcan.gc.ca/pub/75-006-x/2014001/article/14035-eng.htm.

Gao, George. "How Do Americans Stand Out from the Rest of the World?" Pew Research Center, March 12, 2015. http://www.pewresearch.org/fact-tank/2015/03/12/how-do-americans-stand-out-from-the-rest-of-the-world/.

Garreau, Joel. *The Nine Nations of North America*. Boston: Houghton Mifflin, 1981.

Gauthier, James. *The Canada Social Transfer: Past, Present, and Future Considerations*. Social Affairs Division, Parliamentary Information and Research Service, Publication No. 2012-48-E, September 13. Ottawa: Library of Parliament, 2012.

Gavett, Gretchen. "CEOs Get Paid Too Much, According to Pretty Much Everyone in the World." *Harvard Business Review*, September 23, 2014. https://hbr.org/2014/09/ceos-get-paid-too-much-according-to-pretty-much-everyone-in-the-world/.

Gee, Ellen, Karen M. Kobayashi, and Steven G. Prus. "Ethnic Inequality in Canada: Economic and Health Dimensions." In *Dimensions of Inequality in Canada*, edited by David E. Green and Jonathan R. Kesselman, 249–72. Vancouver: UBC Press, 2006.

Gelman, Andrew. *Red State, Blue State, Rich State, Poor State*. Princeton: Princeton University Press, 2010.

Gerson, Michael. "Economic Inequality Is the Wrong Issue." *Washington Post*, November 3, 2011. https://www.washingtonpost.com/opinions/economic-inequality-is-the-wrong-issue/2011/11/03/gIQATYUqjM_story.html?utm_term=.aaf8373a2cae.

Gilens, Martin. *Affluence and Influence: Economic Inequality and Political Power in America.* Princeton: Princeton University Press, 2012.

Gilens, Martin. *Why Americans Hate Welfare: Race, Media, and the Politics of Antipoverty Policy.* Chicago: University of Chicago Press, 1999. https://doi.org/10.7208/chicago/9780226293660.001.0001.

Gilens, Martin, and Benjamim I. Page. "Testing Theories of American Politics: Elites, Interest Groups, and Average Citizens." *Perspectives on Politics* 12, no. 3 (September 2014): 564–81. https://doi.org/10.1017/S1537592714001595.

Gill, Vijay, James Knowles, and David Stewart-Patterson. *The Buck Stops Here: Trends in Income Inequality between Generations.* Ottawa: The Conference Board of Canada, 2014.

Gimpelson, Vladimir, and Daniel Treisman. "Misperceiving Inequality." IZA Discussion Paper no. 9100, Institute for the Study of Labor, June 2015. http://ftp.iza.org/dp9100.pdf. https://doi.org/10.3386/w21174.

Giovannoni, Olivier. "What Do We Know about the Labor Share and the Profit Share? Part III: Measures and Structural Factors." Levy Economics Institute of Bard College, Working Paper no. 805, May 2014. http://www.levyinstitute.org/pubs/wp_805.pdf.

Glynn, Sarah Jane. "Fact Sheet: Child Care." Center for American Progress, August 16, 2012. https://www.americanprogress.org/issues/labor/news/2012/08/16/11978/fact-sheet-child-care/.

Goldstein, Dana. "School Choice in Iowa May Preview the One Facing Trump." *New York Times*, March 21, 2017, https://www.nytimes.com/2017/03/21/us/school-choice-fight-in-iowa-may-preview-the-one-facing-trump.html?hp&action=click&pgtype=Homepage&clickSource=story-heading&module=second-column-region&region=top-news&WT.nav=top-news.

Goldthorpe, John H. "Analysing Social Inequality: a Critique of Two Recent Contributions from Economics and Epidemiology." *European Sociological Review* 26, no. 6 (2010): 731–44. https://doi.org/10.1093/esr/jcp046.

Gordon, Robert J. *The Rise and Fall of American Growth.* Princeton: Princeton University Press, 2016. https://doi.org/10.1515/9781400873302.

Gornick, Janet C., and Branko Milanovic. "Income Inequality in the United States in Cross-National Perspective: Redistribution Revisited." Luxembourg Income Study Center, LIS Center Research Brief (1/2015), May 4, 2015. https://www.gc.cuny.edu/CUNY_GC/media/CUNY-Graduate-Center/PDF/Centers/LIS/LIS-Center-Research-Brief-1-2015.pdf.

Gould, Elise. "Wage Inequality Continued Its 35-Year Rise in 2015." Economic Policy Institute briefing paper, no. 421, March 10, 2016. http://www.epi.org/files/2016/wage-inequality-2015.pdf.

Gould, Elise. "Why America's Workers Need Faster Wage Growth—And What We Can Do about It." Economic Policy Institute Briefing Paper #382, August 27, 2014. http://www.epi.org/files/2014/why-americas-workers-need-faster-wage-growth-final.pdf.

Grabb, Edward, and James Curtis. *Regions Apart: The Four Societies of Canada and the United States.* Oxford: Oxford University Press, 2010.

Graham, Bryan S., Jinyong Hahn, Alexandre Poirier, and James L. Powell. "Quantile Regression with 12 Panel Data." NBER Working Paper No. 21034, 2015. http://www.nber.org/papers/w21034.pdf.

Graham, Bryan S., and Patrick Sharkey. "Mobility and the Metropolis: How Communities Factor into Economic Mobility." Pew Charitable Trusts, Economic Mobility Project, December 2013. http://eml.berkeley.edu/~bgraham/Published/PewMobilityReport_2013/PewMobilityReport_2013.pdf.

Graham, Carol. *Happiness around the World: The Paradox of Happy Peasants and Miserable Millionaires*. Oxford: Oxford University Press, 2009. https://doi.org/10.1093/acprof:osobl/9780199549054.001.0001.

Graham, Carol. *The Pursuit of Happiness: An Economy of Well-Being*. Washington, DC: Brookings Institution Press, 2011.

Gravelle, Jane G. "International Corporate Tax Rate Comparisons and Policy Implications." Congressional Research Service, January 6, 2014. http://www.fas.org/sgp/crs/misc/R41743.pdf.

Gravelle, Jane G. "Tax Havens: International Tax Avoidance and Evasion." Congressional Research Service, January 15, 2015. https://www.fas.org/sgp/crs/misc/R40623.pdf.

Greenberg, Lawson, and Claude Normandin. "Disparities in Life Expectancy at Birth." Statistics Canada, April 2011. http://www.statcan.gc.ca/pub/82-624-x/2011001/article/11427-eng.pdf.

Grogger, Jeffrey. "Welfare Transitions in the 1990s: The Economy, Welfare Policy, and the EITC." National Bureau of Economic Research Working Paper, No. 9472, February 2003. http://www.nber.org/papers/w9472. https://doi.org/10.3386/w9472.

Guatieri, Sal. "Household Finances: Are Young People Worse Off than Their Parents Were?" BMO Capital Markets, *Focus*, October 26, 2012.

Gurr, Ted Robert. *Why Men Rebel*. Princeton: Princeton University Press, 1970.

Guttman, Amy. "Equality." In *The Blackwell Encyclopedia of Political Thought*, edited by David Miller, Janet Coleman, William Connolly, and Alan Ryan, 136–39. Oxford: Basil Blackwell, 1987.

Hacker, Jacob S. "The Institutional Foundations of Middle-Class Democracy." *Social Europe: The Journal of the European Left* 7, no. 1 (Summer/Autumn 2012): 24–87.

Hacker, Jacob S., and Paul Pierson. *American Amnesia: How the War on Government Led Us to Forget What Made America Prosper*. New York: Simon and Schuster, 2016.

Hacker, Jacob S., and Paul Pierson. *Winner-Take-All Politics: How Washington Made the Rich Richer—and Turned Its Back on the Middle Class*. New York: Simon and Schuster, 2011.

Haidt, Jonathan. *The Righteous Mind: Why Good People Are Divided by Politics and Religion*. New York: Pantheon, 2012.

Hardoon, Deborah, Sophia Ayele, and Ricardo Fuentes-Nieva. "An Economy for the 1%." Oxfam Briefing Paper No. 210. January 18, 2016. https://www.oxfam.org/sites/www.oxfam.org/files/file_attachments/bp210-economy-one-percent-tax-havens-180116-en_0.pdf.

Harles, John C. "Immigrant Integration in Canada and the United States." *American Review of Canadian Studies* 34, no. 2 (Summer 2004): 223–58. https://doi.org/10.1080/02722010409481199.

Harles, John C. "Multiculturalism, National Identity, and National Integration: The Canadian Case." *International Journal of Canadian Studies* 17 (Spring 1998): 217–45.

Harles, John C. *Politics in the Lifeboat: Immigrants in the American Democratic Order*. Boulder, CO: Westview Press, 1993.

Harris, Edward, and Joshua Shakin. "The Distribution of Major Tax Expenditures in the Individual Income Tax System." Congressional Budget Office, May 2013. https://www.cbo.gov/sites/default/files/113th-congress-2013-2014/reports/TaxExpenditures_One-Column.pdf.

Hartman, Mitchell. "Fewer Homeowners Are Now 'Underwater,'" *Marketplace*, March 17, 2015. http://www.marketplace.org/2015/03/17/economy/fewer-homeowners-are-now-underwater.

Hartshorne, Joshua K. "How Birth Order Affects Your Personality." *Scientific American*, January 1, 2010. http://www.scientificamerican.com/article/ruled-by-birth-order/.

Hartz, Louis. *The Founding of New Societies*. New York: Harcourt, Brace and World, 1964.

Hartz, Louis. *The Liberal Tradition in America: An Interpretation of American Political Thought since the Revolution*. New York: Harcourt, Brace and World, 1964.

Harwood, John. "Don't Dare Call the Health Law 'Redistribution.'" *New York Times*, November 23, 2013. http://www.nytimes.com/2013/11/24/us/dont-dare-call-the-health-law-redistribution.html.

Haskins, Ron, and Isabell Sawhill. *Creating an Opportunity Society*. Washington, DC: The Brookings Institution, 2009.

Hayes, Christopher. *The Twilight of the Elites: America after Meritocracy*. New York: Random House, 2012.

Heckman, James J. "Skill Formation and the Economics of Investing in Disadvantaged Children." *Science* 312, no. 5782 (2006): 1900–1902. https://doi.org/10.1126/science.1128898.

Hershbein, Brad, Melissa S. Kearney, and Lawrence H. Summers. "Increasing Education: What It Will and Will Not Do for Earnings and Earnings Inequality." The Hamilton Project, March 30, 2015. http://www.hamiltonproject.org/assets/legacy/files/downloads_and_links/impact_of_edu_earnings_inequality_hershbein_kearney_summers.pdf.

Heuer, Ruth, and Stephanie Stullich. "Comparability of State and Local Expenditures among Schools within Districts: A Report from the Study of School-Level Expenditures." US Department of Education, 2011. https://www2.ed.gov/rschstat/eval/title-i/school-level-expenditures/school-level-expenditures.pdf.

Hoberg, George, Keith G. Banting, and Richard Simeon. "The Scope for Domestic Choice: Policy Autonomy in a Globalizing World." In *Capacity for Choice: Canada in a New North America*, edited by George Hoberg, 252–98. Toronto: University of Toronto Press, 2002. https://doi.org/10.3138/9781442672697-012.

Hobhouse, L.T. *The Elements of Social Justice*. New York: Henry Holt and Company, 1922.

Hochschild, Jennifer L. *What's Fair: American Beliefs about Distributive Justice*. Cambridge, MA: Harvard University Press, 1986.

Hofstadter, Richard. *The American Political Tradition and the Men Who Made It*. New York: Alfred A. Knopf, 1948.

Holt-Lunstad, Julianne, Timothy B. Smith, and J. Bradley Layton. "Social Relationships and Mortality Risk: A Meta-analytic Review." *Public Library of Science: Medicine* 7, no. 7 (2010). http://journals.plos.org/plosmedicine/article/file?id=10.1371/journal.pmed.1000316&type=printable; https://doi.org/10.1371/journal.pmed.1000316.

Horowitz, Gad. "Conservatism, Liberalism, and Socialism in Canada: An Interpretation." *Canadian Journal of Economics and Political Science* 32, no. 2 (1966): 143–71. https://doi.org/10.2307/139794.

House of Commons. *Special Committee on Radio Broadcasting: Minutes and Proceedings of Evidence*. Ottawa: F.A. Acland, 1932.

Howard-Hassmann, Rhoda E. *Compassionate Canadians: Civic Leaders Discuss Human Rights*. Toronto: University of Toronto Press, 2003. https://doi.org/10.3138/9781442673182.

Huang, Jon, Samuel Jacoby, Michael Strickland, and K.K. Rebecca Lai. "Election 2016: Exit Polls." *New York Times*, November 8, 2016. https://www.nytimes.com/interactive/2016/11/08/us/politics/election-exit-polls.html.

Huber, Erika, Elissa Cohen, Amanda Briggs, and David Kassabian. "Welfare Rules Databook: State TANF Policies as of July 2014." Urban Institute, OPRE Report 2015-81, August 2015. http://www.urban.org/research/publication/welfare-rules-databook-state-tanf-policies-july-2014.

Human Resources and Skills Development Canada. *Social Assistance Statistical Report: 2008*. June 4, 2012. http://publications.gc.ca/site/archivee-archived.html?url=http://publications.gc.ca/collections/collection_2011/rhdcc-hrsdc/HS25-2-2008-eng.pdf.

Huntington, Samuel. *American Politics: The Promise of Disharmony*. Cambridge, MA: Harvard University Press, 1984.

Immigration, Refugees and Citizenship Canada. *Discover Canada: The Rights and Responsibilities of Citizenship*. http://www.cic.gc.ca/english/resources/publications/discover/section-05.asp.

Inglehart, Ronald. *Culture Shift in Advanced Industrial Society*. Princeton: Princeton University Press, 1990.

Inglehart, Ronald, and Christian Welzel. *Modernization, Cultural Change, and Democracy: The Human Development Sequence*. Cambridge: Cambridge University Press, 2005. https://doi.org/10.1017/CBO9780511790881.

Inglehart, Ronald, and Christian Welzel. "WVS Cultural Map (1981–2015)." http://www.worldvaluessurvey.org/wvs.jsp.

Inkeles, Alex. *National Character: A Psycho-Social Perspective*. New Brunswick, NJ: Transaction Publishers, 1997.

Institute for College Access and Success. "Student Debt and the Class of 2014: Project on Student Debt, Tenth Annual Report." October 2015. http://ticas.org/sites/default/files/pub_files/classof2014.pdf.

International Monetary Fund. "Public Expenditure Reform: Making Difficult Choices (2014)." *Fiscal Monitor*. http://www.imf.org/external/pubs/ft/fm/2014/01/pdf/fm1401.pdf.

Ipsos-Reid. "Half (48%) of Canadians Are Less than $200 Away Monthly from Being Financially Insolvent." February 19, 2016. http://www.ipsos-na.com/news-polls/pressrelease.aspx?id=7148.

Ipsos-Reid. "Nine in Ten Canadians Support Taxing the Rich More." May 30, 2013. http://www.ipsos-na.com/news-polls/pressrelease.aspx?id=6129.

Isaacs, Julia B. "Economic Mobility of Black and White Families." Pew Charitable Trusts, Economic Mobility Project, November 2007. http://www.brookings.edu/~/media/research/files/papers/2007/11/blackwhite-isaacs/11_blackwhite_isaacs.pdf.

Isaacs, Julia B. "Economic Mobility of Families across Generations." In *Getting Ahead or Losing Ground: Economic Mobility in America*, edited by Julia B. Isaacs, Isabel V. Sawhill, and Ron Haskins, 15–26. Washington: Brookings Institution, 2008. https://www.brookings.edu/wp-content/uploads/2016/06/02_economic_mobility_sawhill.pdf.

Jacobson, Louis. "Putting Mitt Romney's Attacks on 'You Didn't Build That' to the Truth-O-Meter." *Tampa Bay Times*, July 26, 2012. http://www.politifact.com/truth-o-meter/statements/2012/jul/26/mitt-romney/putting-mitt-romneys-attacks-you-didnt-build-truth/.

James, Jonathan. "The College Wage Premium." Federal Reserve Bank of Cleveland, August 8, 2012. https://www.clevelandfed.org/newsroom-and-events/publications/economic-commentary/2012-economic-commentaries/ec-201210-the-college-wage-premium.aspx.

Jäntti, Markus, Brent Bratsberg, Knut Røed, et al. "American Exceptionalism in a New Light: A Comparison of Intergenerational Earnings Mobility in the Nordic Countries, the United Kingdom and the United States." IZA Discussion Paper no. 1938, Institute for the Study of Labor, 2006. http://ftp.iza.org/dp1938.pdf.

Jencks, Christopher. "The War on Poverty: Was It Lost?" *New York Review of Books*, April 2, 2015. http://www.nybooks.com/articles/2015/04/02/war-poverty-was-it-lost/.

Jencks, Christopher. "What Happened to Welfare?" *New York Review of Books*, December 15, 2005. http://www.nybooks.com/articles/2005/12/15/what-happened-to-welfare/.

Jenson, Jane. "Redesigning the 'Welfare Mix' for Families: Policy Challenges." Report for the Canadian Policy Research Networks, 2003. http://rcrpp.org/documents/17519_en.pdf.

Jiang, Yang, Mercedes Ekono, and Curtis Skinner. "Basic Facts about Low-Income Children: Children Under 6 Years, 2013." National Center for Children in Poverty, January 2015. http://www.nccp.org/publications/pdf/text_1097.pdf.

Johansen, David. "Property Rights and the Constitution, Law and Government Division." Parliamentary Information and Research Service, Canada, October 1991. http://publications.gc.ca/Collection-R/LoPBdP/BP/bp268-e.htm#%283%29txt.

Joint Center for Housing Studies of Harvard University. "America's Rental Housing: Evolving Markets and Needs." December 12, 2013. http://www.jchs.harvard.edu/sites/jchs.harvard.edu/files/ahr2013_05-affordability.pdf.

Jones, Owens. "It's Socialism for the Rich and Capitalism for the Rest of Us in Britain." *The Guardian*, August 29, 2014. https://www.theguardian.com/books/2014/aug/29/socialism-for-the-rich.

Jones, Robert P., Daniel Cox, Betsy Cooper, and Rachel Lienesch. "Anxiety, Nostalgia, and Mistrust: Findings from the 2015 American Values Survey." Public Religion Research Institute, November 17, 2015. http://publicreligion.org/site/wp-content/uploads/2015/11/PRRI-AVS-2015.pdf.

Judt, Tony. *Ill Fares the Land*. London: Penguin Books, 2010.

Kaiser Family Foundation and the John F. Kennedy School of Government. "National Survey on Poverty in America." April 29, 2001. http://kff.org/medicaid/poll-finding/national-survey-on-poverty-in-america/.

Karabarbounis, Loukas, and Brent Neiman. "The Global Decline of the Labor Share." *Quarterly Journal of Economics* 129, no. 1 (2014): 61–103. https://doi.org/10.1093/qje/qjt032.

Keister, Lisa A. *Getting Rich: America's New Rich and How They Got That Way.* Cambridge: Cambridge University Press, 2005. https://doi.org/10.1017/CBO9780511807589.

Kellermann, Michael. "Power Resources Theory and Inequality in the Canadian Provinces." Paper prepared for the Annual Meeting of the Midwest Political Science Association, Chicago, Illinois, March 29, 2007. http://mkellermann.org/can_inequality.pdf.

Kelly, Nathan J., and Peter K. Enns. "Inequality and the Dynamics of Public Opinion: The Self-Reinforcing Link between Economic Inequality and Mass Preferences." *American Journal of Political Science* 54, no. 4 (2010): 855–70. https://doi.org/10.1111/j.1540-5907.2010.00472.x.

Kena, Grace, et al. "The Condition of Education 2015." NCES 2015-144, U.S. Department of Education, National Center for Education Statistics, May 2015. https://nces.ed.gov/pubs2015/2015144.pdf.

Kennickell, Arthur B. "Ponds and Streams: Wealth and Income in the U.S., 1989 to 2007." FEDS Working Paper 2009-13, January 2009. https://www.federalreserve.gov/pubs/feds/2009/200913/200913pap.pdf.

Kenworthy, Lane. "Has Rising Inequality Reduced Middle-Class Income Growth?" In *Income Inequality: Economic Disparities and the Middle Class in Affluent Countries*, edited by Janet C. Gornick and Markus Jäntti, 101–14. Stanford, CA: Stanford University Press, 2013. https://doi.org/10.11126/stanford/9780804778244.003.0004.

Kenworthy, Lane, and Jonas Pontusson. "Rising Inequality and the Politics of Redistribution in Affluent Countries." *Perspectives on Politics* 3, no. 3 (2005): 449–71. https://doi.org/10.1017/S1537592705050292.

Kessler, Glenn. "Trump's False Claim He Built His Empire with a 'Small Loan' from His Father." *Washington Post*, March 3, 2016. https://www.washingtonpost.com/news/fact-checker/wp/2016/03/03/trumps-false-claim-he-built-his-empire-with-a-small-loan-from-his-father/.

Ketcham, Ralph. *Individualism and Public Life: A Moral Dilemma.* Oxford: Basil Blackwell, 1987.

Key, V.O. *Public Opinion and American Democracy.* New York: Alfred A. Knopf, 1961.

Keynes, John Maynard. *The General Theory of Employment, Interest, and Money.* New York: Harcourt, Brace and Company, 1935.

Kheiriddin, Tasha. "Will Property Rights Finally Get Charter Protection?" *National Post*, February 24, 2011. http://news.nationalpost.com/full-comment/tasha-kheiriddin-will-property-rights-finally-get-charter-protection.

Kilibarda, Konstantin, and Daria Roithmayr. "The Myth of the Rust Belt Revolt." *Slate,* December 1, 2016. http://www.slate.com/articles/news_and_politics/politics/2016/12/the_myth_of_the_rust_belt_revolt.html.

Kirkup, Kristy. "60% of First Nation Children on Reserve Live in Poverty, Institute Says." *CBC News,* May 17, 2016. http://www.cbc.ca/news/indigenous/institute-says-60-percent-fn-children-on-reserve-live-in-poverty-1.3585105.

Kneebone, Ronald, and Katherine White. "An Overview of Social Assistance Trends in Canada." In *Welfare Reform in Canada: Provincial Social Assistance in*

Comparative Perspective, edited by Daniel Béland and Pierre-Marc Daigneault, 53–92. Toronto: University of Toronto Press, 2015.
Kochar, Rakesh, and Richard Fry. "Wealth Inequality Has Widened along Racial, Ethnic Lines since End of Great Recession." Pew Research Center, December 12, 2014. http://www.pewresearch.org/fact-tank/2014/12/12/racial-wealth-gaps-great-recession/.
Kohut, Andrew. "Partisan Polarization Surges in Bush, Obama Years: Trends in American Values, 1987–2012." Pew Research Center, June 4, 2012. http://www.people-press.org/files/legacy-pdf/06-04-12%20Values%20Release.pdf.
Kondo, Naoki, Grace Sembajwe, Ichiro Kawachi, Rob M. van Dam, S.V. Subramanian, and Zentaro Yamagata. "Income Inequality, Mortality and Self-Rated Health: Meta-analysis of Multilevel Studies." British Medical Journal 339, no. 7731 (November 2009): 1178–81.
Kopczuk, Wojciech, Emmanuel Saez, and Jae Song. "Earnings Inequality and Mobility in the United States: Evidence from Social Security Data since 1937." Quarterly Journal of Economics 125, no. 1 (February 2010): 91–128. https://doi.org/10.1162/qjec.2010.125.1.91.
Korpi, Walter. "Social Policy and Distributional Conflict in the Capitalist Democracies: A Preliminary Comparative Framework." West European Politics 3, no. 3 (1980): 296–316. https://doi.org/10.1080/01402388008424288.
Krueger, Alan B. "Land of Hope and Dreams: Rock and Roll, Economics and Rebuilding the Middle Class." Speech delivered at the Rock and Roll Hall of Fame, Cleveland, Ohio, June 12, 2013. https://www.whitehouse.gov/sites/default/files/docs/hope_and_dreams_-_final.pdf.
Krugman, Paul. "Inequality Is a Drag." New York Times, August 7, 2014. http://www.nytimes.com/2014/08/08/opinion/paul-krugman-inequality-is-a-drag.html.
Krugman, Paul. "Why We're in a New Gilded Age." New York Review of Books, May 8, 2014. http://www.nybooks.com/articles/2014/05/08/thomas-piketty-new-gilded-age/.
Kuziemko, Ilyana, Michael I. Norton, Emmanuel Saez, and Stefanie Stantcheva. "How Elastic Are Preferences for Redistribution? Evidence from Randomized Survey Experiments." Working Paper 18865, National Bureau of Economic Research, March 2013. https://doi.org/10.3386/w18865.
Lafrance, Amélie, and Sébastien LaRochelle-Côté. "The Evolution of Wealth over the Life Cycle." Perspectives on Labor and Income, no. 75-001-X. Statistics Canada, June 22, 2012. http://www.statcan.gc.ca/pub/75-001-x/2012003/article/11690-eng.pdf.
Lakner, Christoph, and Branko Milanovic. "Global Income Distribution: From the Fall of the Berlin Wall to the Great Recession." World Bank Working Paper No. 6719, December 2013. https://openknowledge.worldbank.org/bitstream/handle/10986/16935/WPS6719.pdf?sequence=1&isAllowed=y; https://doi.org/10.1596/1813-9450-6719.
Lammam, Charles. "Why Income Mobility Needs Closer Study." Globe and Mail, November 29, 2012. http://www.theglobeandmail.com/report-on-business/economy/economy-lab/why-income-mobility-needs-closer-study/article5789888/.

Lammam, Charles, Amela Karabegović, and Niels Veldhuis. "Measuring Income Mobility in Canada, Studies in Economic Prosperity." Fraser Institute, November 2012. http://www.fraserinstitute.org/uploadedFiles/fraser-ca/Content/research-news/research/publications/measuring-income-mobility-in-canada.pdf.

Lammam, Charles, and Hugh MacIntyre. "An Introduction to the State of Poverty in Canada." Fraser Institute, January 2016. https://www.fraserinstitute.org/sites/default/files/an-introduction-to-the-state-of-poverty-in-canada.pdf.

Lang, Eugene, and Frank Graves. "Closer Reading of StatsCan Report Troubling for Middle Class." *Toronto Star,* March 2, 2014. http://www.thestar.com/opinion/commentary/2014/03/02/closer_reading_of_statscan_report_troubling_for_middle_class.html.

Lansley, Stewart. *The Cost of Inequality: Three Decades of the Super-Rich and the Economy.* London: Gibson Square, 2012.

Laski, Harold J. *The American Democracy: A Commentary and Interpretation.* New York: Viking, 1948.

Lasswell, Harold D. *Politics: Who Gets What, When, How.* New York: Whittelsey House, 1936.

Lauff, Eric, and Stephen J. Ingels. "Education Longitudinal Study of 2002 (ELS:2002): A First Look at 2002 High School Sophomores 10 Years Later." NCES 2014-363, U.S. Department of Education. Washington, DC: National Center for Education Statistics, 2013. https://nces.ed.gov/pubs2014/2014363.pdf.

Lee, Chul-In, and Gary Solon. "Trends in Intergenerational Income Mobility." *Review of Economics and Statistics* 91, no. 4 (2009): 766–72. https://doi.org/10.1162/rest.91.4.766.

Lee, Donghoon. "Household Debt and Credit: Student Debt." Federal Reserve Bank of New York, October 28, 2013. https://www.newyorkfed.org/medialibrary/media/newsevents/mediaadvisory/2013/Lee022813.pdf.

Lee, Michelle Ye Hee. "Yes, US Locks Up People at a Higher Rate than Any Other Country." *Washington Post,* July 7, 2015. https://www.washingtonpost.com/news/fact-checker/wp/2015/07/07/yes-u-s-locks-people-up-at-a-higher-rate-than-any-other-country/.

Lemieux, Thomas, and W. Craig Riddell. "Top Incomes in Canada: Evidence from the Census." Paper presented at the IRPP/CLSRN conference on Inequality in Canada: Driving Forces, Outcomes and Policy, Ottawa, February 2014. http://www.economics.ubc.ca/files/2014/12/Lemieux-Riddell-Top-Incomes.pdf.

Leonhardt, David, and Kevin Quealy. "The American Middle Class Is No Longer the World's Richest." *New York Times,* April 22, 2014. http://www.nytimes.com/2014/04/23/upshot/the-american-middle-class-is-no-longer-the-worlds-richest.html?abt=0002&abg=1.

Lerner, Max. *America as a Civilization: Life and Thought in the United States Today.* 2nd ed. New York: Henry Holt, 1987.

Levine, Linda. "An Analysis of the Distribution of Wealth across Households, 1989–2010." Congressional Research Service Report, July 2012. https://fas.org/sgp/crs/misc/RL33433.pdf.

Levitt, Steven D. "Using Repeat Challengers to Estimate the Effect of Campaign Spending on Election Outcomes in the US House." *Journal of Political Economy* 102, no. 4 (1994): 777–98. https://doi.org/10.1086/261954.

Lewis, Michael. *Flash Boys: A Wall Street Revolt.* New York: W.W. Norton, 2013.

Lewis, Timothy. *In the Long Run We're All Dead: The Canadian Turn to Fiscal Restraint.* Vancouver: UBC Press, 2003.

Lindblom, Charles E. *Politics and Markets: The World's Political-Economic Systems.* New York: Basic Books, 1977.

Linden, Michael. "The Federal Tax Code and Income Inequality: How Federal Tax Policy Changes Have Affected and Will Affect Income Inequality." Center for American Progress, April 19, 2012. http://www.americanprogress.org/issues/tax-reform/report/2012/04/19/11404/the-federal-tax-code-and-income-inequality/.

Lipset, Seymour Martin. *American Exceptionalism: A Double Edged Sword.* New York: W.W. Norton, 1996.

Lipset, Seymour Martin. *Continental Divide: The Values and Institutions of the United States and Canada.* New York: Routledge, 1990.

Lipset, Seymour Martin. *The First New Nation: The United States in Historical and Comparative Perspective.* New York: Basic Books, 1963.

Lipset, Seymour Martin, *Political Man: The Social Bases of Politics.* Baltimore: Johns Hopkins University Press, 1959.

Lipset, Seymour Martin, and Reinhard Bendix. *Social Mobility in Industrial Society.* Los Angeles: University of California Press, 1963.

Logan, John R., and Brian Stults. "The Persistence of Segregation in the Metropolis: New Findings from the 2010 Census." Census brief prepared for Project US2010, 2011. http://www.s4.brown.edu/us2010.

Looney, Adam, and Kevin B. Moore. "Changes in the Distribution of After-Tax Wealth: Has Income Tax Policy Increased Wealth Inequality?" Finance and Economics Discussion Series 2015–058. Washington: Board of Governors of the Federal Reserve System, 2015. http://dx.doi.org/10.17016/FEDS.2015.058.

Lower-Basch, Elizabeth. "Cash Assistance: Temporary Assistance for Needy Families." Center for Law and Social Policy, May 2015. http://www.clasp.org/resources-and-publications/publication-1/TANF-101-Cash-Assistance.pdf.

Lowi, Theodore. *The End of Liberalism: Ideology, Policy, and the Crisis of Public Authority.* New York: W.W. Norton, 1969.

Luttig, Matthew. "The Structure of Inequality and Americans' Attitudes toward Redistribution." *Public Opinion Quarterly* 77, no. 3 (Fall 2013): 811–21. https://doi.org/10.1093/poq/nft025.

Luxembourg Income Study. "Inequality and Poverty: Key Figures." June 18, 2015. http://www.lisdatacenter.org.

MacDonald, Forrest. *Novus Ordum Seclorum: The Intellectual Origins of the Constitution.* Lawrence: University Press of Kansas, 1985.

MacDorman, Marian F., T.J. Mathews, Ashna D. Mohangoo, and Jennifer Zeitlin. "International Comparisons of Infant Mortality and Related Factors: United States and Europe, 2010." *National Vital Statistics Reports* 63, No. 5, September 24, 2014. http://www.cdc.gov/nchs/data/nvsr/nvsr63/nvsr63_05.pdf.

MacPherson, C.B. *Democratic Theory: Essays in Retrieval.* Oxford: Clarendon Press, 1973.

MacPherson, C.B. *The Political Theory of Possessive Individualism: Hobbes to Locke.* Oxford: Clarendon Press, 1969.

Mankiw, N. Gregory. "Defending the One Percent." *Journal of Economic Perspectives* 27, no. 3 (2013): 21–34. https://doi.org/10.1257/jep.27.3.21.

Maoni, Antonia. "Health Care in Canada and the United States." In *Canada and the United States: Differences that Count*, 4th ed., edited by David M. Thomas and David N. Biette, 254–72. Toronto: University of Toronto Press, 2014.

Marmot, Michael. *The Status Syndrome: How Social Standing Affects Our Health and Longevity*. New York: Henry Holt and Company, 2004.

Marr, Garry. "Canada Household Debt Ratio Hits New Record of 163.3%." *Financial Post*, March 12, 2015. http://business.financialpost.com/personal-finance/debt/canada-household-debt-ratio-hits-new-record-of-163-3.

Marshall, T.H. *Citizenship and Social Class and Other Essays*. Cambridge: Cambridge University Press, 1950.

Martineau, Harriet. *Society in America*. Edited by Seymour Martin Lipset. 1837. Garden City, NJ: Anchor-Doubleday, 1962.

Massing, Michael. "How to Cover the One Percent." *New York Review of Books*, January 14, 2016. http://www.nybooks.com/articles/2016/01/14/how-to-cover-the-one-percent/.

Masters, Jonathan. "US Gun Policy: Global Comparisons." Council on Foreign Relations, January 12, 2016, http://www.cfr.org/society-and-culture/us-gun-policy-global-comparisons/p29735.

Mayer, Jane. *Dark Money: The Hidden History of the Billionaires behind the Rise of the Radical Right*. New York: Doubleday, 2015.

Mazumder, Bhashkar. "The Apple Falls Even Closer to the Tree than We Thought: New and Revised Estimates of the Intergenerational Inheritance of Earnings." In *Unequal Chances: Family Background and Unequal Success*, edited by Samuel Bowles, Herbert Gintis, and Melissa Osborne Groves, 80–99. Princeton: Princeton University Press, 2005.

Mazumder, Bhashkar. "Black-White Differences in Intergenerational Economic Mobility in the US." Discussion Paper CES 11–40, US Census Bureau, Center for Economic Studies, December 2011. https://www2.census.gov/ces/wp/2011/CES-WP-11-40.pdf. https://doi.org/10.2139/ssrn.1966690.

Mazzucato, Mariana. *The Entrepreneurial State: Debunking Private Sector versus Public Sector Myths*. New York: Public Affairs, 2015.

McCall, Leslie. *The Undeserving Rich: American Beliefs about Inequality, Opportunity, and Redistribution*. Cambridge: Cambridge University Press, 2013. https://doi.org/10.1017/CBO9781139225687.

McCarty, Nolan, Keith Poole, and Howard Rosenthal. *Polarized America: The Dance of Ideology and Unequal Riches*. Boston: MIT Press, 2006.

McGee, Suzanne. "How America's Middle Class Fell Behind Its Canadian Neighbours." *The Guardian*, April 27, 2014. http://www.theguardian.com/money/us-money-blog/2014/apr/27/america-canada-middle-class-college-healthcare-taxes.

McHugh, James T. "Toward a Grand Theory of the Study of Canadian Political Thought." *American Review of Canadian Studies* 43, no. 1 (March 2013): 123–43. https://doi.org/10.1080/02722011.2013.766806.

MacIntyre, Hugh, Charles Lammam, and Feixue Ren. "Generosity in Canada and the United States: The 2015 Generosity Index." Fraser Institute, 2015. https://www.fraserinstitute.org/studies/generosity-in-canada-and-the-united-states-the-2015-generosity-index.

McKenzie, Evan. *Beyond Privatopia: Rethinking Residential Private Government*. Washington, DC: The Urban Institute Press, 2011.

McRae, Kenneth. "The Structure of Canadian History." In *The Founding of New Societies: Studies in the History of the United States, Latin America, South Africa, Canada, and Australia*, edited by Louis Hartz, 234–44. Orlando: Harcourt Brace Jovanovich, 1964.

Mettler, Suzanne. *Degrees of Inequality: How the Politics of Higher Education Sabotaged the American Dream*. New York: Basic Books, 2014.

Milanovic, Branko. *The Haves and the Have Nots: A Brief and Idiosyncratic History of Global Inequality*. New York: Basic Books, 2012.

Miller, David. "In Defence of Nationality." *Journal of Applied Philosophy* 10, no. 1 (1993): 3–16. https://doi.org/10.1111/j.1468-5930.1993.tb00058.x.

Miller, David. *Social Justice*. Oxford: Clarendon Press, 1976.

Mishel, Lawrence. "Declining Value of the Federal Minimum Wage Is a Major Factor Driving Inequality." Economic Policy Institute, Issue Brief no. 1351, February 21, 2013. http://s1.epi.org/files/2013/minimum-wage.pdf.

Moffat, Mike. "8 Charts Explain Why Canada's Middle Class Is Richer than America's." *Maclean's*, April 29, 2014. http://www.macleans.ca/economy/economicanalysis/8-charts-that-explain-why-canadas-middle-class-is-richer-than-americas/.

Monaghan, Angela. "IMF Chief Says Banks Haven't Changed since Financial Crisis." *The Guardian*, May 27, 2014. https://www.theguardian.com/business/2014/may/27/imf-chief-lagarde-bankers-ethics-risks.

Monsma, Stephen V., and Carolyn M. Mounts. "Working Faith: How Religious Organizations Provide Welfare–to-Work Services." Davenport Institute, Pepperdine University School of Public Policy, 2002. http://publicpolicy.pepperdine.edu/davenport-institute/reports/workingfaith/working2.html.

Montiel, Lisa M., and David J. Wright. "Getting a Piece of the Pie: Federal Grants to Faith-Based Social Service Organizations." Report for the Roundtable on Religion and Social Welfare Policy, Rockefeller Institute of Government, February 2006. http://features.pewforum.org/roundtable/docs/research/federal_grants_report_2-14-06.pdf.

Mood, Carina, Jan O. Jonsson, and Erik Bihagen. "Socio-economic Persistence across Generations: Cognitive and Noncognitive Processes." In *From Parents to Children: The Intergenerational Transmission of Advantage*, edited by John Ermisch, Markus Jäntti, and Timothy Smeeding, 53–83. New York: Russell Sage Foundation, 2012.

Moore, Peter. "Poll Results: Poverty." YouGov US, April 16, 2014. https://today.yougov.com/news/2014/04/16/poll-results-poverty/.

Moos, Markus. "Generational Dimensions of Neoliberal and Post-Fordist Restructuring: The Changing Characteristics of Young Adults and Growing Income Inequality in Montreal and Vancouver." *International Journal of Urban and Regional Research* 38, no. 6 (November 2014): 2078–102. https://doi.org/10.1111/1468-2427.12088.

Morales, Lymari. "Fewer Americans See US Divided into 'Haves,' 'Have Nots.'" Gallup, December 15, 2011. http://www.gallup.com/poll/151556/fewer-americans-divided-haves-nots.aspx.

Morin, Rich, and Seth Motel. "A Third of Americans Now Say They Are in the Lower Classes." Pew Research Center. September 10, 2012. http://www.pewsocialtrends.org/2012/09/10/a-third-of-americans-now-say-they-are-in-the-lower-classes/.

Morris, Charles R. "Economic Injustice for Most: From the New Deal to the Raw Deal." *Commonweal* 131, no. 14 (August 13, 2004): 12–17.

Morton, W.L. *The Canadian Identity*. 2nd ed. Toronto: University of Toronto Press, 1972.

Moscovitch, Allan. "The Canada Assistance Plan: A Twenty Year Assessment, 1966–1986." In *How Ottawa Spends, 1988–1989: The Conservatives Heading into the Stretch*, edited by Katherine Graham, 260–307. Ottawa: Carleton University Press, 1988.

Motel, Seth. "5 Facts on How Americans View Taxes." Pew Research Center, April 10, 2015. http://www.pewresearch.org/fact-tank/2015/04/10/5-facts-on-how-americans-view-taxes/.

Murphy, Brian, Andrew Heisz, and Xuelin Zhang. "Low Income and Inequality Trends in Canada." In *Welfare Reform in Canada: Provincial Social Assistance in Comparative Perspective*, edited by Daniel Béland and Pierre-Marc Daigneault, 93–109. Toronto: University of Toronto Press, 2015.

Murphy, Brian, and Michael Wolfson. "Income Trajectories of High Income Canadians, 1982–2010." Unpublished paper prepared for the Canadian Economics Association meeting, Montreal, May 21, 2013. http://citeseerx.ist.psu.edu/viewdoc/download?doi=10.1.1.663.4211&rep=rep1&type=pdf.

Murphy, Brian, Xuelin Zhang, and Claude Dionne. "Low Income in Canada: a Multi-line and Multi-index Perspective," Statistics Canada, Income Statistics Division, Income Research Paper Series, Catalogue no. 75F0002M—No. 001, March 2012. http://www.statcan.gc.ca/pub/75f0002m/75f0002m2012001-eng.pdf.

Murray, Charles. *Coming Apart: The State of White America*. New York: Crown Forum, 2012.

Myrdal, Gunnar. *An American Dilemma: The Negro Problem and Modern Democracy*. New York: Harper and Brothers, 1944.

National Aboriginal Economic Development Board. "The Aboriginal Economic Progress Report 2015." June 2015. http://www.naedb-cndea.com/reports/NAEDB-progress-report-june-2015.pdf.

National Academies of Sciences, Engineering, and Medicine. *The Growing Gap in Life Expectancy by Income: Implications for Federal Programs and Policy Responses*. Washington, DC: The National Academies Press, 2015.

National Council of Welfare. "Total Welfare Incomes (for 1996–2011)." July 19, 2012. http://www.ncw.gc.ca/m.1p1data@-eng.jsp.

Neate, Rupert. "Trump's Tax Plan: Massive Cuts for the 1% Will Usher 'Era of Dynastic Wealth.'" *The Guardian*, November 23, 2016. https://www.theguardian.com/us-news/2016/nov/23/trump-tax-plan-cuts-wealthy-low-income-inequality.

Nevitte, Neil. *The Decline of Deference: Canadian Value Change in Cross-National Perspective*. Toronto: University of Toronto Press, 1996.

Newport, Frank. "Americans Continue to Say US Wealth Distribution Is Unfair." Gallup, May 4, 2015. http://www.gallup.com/poll/182987/americans-continue-say-wealth-distribution-unfair.aspx.

Newport, Frank. "Americans Favor Jobs Plan Proposals, Including Taxing Rich." Gallup, September 20, 2011. http://www.gallup.com/poll/149567/americans-favor-jobs-plan-proposals-including-taxing-rich.aspx.

Newport, Frank. "Americans Prioritize Economy over Reducing Wealth Gap." Gallup, December 16, 2011. http://www.gallup.com/poll/151568/americans-prioritize-growing-economy-reducing-wealth-gap.aspx.

Newport, Frank. "Americans' Satisfaction with Ability to Get Ahead Edges Up." Gallup, January 21, 2016. http://www.gallup.com/poll/188780/americans-satisfaction-ability-ahead-edges.aspx?g_source=income%20inequality&g_medium=search&g_campaign=tiles.

Newport, Frank. "Americans Continue to Say US Wealth Distribution Is Unfair." Gallup, May 4, 2015. http://www.gallup.com/poll/182987/americans-continue-say-wealth-distribution-unfair.aspx.

Newport, Frank, and Brandon Busteed. "Americans Still See College Education as Very Important." Gallup, December 17, 2013. http://www.gallup.com/poll/166490/americans-college-education-important.aspx.

Noah, Timothy. *The Great Divergence: America's Growing Inequality Crisis and What We Can Do about It.* New York: Bloomsbury Press, 2012.

Norris, Floyd. "Young Households Are Losing Ground in Income, Despite Education." *New York Times*, September 12, 2014. http://www.nytimes.com/2014/09/13/business/economy/young-households-are-losing-ground-in-income-despite-education.html.

Northrup, David, and Lesley Jacobs. "The Growing Income Inequality Gap in Canada: A National Survey." Institute for Social Research, York University, Toronto, January 31, 2014. http://www.isr.yorku.ca/events/Jacobs%20Northrup%20Canada%202014%20Survey%20IncomeGap_Full2014.pdf.

Norton, Anne. *Alternative Americas: A Reading of Antebellum Political Culture.* Chicago: University of Chicago Press, 1986.

Norton, Michael I., and Dan Ariely. "Building a Better America—One Wealth Quintile at a Time." *Perspectives on Psychological Science* 6, no. 1 (2011): 9–12. https://doi.org/10.1177/1745691610393524.

Nozick, Robert. *Anarchy, State, and Utopia.* New York: Basic Books, 1974.

Nussbaum, Martha C. *Creating Capabilities: The Human Development Approach.* Cambridge, MA: The Belknap Press of Harvard University Press, 2011. https://doi.org/10.4159/harvard.9780674061200.

Nyhan, Brendan. "Why Republicans Are Suddenly Talking about Economic Inequality." *New York Times*, February 13, 2015. http://www.nytimes.com/2015/02/14/upshot/why-republicans-are-suddenly-talking-about-economic-inequality.html.

"Obama's Second Inaugural Speech." *New York Times*, January 21, 2013. http://www.nytimes.com/2013/01/21/us/politics/obamas-second-inaugural-speech.html.

OECD. "CO2.2: Child Poverty." OECD Family Database, August 28, 2016. http://www.oecd.org/els/soc/CO_2_2_Child_Poverty.pdf.

OECD. *Divided We Stand: Why Inequality Keeps Rising.* Paris: OECD Publishing, 2011. http://www.oecd.org/els/soc/dividedwestandwhyinequalitykeepsrising.htm.

OECD. *Economic Policy Reforms: Going for Growth 2010.* Washington, DC: OECD Publishing, 2010. https://www.oecd.org/eco/monetary/economicpolicyreformsgoingforgrowth2010.htm.

OECD. *Education at a Glance 2015: OECD Indicators.* Paris: OECD Publishing, 2015. https://www.oecd.org/edu/education-at-a-glance-2015.htm.

OECD. "Focus on Inequality and Growth." December 2014. http://www.oecd.org/els/soc/Focus-Inequality-and-Growth-2014.pdf.

OECD. "Focus on Top Incomes and Taxation in OECD Countries: Was the Crisis a Game Changer?" Paris: OECD Publishing, 2014. www.oecd.org/social/OECD2014-FocusOnTopIncomes.pdf.

OECD. "General Government Spending." https://data.oecd.org/gga/general-government-spending.htm.
OECD. *Government at a Glance: 2015.* Paris: OECD Publishing, 2015.
OECD. "Income Distribution and Poverty." Social Protection and Well-Being database. http://stats.oecd.org.
OECD. *In It Together: Why Less Inequality Benefits All.* Paris: OECD Publishing, 2015. http://www.oecd.org/social/in-it-together-why-less-inequality-benefits-all-9789264235120-en.htm.
OECD. "In It Together: Why Less Inequality Benefits All … in Canada." May 21, 2015. http://www.oecd.org/canada/OECD2015-In-It-Together-Highlights-Canada.pdf.
OECD. "OECD Income Distribution Database (IDD): Gini, Poverty, Income, Methods and Concepts." July 2016. http://www.oecd.org/social/income-distribution-database.htm.
OECD. "Overall Statutory Tax Rates on Dividend Income." 2016, Table II.4. http://stats.oecd.org/Index.aspx?QueryId=59615.
OECD. *Pensions at a Glance 2015: OECD and G20 indicators.* Paris: OECD Publishing, 2015.
OECD. *Revenue Statistics, 2015 Edition.* Paris: OECD Publishing, 2015. http://www.oecd-ilibrary.org/taxation/revenue-statistics-2015_rev_stats-2015-en-fr.
OECD. *Revenue Statistics, 2016 Edition.* Paris: OECD Publishing, 2016. https://stats.oecd.org/Index.aspx?DataSetCode=REV.
OECD. "Social Spending Is Falling in Some Countries, but in Many Others It Remains at Historically High Levels." OECD Directorate for Employment, Labour, and Social Affairs, November 2014.
OECD. "Top Statutory Personal Income Tax Rate and Top Marginal Tax Rates for Employees." 2015, Table I.7. http//stats.oecd.org/index.aspx?DataSetCode=TABLE_17 .
OECD. "Wealth Shares of the Top Percentiles of the Wealth Distribution." Wealth Distribution Database, Figure 6.7. http://dx.doi.org/10.1787/888933208539
Office of Family Assistance. "TANF Financial Data—FY 2014." https://www.acf.hhs.gov/ofa/resource/tanf-financial-data-fy-2014.
Oishi, Shigehiro, and Selin Kesebir. "Income Inequality Explains Why Economic Growth Does Not Always Translate to an Increase in Happiness." *Psychological Science* 26, no. 10 (2015): 1630–38. https://doi.org/10.1177/0956797615596713.
Oishi, Shigehiro, Selin Kesebir, and Ed Diener. "Income Inequality and Happiness." *Psychological Science* 22, no. 9 (2011): 1095–100. https://doi.org/10.1177/0956797611417262.
Okun, Arthur M. *Equality and Efficiency: The Big Tradeoff.* Washington, DC: The Brookings Institution, 1975.
Olasky, Martin. *Renewing American Compassion.* New York: The Free Press, 1993.
Olasky, Martin. *The Tragedy of American Compassion.* Washington, DC: Regnery Press, 1992.
Orfield, Gary, John Kucsera, and Genevieve Siegel-Hawley. "*E Pluribus* … Separation: Deepening Double Segregation for more Students." The Civil Rights Project, UCLA, September 2012. https://civilrightsproject.ucla.edu/research/k-12-education/integration-and-diversity/mlk-national/e-pluribus…separation-deepening-double-segregation-for-more-students/orfield_epluribus_revised_omplete_2012.pdf.

Osberg, Lars, and Timothy Smeeding. "'Fair' Inequality? Attitudes toward Pay Differentials: The United States in Comparative Perspective." *American Sociological Review* 71, no. 3 (June 2006): 450–73. https://doi.org/10.1177/000312240607100305.

Ostry, Jonathan D., Andrew Berg, and Charalambos G. Tsangarides. "Redistribution, Inequality, and Growth." IMF Staff Discussion Note, International Monetary Fund, February 2014. https://www.imf.org/external/pubs/ft/sdn/2014/sdn1402.pdf. https://doi.org/10.5089/9781484352076.006.

Otani, Akane. "Ten Elite Schools Where Middle-Class Kids Don't Pay Tuition." *Bloomberg Business*, April 1, 2015. http://www.bloomberg.com/news/articles/2015-04-01/ten-elite-schools-where-middle-class-kids-don-t-pay-tuition.

Page, Benjamin I., and Lawrence R. Jacobs. *Class War? What Americans Really Think about Economic Inequality*. Chicago: University of Chicago Press, 2009. https://doi.org/10.7208/chicago/9780226644561.001.0001.

Page, Benjamin I., and Robert Y. Shapiro. "Effects of Public Opinion on Policy." *American Political Science Review* 77, no. 1 (1983): 175–90. https://doi.org/10.2307/1956018.

Paine, Thomas. *Common Sense and Other Political Writings*. Edited by Nelson F. Adkins. New York: The Liberal Arts Press, 1953.

Pal, Leslie A. *Beyond Policy Analysis: Public Issue Management in Turbulent Times*. 3rd ed. Toronto: Thomas Nelson, 2013.

Palameta, Boris. "Low Income among Immigrants and Visible Minorities." *Perspectives* 5, no. 4 (April 2004): 12–17. http://www.statcan.gc.ca/pub/75-001-x/10404/6843-eng.pdf.

Pangle, Thomas L. *The Spirit of Modern Republicanism: The Moral Vision of the American Founders and the Philosophy of Locke*. Chicago: University of Chicago Press, 1988.

Parker, Kim. "Yes, the Rich Are Different." Pew Research Center, Social and Demographic Trends, August 27, 2012. http://www.pewsocialtrends.org/2012/08/27/yes-the-rich-are-different/.

Parlapiano, Alicia, Robert Gebeloff, and Shan Carter. "The Shrinking American Middle Class." *New York Times*, January 26, 2015. http://www.nytimes.com/interactive/2015/01/25/upshot/shrinking-middle-class.html?abt=0002&abg=0.

Pell Institute. "Indicators of Higher Education Equity in the United States: 2016 Historical Trend Report." The Pell Institute Study for Opportunity in Higher Education, 2016. http://www.pellinstitute.org/downloads/publications-Indicators_of_Higher_Education_Equity_in_the_US_2016_Historical_Trend_Report.pdf.

Perrsson, Torsten, and Guido Tabellini. "Is Inequality Harmful for Growth?" *American Economic Review* 84, no. 3 (1994): 600–621.

Pew Charitable Trusts. "Economic Mobility and the American Dream—Where Do We Stand in the Wake of the Great Recession?" Economic Mobility Project, May 2011.

Pew Charitable Trusts. "Moving on Up: Why Do Some Americans Leave the Bottom of the Economic Ladder, but Not Others?" November 2013. http://www.pewtrusts.org/~/media/assets/2013/11/01/movingonuppdf.pdf.

Pew Charitable Trusts. "A New Financial Reality: The Balance Sheets and Economic Mobility of Generation X." September 2014. http://www.pewtrusts.org/~/media/Assets/2014/09/Pew_Generation_X_report.pdf.

Pew Charitable Trusts. "Pursuing the American Dream: Economic Mobility across Generations." July 2012. http://www.pewtrusts.org/~/media/legacy/uploadedfiles/wwwpewtrustsorg/reports/economic_mobility/pursuingamericandreampdf.pdf.

Pew Research Center. "The American-Western Values Gap." February 29, 2012. http://www.pewglobal.org/2011/11/17/the-american-western-european-values-gap/.

Pew Research Center. "America's Changing Religious Landscape." Religion and Public Life, May 12, 2015. http://www.pewforum.org/2015/05/12/americas-changing-religious-landscape/.

Pew Research Center. "Canada's Changing Religious Landscape." Religion and Public Life, June 27, 2013. http://www.pewforum.org/2013/06/27/canadas-changing-religious-landscape/.

Pew Research Center. "Continued Bipartisan Support for Expanded Background Checks on Gun Sales." August 13, 2015. http://www.people-press.org/2015/08/13/continued-bipartisan-support-for-expanded-background-checks-on-gun-sales/.

Pew Research Center. "Emerging and Developing Economies Much More Optimistic than Rich Countries about the Future." October 9, 2014. http://www.pewglobal.org/2014/10/09/emerging-and-developing-economies-much-more-optimistic-than-rich-countries-about-the-future/.

Pew Research Center. "For the Public, It's Not about Class Warfare, but Fairness." March 2, 2016. http://www.people-press.org/2012/03/02/for-the-public-its-not-about-class-warfare-but-fairness/.

Pew Research Center. "Middle Easterners See Religious and Ethnic Hatred as Top Global Threat." October 16, 2014. http://www.pewglobal.org/2014/10/16/middle-easterners-see-religious-and-ethnic-hatred-as-top-global-threat/.

Pew Research Center. "Most See Inequality Growing, but Partisans Differ over Solutions." January 23, 2014. http://www.people-press.org/files/legacy-pdf/1-23-14%20Poverty_Inequality%20Release.pdf.

Pew Research Center. "Parenting in America." December 17, 2015. http://www.pewsocialtrends.org/2015/12/17/parenting-in-america/.

Pew Research Center. "Public Views about Guns." August 26, 2016. http://www.people-press.org/2016/08/26/gun-rights-vs-gun-control/#total.

Pew Research Center for the People and the Press. "Raising Taxes on the Rich Seen as Good for Economy, Fairness." July 16, 2012. http://www.people-press.org/2012/07/16/raising-taxes-on-rich-seen-as-good-for-economy-fairness/.

Picot, Garnett, and John Myles. "Poverty and Exclusion: Income Inequality and Low Income in Canada." Report prepared for the Government of Canada, Policy Research Initiative 7, no. 2, December 2004. http://policyresearch.gc.ca/page.asp?pagenm=v7n2_art_03.

Pierson, Paul. "Fragmented Welfare States: Federal Institutions and the Development of Social Policy." *Governance: An International Journal of Policy, Administration and Institutions* 8, no. 4 (1995): 449–68. https://doi.org/10.1111/j.1468-0491.1995.tb00223.x.

Piff, Paul K., Michael W. Kraus, Stéphane Côté, Bonnie Hayden Cheng, and Dacher Keltner. "Having Less, Giving More: The Influence of Social Class on Prosocial Behavior." *Journal of Personality and Social Psychology* 99, no. 5 (2010): 771–84. https://doi.org/10.1037/a0020092.

Piketty, Thomas. *Capital in the Twenty-First Century*. Cambridge, MA: The Belknap Press of Harvard University Press, 2014. https://doi.org/10.4159/9780674369542.

Piketty, Thomas, and Emanuel Saez. "How Progressive Is the US Federal Tax System? A Historical and International Perspective." *Journal of Economic Perspectives* 21, no. 1 (Winter 2007): 3–24. https://doi.org/10.1257/jep.21.1.3.

Piketty, Thomas, Emmanuel Saez, and Gabriel Zucman. "Distributional National Accounts: Methods and Estimates for the United States." National Bureau of Economic Research, Working Paper 22945. December 2016. http://www.nber.org/papers/w22945. https://doi.org/10.3386/w22945.

Polanyi, Karl. *The Great Transformation: The Political and Economic Origins of Our Time*. Boston: Beacon Press, 1944.

"Poll Finds a More Bleak View of American Dream." *New York Times*, December 10, 2014. https://assets.documentcloud.org/documents/1377502/poll-finds-a-more-bleak-view-of-american-dream.pdf.

Porter, John. *The Vertical Mosaic: An Analysis of Social Class and Power in Canada*. Toronto: University of Toronto Press, 1965. https://doi.org/10.3138/9781442683044.

Press, Jordan, and Joan Bryden. "Money No Guarantee of Success in 2015 Federal Election: Almost Half of Top 100 Spenders Lost, Analysis Finds." *National Post*, April 3, 2016. http://news.nationalpost.com/news/canada/money-no-guarantee-of-success-in-2015-federal-election-almost-half-of-top-100-spenders-lost-analysis-finds.

Przeworski, Adam, and Henry Teune. *The Logic of Comparative Social Inquiry*. New York: John Wiley and Sons, 1970.

Public Religion Research Institute. "Race and America's Social Networks." Analysis of the American Values Survey 2013. August 28, 2014, http://prri.org/research/2014/08/analysis-social-network/.

Putnam, Robert. *Bowling Alone: The Collapse and Revival of American Community*. New York: Simon and Schuster, 2000. https://doi.org/10.1145/358916.361990.

Putnam, Robert D. *Our Kids: The American Dream in Crisis*. New York: Simon and Schuster, 2015.

Qvortrup, Matt, ed. *Referendums around the World: The Continued Growth of Direct Democracy*. Basingstoke: Palgrave MacMillan, 2014. https://doi.org/10.1057/9781137314703.

Rae, Douglas. *Equalities*. Cambridge, MA: Harvard University Press, 1981.

Raj, Althia. "Income Inequality Back in Focus for Liberals, NDP as Parliament Returns." *Huffington Post,* January, 27, 2016. http://www.huffingtonpost.ca/2016/01/25/income-inequality-canada-npd-liberals_n_9068020.html.

Rajan, Raghuram. *Fault Lines: How Hidden Fractures Still Threaten the World Economy*. Princeton: Princeton University Press, 2010.

Raphael, D.D. *Problems of Political Philosophy*. London: The MacMillan Press, 1976.

Rasmussen Report. "83% Favor Work Requirement for Welfare Recipients." July 18, 2012. http://www.rasmussenreports.com/public_content/business/

jobs_employment/july_2012/83_favor_work_requirement_for_welfare_recipients.

Rattner, Steven. "2016 in Charts." *New York Times*, January 3, 2017. https://www.nytimes.com/2017/01/03/opinion/2016-in-charts-and-can-trump-deliver-in-2017.html?emc=eta1.

Ravitch, Diane. *Reign of Error: The Hoax of the Privatization Movement and the Danger to America's Public Schools*. New York: Vintage, 2014.

Reardon, Sean F., and Kendra Bischoff. "Growth in the Residential Segregation of Families by Income, 1970–2009." US2010 Project, Russell Sage Foundation, November 2011. https://s4.ad.brown.edu/Projects/Diversity/Data/Report/report111111.pdf.

Reeves, Richard V., and Emily Cuddy. "Stretchy Ends: The Shape of Income Inequality." *Social Mobility Memos*, The Brooking Institution, July 9, 2015. http://www.brookings.edu/blogs/social-mobility-memos/posts/2015/07/09-stretchy-ends-inequality-reeves.

Reich, Robert B. *Aftershock: The Next Economy and America's Future*. New York: Random House, 2010.

Reich, Robert B. *Saving Capitalism: For the Many, Not the Few*. New York: Vintage Books, 2016.

"Remarks by the President at a Campaign Event in Roanoke, Virginia." Office of the Press Secretary, White House, July 13, 2012. https://obamawhitehouse.archives.gov/the-press-office/2012/07/13/remarks-president-campaign-event-roanoke-virginia.

Ren, Zhe, and Kuan Xu. "Low-Income Dynamics and Determinants under Different Thresholds: New Findings for Canada in 2000 and Beyond." Statistics Canada, Income Statistics Division, Income Research Paper Series, Catalogue no. 75F0002M, no. 00, October 2011. http://www.statcan.gc.ca/pub/75f0002m/75f0002m2011003-eng.pdf.

Resnick, Philip. *The European Roots of Canadian Political Identity*. Peterborough, ON: Broadview Press, 2005.

Resnick, Philip. *The Labyrinth of North American Identity*. Toronto: University of Toronto Press, 2015.

Rice, James J., and Michael Prince. *The Changing Politics of Canadian Social Policy*. Toronto: University of Toronto Press, 2000.

Richler, Mordecai. "Canadian Identity." In *The Future of North America: Canada, the United States, and Quebec Nationalism*, edited by Elliot J. Feldman and Neil Nevitte, 37–55. Cambridge, MA: Harvard University, the Center for International Affairs, 1979.

Rocheleau, Matt. "Trump's Cabinet Picks so Far Worth a Combined $13b." *Boston Globe*, December 20, 2016. https://www.bostonglobe.com/metro/2016/12/20/trump-cabinet-picks-far-are-worth-combined/XvAJmHCgkHhO3lSxgIKvRM/story.html.

Rogers, Alex. "New Welfare Reform Directive Creates Unlikely Political Issue for Obama." *Time*, July 31, 2012. http://swampland.time.com/2012/07/31/new-welfare-reform-directive-creates-unlikely-political-issue-for-obama/#ixzz2GGx7etOJhttp://swampland.time.com/2012/07/31/new-welfare-reform-directive-creates-unlikely-political-issue-for-obama/.

Rothstein, Bo, and Eric M. Uslaner. "All for All: Equality, Corruption and Social Trust." *World Politics* 58, no. 3 (2006): 41–72.

Rowlingson, Karen. "Does Inequality Cause Health and Social Problems?" A report for the Joseph Rowntree Foundation, September 2011. https://www.jrf.org.uk/sites/default/files/jrf/migrated/files/inequality-income-social-problems-full.pdf.

Roy-César, Édison. "Canada's Equalization Formula." Library of Parliament, Parliament of Canada, September 4, 2013. http://www.lop.parl.gc.ca/content/lop/ResearchPublications/2008-20-e.htm.

Rushe, Dominic. "Obama's Millionaire Tax Is Class War, Say Republicans." *The Guardian*, September 18, 2011. https://www.theguardian.com/world/2011/sep/18/obama-millionaire-tax-war.

Saez, Emanuel. "Striking It Richer: The Evolution of Top Incomes in the United States (Updated with Preliminary 2013 Estimates)." Methodological note in the World Top Incomes Database, March 21, 2015.

Saez, Emanuel, and Thomas Piketty. "Why the 1% Should Pay Tax at 80%." *The Guardian*, October 24, 2013. https://www.theguardian.com/commentisfree/2013/oct/24/1percent-pay-tax-rate-80percent.

Saez, Emmanuel, and Gabriel Zucman. "Wealth Inequality in the United States since 1913: Evidence from Capitalized Income Tax Data." National Bureau of Economic Research Working Papers Series 20625, October 2014. https://gabriel-zucman.eu/files/SaezZucman2014.pdf. https://doi.org/10.3386/w20625.

Salvation Army. "The Dignity Project: Debunking Myths about Poverty in Canada." March 2011. http://salvationarmy.ca/DPresources/DebunkingMyths_report_Mar2011.pdf.

Sandel, Michael J. *Justice: What's the Right Thing to Do?* New York: Farrar, Straus, and Giroux, 2009.

Sargent, Greg. "The Bernie Effect? A New Poll Shows Young Voters See a Big Role for Government." *Washington Post*, April 25, 2016. https://www.washingtonpost.com/blogs/plum-line/wp/2016/04/25/the-bernie-effect-a-new-poll-shows-young-voters-see-a-big-role-for-government/.

Saunders, Doug. "The Rich Do Get Richer. Why Can't the Poor Also Get Richer?" *Globe and Mail*, January 24, 2015. http://www.theglobeandmail.com/opinion/its-not-about-inequality-its-about-social-mobility/article22590971/.

Sawhill, Isabel V. "Do We Face a Permanently Divided Society?" In *The Economics of Inequality, Poverty, and Discrimination in the 21st Century*, edited by Robert S. Rycroft, 79–106. New York: Praeger, 2013.

Sawhill, Isabel V., and Quentin Karpilow. "Raising the Minimum Wage and Redesigning the EITC." Center on Children and Families at Brookings, January 30, 2014. https://www.brookings.edu/wp-content/uploads/2016/06/30-Raising-Minimum-Wage-Redesigning-EITC-sawhill.pdf.

Sayer, Andrew. *Why We Can't Afford the Rich*. Bristol: Policy Press, 2016.

Schattschneider, E.E. *The Semi-Sovereign People*. New York: Holt, Rinehart and Winston, 1960.

Schlesinger, Joel. "A Taxing Question: How Does Canada Stack Up?" *Winnipeg Free Press*, April 11, 2015. http://www.winnipegfreepress.com/business/finance/a-taxing-question-299436781.html.

Schmitt, John, Heidi Shierholz, and Lawrence Mishel. "Don't Blame the Robots: Assessing the Job Polarization Explanation of Growing Wage Inequality." Economic Policy Institute, November 19, 2013. http://www.epi.org/publication/technology-inequality-dont-blame-the-robots/.

Schram, Sanford F., Joe Soss, and Richard Fording, eds. *Race and the Politics of Welfare Reform*. Ann Arbor: University of Michigan Press, 2003. https://doi.org/10.3998/mpub.11932.

Scott, Amy. "Forget Tuition, Just Applying to College Can Cost Thousands." *Marketplace*, April 1, 2013. http://www.marketplace.org/2013/04/01/education/forget-tuition-just-applying-college-can-cost-thousands.

Searcey, Dionne. "More Americans Are Renting and Paying More, as Homeownership Falls." *New York Times*, June 24, 2015. http://www.nytimes.com/2015/06/24/business/economy/more-americans-are-renting-and-paying-more-as-homeownership-falls.html.

Seligson, Mitchell A., Amy Erica Smith, and Elizabeth J. Zechmeister, eds. "The Political Culture of Democracy in the Americas, 2012: Towards Equality of Opportunity." AmericasBarometer, Latin America Pubic Opinion Poll, November 2012. http://www.vanderbilt.edu/lapop/ab2012/AB2012-comparative-report-v3-PreliminaryVersion.pdf.

Sen, Amartya. *The Idea of Justice*. Cambridge, MA: The Belknap Press of the Harvard University Press, 2009.

Sen, Amartya. *Inequality Reexamined*. Cambridge, MA: Harvard University Press, 1992.

Shaefer, H. Luke, and Kathryn Edin. "Rising Extreme Poverty in the United States and the Response of Federal Means-Tested Transfer Programs." *Social Service Review* 87, no. 2 (2013): 250–68. https://doi.org/10.1086/671012.

Shafer, Byron. "'Exceptionalism' in American Politics?" *PS, Political Science & Politics* 22, no. 3 (1989): 592–94.

Shapiro, Thomas, Tatjana Meschede, and Sam Osoro. "The Roots of the Widening Racial Wealth Gap: Explaining the Black-White Economic Divide." Institute on Assets and Social Policy, Brandeis University, Research and Policy Brief, February 2013. http://iasp.brandeis.edu/pdfs/Author/shapiro-thomas-m/racialwealthgapbrief.pdf.

Shierholz, Heidi. "Immigration and Wages: Methodological Advancements Confirm Modest Gains for Native Workers." Economic Policy Institute, February 4, 2010. http://www.epi.org/publication/bp255/.

Shiller, Robert J. "Better Insurance against Inequality." *New York Times*, April 12, 2014. http://www.nytimes.com/2014/04/13/business/better-insurance-against-inequality.html?_r=0.

Shorrocks, Anthony, James B. Davies, and Rodrigo Lluberas. *Global Wealth Report, 2014*. Zurich: Credit Suisse Group AG, Credit Suisse Research Institute, 2014.

Short, Kathleen. "The Supplemental Poverty Measure: 2014." *Current Population Reports*, September 2015. http://www.census.gov/content/dam/Census/library/publications/2015/demo/p60-254.pdf.

Shufelt, Tim. "Canada's Productivity Gap Is Looking Worse than Ever." *Financial Post*, May 29, 2012. http://business.financialpost.com/executive/canadas-productivity-gap-is-looking-worse-than-ever.

Simon, Jeff. "Raising the Minimum Wage Doesn't Affect Employment, in 3 Charts (and 2 McDonald's Meals)." *Washington Post*, January 8, 2014. https://www.washingtonpost.com/blogs/govbeat/wp/2014/01/08/raising-minimum-wage-doesnt-seem-to-affect-employment-in-3-charts-and-2-mcdonalds-meals/.

Skidelsky, Robert, and Edward Skidelsky. *How Much Is Enough? Money and the Good Life*. New York: Other Press, 2012.

Skogstad, Grace. "Globalization and Public Policy: Situating Canadian Analyses." *Canadian Journal of Political Science* 33, no. 4 (December 2000): 811–20.

Smith, Adam. *An Inquiry into the Nature and Causes of the Wealth of Nations*. 1776. Edited by Edwin Cannan. Chicago: University of Chicago Press, 1976.

Smith, Adam. *The Theory of Moral Sentiments*. 1759. New York: Penguin Books, 2010.

Smith, Jessica C., and Carla Medalia. "Health Insurance Coverage in the United States: 2013." *Current Population Reports*, P60-250, US Census Bureau. Washington, DC: US Government Printing Office, 2014.

Snider, Susannah. "Colleges that Report Meeting Full Financial Need." *U.S. News & World Report*, September 14, 2015. http://www.usnews.com/education/best-colleges/paying-for-college/articles/2015/09/14/colleges-that-report-meeting-full-financial-need.

Solon, Gary. "Cross-Country Differences in Intergenerational Earnings Mobility." *Journal of Economic Perspectives* 16, no. 3 (Summer 2002): 59–66. https://doi.org/10.1257/089533002760278712.

Solon, Gary. "A Model of Intergenerational Mobility Variation over Time and Place." In *Generational Income Mobility in North America and Europe*, edited by Miles Corak, 38–47. Cambridge: Cambridge University Press, 2011.

Sombart, Werner. *Warum gibt es in den Vereinigten Staaten keinen Sozialismus?* Tübingen: J.C.B. Mohr, 1906.

Song, Jean. "Goldman Sachs CEO: Income Inequality Is 'Destabilizing.'" *CBS News*. June 10, 2014. http://www.cbsnews.com/news/goldman-sachs-ceo-lloyd-blankfein-income-inequality-is-destabilizing/.

Soucy, Jean, and Marion G. Wrobel. "Federal Spending: Changing Trends." Government of Canada, Economics Division, March 27, 2000. http://publications.gc.ca/Collection-R/LoPBdP/CIR/872-e.htm.

Squires, Judith. "Equality and Difference." In *The Oxford Handbook of Political Theory*, edited by John Dryzek, Bonnie Honig, and Anne Phillips, 470–87. Oxford: Oxford University Press, 2006.

Stabile, Mark, and Lauren Jones. "The Shrinking Middle Class: So Far, Just a U.S. Story." *Globe and Mail*, February 6, 2015. http://www.theglobeandmail.com/globe-debate/the-shrinking-middle-class-so-far-just-a-us-story/article22828747/.

Stanley, Alessandra. "It's a Small World of Real Housewives." *New York Times*, June 6, 2013. http://www.nytimes.com/2013/06/09/arts/television/real-housewives-in-greece-israel-and-canada.html.

Statistics Canada. "Canadian Financial Capability Survey, 2014." http://www.statcan.gc.ca/daily-quotidien/141106/dq141106b-eng.htm.

Statistics Canada. "Donor Rate and Distribution of Donations, by Household Income, Canada, Provinces, Occasional." CANSIM, Table 119–0006.

Statistics Canada. "Economic Family." April 21, 2015. http://www.statcan.gc.ca/eng/concepts/definitions/famecon.

Statistics Canada. "High Income Trends of Tax Filers in Canada, Provinces and Census Metropolitan Areas (CMA), Specific Geographic Area Thresholds, 2011 Constant Dollars." CANSIM, Table 204–0002.
Statistics Canada. "Homeownership and Shelter Costs in Canada: National Household Survey 2011." Ministry of Industry, 2013. http://www12.statcan.gc.ca/nhs-enm/2011/as-sa/99-014-x/99-014-x2011002-eng.cfm.
Statistics Canada. "Income in Canada: 2010." November 27, 2015. http://www.statcan.gc.ca/pub/75-202-x/2010000/analysis-analyses-eng.htm.
Statistics Canada. "Income of Individuals, by Sex, Age Group and Income Source, 2011 Constant Dollars, Annual." CANSIM, Table 202–0407.
Statistics Canada. "Labour Force Survey Estimates (LFS), by Sex and Age Group, Seasonally Adjusted and Unadjusted, Monthly." CANSIM, Table 282–0087.
Statistics Canada. "Market, Total and After-Tax Income, by Economic Family Type and Income Quintiles, 2011 Constant Dollars, Annual." CANSIM, Table 202–0701.
Statistics Canada. "Market, Total and After-Tax Income, by Economic Family Type and After-Tax Income Quintiles, 2011 Constant Dollars, Annual." CANSIM, Table 202–0703.
Statistics Canada. "Market Income, Government Transfers, Total Income, Income Tax and After-Tax Income, by Economic Family Type, 2011 Constant Dollars, Annual." CANSIM, Table 202–0702.
Statistics Canada. "Persons in Low Income, by Economic Family Type, Annual." CANSIM, Table 202–0804.
Statistics Canada. "Persons in Low Income Families, Annual." CANSIM, Table 202–0802.
Statistics Canada. "Persons Living in Low-Income Neighborhoods." National Household Survey (2011), Catalogue no. 99014-X201100. http://www12.statcan.gc.ca/nhs-enm/2011/as-sa/99-014-x/99-014-x2011003_3-eng.pdf.
Statistics Canada. "Quarterly Balance Sheet and Income Statement, by North American Industry Classification System (NAICS)." CANSIM, Table 187–0001.
Statistics Canada. "Summary of Charitable Donors, Annual." CANSIM, Table 111–0001.
Statistics Canada. "Survey of Financial Security (SFS), Composition of Assets (Including Employer Pension Plans Valued on a Termination Basis) and Debts Held by All Family Units, by Age Group, Canada and Provinces." CANSIM, Table 205–0002.
Statistics Canada. "Survey of Financial Security (SFS), Composition of Assets (Including Employer Pension Plans Valued on a Termination Basis) and Debts Held by All Family Units, by Net Worth Quintiles, Canada and Provinces, occasional (2012 Constant Dollars)." CANSIM, Table 205–0003.
Statistics Canada. "Survey of Household Spending (SHS), Dwelling Characteristics and Household Equipment at Time of Interview, Canada, Regions and Provinces, Annual," CANSIM, Table 203–0027.
Statistics Canada. *2011 National Household Survey*. Catalogue no. 99–014–X2011041.
Statistics Canada. "Weighted Average Tuition Fees for Full-time Canadian Undergraduate Students, by Field of Study, Annual (Dollars)." CANSIM, Table 477–0021.

Stepan, Alfred, and Juan J. Linz. "Comparative Perspectives on Inequality and the Quality of Democracy in the United States." *Perspectives on Politics* 9, no. 4 (2011): 841–56. https://doi.org/10.1017/S1537592711003756.

Stevenson, Betsey, and Justin Wolfers. "Economic Growth and Subjective Well-Being: Reassessing the Easterlin Paradox." NBER Working Paper No. 14282, August 2008. http://www.nber.org/papers/w14282.pdf; https://doi.org/10.3386/w14282.

Stewart, Gordon T. *The Origins of Canadian Politics: A Comparative Approach*. Vancouver: UBC Press, 1986.

Stiglitz, Joseph. *The Price of Inequality: How Today's Divided Society Endangers Our Future*. New York: W.W. Norton, 2012.

Stiglitz, Joseph E. "Reforming Taxation to Promote Growth and Equity." White paper for the Roosevelt Institute, May 28, 2014. http://rooseveltinstitute.org/wp-content/uploads/2014/05/Stiglitz_Reforming_Taxation_White_Paper_Roosevelt_Institute.pdf.

"Stop Whacking the One Per cent." *Globe and Mail*, February 11, 2016. http://www.theglobeandmail.com/opinion/editorials/stop-whacking-the-one-per-cent/article28731337/?click=sf_globefb.

Sutton Trust. "What Prospects for Mobility in the UK? A Cross-National Study of Educational Inequalities and Their Implications for Future Education and Earnings Mobility." November 2011. http://www.suttontrust.com/research/summary-what-prospects-for-mobility-in-the-uk.

Tal, Benjamin, and Emanuella Enenajor. "Degrees of Success: The Payoff to Higher Education in Canada." *In Focus*, CIBC Economics, August 26, 2013. http://research.cibcwm.com/economic_public/download/if_2013-0826.pdf.

Tawney, R.H. *Equality*. 1931. Revised edition. London: George Allen and Unwin, 1964.

Tax Policy Center. "Tax Policy Center Briefing Book: Key Elements of the US Tax System." http://www.taxpolicycenter.org/briefing-book/what-are-flow-through-enterprises-and-how-are-they-taxed.

Taylor, Charles. "Democratic Exclusion (and Its Remedies?)." In *Citizenship, Diversity and Pluralism: Canadian and Comparative Perspectives*, edited by Alan C. Cairns, et al., 265–87. Montreal, Kingston: McGill-Queen's University Press, 1999.

Taylor, Charles. *Reconciling the Solitudes: Essays on Canadian Federalism and Nationalism*. Montreal, Kingston: McGill-Queen's University Press, 1993.

Terry, Matt. "Canadians More Upbeat than US Neighbours, at Least on Twitter." *Daily News*, January 6, 2016. http://dailynews.mcmaster.ca/article/canadians-more-upbeat-than-us-neighbours-at-least-on-twitter.

Therborn, Goran. *The Killing Fields of Inequality*. Cambridge: Polity Press, 2013.

Thompson, Derek. "How Did Canada's Middle Class Get So Rich?" *The Atlantic*, April 22, 2014. http://www.theatlantic.com/business/archive/2014/04/how-did-canadas-middle-class-get-so-rich/361053/.

Thompson, Derek. "How Low Are US Taxes Compared to Other Countries?" *Atlantic*, January 14, 2013. http://www.theatlantic.com/business/archive/2013/01/how-low-are-us-taxes-compared-to-other-countries/267148/.

Thompson, Michael J. *The Politics of Inequality: A Political History of the Idea of Economic Inequality in America*. New York: Columbia University Press, 2007.

Toikka, Richard, Thomas Gais, Plamen V. Nikolov, and Patricia Billen. "Spending on Social Welfare Programs in Rich and Poor States." Study for the US Department

of Health and Human Services, Office of the Assistant Secretary for Planning and Evaluation, June 2004.
Tomasi, John. *Free Market Fairness*. Princeton: Princeton University Press, 2013.
Torche, Florencia. "Analyses of Intergenerational Mobility: An Interdisciplinary Review." *Annals of the American Academy of Political and Social Science* 657, no. 1 (2015): 37–62. https://doi.org/10.1177/0002716214547476.
Trollope, Fanny. *Domestic Manners of the Americans*. Edited by Richard Mullen. 1939. Oxford: Oxford University Press, 1984.
Truman, David B. *The Governmental Process: Political Interests and Public Opinion*. New York: Alfred A. Knopf, 1965.
Tsalikis, Catherine. "What Canada's Election Campaign Has Missed: The Inequality Debate." Opencanada.org, October 14, 2015. https://www.opencanada.org/features/what-canadas-election-campaign-has-missed-inequality-debate/.
Tweddle, Anne, Ken Battle, and Sherri Torjman. *Welfare in Canada 2014*. The Caledon Institute of Social Policy, November 2015. http://www.caledoninst.org/Publications/PDF/1086ENG.pdf.
Tyson, Alec, and Shiva Maniam. "Behind Trump's Victory: Divisions by Race, Gender, Education." Pew Research Center. November 9, 2016. http://www.pewresearch.org/fact-tank/2016/11/09/behind-trumps-victory-divisions-by-race-gender-education/.
UNICEF. "Child Poverty in Rich Countries, 2005." Innocenti Report Card, No. 6. Innocenti Research Centre. https://www.unicef-irc.org/publications/pdf/repcard6e.pdf.
Uppal, Sharanjit. "Unionization 2011." Statistics Canada, 2012. http://www.statcan.gc.ca/pub/75-001-x/2011004/article/11579-eng.htm.
Uppal, Sharanjit, and Sébastien LaRochelle-Côté. "Changes in Wealth across the Income Distribution, 1999 to 2012." Report for Statistics Canada, June 3, 2015. http://www.statcan.gc.ca/pub/75-006-x/2015001/article/14194-eng.pdf.
US Bureau of Labor Statistics. "Average Hours and Earnings of Production and Non-supervisory Employees on Private Non-farm Payrolls, 2012." Current Employment Statistics Survey, Table B-2.
US Bureau of Labor Statistics. "Quintiles of Income before Taxes: Annual Means, Standard Errors, and Coefficient of Variation" (2011 and 2006). Consumer Expenditure Survey, Table 1101.
US Bureau of Labor Statistics. "Quintiles of Income before Taxes: Average Annual Expenditures and Characteristics" (1996, 1986). Consumer Expenditure Survey, Table 1.
US Bureau of Labor Statistics. "Quintiles of Income before Taxes: Shares of Aggregate Expenditures and Sources of Income" (2001). Consumer Expenditure Survey, Table 55.
US Bureau of Labor Statistics. "Unemployment Rates by Age, Sex, Race, and Hispanic or Latino Ethnicity." Current Population Survey, Table E-16.
US Census Bureau. "Current Population Survey: Subject Definitions." August 25, 2015. https://www.census.gov/programs-surveys/cps/technical-documentation/subject-definitions.html#household.
US Census Bureau. "Families in Poverty by Type of Family: 2012 and 2013." Current Population Survey, Annual Social and Economic Supplements, Table 4.

Bibliography   267

US Census Bureau. "Median Household Income, by Definition of Income: 1979 to 2003." Table RDI-4. Current Population Survey, Annual Social and Economic Supplements, 2005–2014.

US Census Bureau. "People in Poverty by Selected Characteristics: 2012 and 2013." Current Population Survey, 2013 and 2014 Annual Social and Economic Supplements, Table 3.

US Census Bureau. "Poverty Status, by Type of Family, Presence of Related Children, Race and Hispanic Origin: 1959–2013." Current Population Survey, 2013 and 2014 Annual Social and Economic Supplements, Historical Poverty Tables, Families, Table 4.

US Census Bureau. "Poverty Status of People by Age, Race and Hispanic Origin, 1959–2013." Current Population Survey, Annual Social and Economic Supplements, Historical Poverty Tables, Table 4.

US Census Bureau. "Poverty Status of People by Family Relationship, Race, and Hispanic Origin." Current Population Survey, Annual Social and Economic Supplements, Historical Poverty Tables, Table 2.

US Census Bureau. "Quarterly Homeownership Rates for the U.S. and Regions: 1965 to Present." Housing Vacancies and Homeownership (CPS/HVS), Table 14. http://www.census.gov/housing/hvs/data/histtabs.html.

US Census Bureau. "Selected Measures of Household Income Dispersion, 1967–2013." www.census.go/hhes/www/income/data/incpovhlth/2013/tableA2.

US Department of Agriculture Economic Research Service. "Rural Poverty and Well-being." March 1, 2017. http://www.ers.usda.gov/topics/rural-economy-population/rural-poverty-well-being/poverty-overview.aspx.

US Department of Commerce. "Corporate Profits by Industry, 2015." Table 6.16D. Bureau of Economic Analysis.

US Department of Education, National Center for Education Statistics. *Digest of Education Statistics, 2013*. NCES 2015-011.

US Department of Labor, Bureau of Labor Statistics. "Employee Benefits in the United States—March 2015," http://www.bls.gov/news.release/pdf/ebs2.pdf.

US Department of Labor, Bureau of Labor Statistics. "Seasonal Unemployment Rate." Labor Force Statistics from the Current Population Survey, Series LNS14000000, June 22, 2015.

US Department of Labor, Bureau of Labor Statistics. "Union Members Summary." January 27, 2012. http://www.bls.gov/news.release/union2.nr0.htm.

US Department of the Treasury. "Income Mobility in the US from 1996 to 2005." *Report of the Department of the Treasury*, November 13, 2007.

US Federal Reserve. *2013 Survey of Consumer Finances Chartbook*. http://www.federalreserve.gov/econresdata/scf/files/BulletinCharts.pdf.

Uslaner, Eric M., and Mitchell Brown. "Inequality, Trust, and Civic Engagement." *American Politics Research* 31, no. 10 (2003): 1–28.

United States Department of Health and Human Services, "National Data: TANF and MOE Spending and Transfers by Activity, FY 2014." https://acf.hhs.gov/sites/default/files/ofa/2014_tanf_moe_national_data.pdf?nocache=1447434621.

Veall, M.R. "Top Income Shares in Canada: Recent Trends and Policy Implications." *Canadian Journal of Economics* 45, no. 4 (2012): 1247–72. https://doi.org/10.1111/j.1540-5982.2012.01744.x.

Veiga, Alex. "Economic Recovery: Foreclosure Rates Drop to Lowest Level since Great Recession." *Christian Science Monitor*, January 15, 2015. http://www.csmonitor.com/Business/Latest-News-Wires/2015/0115/Economic-recovery-Foreclosure-rates-drop-to-lowest-level-since-Great-Recession.

Verhaege, Paul. *What about Me? The Struggle for Identity in a Market-Based Society*. Melbourne: Scribe, 2014.

Verney, Douglas V. *Three Civilizations, Two Cultures, One State: Canada's Political Traditions*. Durham, NC: Duke University Press, 1986.

Vogel, Kenneth P. *Big Money: 2.5 Billion Dollars, One Suspicious Vehicle, and a Pimp—on the Trail of the Ultra-Rich Hijacking American Politics*. New York: Public Affairs, 2014.

Voorheis, John, Nolan McCarty, and Boris Shor. "Unequal Incomes, Ideology and Gridlock: How Rising Inequality Increases Political Polarization." Working paper, August 31, 2015. https://doi.org/10.2139/ssrn.2649215.

Vornovitsky, Marina, Alfred Gottschalk, and Adam Smith. "Distribution of Household Wealth in the US: 2000–11." US Census Bureau. Washington, DC: US Government Printing Office, 2013.

Walker, Christina. "Head Start Participants, Programs, Families and Staff in 2013." Center for Law and Social Policy, August 2014. http://www.clasp.org/resources-and-publications/publication-1/HSpreschool-PIR-2013-Fact-Sheet.pdf.

Wang, Wendy, Kim Parker, and Paul Taylor. "Breadwinner Moms." Pew Research Center, May 29, 2013. http://www.pewsocialtrends.org/2013/05/29/breadwinner-moms/.

Warner, Kris. *Protecting Fundamental Labor Rights: Lessons from Canada for the United States*. Washington, DC: Center for Economic and Policy Research, August 2012. http://cepr.net/documents/publications/canada-2012-08.pdf.

"The War over Class War." *The Economist*, June 2, 2012. http://www.economist.com/node/21556243.

Watson, William. *The Inequality Trap: Fighting Capitalism Instead of Poverty*. Toronto: University of Toronto Press, 2015.

Weaver, R. Kent. *Ending Welfare as We Know It*. Washington, DC: Brookings Institution Press, 2000.

Weaver, Robert D., Nazim Habibov, and Lida Fan. "Devolution and the Poverty Reduction Effectiveness of Canada's Provincial Social Welfare Programs: Results from a Time-Series Investigation of a Canadian National Survey." *Journal of Policy Practice* 9, no. 2 (2010): 80–95. https://doi.org/10.1080/15588741003602155.

Western, Bruce, and Jake Rosenfeld. "Unions, Norms, and the Rise in U.S. Wage Inequality." *American Sociological Review* 76, no. 4 (2011): 513–37. https://doi.org/10.1177/0003122411414817.

Weston, Liz. "How Many Applications Is Too Many?" Reuters, April 25, 2014. http://www.reuters.com/article/us-column-weston-applications-idUSBREA3O1VU20140425.

The White House. "Worker Voice in a Time of Rising Inequality." Council of Economic Advisers Issue Brief, October 2015. https://www.whitehouse.gov/sites/default/files/page/files/worker_voice_issue_brief_cea.pdf.

Wilkinson, Richard, and Kate Pickett. *The Spirit Level: Why Greater Equality Makes Societies Stronger*. New York: Bloomsbury Press, 2009.

Wilmoth, J., C. Boe, and M. Barbieri. "Geographic Differences in Life Expectancy at Age 50 in the United States Compared with Other High-Income Countries." In *International Differences in Mortality at Older Ages: Dimensions and Sources*, edited by E.M. Crimmins, S.H. Preston, and B. Cohen, 333–66. Washington: National Academies Press, 2010.

Wilson, Daniel, and David Macdonald. "The Income Gap between Aboriginal Peoples and the Rest of Canada." Canadian Centre for Policy Alternatives, April 2010. http://ywcacanada.ca/data/research_docs/00000121.pdf.

Winship, Scott. "The Great Gatsby Curve: All Heat, No Light." Social Mobility Memos, Brookings Institution, May 20, 2015. http://www.brookings.edu/blogs/social-mobility-memos/posts/2015/05/20-opposition-great-gatsby-curve-winship.

Wimer, Christopher, et al. "Trends in Poverty with an Anchored Supplemental Poverty Measure." Columbia Population Research Center, 2013. https://courseworks.columbia.edu/access/content/group/c5a1ef92-c03c-4d88-0018-ea43dd3cc5db/Articles/Anchored%20SPM%20December7.pdf.

Wolf, Martin. "'Capital in the 21st Century,' by Thomas Piketty." *Financial Times*, April 15, 2014. https://www.ft.com/content/0c6e9302-c3e2-11e3-a8e0-00144feabdc0#axzz4HXKBR0jE.

Wolff, Edward. "The Asset Price Meltdown, Rising Leverage, and the Wealth of the Middle Class." *Journal of Economic Issues* 47, no. 2 (2013): 333–42. https://doi.org/10.2753/JEI0021-3624470205.

Wolfson, Michael. "Income Mobility Is Still a Problem in Canada." *Globe and Mail*, November 26, 2012. http://www.theglobeandmail.com/report-on-business/economy/economy-lab/income-mobility-is-still-a-problem-in-canada/article5663444/.

Wood, Gordon S. *The Creation of the American Republic, 1776–1787*. Chapel Hill: University of North Carolina Press, 1969.

Wood, Gordon S. *The Radicalism of the American Revolution*. New York: Alfred A. Knopf, 1992.

Woodward, Colin. *American Nations: A History of the Eleven Rival Regional Cultures of North America*. New York: Viking, 2011.

Woolf, Steven H., and Laudan Aron, eds. *U.S. Health in International Perspective: Shorter Lives, Poorer Health*. Panel on Understanding Cross-National Health Differences among High-Income Countries, National Research Council and Institute of Medicine. Washington, DC: The National Academies Press, 2013.

World Bank. "Price Level Ratio of PPP Conversion Factor (GDP) to Market Exchange Rate." http://data.worldbank.org/indicator/PA.NUS.PPPC.RF?locations=CA&name_desc=false&page=4.

World Bank. "World Development Indicators, GDP Growth (Annual %)." http://data.worldbank.org/indicator/NY.GDP.MKTP.KD.ZG/countries/US-CA?display=graph.

World Health Organization and Calouste Gulbenkian Foundation. *Social Determinants of Mental Health*. Geneva: World Health Organization, 2014.

World Wealth and Income Database. http://wid.world/data/#countriestimeseries/sfiinc_p99p100_z/US;CA/1930/2015/eu/k/p/yearly/s.

Yakabuski, Konrad. "There Is No Middle in the Middle Class Debate." *Globe and Mail*, June 8, 2015. http://www.theglobeandmail.com/opinion/there-is-no-middle-in-the-middle-class-debate/article24827509/.

Yellen, Janet. "Perspectives on Inequality and Opportunity from the Survey of Consumer Finances." Conference on Economic Opportunity and Inequality, Federal Reserve Bank of Boston, Boston, Massachusetts, October 17, 2014. http://www.federalreserve.gov/newsevents/speech/yellen20141017a.pdf.

Zeman, Klarka. "A First Look at Provincial Differences in Educational Pathways from High School to College and University." *Education Matters: Insights on Education, Learning and Training in Canada* 4, no. 2 (June 2007). http://www.statcan.gc.ca/pub/81-004-x/2007002/9989-eng.htm.

Zuberi, Dan. *Differences That Matter: Social Policy and the Working Poor in the United States and Canada*. Ithaca, NY: ILR Press, 2006.

Zucman, Gabriel. *The Hidden Wealth of Nations: The Scourge of Tax Havens*. Chicago: University of Chicago Press, 2015. https://doi.org/10.7208/chicago/9780226245560.001.0001.

Databases/Statistical Sources Consulted

Canadian Opinion Research Archive. Queen's University, Kingston, Ontario. http://www.queensu.ca/cora.

Center for Responsive Politics. Lobbying Database. https://www.opensecrets.org/lobby/.

Conference Board. International Labor Comparisons Program. https://www.conference-board.org/ilcprogram/.

Google Books Ngram Viewer. https//books.google.com/ngrams.

Luxembourg Income Study. http://www.lisdatacenter.org.

National Conference of State Legislatures. Ballot Measures Database. http://www.ncsl.org/research/elections-and-campaigns/initiative-and-referendum.aspx.

OECD Better Life Index: Education. http://www.oecdbetterlifeindex.org/topics/education/.

OECD Better Life Index: Safety. http://www.oecdbetterlifeindex.org/topics/safety/.

OECD Employment Database. http://www.oecd.org/employment/emp/onlineoecdemploymentdatabase.htm.

OECD Family Database. http://www.oecd.org/social/family/database.htm.

OECD Health Statistics 2015. http://stats.oecd.org/index.aspx?DataSetCode=HEALTH_STAT.

OECD Income Distribution Database. http://www.oecd.org/social/income-distribution-database.htm.

OECD Social Expenditure Database. https://www.oecd.org/social/expenditure.htm.

OECD Statistical Extracts Database, "Average Annual Wages." https://stats.oecd.org/Index.aspx?DataSetCode=AV_AN_WAGE.

OECD Statistical Extracts Database, "Unit Labor Costs—Annual Indicators." http://stats.oecd.org/Index.aspx?DataSetCode=ULC_ANN.

OECD Wealth Distribution Database. https://stats.oecd.org/Index.aspx?DataSetCode=WEALTH.

Statistics Canada. CANSIM Database. http://www5.statcan.gc.ca/cansim/.
Statistics Canada. 2011 National Household Survey. https://www12.statcan.gc.ca/nhs-enm/2011/dp-pd/prof/index.cfm?Lang=E.
UN Development Programme. International Human Development Indicators. http://hdr.undp.org/en/data/profiles/.
United Nations Office on Drugs and Crime, "Homicide Statistics." https://www.unodc.org/gsh/en/data.html.
US Census Bureau. American Community Survey. https://www.census.gov/programs-surveys/acs/.
US Census Bureau. Current Population Survey. https://www.census.gov/programs-surveys/cps.html.
US Census Bureau. Historical Poverty Tables: People and Families 1959 to 2014. https://www.census.gov/data/tables/time-series/demo/income-poverty/historical-poverty-people.html.
US Department of Commerce. Census of Governments. https://www.census.gov/govs/cog/.
US Department of Commerce, Bureau of Economic Analysis. National Income and Product Accounts Tables. https://www.bea.gov/bea/nipaweb/TableViewFixed.asp.
US Department of Education. National Center for Education Statistics. https://nces.ed.gov/.
US Department of Labor. Bureau of Labor Statistics. https://www.bls.gov/.
US Federal Reserve. Survey of Consumer Finances. http://www.federalreserve.gov/econresdata/scf/files/BulletinCharts.pdf.
US Office of Family Assistance, Administration for Family and Children. TANF Caseload Data 2014. https://www.acf.hhs.gov/ofa/resource/caseload-data-2014.
World Bank. http://data.worldbank.org/.
World Values Survey. http://www.worldvaluessurvey.org/WVSOnline.jsp.
World Wealth and Income Database. http://wid.world/.

Index

absolute intergenerational mobility, 57, 64–67
absolute intra-generational mobility, 57–61
Adelson, Sheldon, 190
African-Americans, 160–61, 185–86
Aid to Families with Dependent Children (AFDC), 146, 148
Aristotle and Aristotelean views, 174, 196–97
Atkinson, Anthony, 12n25, 215–16
The Atlantic, middle class and income, 25–26

bachelor programs, 78, 98n103
banking, deregulation, 41–42
Bartels, Larry, 191
basic material needs, and equality, 8–9
Bischoff, Kendra, 187
Bowling for Columbine (Moore), 102–3
Bradbury, Katherine, 60, 89n19
Brandenburg v. Ohio (US, 1969), 111
British North America (BNA) Act of 1867, 109, 113
Brooks, David, 190
Bryce, James, 112–13
Buffett, Warren, and "Buffett Rule," 12n36
business ownership, 125–26

Canada
    community in politics and law, 109–11
    creation myth, 109
    economic development and Crown corporations, 113–14
    election of 2015, 189
    equality advantage over US, 4, 214–15, 220–21
    equality in, 117–18, 214
    equality initiatives, 221
    inequality as issue in politics, 2–3
    multiculturalism, 109–10
    political power and processes, 132–33
    poverty rates, 35–36, 154, 163
    vs. United States (*See* comparison Canada–United States)
    welfare reform, 146–48, 151–54, 156, 157, 161–62, 163, 166
Canada Assistance Plan (CAP), 146, 148, 153
Canada Health and Social Transfer (CHST)
    changes in, 148, 152, 157
    decision making in welfare disbursement, 145
    description, 151–52
Canada Health Transfer (CHT), in welfare reform, 152, 153
Canada Social Transfer (CST), in welfare reform, 152, 153, 157

capabilities perspective of equality, 8–9
capital, and wealth, 27–28
capital gains, taxation, 218, 227n31
Capital in the Twenty-First Century (Piketty), 3
CEO compensation, 43, 220
charitable giving, 159
Charter of Rights and Freedoms (Canada), 109–10, 111, 113, 138n42
charter schools, 114–15
Chen, Wen-Hao, 60
Chetty, Raj, and colleagues, 68–69
Child Care and Development Block Grant (CCDBG), 149, 167n13
children and parents, and mobility, 64–72
child support, 149
citizens in US
    initiatives for equality, 223–25
    rights in Constitution, 107–8, 110–11
class
    and income inequality, 25
    and inequality, 10, 183–84
    self-identification, 23, 48n16
Clinton, Bill, 148
Clinton, Hillary
    election of 2016, 2, 10–11n10
    on inequality, 11–12n24
college. *See* university education
community
    and justice, 199–201
    and politics and politicians, 109–12
    values in, 106–11
comparison Canada–United States
    class self-identification, 23, 48n16
    debt, 32, 33
    distribution of inequality (*See* distribution of equality)
    education and income, 42–43
    equality advantage in Canada, 4, 214–15, 220–21
    fairness and opportunity, 122–23
    female-headed households, 43
    financial sector, 41–42
    Gini coefficient, 15, 20–22, 23
    government redistribution against inequality, 125, 128–31, 133–34
    homes and wealth, 33–34
    household income, 18–20, 21, 24, 47n9
    household income growth, 58–61
    income inequality, 15–22, 43–44, 46, 123–25
    of inequality, 4–5, 9–10
    longevity gap and income, 179–80

market income, 48n14
markets, 125–31
measures of equality, 4
middle class distribution of equality, 22–27
minimum wage, 44
mobility, 62–72, 75–76, 87, 89–90n25, 120–22
niceness, 102–3
overview of argument, 5–7
policy (*See* policy on equality)
political culture, 104, 105–6, 112–13
politics and politicians, 6, 105–6, 107–11
poverty rates and gaps, 35–37, 39–40
retirement preparation, 34–35
statistics and statistical agencies, 9, 13–14, 46–47n2
taxation, 115, 220, 227nn30–31
university enrollment and graduation, 82–83, 84–85
university fees and debt, 78–79, 100n116
values, 102–3, 214
wealth and income, 28–34
welfare and social assistance, 45, 118, 133
See also specific topics
competition, public opinion on, 125, 127
computers, in finance sector, 42
Continental Divide (Lipset), 118
Corak, Miles, 69
corporate tax, in US, 217
Crèvecoeur, J. Hector St. John de, 107
culture. *See* values and culture

daycare, and mobility, 77
Deaton, Angus, 38
debt
　Canada *vs.* US, 32, 33
　indices and measure, 33, 51n52
　from university fees, 79, 100n116
　and wealth, 32, 33
debt-to-asset ratios, 33
debt-to-income ratios, 33
democracy, and initiatives for equality, 223–25
democratic integrity, 188–95, 206
democratic solidarity, 182–88
Denmark, wealth in, 29, 49–50n35
Diener, Ed, 182
disposable income
　definition, 13
　global inequality, 15–16, 22
　as measure of inequality, 48n14
distribution of equality
　and income, 14–22
　and middle class, 22–27
　overview, 6
　in poverty and low-income status, 35–40
　and rising levels of inequality, 13, 40–45
　and wealth, 27–35
District of Columbia v. Heller (US, 2008), 108
diversity in employment, 110–11

Dodd–Frank Wall Street Reform and Consumer Protection Act (2010), 42, 52n79, 220

earned income tax credit (EITC), 151
Easterlin, Richard, 182
economic equality. *See* equality
"economic family", definition, 46–47n2
economic freedom, 203
economic growth, and equality, 175–77
economic inequality. *See* inequality
economic mobility. *See* mobility
economy. *See* markets
education
　charter schools, 114–15
　initiatives for equality, 219
　and mobility, 76, 77–78
　and race, 186–87
　See also university education
elections
　campaign financing, 188–91
　Canadian election of 2015, 189
　US election of 2012, 188–89
　US election of 2016, 2, 10–11n10
employment, equality and diversity in, 110–11
Employment Equity Act (Canada), 110
equality (economic)
　and basic material needs, 8–9
　Canada *vs.* United States (*See* comparison Canada–United States)
　Canadian advantage, 4, 214–15, 220–21
　in Charter of Rights and Freedoms, 110, 111
　and democratic integrity, 188–95, 206
　distribution (*See* distribution of equality)
　and economic growth, 175–77
　in employment, 110–11
　future direction, 214
　and government, 200–201, 221–25
　in humanity and of people, 195–97
　as ideal, 7–8
　importance of, 174–75
　initiatives for, 215–25
　and institutions, 103, 104, 131–34
　as issue, 1–3
　and justice, 195–206
　and law, 117–18
　and markets, 9, 175–76, 201–3
　policy (*See* policy on equality)
　from politics and politicians, 221–25
　psychosocial stress for, 181
　and public health, 177–82, 218–19
　and public opinion, 119–31
　sameness of equality paradox, 8
　and solidarity, 182–88
　and values, 103–4, 115–18
　and welfare, 160–63, 166
　See also inequality
equalization, in welfare reform, 153, 160, 168n28

fairness and opportunity, public opinion on, 122–23, 130–31
family
   "economic family," 46–47n2
   and mobility, 67–70, 74–80, 86
   and university education, 80–82, 83–84
   in welfare reform, 149, 150
fathers and sons, and mobility, 69–72, 92n44, 94n59, 94n62
Federalist Paper #10, 114
female-headed households, income inequality, 43
finance sector, 41–42, 220
   See also markets
fiscal policy, and income inequality, 21–22, 23, 44–45
Flash Boys: A Wall Street Revolt (Lewis), 102
food stamps (Supplemental Nutrition Assistance Program (SNAP)), 151, 162, 168n24
Francophones in welfare, 161
Frank, Robert, 181
Fraser Institute, on mobility, 62–63, 64, 88–89nn15–16, 89n24, 90n31
freedom, in political culture, 111–12
Freeman, Richard, 176
Friedman, Thomas, 40

gender, and long-term income growth, 61
General Social Survey (GSS), 119
Gilens, Martin, 193
Gini coefficient
   Canada *vs.* US, 15, 20–22, 23
   globally, 14–15
   income inequality, 29, 30
   as measure, 14
Glass-Steagall Act (1933), repeal, 41
globalization, 40–41
Global Wealth Databook (GWD), 32, 33
governments (states)
   and equality, 200–201, 221–25
   initiatives for equality, 221–25
   interference in personal affairs, 107–8
   and markets, 9, 113–15, 193, 222–23
   in political culture, 112–13
   political power and change, 131–34
   redistribution by, 125, 128–31, 133–34, 222–23
   restrained in US, 112
   and values, 103, 104, 112–13
Great Divergence
   and income inequality, 17, 18
   and mobility, 73–74
   wealth and net worth, 29, 31
gross income, definition, 13
The Guardian, middle class and income, 25–26
gun rights and ownership, 108

happiness, and inequality, 181–82
Harper v. Canada (Attorney General) (2004), 108
Head Start program, 77

health and income, 178–80
   See also public health
higher education. *See* university education
Hispanics, 185–86
Hobhouse, L.T., 195–96
home ownership levels, 34
household, definition, 46n2
household income
   and income inequality, 18–20, 21, 24, 47n9
   and middle class, 23–24
household income growth, and mobility, 58–61
housing and homes, as wealth, 33–34
housing associations, 187–88
Human Development Indicator (HDI), and mobility, 65

immigrants, social inequalities, 184–85
income
   and health, 178–80
   and longevity, 179–80
   middle class differences factors, 25–26, 49n25
   and mobility, 27, 57
   public opinion on, 123–25
   types, 13
   as wealth, 27–29
   and wealth distribution, 29–32
income elasticity, and mobility, 70–71, 74
income growth. *See* mobility
income inequality
   Canada *vs.* US, 15–22, 43–44, 46, 123–25
   and class, 25
   distribution, 14–22
   and education, 42–43
   globally, 14–16, 17, 21–22
   and household income, 18–20, 21, 24, 47n9
   1920–30s *vs.* current situation, 16–17
   one percent and top earners, 15–18, 21
   and poverty, 39
   public policy, 43–44, 45
   and race, 184–86, 187
   and taxation, 21–22, 23, 44–45
   visible minorities and immigrants, 184–85
   and wealth distribution, 29, 30
   and women, 43
indebtedness. *See* debt
independent education consultants (IEC), 84
Indigenous people, social inequalities, 184
individualism and values, 106–11
inequality (economic)
   Canada *vs.* US (*See* comparison Canada–United States)
   and class, 10, 183–84
   correlation with mobility, 72–73
   and economic growth, 175–77
   factors in, 13, 40–45
   and government redistribution, 125, 128–31, 133–34, 222–23

and happiness, 181–82
of income (*See* income inequality)
and infant mortality, 179, 180
as issue, 1–3
and justice, 199–201, 205–6
measure of, 48n14
in media and online, 3
and mobility, 55, 72–86, 177, 182
and neighborhoods, 187–88
and politics, 1–3, 105, 188, 221–25
and public health, 177–82
public opinion on, 119–20, 123
reduction and initiatives for, 174–75, 214, 215–16
social aspects, 3–4
values about, 119–20
See also equality
infant mortality, 179, 180
inheritance, and wealth, 28, 218
institutions, and equality, 103, 104, 131–34
Intergenerational Income Database (IID), 60
intergenerational mobility, 57, 64–72
intra-generational mobility, 57–64
IT, in finance sector, 42

Jacobs, Lawrence R., 120, 131
Judt, Tony, 200
justice
capabilities approach, 197–201, 206
and community, 199–201
and equality, 195–206
humanity and people in, 195–97
and inequality, 199–201, 205–6
and markets, 201–5, 206
and monetary resources, 199

Katsuyama, Brad, 102
Kesebir, Sele, 182
Key, V.O., 119
King Solomon morality tale, 7–8
Koch, David, and Charles, 190
Kopczuk, Wojciech, 61

labor unions, 44, 113–14, 220
language rights in Canada, 109, 138n43
law
community in, 109, 110, 111
and equality, 117–18
individualism in, 108–9, 111
less wealthy, wealth and net worth, 29, 31, 32–33
Liberal Party, actions on inequality, 2, 11n12
Lindblom, Charles, 194
Lipset, Seymour Martin, 118
lobbying in politics, 192, 193
longevity (life expectancy), and income, 179–80
"low-income cut-off" (LICO), as measure, 35–36

low-income status. *See* poverty and low-income status
Luxembourg Income Study (LIS), 25–26, 35

Maclean's, middle class and income, 25–26
MacPherson, C.B., 201
Madison, James, 114
"Maintenance of Effort" (MOE) clause, 149, 150–51
"market basket measure" (MBM), as measure, 35–36
market income, 13, 22, 47n14, 48n14
markets
and equality, 9, 175–76, 201–3
government role, 9, 113–15, 193, 222–23
initiatives for equality, 220, 222–23
and justice, 201–5, 206
and politics, 193–94
public opinion on, 125–31
Martin, Paul, 156
McCall, Leslie, 123, 131
median household income, 24
middle class
distribution of equality, 22–27
and household income, 23–24
housing as wealth, 33–34
income differences factors, 25–26, 49n25
and income mobility, 27
self-identification in, 23, 48n16
Millennials, and mobility, 66–67
minimum wage, 44
mobility (economic)
absolute intergenerational mobility, 57, 64–67
absolute intra-generational mobility, 57–61
Canada *vs.* US, 62–72, 75–76, 87, 89–90n25, 120–22
as concept, 55
correlation with inequality, 72–73
and education, 76, 77–78
equal opportunity in, 86
and family background, 67–70, 74–80, 86
fathers and sons, 69–72, 92n44, 94n59, 94n62
Great Gatsby Curve, 72–73
and household income growth, 58–61
and household surveys, 60, 90n31
and income, 27
and income elasticity, 70–71, 74
and inequality, 55, 72–86, 87, 177, 182
influences on, 58
measurement, 57, 70–71
narrative of, 55–56
overview, 6
panel studies, 60
of parents and children, 64–72
of poor and low-income earners, 62–64, 76
public opinion on, 120–22
and race, 185, 187

relative intergenerational mobility, 57, 67–72
relative intra-generational mobility, 57, 61–64
and social factors, 75–76
and social status, 61–62
timeframe of analysis, 60, 88–89nn15–16
types, 57
and university education, 80–86
values about, 120–22
Moore, Michael, 102–3
mortgage as debt, 33, 34
multiculturalism, 109–10

neighborhoods and inequality, 187–88
neoliberalism, 41
net worth
  definition, 27
  of politicians, 189
  top earners, 29, 30–33
  and wealth distribution, 32–33
New Deal, 118
niceness, Canada vs. US, 102–3
Nussbaum, Martha C., 197, 198

Oakes test, 138n42
Obama, Barack, 1–2, 56
OECD countries
  debt, 32, 33, 51n52
  income elasticity, 71
  income inequality, 14–16, 29, 30
  poverty rates, 35, 36
  wealth distribution, 30, 31–32
Oishi, Shigehiro, 182
Okun, Arthur, 175
one percent (1%)
  and income inequality, 15–16, 17, 18, 21
  source of income, 17
  wealth and net worth, 29, 30–31
  See also top earners
opportunity and fairness, public opinion on, 122–23, 130–31
organized labor, 44, 113–14, 220
Osberg, Lars, 125

Page, Benjamin I., 120, 131, 193
Paine, Thomas, 107
Panel Study of Income Dynamics (PSID), 60, 89n19, 91–92n41
parents and children, and mobility, 64–72
Personal Responsibility and Work Opportunity Reconciliation Act (US), 155
philanthropy, 159
Pickett, Kate, 177–78, 179, 207n18
Piketty, Thomas, 3, 27–28, 29, 216
policy on equality
  and income inequality, 43–44, 45
  influences on decision making, 146
  overview, 6–7

privatization of welfare, 156, 158–59
safety net, 163–65
in United States, 215, 224–25
welfare reform in Canada, 146–48, 151–54, 156, 157, 161–62, 163, 166
welfare reform in US, 146–51, 155, 156–58, 161–62, 166
political culture
  assemblies and legislatures, 113
  Canada vs. US, 104, 105–6, 112–13
  community in Canada, 109–11
  criticisms of, 134, 135
  government in, 112–13
  individualism, 107–9, 111
  and market, 113–15
  regional specificities, 104–5
  and sovereignty, 112
  and values, 104, 105–18
political power and change, 131–34
politics and politicians
  campaign financing, 188–91
  and community, 109–12
  equality from, 221–25
  individualism, 107–9
  and inequality, 1–3, 105, 188, 221–25
  and markets, 193–94
  mobility as narrative, 56
  net worth of politicians, 189
  pluralism in, 192–93
  policymaking and money, 191–95
  pressure groups and lobbying, 192, 193
  spending on, 188–89
  systems in Canada and US, 6, 105–6, 107–11
polls. See public opinion
Pope Francis, 1
populism, 116
poverty and low-income status
  distribution of equality, 35–40
  factors in, 40
  and female-headed households, 43
  and government redistribution, 125, 128–31
  improvements on, 38
  income and wealth, 32–33
  income inequality, 39
  increases in, 38–39
  measure and definition, 35–38
  mobility, 62–64, 76
  need for reduction, 174
  political choices, 191
  public opinion on, 121, 128–31
  and race, 185, 209n55
  rates and gaps, 35–37, 39–40, 209n55
  rates and welfare, 151, 161–63, 171n69
  and university, 79, 97n100
"poverty gaps", 35, 36
pressure groups in politics, 192, 193
private education, 78, 114–15
privatization of welfare, 156, 158–59

productivity vs. wages, 176
property rights, 114
provinces
    equalization program, 153, 160, 168n28
    welfare policy and programs, 133, 147, 148, 152–54, 156, 157, 161
psychosocial stress for equality, 181
public health, 177–82, 218–19
public opinion
    on business ownership, 125–26
    on competition, 125, 127
    on equality, 119–31
    on fairness and opportunity, 122–23, 130–31
    on government redistribution, 125, 128–31, 133–34
    on income, 123–25
    on inequality, 119–20, 123
    interpretation, 119
    on markets, 125–31
    on mobility, 120–22
    on poverty, 121, 128–31
    on top earners, 122–23
public policy. *See* policy on equality
purchasing power parity (PPP), 20, 26, 47n12
Putnam, Robert, 75, 107

Quebec, welfare policy, 161

race
    and education, 186–87
    and female-headed households, 43
    income inequality and wealth, 184–86, 187
    and mobility, 185, 187
    and poverty, 185, 209n55
Raphael, D.D., 197
Reardon, Sean F., 187
recession of 2008–09, 33–34, 41–42
redistribution by government, 125, 128–31, 133–34, 222–23
Reich, Robert, 193
relative intergenerational mobility, 57, 67–72
relative intra-generational mobility, 57, 61–64
religion
    influence on culture, 134–35
    in welfare, 158–59
retirement, financial preparation, 34–35
rich people. *See* top earners
right to vote, 116, 118, 140n70
R. v. Keegstra (Canada, 1990), 111
R. v. Oakes (Canada, 1986), 138n42

Saez, Emmanuel, 61
safety net, 163–65
Sanders, Bernie, on inequality, 2, 11–12n24
savings rate, 28, 49n32
Schattschneider, E.E., 192
sectarian schools, 114–15
Sen, Amartya, 195, 197, 198–99

Smeeding, Timothy, 125
Smith, Adam, 52n67
social assistance
    Canada vs. US, 45, 118, 133
    distribution of benefits, 164–65
    initiatives for equality, 216, 218–19
    privatization, 156, 158–59
    as safety net, 163–65
    See also welfare
social disparities, 183–84
social justice, 200
social networks, and race, 186
social safety net, 163–65
Social Security program (US) and Act, 155, 160
social status, and mobility, 61–62
solidarity, 182–88
Song, Jae, 61
sons and fathers, and mobility, 69–72, 92n44, 94n59, 94n62
Soros, George, 190
sovereignty, 112
The Spirit Level (Wilkinson and Pickett), 177, 179
state. *See* governments
states (of US), welfare policy and programs, 147–51, 156–58, 161
statistics and statistical agencies
    Canada vs. US, 9, 13–14, 46–47n2
    and household surveys of mobility, 60, 90n31
    retirement preparation, 34–35
    See also Statistics Canada; US Census Bureau
Statistics Canada
    definitions, 46–47n2
    on mobility, 64
    poverty measure, 35
Steyer, Tom, 190
super PACs, 189, 190
Supplemental Nutrition Assistance Program (SNAP—food stamps), 151, 162, 168n24
supplemental poverty measure (SPM), 37
Supreme Court of Canada, Charter cases, 111
Supreme Court of US, 111
Survey of Labour and Income Dynamics (SLID), 60, 90n31
surveys. *See* public opinion

Tawney, R.H., 1, 8, 103
taxation
    Canada vs. US, 115, 220, 227nn30–31
    and income inequality, 21–22, 23, 44–45
    against inequality, 2–3
    initiatives for equality, 216, 217–18
    middle class income differences, 49n25
    and solidarity, 183
    of top earners, 12n36, 217–18, 225–26n11

Taylor, Charles, 108
Temporary Assistance for Needy Families (TANF), 148–51, 155, 161–62
territories, welfare policy and programs, 152–54, 156
Tocqueville, Alexis de, 116, 223, 227n38
top earners
 happiness, 181–82
 and household income, 18–20, 21
 and income inequality, 15–18, 21
 need for redistribution of wealth, 174–75
 net worth and wealth, 29, 30–33
 public opinion on, 122–23
 taxation, 12b36, 217–18, 225–26n11
 and wealth increase, 28
 See also one percent (1%)
trading, advantage in, 102
Trudeau government, 2–3, 227n30
Trump, Donald
 election of 2016, 10–11n10, 191
 and inequality, 2, 224

unemployment, initiatives for equality, 215–16
unions, 44, 113–14, 220
United States
 affirmative action, 110–11
 vs. Canada (*See* comparison Canada–United States)
 election of 2012, 188–89
 election of 2016, 2, 10–11n10
 equality advantage of Canada, 4, 214–15, 220–21
 equality in, 115–17, 215
 equality initiatives, 217–20, 223–24
 financial sector, 41–42
 freedom in, 111–12
 government interference, 107–8, 111
 happiness and inequality, 181–82
 individualism in politics and law, 107–9, 110–11
 inequality as issue in politics, 1–2
 mobility and inequality, 72, 73–74, 75
 mobility as narrative, 55–56
 neighborhoods and housing, 187–88
 net worth of politicians, 189
 pluralism in politics, 192–93
 policy choices, 215, 224–25
 political power and processes, 131–32
 poverty rates, 37, 151, 161–62
 race and minorities, 160–61, 185–86
 restrained government, 112
 taxation initiatives, 217–18
 university policy, 85–86
 welfare initiatives, 218–19
 welfare reform, 146–51, 155, 156–58, 161–62, 166
university education
 academic quality, 83
 application for, 84–85, 100n123

 economic return and earnings, 79, 85, 98n103
 enrollment and graduation, 82–84
 and family wealth, 80–82, 83–84
 fees and debt, 78–79, 85, 100n116
 and income inequality, 42–43
 and low-income families, 79, 97n100
 and mobility, 80–86
 policy in US, 85–86
US Census Bureau
 definitions, 46–47n2
 poverty measure, 36–37
US Constitution, citizens rights, 107–8, 110–11
US Department of Treasury, on mobility, 63–64
US Personal Responsibility and Work Opportunity Reconciliation Act (PRWORA), 145, 148, 157

values and culture
 Canada *vs.* US, 102–3, 214
 criticisms of, 134, 135
 and equality, 103–4, 115–18
 and governments, 103, 104, 112–13
 individualism and community, 106–11
 on inequality, 119–20
 initiatives for equality, 223–24
 and institutions, 103, 104, 131–34
 on mobility, 120–22
 niceness, 102–3
 overview, 6
 and political culture, 104, 105–18
 political differences, 6
 and public opinion on, 119–31
 regional specificities, 104–5
 and religion, 134–35
 wealth in, 116–17
 and welfare policy, 145, 154–55, 158–59, 165–66
visible minorities, social inequalities, 184–85
voting rights, 116, 118, 140n70

wages *vs.* productivity, 176
Watson, William, 174
wealth
 definition, 27
 housing and homes as, 33–34
 income and capital in, 27–29
 initiatives for equality, 216
 and policymaking, 191–95
 and race, 185–86
 as safety, 34
 as value, 116–17
 See also less wealthy; poverty and low-income status; top earners
wealth distribution
 and equality, 27–35
 and income, 29–32
 and income inequality, 29, 30
 inequality in, 27–28, 29–32

need for, 174–75, 177
wealthy. *See* one percent (1%); top earners
welfare
    access to and conditions in US, 148–49
    Canada *vs.* US, 45, 118, 133
    caseloads, 154, 162, 169n34
    cuts in, 145
    decision making in disbursement, 145
    definition, 145
    distribution of benefits, 164–65
    and equality, 160–63, 166
    equalization program, 153, 160, 168n28
    initiatives for equality, 218–19
    main programs, 146–47
    and minority groups, 160–61
    policy and change, 133
    and poverty rates, 151, 161–63, 171n69
    privatization, 156, 158–59
    rates in Canada, 154, 163
    reform in Canada, 146–48, 151–54, 156, 157, 161–62, 163, 166
    reform in US, 146–51, 155, 156–58, 161–62, 166
    religion in, 158–59
    role of, 145–46
    rules in Canada and US, 156, 157
    in safety net, 163–65
    and values, 145, 154–55, 158–59, 165–66
    work provisions and participation, 148, 149–50, 154, 158, 162, 167n15–16
    See also social assistance
Wilkinson, Richard, 177–78, 179, 207n18
women, and income inequality, 43
Wood, Gordon, 115
workplace, initiatives for equality, 215, 219
work provisions and participation in welfare, 148, 149–50, 154, 158, 162, 167n15–16
World Bank and PPP, 47n12
World Values Survey, 123–25
World Wealth and Income Database (WID), 18

www.ingramcontent.com/pod-product-compliance
Lightning Source LLC
Chambersburg PA
CBHW020247030426
42336CB00010B/649